D0064893

Consumerism

Consumerism:

Search for the
Consumer Interest

Edited by

David A. Aaker and George S. Day

The Free Press, New York
Collier-Macmillan Ltd., London

The Free Press
`A Division of The Macmillan Company
866 Third Avenue, New York, New York 10022

Collier-Macmillan Canada Ltd., Toronto, Ontario

Library of Congress Catalog Card Number: 72–148737

printing number
1   2   3   4   5   6   7   8   9   10

To Kay and Marilyn

Contents

Part One

The Scope of the Problem

Part Two

The Pre-Purchase Phase: The Availability and Quality of Information

C. Possibilities for Solution

Preface

A content analysis of books dealing with the American marketplace in the late 1960's would likely show that the ancient
maxim "caveat emptor," let the buyer beware, has been dis-
placed by a newer maxim, "caveat venditor," let the seller
beware. This would be but one symptom of consumerism, the
most recent manifestation of the concern for consumer protection that has ebbed and flowed in the United States and
Europe for more than 60 years. The sudden emergence of consumerism has often outstripped the capacity to understand and
respond effectively. Thus, the objective of this book is to present
an organized collection of materials that will facilitate the
necessary understanding. The primary audience is managers
and students of business who will be dealing with consumerism
as a significant part of their future environment. We hope that
others who are interested in furthering the contemporary consumer movement will also find helpful and broadening
perspectives.

The choice of materials was largely guided by a desire to
present a balanced and well structured discussion of the key
issues. This goal eliminated a distressing number of articles
and books that have treated these issues in a sensational,
superficial or excessively partisan fashion. We don't claim that

the articles in this volume are not partisan. However, they generally have the good grace to recognize that there are two or three sides to the question. We hope that the reader will come away with an appreciation of the complexities of the situation, and the validity of the competing points of view.

The introduction to the book serves to position the articles in an overall context by first defining the meaning of consumerism, then identifying the major causal forces, and finally speculating about the future. Part One of the book is a continuation and elaboration of the introduction. It presents the scope of the problem from several perspectives. The remaining four parts of the book follow the problems that concern the consumer as he moves through the purchasing decision process.

Part Two deals with the availability and quality of the pre-purchase information. This information may come through many channels. Advertising and personal selling are the most visible, but packaging is also a powerful communication vehicle. The brand name and what it represents is a most relevant information source for the consumer, yet it is easy to forget its role in the communication process. Other marketer controlled information sources such as labels, instructional materials, industry performance standards and credit contracts are also relevant. Finally, there are issues surrounding the role of non-commercial information sources, such as consumer testing organizations.

Part Three considers various concerns with the conditions of the purchase decision, including prices and credit terms. Here, we consider the issues of trading stamps, games and other forms of non-price, basically non-informative promotions. Does the consumer have a satisfactory alternative to participating in the promotion? Does he have an adequate economic choice at the trading stamp redemption center? Also discussed here are the vast variety of schemes to knowingly defraud and deceive the consumer, or precipitate an unwanted purchase decision.

The post-purchase experience, covered in Part Four, deals with the adequacy of the performance. This includes the manufacturers' efforts to insure quality and safety, to meet performance claims, and to service the product. The courts have been instrumental in this aspect of consumerism by constantly broadening the manufacturers' liability for unsafe or inadequate performance.

Part Five recognizes that the purchase decision process cannot be applied uniformly to all buyers. The ghetto consumer segment is particularly differentiable from the public as a whole because of the "deviant" nature of the ghetto marketplace, and the relative inability of these consumers to cope with their problems. Consumers in this segment also deserve special attention because they have the most to gain from the protection of their rights as consumers.

The completion of this book, and in particular the introduction, would not have been possible without the encouragement, advice and criticism of our colleagues at Stanford and Berkeley. We think particularly of Harper W. Boyd and Lee E. Preston in this regard. Our greatest debt is to Richard H. Holton who brought his experience with the Consumer Advisory Council to bear on our problems, provided much-needed inspiration, and made his own special contribution in the foreword. Lastly we acknowledge Kay and Marilyn who are exceptional consumers and wives, but need protection nonetheless.

David A. Aaker
George S. Day

Foreword

The consumer movement in the United States historically has been a rather feeble animal, one whose presence has been generally known but safely ignored by observers of the economic and political scene. True, campaigns for public office have been marked by the ritualistic bow in the direction of the housewife and some of her problems as a consumer. But seldom was much done about such matters once the newly-elected officials assumed their positions and turned their attention to the more important policy issues of the day.

In recent years, however, vigorous debate about consumer issues has emerged as an important feature of the political scene. This surge in interest can be dated from the appointment of Esther Peterson to the new position of Special Assistant for Consumer Affairs in the Executive Office of the President, early in 1964. The business community was jolted by the announcement. Many saw it as an indication of anti-business sentiment on the part of President Johnson, who had appeared far more friendly to business than had President Kennedy. It was hoped that this apparent high-level interest in consumer affairs would prove to be nothing more than simple window-dressing.

For several reasons, however, the interest in consumer affairs not only survived but grew substantially in political prominence. Although the White House in the six years since Esther Peterson's appointment has been able to control its enthusiasm for the activities of the Special Assistant, regardless of the incumbent appointee, various Congressmen

and Senators have discovered rather substantial public interest in
consumer problems. With every voter also a consumer, talk or action
on high prices, shoddy merchandise, misleading advertising or poor
service was certain to be received sympathetically. Furthermore, the
topic could be worked nicely into discussions of the problems of poverty. With the Vietnam war, the space program and other high priority
demands on Federal funds generating such enormous demands, consumer issues were especially appealing since the remedies, e.g., the
introduction of Federal standards for automobile tires, were, for the
most part, cheap.

The initial impression that the attention given consumer matters
would be quite short-lived has proven to be in error. Interested legislators, reinforced by Ralph Nader and other (mostly young) lawyers
and writers, have built up a base of support which assures visibility
for consumer problems for several years to come.

Meanwhile, as is so often the case with problems in the social sciences, we have done a poor job of anticipating the problems to be
faced. Consequently policy solutions may come tumbling out of the
legislative mill before the researcher has had time to do his homework.
The researcher alone cannot be held responsible for this. Even if he
were interested before the problem surfaced as a major public policy
issue, his possible sources of research funding might not be moved
until the topic appeared in the policy spotlight. If we were to do the
basic research needed for optimum policy design in the social sciences
with the same care that the basic R&D precedes a manned lunar flight,
Congress might be more pleased with the results of its legislative
handiwork in the field of social policy, including the general field of
"consumerism."

At the present writing it appears that consumer legislation of one
variety or another will be under discussion into the indefinite future.
It would seem wise, therefore, not only to press forward with the
research needed to make judgments about certain policy questions,
but also to begin to organize the available materials on consumer issues
so they can easily be presented to managers and to the students of
management. No one can pretend to be prepared for the world of management today in this country unless he has a reasonably good idea of
what "the consumer interest" is all about. This collection of readings
is a helpful step toward providing this necessary overview.

What attitude should the businessman take toward this growing
interest in consumer legislation? It does little good, surely, for him

to answer with the knee-jerk response that competition and our present regulations provide ample protection for the consumer. The consumer simply cannot become an expert purchasing agent for all consumer goods. The widening choice of goods and services, which the public welcomes, is accompanied by growing complexity of the performance characteristics of the items available. With the advance of technology, more of the product features fall below the threshold of perception. Consequently the consumer is less able to judge the quality of the product for himself. I have argued elsewhere [1] that competition alone does quite well in providing protection for the consumer in the case of those products (1) which are bought frequently by the individual consumer, (2) which have quality and performance characteristics (readily comparable among brands) which are apparent before purchase or immediately after use, and (3) which are subject to a rate of technological change which is slow, relative to the frequency of purchase. Razor blades and dry cleaning services are product (service) markets which come close to meeting the three criteria. But at the other end of the spectrum are a multitude of products and services which fail to meet one or more of the three criteria: major appliances, automobile tires, automobiles themselves, casualty and life insurance, pharmaceuticals, medical care, appliance repair services, automobile repair services and even supermarket items in which package sizes of alternative brands inhibit comparison of price per ounce or pound or quart. In these latter cases, markets are quite imperfect in the sense that the consumer has difficulty acquiring or assimilating the information he needs to make a satisfactory choice.

The businessman of course sees competition as "working" in all these areas because sellers are clearly fighting for a leading place in the market, and the fortunes of each will rise and fall over time. But this does not necessarily mean that this intensive competition leads to contentment among buyers. Competition among retailers in the market for automobile tires is famous for being as intense as in any product market. Yet the complaints about the nature of competition in the tire market from the consumer's point of view have led to the promulgation of tire standards. Thus we see that intensive competition among sellers does not, in and of itself, assure market conditions which are satisfactory to consumers. In this case the terminology used in the industry ("first line," "second line," etc.) was so nearly meaningless that the consumer, unable to measure tire quality by physical exam-

[1] "Business and Government," *Daedalus* (Winter, 1969), 47–48.

ination, was lost without standardization of that terminology. Without such standardization of usage, what was intensive competition among sellers was not satisfactory competition in the eyes of buyers. The businessman who sees himself engaged in a stiff competitive struggle should not assume that consumers are necessarily happy with the results of that competition.

What is needed in many consumer markets is a more efficient information system. Consumers may complain that not enough information is available, while the businessman complains in turn that consumers don't use the information already at hand. This suggests that the consumer finds the increased cost of search relatively high, as he expends it among competing sellers, compared with the yield of additional information that the increased search provides. If the information system were more efficient, this increased search would yield more knowledge, and consumers would make fewer purchase errors. Much of the government regulation discussed in these readings can be viewed as attempts to improve the efficiency of the information system available to consumers, to improve the productivity, so to speak, of the process of consumer search. The quality of the public discussion of "consumerism" would be enhanced if the problems of consumer markets were seen in this light.

Richard H. Holton

Consumerism

Introduction:
A Guide to Consumerism

David A. Aaker and George S. Day

Consumerism has played an expanding role in the environment of business decision makers during the past decade. Despite wishful thinking by some of these decision makers, the following analysis of consumerism is as relevant today as it was in 1964 when it was written:

(1) As evidenced by consumer agitation at the local-state-federal levels, business has failed to meet the total needs and desires of today's consumers.

(2) Into this business-created vacuum, government forces have quickly moved to answer this consumer need.

(3) The areas of consumer interest are so diverse that they offer government agencies and legislators almost limitless reasons for additional regulation of business and commerce.

(4) If business managers want to avoid such new government regulations (with the attendant possibilities of excessive and punitive legislation), they will have to take positive action to demon-

Reprinted from *Journal of Marketing,* Vol. 34 (July, 1970), pp. 12–19, published by The American Marketing Association.

strate that the business interest is in more general accord with consumer's needs and wants.[1]

The ensuing six years have seen the passage of a great deal of consumerism legislation and a substantial broadening of the scope of the concept. One constant factor during this period has been a lack of agreement on the extent of the influence of consumerism or its long-range implications. Businessmen have suffered from a myopia that comes from perceiving consumerism primarily in terms of markets with which they are very familiar. Their emphasis on the peculiarities of these few markets often leads them to overlook similar problems in other contexts and, thus, to discount the seriousness of the overall problem they face. Legislators and members of the consumer movement are more responsive to the broad problems facing consumers, but their lack of understanding of specific market situations too often leads to inappropriate diagnoses and solutions. Fortunately the two basic perspectives are demonstrating a healthy convergence. The goal of this paper is to encourage this convergence by putting consumerism into a perspective that will facilitate understanding.

The Scope of Consumerism

Consumerism is a term that appears to be uniquely associated with the past decade. Even in this short period it has undergone a number of changes in meaning. One of the earliest adopters of the term was Vance Packard, who linked it with strategies for persuading consumers to quickly expand their needs and wants by making them "voracious, compulsive (and wasteful)." [2] His usage clearly reflected the concerns of the fifties with planned obsolescence, declining quality and poor service in saturated consumer goods markets. The term was not put to wider use

---

[1] Tom M. Hopkinson, "New Battleground—Consumer Interest," *Harvard Business Review* (September–October, 1964), 97.

[2] Vance Packard, *The Waste Makers,* New York: David McKay, 1960, 23.

until 1963 or 1964, when a variety of commentators identified it with the very visible concerns triggered indirectly by Rachel Carson,[3] and directly by Ralph Nader's [4] auto safety investigations and by President Kennedy's efforts to establish the rights of consumers: to safety, to be informed, to choose, and to be heard.[5]

The most common understanding of consumerism is in reference to the *widening* range of activities of government, business and independent organizations that are designed to protect individuals from practices that infringe upon their rights as consumers. This view of consumerism emphasizes the direct relationship between the individual consumer and the business firm. Because it is an evolving concept, there is no accepted list of the various facets of this relationship. The following is representative:

(1) Protection against clear-cut abuses. This encompasses outright fraud and deceit that are a part of the "dark side of the marketplace," [6] as well as dangers to health and safety from *voluntary* use of a product. There is substantial agreement in principle between business and consumer spokesmen that such abuses need to be corrected and prevented, but there is often a wide divergence of opinion on the extent of the problem. As a result the government has taken the initiative in this area; usually after the divulgence of a sensational abuse. This has been the case with much of the legislation dealing with drug, tire, auto and pipeline safety and meat and fish inspection. Even so, this is the least controversial and oldest aspect of consumerism.

(2) Provision of adequate information. The concern here is with the economic interests of the consumer. The question is

[3] Rachel Carson, *Silent Spring,* Boston: Houghton Mifflin, 1962.

[4] Ralph Nader, *Unsafe At Any Speed,* New York: Pocket Books, 1966.

[5] For a discussion, see "Consumer Advisory Council, First Report," Executive Office of the President (Washington, D.C.: United States Government Printing Office, October 1963).

[6] Senator Warren Magnuson and Jean Carper, *The Dark Side of the Marketplace,* Englewood Cliffs: Prentice-Hall, 1968.

whether the right to information goes beyond the right not
to be deceived, to include the provision of performance information that will ensure a wise purchase. Much of the controversy and confusion over consumerism revolves around this
basic issue.[7] The two polar positions identified by Bauer and
Greyser [8] are the business view that the buyer should be
guided by his judgment of the reputation of the manufacturer
and the quality of the brand, versus the view of the consumer
spokesmen that information should be provided by impartial
sources and reveal performance characteristics.

(3) The protection of consumers against themselves and other
consumers. Some of the thrust behind consumerism comes
from the growing acceptance of the position that paternalism
is a legitimate policy. Thus the National Traffic and Motor
Vehicle Safety Act of 1966 is not concerned with the possibility that the buyer has an expressed but unsatisfied need for
safety, and emphasizes instead that carelessness may have
undesirable consequences for innocent participants.[9] There is
a sound basis in economic theory for such intervention whenever the action of a buyer serves his own best interest and
does not account for the effects on others. However, this
principle is being extended to situations of implied consumer
interest where the individual is deemed unable to even identify his own best interest (e.g., the mandatory installation of
seat belts and the provision for a "cooling off" period after a
door-to-door sale). This is a strong justification for the protection of inexperienced, poorly educated and generally disadvantaged consumers. More controversial by far is the
extension of this notion to all consumers, on the grounds that
manipulated preferences may be disregarded when the consumer is not acting in his best interest. So far the idea has
not been adopted with enthusiasm.[9a]

[7] *Freedom of Information in the Market Place,* FOI Center, Columbus,
Missouri, 1967.
[8] Raymond A. Bauer and Stephen A. Greyser, "The Dialogue That Never
Happens," *Harvard Business Review,* 45 (November–December, 1967), 2.
[9] Robert L. Birmingham, "The Consumer As King: The Economics of Pre-
carious Sovereignty," *Case Western Reserve Law Journal,* 20 (1969).
[9a] Birmingham, *op. cit.,* page 374.

The above three facets of consumerism suggest the current thrust of the movement. Yet, it would be naive to portray consumerism as a static entity. It has had a dynamic past and continues to evolve and change at an increasingly rapid rate. For example, the emphasis of the consumer movement of the thirties and later was on dangerous and unhealthy products and "dishonest or questionable practices which are believed to hamper the consumer in making wise decisions . . . and obtaining useful information." [10] The emphasis today is clearly far broader.

There is a high probability that the scope of consumerism will eventually subsume, or be subsumed by, two other areas of social concern: distortions and inequities in the economic environment and the declining quality of the physical environment. The forecast of a greater identity between these social problems and consumerism rests on the fact that they are associated with many of the same basic causes, have common spokesmen, and seem to be moving in the same direction in many respects. Indeed, Yohalem has indicated that the ultimate challenge of consumerism to industry is "toward ending hunger and malnutrition . . . toward alleviating pollution of the air, water and soil . . . toward educating and training the disadvantaged . . . toward solving these and other problems of a society rather than strictly of an industrial nature." [11]

Concern over the *economic* environment dates back to the end of the last century. The long-run manifestation of this concern has been antitrust law and enforcement, which has swung back and forth between protecting competition and protecting competitors. Despite various ambiguities in antitrust interpretation, this has been a major effort to ensure the consumers'

[10] Fred E. Clark and Carrie P. Clark, *Principles of Marketing*, New York: Macmillan, 1942, page 406.
[11] Aaron S. Yohalem, "Consumerism's Ultimate Challenge: Is Business Equal to the Task?", address before the American Management Association, New York, November 10, 1969.

"right to choose" by increasing the number of competitors. Some regard it as "the fundamental consumer edifice on which all other measures are bottomed." [12] Judging from the recent intensification of concern over the economic role of advertising and promotion (insofar as they increase price and raise barriers to entry to new markets), reciprocity, restrictive distributive arrangements, conglomerate mergers, and related topics, it appears that antitrust issues will be a continuing impetus to consumerism. In a period of rapid inflation it is not surprising that advertising and promotion costs have come under additional scrutiny for their role in contributing to high prices, particularly food prices. This promises to be a durable issue, inasmuch as a task force of the White House conference on food, nutrition, and health has recommended lower food prices, by reducing promotion not related to nutritional or other food values, as a major item in a national nutrition policy.[13]

More recently, consumerism has become identified with the widespread concern with the quality of the *physical* environment. The problems of air, water, and noise pollution have become increasingly salient as the tolerance of the public for these abuses has decreased. In effect a "critical mass" of explosive concern has suddenly been created. The consumer movement has rapidly rearranged its priorities to become a part of this critical mass. This shift is not surprising in view of the desire to broaden consumerism to include problems arising from indirect influences on the consumer interest. It also follows naturally from the long standing concern with built-in obsolescence and poor quality and repairability, for these problems contribute to pollution in a "disposable" society.

As the consumer movement joins with conservationists and interested legislators there is a growing likelihood of govern-

[12] Statement of Leslie Dix (on behalf of the Special Committee on Consumer Interests) Federal Trade Commission, *National Consumer Protection Hearings* (Washington: U.S. Government Printing Office, November, 1968), 16.
[13] "Food Ads to Get Wide Ranging Scrutiny at White House Session," *Advertising Age,* 41 (December 1, 1969), 1.

ment action. The argument for such intervention has been well
stated by Andrew Shonfield:

> Increasingly the realization is forced upon us that the market,
> which purports to be the reflection of the way in which people
> spontaneously value their individual wants and efforts, is a poor
> guide to the best means of satisfying the real wishes of consumers.
> That is because market prices generally fail to measure either
> social costs or social benefits. In our civilization these grow con-
> stantly more important. Simply because some amenity—let it be
> a pleasant view or an uncongested road or a reasonably quiet en-
> vironment—is not paid for directly by those who enjoy it, there
> is no measure of the cost of the disinvestment which occurs when
> a profitable economic activity destroys what already exists. Unless
> the State actively intervenes, and on an increasing scale, to compel
> private enterprise to adapt its investment decisions to considera-
> tions such as these, the process of economic growth may positively
> impede the attainment of things that people most deeply want.[14]

The result may well be increased controls on producer controlled emittants and, perhaps, "quality standards . . . or
other regulatory devices in the interest of upgrading product
quality and repairability." [15]

The Underlying Causes of Consumerism

Additional insights come from a consideration of the factors
underlying the recent upsurge of interest in consumerism.
It appears that increasingly discontented and aroused consumers have combined with a growing number of formal and
informal institutions capable of focusing discontent, to create
enough pressure to overcome the advantage of the traditionally
more effective lobbies representing the producer's interests.
Since a particular government action means much more to
the individual producer (who will be totally affected), than to
the individual consumer (who divides his concern among many
items), this clearly involved a significant effort.

---

[14] Andrew Shonfield, *Modern Capitalism: The Changing Balance of Public
and Private Power,* New York: Oxford University Press, 1965, page 227.
[15] Stanley E. Cohen, "Pollution Threat May Do More for Consumers Than
Laws, Regulations," *Advertising Age,* 41 (March 2, 1970), 72.

The discontented consumer

The discontented consumer is not part of an homogeneous group with easily described complaints. The fact is that there exists a great variation among consumers in the extent of their discontent and a wide variety of underlying causes. Nonetheless, it is possible to distinguish specific sources of discontent, that are traceable to the marketing environment, from other more pervasive concerns with the nature of society.

Problems in the marketplace

To some observers [16] the leading problem is imperfections in the state of information in consumer markets. Their argument is that consumers would be adequately cared for by competition *if* they could learn quickly about available brands and their prices and characteristics. However, as products proliferate each consumer is less and less able to make useful price and quality comparisons. This inability leads to "increasing shopper confusion, consequent irritation and consequent resentment." [17] The problem is most severe for products which are purchased infrequently, exhibit a rapid rate of technological change and whose performance characteristics are not readily apparent. Hence we see increasing pressure for tire standards, unit prices, truth-in-lending, truth-in-funds, information about the design-life of durable goods and so on. The truth-in-packaging bill is another manifestation of this problem, for it aims to help the consumer cope with the volume of information available on the thousands of available grocery and drug products. Since advertising has not been notable as a source of adequate, or even accurate, information that could alleviate the problem, it

[16] Richard H. Holton, "Government-Consumer Interest: Conflicts and Prospects" (The University Point of View), in *Changing Market Systems* (Chicago: American Marketing Association, 1967).
[17] E. B. Weiss, "Line Profusion in Consumerism," *Advertising Age,* 40 (April 1, 1968), 72.

has been under continuing attack.[18] To the extent that retailing is becoming more and more impersonal, the whole situation may become worse. Thus,

> . . . as a result of the character of contemporary retail establishments, the vastly increased number of consumer products, and the misleading, deceptive and generally uninformative aspects of advertising and packaging, the consumer simply lacks the information necessary to enable him to buy wisely.[19]

This is not an unusually intemperate charge; nor is it denied by the finding that 53 per cent of a sample of adults disagreed with the statement that "In general, advertisements present a true picture of the product advertised." This response measures both a concern over genuine deception and differences in people's tolerance for fantasy.[20] Nonetheless the potential for dissatisfaction is large.

The proliferation and improvement of products, resulting from attempts to better satisfy specific needs and/or reduce direct competition, has had other consequences as well. As one appliance executive noted, ". . . the public is staging a revolt of rising expectancy. Customers today expect products to perform satisfactorily, to provide dependable functional performance and to be safe. This threshold of acceptable performance is steadily rising . . ."[21] Unfortunately the complexity and malfunction potential of many products has also been rising.[22] The result is an uncomfortable level of dissatisfaction with

[18] Louis L. Stern, "Consumer Information Via Increased Information," *Journal of Marketing,* 31 (April, 1967), 48–52.

[19] Richard J. Barber, "Government and the Consumer," *Michigan Law Review,* 64 (May, 1966), 1226.

[20] Raymond A. Bauer and Stephen A. Greyser, *Advertising in America: the Consumer View,* Boston: Graduate School of Business Administration (Harvard University, 1968), page 345.

[21] Robert C. Wells, quoted in James Bishop and Henry W. Hubbard, *Let The Seller Beware* (Washington: The National Press, 1969), page 14.

[22] "Rattles, Pings, Dents, Leaks, Creaks—and Costs," *Newsweek* (November 25, 1968), 93.

quality, compounded by inadequate service facilities.[23] This situation is not confined to hard goods, for one result of rapidly rising sales is overburdened retail and manufacturing facilities, which leads to deteriorating quality and service for almost all mass merchandised goods.[24]

These problems are occurring at a time when consumers are generally less willing to give industry the benefit of the doubt —an understandable reaction to the well publicized shortcomings of the drug, auto, and appliance manufacturers. Even without these problems, more skepticism is to be expected from consumers who have found that their assumptions about the adequacy of laws covering reasonable aspects of health, safety, and truthfulness are wrong. Recent disclosures involving such vital issues as meat inspection and auto and drug safety have hurt both government and industry by contributing to an atmosphere of distrust. According to Stanley Cohen the meat inspection battle was particularly important here, "because for the first time the public had a clear cut demonstration of the jurisdictional gap (between state and federal governments) that limits the effectiveness of virtually all consumer protection legislation." [25]

Problems in the social fabric

The present imperfections in the marketplace would probably not have generated nearly the same depth of concern in earlier periods. The difference is several changes deep in society, that have served as catalysts to magnify the seriousness of these imperfections.

The first catalyst has been the new visibility of the low-income consumer. These are the consumers who suffer the most from

[23] See, Federal Trade Commission, "Staff Report on Automobile Warranties" (Washington: no date) and "Report of the Task Force on Appliance Warranties and Service" (Washington: January 1969).

[24] "Consumers Upset Experts," *New York Times* (April 13, 1969), f. 17.

[25] Stanley E. Cohen, "Business Should Prepare for Wider Probe of Consumer Protection Laws," *Advertising Age* (January 8, 1968), page 59.

fraud, excessive prices, exorbitant credit charges or poor
quality merchandise and service. Unfortunately, solutions
oriented toward improving the amount and quality of product
information have little relevance to low income buyers who,
as indicated below, lack most of the characteristics of the
prototype middle income consumer.[26]

(1) Low income consumers are often unaware of the benefits of
comparative shopping,

(2) They lack the education and knowledge necessary to choose
the best buy, even if it were available. Because of their low
income they have many fewer opportunities to learn through
experience.

(3) They often lack the freedom to go outside their local community to engage in comparative shopping,

(4) They lack even a superficial appreciation of their rights and
liabilities in post-sale legal conflicts,

(5) Nothing in their experience has reinforced the benefits of
seeking better value for their money; consequently the low
income buyer lacks the motivation to make improvements in
his situation.

Thus the low income consumer environment is a perfect breed-
ing ground for exploitation and fraud. The extent of the distortion in the ghetto marketplace has only recently been widely
comprehended [27] and related to the overall failure of society
to help the disadvantaged.

The second catalyst is best described as a basic dissatisfaction
with the impersonalization of society in general, and the market
system in particular. Evidence for this point of view is not hard
to find, particularly among young people. A survey of college

---

[26] Lewis Schnapper, "Consumer Legislation and the Poor," *The Yale Law
Journal,* 76 (1967).
[27] David Caplovitz, *The Poor Pay More,* New York: The Free Press of
Glencoe, 1963.

student opinion [28] found 65 per cent of the sample were in strong or partial agreement with the statement that "American society is characterized by injustice, insensitivity, lack of candor, and inhumanity." Similar levels of disenchantment were reported among parents and nonstudents of the same age. The need seems to be felt for social organizations that are responsive—and perhaps the impression of responsiveness is as important as the specific responses that are made.

There is little doubt that large American corporations are not regarded as responsive by their customers. According to Weiss,[29] both manufacturers and retailers are "turning a deaf ear," while increasingly sophisticated consumers are demanding more personal relationships and security in their purchases. This situation stems from a whole series of changes in the marketing environment: the rise of self-service and discounting (in part because of the difficulty of obtaining good sales employees), the high cost of trained service personnel and the intervention of the computer into the relationship with consequent rigidifying of customer policies and practices. The prospects for improvement are dim, because the benefits of good service and prompt personal attention to complaints are difficult to quantify and consequently are given low priority when investment decisions are made. As more consumers are seeing the government as being more sympathetic, if not more helpful, the prospect for arbitration procedures to settle complaints is increased.

The most disturbing feature of the catalyzing effects of the recently visible low-income consumer, the growing dissatisfaction with the impersonalization of society and concern over the quality of the physical environment is their intractability. These problems are almost impervious to piecemeal attempts

---

[28] Jeremy Main, "A Special Report on Youth," *Fortune* (June, 1969), 73.
[29] E. B. Weiss, "The Corporate Deaf Ear," *Business Horizons* (December, 1968), 5.

at correction. In view of the small likelihood of large-scale changes in social priorities or social structures, these problems will be a part of the environment for the foreseeable future.

The final and most enduring catalyst is the consequence of an increasingly better educated consumer. As the Chamber of Commerce recently noted, the consumer of the present and future "expects more information about the products and services he buys. He places greater emphasis on product performance, quality and safety. He is more aware of his 'rights' as a consumer and is more responsive than ever before to political initiatives to protect these rights." [30]

The activist consumer

The discontented consumer found many more effective ways to express feelings and press for change during the 1960's than ever before. The development of means of translating discontent into effective pressure distinguishes recent consumer efforts from those of the 1910 and 1935 eras.

The consumer has been more ably represented by advocates such as Ralph Nader, Senator Warren Magnuson and a number of journalists who pursue similar interests. These men are able to identify and publicize problems, and follow up with workable programs for improvement. In a real sense, they are self-elected legal counsels to a typically unrepresented constituency. Many consumer problems would have remained smoldering but unfocused discontents without their attention. As new product researchers have frequently found, consumers don't know what is bothering them or realize that others are similarly troubled until the extent of the problem is publicized or an alternative is provided.

[30] Report of Council on Trends and Perspective on, "Business and the Consumer—A Program for the Seventies," Washington, D.C.: Chamber of Commerce of the United States, 1969.

The institutional framework has also been expanded and
strengthened in recent years. Traditional bodies, such as Consumers Union and Consumers Research, Inc., have now received support from permanent bodies in the government such
as the Consumer Advisory Council and the Office of the Special
Assistant to the President for Consumer Affairs. These agencies
have been specifically developed to avoid the problems of
excessive identification with regulated industries which plague
some of the older regulated bodies.

This decade has also seen greater willingness on the part of
consumers to take direct action. Consider the protest of the
housewives in Denver over the costs of trading stamps and
games. While this was probably due to general dissatisfaction
over the effects of inflation on food prices, it did represent an
important precedent. More sobering is the extreme form of
protest documented by the National Commission on Civil Disorders. "Much of the violence in recent civil disorders has been
directed at stores and other commercial establishments in disadvantaged Negro areas. In some cases, rioters focused on
stores operated by white merchants who, they apparently
believed, had been charging exorbitant prices or selling inferior
goods. Not all the violence against these stores can be attributed
to 'revenge' for such practices. Yet, it is clear that many residents of disadvantaged Negro neighborhoods believe they suffer
constant abuses by local merchants." [31]

The changing legal and political scene

The pressures for change have been directed at a legal and
political structure that is much more willing to take action than
before:

(1) Overall, there is more acceptance of government involvement
in issues of consumer protection. Also, the Federal govern-

[31]"Exploitation of Disadvantaged Consumers by Retail Merchants," *Report
of the National Commission on Civil Disorders,* New York: Bantam Books,
1968, page 274.

ment has been more prepared to take action, because the state and local governments have generally defaulted their early legal responsibility in this area.[32]

(2) A combination of factors has contributed to the expanded role of the Federal government: Congress is no longer so dominated by the rural constituencies who appear less interested in these matters; consumer legislation is relatively cheap and appears to generate goodwill among voters; and various tests of the influence of business lobbyists have shown that their power is not as great as originally feared.[33] In fact, many observers feel that industry may have been its own worst enemy by often opposing all consumer legislation without admitting any room for improvement or providing constructive alternatives.[34] Worse, they may have demonstrated that industry self-regulation is not workable.[35]

(3) The consequence is a Congress that is responsive to the economic interests of consumers. A significant proportion of the enacted or pending legislation is a result of Congressional initiative and is directed toward ensuring that consumers have adequate and accurate shopping information. This is very different from earlier legislation which was enacted because a tragedy dramatized the need to protect health and safety.[36]

(4) Finally, a large number of legal reforms have been slowly instituted which attempt to correct the imbalance of power held by the manufacturers, e.g., the expansion of the implied warranty, and the elimination of privity of contract.[37] Of special interest are current efforts to give the individual consumer more leverage by making the practice of consumer law

[32] Ralph Nader, "The Great American Gyp," *New York Review of Books,* 9 (November 21, 1968), 28.

[33] Stanley E. Cohen, " 'Giant Killers' Upset Notions That Business 'Clout' Runs Government," *Advertising Age,* 41 (July 14, 1969), 73.

[34] Jeremy Main, "Industry Still Has Something to Learn about Congress," *Fortune* (February, 1967), 128–135.

[35] Harper W. Boyd, Jr., and Henry J. Claycamp, "Industrial Self-Regulation and the Consumer Interest," *Michigan Law Review,* 64 (May, 1966), 1239.

[36] Philip A. Hart, "Can Federal Legislation Affecting Consumers' Economic Interests Be Enacted?" *Michigan Law Review,* 64 (May, 1966), 1255.

[37] David L. Rados, "Product Liability: Tougher Ground Rules," *Harvard Business Review,* 47 (July–August, 1969), 144.

profitable for attorneys. The mechanism being promoted is the consumer class action which permits suits by one or a few consumers on behalf of all consumers similarly abused.[38] This will make fraud cases, where individual claims are smaller than legal costs, much more attractive to investigate and litigate.

The Future of Consumerism

One of the main conclusions from past efforts to forecast social phenomena is that naive extrapolations are likely to be wrong. A better approach in this situation is to utilize the interpretation that consumerism is at least partially a reflection of many social problems that are certain to persist, and perhaps be magnified in the future. This diagnosis rules out the possibility that consumerism activity will decline significantly in the future; the unanswered questions concern the rate of increase in this activity and the areas of greatest sensitivity.

One index of activity, the amount of Federal consumer legislation pending, should slow its rate of increase. Only a limited number of consumer bills can be considered at a time, and over 400 such bills were pending in Congressional committees at the end of 1969.[39] Also more attention will have to be given to implementing and improving existing legislation rather than writing new legislation. For example, there is evidence that the truth-in-lending bill will not achieve its original goals, partly because of lack of understanding of the problem and partly because of inadequacies and confusion in the enacted legislation.[40] Similarly it is dismaying that after two years of experience with the truth-in-packaging bill it is being referred to as "one

[38] David Sanford, "Giving the Consumer Class," *The New Republic* (July 26, 1969), 15. Partial support for this concept was given by President Nixon in his "Buyer's Bill of Rights" proposal of October 30, 1969.
[39] This estimate appeared in *Business Week* (November 1, 1969), 32.
[40] "A Foggy First Week for the Lending Law," *Business Week* (July 5, 1969), 13. This result was accurately forecasted by Homer Kripke, "Gesture and Reality in Consumer Credit Reform," *New York University Law Review*, 44 (March, 1969), 1.

of the best non-laws in the book." [41] In this particular situation
the problem seems to lie with the interest and ability of the
various regulatory agencies to implement the law. This is not
an isolated example of enforcement failures. The Food and
Drug Administration (FDA) recently estimated that fewer than
two-thirds of all food processors have complied with standards
to prevent some forms of food contamination. One result has
been an increased pressure for a powerful central consumer
agency [42] to implement, modify and coordinate the 269 consumer programs that are presently administered by 33 different
Federal agencies.[43]

The very nature of the contemporary marketplace will probably
continue to inhibit basic changes in business operations.
Weiss [44] points out that some manufacturers and retailers will
always equate responsible with legal behavior. These tenden-
cies are reinforced by the competitive structure of many markets
where success depends on an ability to appeal directly to the
"marginal float." One view of this group,[45] is that they constitute
a minority who are "fickle . . . particularly susceptible to
innovation that may not be relevant, and to attention getters
such as sexy TV jokes or giveaway games." While research
support is lacking, this widely held view helps explain some of
the behavior that consumerists complain about.

There are signs that concerned parties are making efforts to
rise above emotion to rationally identify and realistically attack
the problems. Two major, if embryonic, research efforts are

[41] Stanley E. Cohen, "Packaging Law Is on Books, But Ills It Aimed to
Cure Are Still Troublesome," *Advertising Age,* 41 (September 1, 1969), 10.
[42] See Richard J. Barber, *op. cit.,* and Louis M. Kohlmeier, Jr., "The Regulatory Agencies: What Should Be Done?" *Washington Monthly,* 1 (August,
1969), 42.
[43] "Wide Gaps Exist in Consumer Food Safety," *Congressional Quarterly*
(November, 1969).
[44] E. B. Weiss, "Marketeers Fiddle While Consumers Burn," *Harvard Business Review,* 46 (July–August, 1968), 45.
[45] See Stanley E. Cohen, "Consumer Interests Drift in Vacuum as Business
Pursues Marginal Float," *Advertising Age,* 41 (March 24, 1969), 112.

underway which aim at providing decision makers in business and government with empirically based knowledge to supplement the intuition on which they now too often solely rely. The first is the Consumer Research Institute sponsored by the Grocery Manufacturers Association.[46] The second is an effort by the Marketing Science Institute.[47] Although both research organizations have close ties with business, neither was established to justify or defend vested interests. Their objectives are to promote basic, academic research that will be respected by all parties. The MSI group specifically proposes to obtain participation at the research design phase of each project of those who would potentially disagree about policy. Although the government now has no comparable effort, it is reasonable to expect movement in this direction. Cohen has suggested that the FTC should establish a Bureau of Behavioral Studies "whose function would be to gather and analyze data on consumer buying behavior relevant to the regulations of advertising in the consumer interest." [48]

An early study, which might be regarded as a prototype to the CRI and MSI efforts, experimentally examined the relationship between deceptive packaging (with respect to content weight) and brand preference.[49] It demonstrated that experimentation can provide useful information to policy makers.

These research approaches and the forces behind them should not only generate influential information but should also help stimulate some basic changes in orientation. We can expect to see, for example, the simplistic "economic man" model of

[46] "Business Responds to Consumerism," *Business Week* (September 6, 1969), p. 98.

[47] Robert Moran, "Consumerism and Marketing," *Marketing Science Institute Preliminary Statement* (May, 1969).

[48] Dorothy Cohen, "The Federal Trade Commission and the Regulation of Advertising in the Consumer Interest," *Journal of Marketing*, 33 (January, 1969), 40.

[49] James C. Naylor, "Deceptive Packaging: Are Deceivers Being Deceived?" *Journal of Applied Psychology*, 6 (December, 1962), 393.

consumer behavior enriched.[50] The last decade has seen great progress made in the study of consumer behavior. This progress should contribute directly to a deeper analysis of consumerism issues. We can also hope that the dissemination of relevant knowledge will help eliminate the present semantic problems.[51] Such a development must accompany rational discourse.

Finally, we can expect business managers, whether progressive or defensive, to develop new, flexible approaches toward insuring that the rights of the consumer will be protected. Even though the motives may be mixed there is no reason why effective programs cannot be developed.

[50] David M. Gardner, "The Package, Legislation, and the Shopper," *Business Horizons*, 2 (October, 1968), 53.
[51] Raymond A. Bauer and Stephen A. Greyser, "The Dialogue That Never Happens," *op. cit.*

Part One
The Scope of the Problem

1. First Report

Consumer Advisory Council

The Consumer Advisory Council's first year

On March 15, 1962, President John F. Kennedy sent to the Congress a *Special Message on Protecting the Consumer Interest*. In this message, the first ever delivered by a president on this topic, President Kennedy took note of the important role played by consumers in the American economy and the challenging problems that confront them. And he pointed to the potential for improving the well-being of American families—not only by increasing the size of their incomes, but by making the best possible use of their incomes as consumers.

The President's directive

The President called attention to the complex, rapidly changing nature of consumer problems.

> The march of technology—affecting, for example, the foods we eat, the medicines we take, and the many appliances we use in our homes—has increased the difficulties of the consumer along with his opportunities; and it has outmoded many of the old laws and regulations and made new legislation necessary. The typical supermarket before World War II stocked about 1,500 separate

Reprinted from "Consumer Advisory Council, First Report," Executive Office of the President (Washington, D.C.: United States Government Printing Office, October, 1963), 5–8, 18–31.

23

food items—an impressive figure by any standard. But today it carries over 6,000. Ninety percent of the prescriptions written today are for drugs that were unknown 20 years ago. Many of the new products used every day in the home are highly complex. The housewife is called upon to be an amateur electrician, mechanic, chemist, toxicologist, dietitian, and mathematician—but she is rarely furnished the information she needs to perform these tasks proficiently.

Marketing is increasingly impersonal. Consumer choice is influenced by mass advertising utilizing highly developed arts of persuasion. The consumer typically cannot know whether drug preparations meet minimum standards of safety, quality, and efficacy. He usually does not know how much he pays for consumer credit; whether one prepared food has more nutritional value than another; whether the performance of a product will in fact meet his needs; or whether the "large economy size" is really a bargain.

In this same message, the President stressed the importance of the long-established role of the Federal Government in promoting the consumer interest. He pointed out that:

> Nearly all of the programs offered by this Administration— e.g., the expansion of world trade, the improvement of medical care, the reduction of passenger taxes, the strengthening of mass transit, the development of conservation and recreation areas and low-cost power—are of direct or inherent importance to consumers.

He went on to say that:

> Additional legislative and administrative action is required, however, if the Federal Government is to meet its responsibility to consumers in the exercise of their rights. These rights include—
>
> 1. *The right to safety*—to be protected against the marketing of goods which are hazardous to health or life.
>
> 2. *The right to be informed*—to be protected against fraudulent, deceitful, or grossly misleading information, advertising, labeling, or other practices, and to be given the facts he needs to make an informed choice.
>
> 3. *The right to choose*—to be assured, wherever possible, access to a variety of products and services at competitive prices and in those industries in which competition is not workable and

Government regulation is substituted, to be assured satisfactory quality and service at fair prices.

4. *The right to be heard*—to be assured that consumer interests will receive full and sympathetic consideration in the formulation of Government policy, and fair and expeditious treatment in its administrative tribunals.

With respect to the fourth right—the right to be heard—the President emphasized the need for new arrangements for participation by consumers in government. This was one of the recurring themes of the Consumer Message. In the opening paragraph he noted that consumers "are the only important group in the economy who are not effectively organized, whose views are often not heard." In the closing paragraph he said, "Their voice is not always as loudly heard in Washington as the voices of smaller and better-organized groups—nor is their point of view always defined and presented." He also referred in the same message to "the failure of governmental machinery to assure specific consideration of the consumers' needs and point of view."

It was this "failure of governmental machinery" that prompted the President to direct that the Council of Economic Advisers create a Consumer Advisory Council to "examine and provide advice to the Government on issues of broad economic policy, on governmental programs protecting consumer needs, and on needed improvements in the flow of consumer research material to the public; . . ." He further stated that this new Council should ". . . give interested individuals and organizations a voice in these matters."

The President also directed the head of each agency whose activities bear significantly on consumer welfare to designate a special assistant in his office "to advise and assist him in assuring adequate and effective attention to consumer interests in the work of the agency, to act as liaison with consumer and related organizations, and to place increased emphasis on preparing and making available pertinent research findings for consumers in clear and usable form. . . ."

The first Consumer Advisory Council was appointed . . . in July 1962. . . . [G]uided by the broad terms used by the President in his Consumer Message, . . . [t]he Council approached its planning from the standpoint of the actual and ideal roles of the consumer in the American economy. After considering a wide range of topics, the Council identified ten fields of pressing interest to consumers. It specified, for the first six of these fields, issues which the members felt should receive primary attention. The ten fields are:

(1) Consumer standards, grades, and labels: To study governmental consumer standards of identity, quality, quantity, safety, and product performance, including assessment from the consumer point of view of systems of grades, labels, and quality designation.

(2) Two-way flow of information and opinion between government and the consumer: To prepare recommendations for improving the two-way flow of information and opinion between government and the consumer public.

(3) Effective consumer representation in government: To examine and advise on different structures and procedures for achieving effective representation of, and participation by, the consumer in government.

(4) Consumer credit: To examine consumer credit (including mortgage credit) in order to assess its effect on the family and the Nation, to evaluate contract terms as they facilitate or inhibit efficient and intelligent use of credit by consumers, and to appraise procedures used in cases where consumers have made excessive use of credit.

(5) Interrelation among Federal agencies and between Federal and State agencies in areas of consumer protection: To examine and advise on such relationships with a view to improving the effective administration, enforcement, and scope of their programs.

(6) Acceleration of economic growth: To examine and advise on the process of economic growth with the objective of submitting the consumer's point of view on basic economic policies designed to promote a higher level of national product, income, and employment—with special attention to the factors determining consumer decisions to save or consume and the improvement of economic opportunities.

(7) Improvement of levels of consumption of low-income groups.

(8) Antitrust action and prevention of price fixing.

(9) Provision of adequate housing for the Nation's families.

(10) Medical care.

. . . The Consumer Advisory Council has issued statements favoring "truth-in-packaging," "truth-in-lending," and wood labeling. It has also gone on record as opposing "quality stabilization" bills and has urged that the consumer's right to choose should be respected in public accommodations without regard to race. It has taken a position favoring tax revision. And, through the Chairman of the Council of Economic Advisers, it has made recommendations to the Food and Drug Administration. It has endorsed proposals to promote safety with regard to health devices, cosmetics, and hazardous substances. It has set forth a list of principles which it would like to see used as guides in housing policy. It has supported agency requests for more funds for consumer research and information work. It has urged a program of improvement in government publications and field services for consumers.[1]

The Council has expressed interest in seeing studies or investigations undertaken on such topics as the following, some of which have been or are now the subject of active inquiry: the nature of guarantees and warranties in major areas of consumer expenditure; the level of electricity charges under State regulation; establishment of standards for sizes of clothing and clothing patterns, especially for children's clothing and knit garments; possible adoption of Federal safety standards for electrical equipment; possibilities for more work by private and governmental agencies on standards of highway safety; and the development of uniform warning labels on toxic substances.

Government and the Consumer

In this chapter the Consumer Advisory Council presents some of the results of the studies it has made during the year to inform itself on the wide range of Federal Government activities on behalf of the consumer. It begins with a discussion of consumption expenditures. This

---

[1] The Chairman of the Council of Economic Advisers issued releases to the press on the work of the CAC on the following dates: July 18, July 19, and September 14, 1962; and January 31, March 20, March 25, and June 5, 1963.

is followed by a review of the historical development of Federal programs to protect and promote the interests of consumers and a detailed account of the range of such programs today.

Consumption expenditures

In a sense, consumption—the final use of goods and services—is the end purpose of all economic activity. In any given year, however, the use of output is divided between consumption and investment (or real capital formation). While not all consumption is private in peace time, private consumption expenditures alone consistently absorb more than three-fifths of the gross national product in the United States. In 1962 purchases of goods and services by private consumers accounted for 64 percent of the GNP. Gross expenditures for private domestic investment, which include outlays by households for new residential construction, were 14 percent of the total; Federal, State, and local governments purchased 21 percent. Finally, about five percent of our total product was claimed by foreigners; but this was largely offset by imports from foreign producers, leaving a net export figure of less than one percent of GNP.

About 59 percent of personal consumption expenditures are for goods while 41 percent are for services. Food at 21 percent, clothing at eight percent, and housing services and household operation at 19 percent, together account for slightly less than half the total of private consumer expenditures.

The bulk of private consumer outlays is financed out of personal income, which is the sum of wages and salaries, rent, interest, dividends, proprietors' income, and transfer payments (less personal contributions for social insurance) received by individuals. (Transfers are payments other than for current production, the largest part of these being social insurance benefits.) In 1962 personal income aggregated $442 billion. After payment of personal taxes, there remained $384 billion of total disposable personal income, or $2,060 per capita.

With per capita disposable income at $2,060, the average after tax income of a consumer unit was $6,400 in 1962. It was $6,210 in 1961. In that year, however, individual families had incomes (after tax) ranging widely in both directions from the median of approximately $5,230. Starting from the top, five percent of families had incomes in excess of $14,360. On the other hand, the lowest 20 percent of such families had less than $2,700.

During recent years, consumers as a group have spent between 92 and 94 percent of disposable personal income on personal consumption. In 1962 such expenditures amounted to $355 billion. This means that, as a group, they have saved between six and eight percent of disposable personal income. Consumers hold tangible assets, such as cars and houses, and intangible assets, such as bank deposits, insurance policies, corporate securities, and government bonds. Total assets, tangible and intangible, in the hands of consumers were estimated to be more than $2,000 billion, or more than $10,000 per capita, in 1962. At the same time consumers have substantial liabilities—in 1962, about $246 billion, or $1,300 per capita. Installment and other consumer credit totaled $63 billion in 1962; mortgage credit for one- to four-family houses stood at $168 billion.

As was noted above, governments purchased about one-fifth of the total product in 1962. Some of these purchases, e.g., for the provision of park services, are for the purpose of collective consumption, with the government functioning as a purchasing agent for private consumers. Some, e.g., land reclamation, are purchases for the purpose of facilitating or promoting production. Still other government purchases, e.g., those for national defense, are directed primarily to the achievement of national goals and are only indirectly related to consumption.

Purchases by Federal, State, and local governments totaled $117.0 billion in 1962. Of this total, $53.6 billion was spent for national defense, $21.4 billion for education, $9.7 for highways, roads, and streets, and $6.8 for health services. How much of these government purchases can be labeled "consumption expenditures" is necessarily a matter of somewhat arbitrary definition, and there is no such official classification in the United States.

The consumer interest, the market, and the roles of government

Broadly construed, the goals of American consumers call for a highly productive economy, wherein a balance is struck between added effort to produce more and added satisfaction from consuming more, and wherein there is a desirable sharing of total output among all persons. The consumer point of view—as distinct from a producer point of view—places a high priority on arrangements to assure that what is most wanted is in fact produced, that it is produced to give choice of quality at lowest possible cost, and that what is produced is channeled to those who want it.

THE MARKET. The American economy relies to a high degree on the private market to achieve this result. Consumers and producers make their own choices. The individual consumer still decides what he wants to buy and reaps both the satisfactions and the dissatisfactions of his choices, even though the harshness of the principle of *caveat emptor* (Let the buyer beware!) has been eroded over the years. The consumer's choice is, of course, limited by his income and to those goods and services that producers are able and willing to supply at prices consumers can pay. Moreover, the producer is free to try to influence the consumer—not only anticipating consumer wants, but stimulating and even creating them, subject to legal restraints on unfair and misleading practices.

THE ROLES OF GOVERNMENT. Government intervenes to affect consumption in a number of ways. It provides the legal framework within which economic activity is carried on. In many cases it leaves the parties relatively free to offer, choose, negotiate, make contracts, and make use of property (but it should be noted that the legal terms "contract" and "property" imply the prior existence of government). In other cases American governments, through ordinances, statutes, administrative rules, and judicial decrees, have set limits on the free choice of consumers as well as producers—in the forms, for example, of narcotics control, zoning, regulation of public utilities, licensing of occupations, traffic and public health statutes, and laws to limit pollution of air and water and to conserve natural resources.

Besides conditioning the structure and operation of the market, government participates actively in the economy as a producer, a buyer, and a redistributor of income. As a producer—for example, of postal service or highway services—it resembles a private business firm in its effort to organize and offer a service that is of value to consumers. But unlike the typical private business, it may not cover the full cost of the product out of charges paid by the direct users.

The government also buys some privately produced goods for "free" distribution to consumers. It may buy an artist's painting to put on display in a public museum or contract with private physicians to supply medical services without charge to veterans. Or it may partially buy a product, i.e., subsidize it (or exempt it from taxation) and thereby lower its price to private purchasers or users. This is the intent in the case of the subsidy to private air transport.

Public education and health programs, along with national parks, monuments, and museums, constitute the best examples of public consumption. Federal participation in the former dates from the land grants to education in 1862. Currently Federal grants to States for education and health purposes support a wide range of public consumption, including such environmental improvements as the control of water pollution.

The Federal Government has encouraged housing, particularly since the 1930's. The Home Owners' Loan Corporation (since liquidated) was first established to refinance home mortgages. The Federal Home Loan Bank System and the Federal Savings and Loan Insurance Corporation are now major factors in the field of housing finance. The Federal Housing Administration (FHA) insures loans made by financial institutions for the purchase, construction, and modernization of residential properties. The Veterans Administration (VA) has similarly underwritten housing loans. The Federal National Mortgage Association (FNMA) adds further to housing credit by purchasing mortgages insured by FHA or guaranteed by the VA and selling them to institutional or other investors.

HISTORY OF CHANGING ROLES OF GOVERNMENT. Basic provisions of the common law relating to orderly marketing antedate our Constitution. The Constitution itself provides for a strong role for the Federal Government in economic affairs, authorizing it, for example, to lay and collect taxes and provide for the general welfare, to regulate commerce, to establish uniform laws on the subject of bankruptcies, to coin and regulate the value of money, to standardize weights and measures, establish post offices and post roads, and promote the progress of science and useful arts. Under the Constitution these powers take precedence over the powers of the States, which are specifically prohibited from impairing the obligation of contracts. But, in general, the powers States are left with give them an inclusive police authority, modified only by the due process clause of the 14th amendment, to influence the consumption process in many ways.

In the early days of this Nation courts took the lead in expressing public policy on private consumption. They marked out, case by case, the limits of the seller's liability for fraudulent and deceptive practice. They refused to enforce contracts in restraint of trade. At the same time, State and local governments were active in encouraging and providing for the public health and safety, transport, communications, and other essential services, and gradually, at the State level, legislative enactment superseded the common law as developed in the courts.

Toward the end of the nineteenth century another trend evidenced itself—the shift toward the specialized administrative agency. Railroad and public utilities commissions at the State level presaged the practice also in the Federal Government of delegating authority to an expert body to find facts, adjudicate disputes, and make rules within a particular industry or with reference to a particular function.

Near the turn of the century, the Federal Government also began to enter the consumer field on a large scale with legislation and specialized agencies—for example, the Mail Frauds Statute of 1872, the Sherman Anti-Trust Act of 1890, establishment of the National Bureau of Standards in 1901, and the Pure Food and Drug Law of 1906. Each of these measures became a precedent and model for others.

It is interesting to note that subsequently the rate of expansion of Federal consumer-related activities has varied markedly. Around the time of World War I, there was a burst of new regulations that included the Clayton and Federal Trade Commission Acts of 1914, the Standard Container Act of 1916, and the Transportation and Water Power Acts of 1920. The latter law established the Federal Power Commission. The next great surge of legislative activity came in the 1930's, bringing extensive amendment to the regulation of food and drugs, utilities, transportation, communications, trade practices, and advertising, as well as the creation of several new regulatory agencies, including the Civil Aeronautics Board, the Federal Communications Commission, and the Securities and Exchange Commission. Moreover, in that decade the Federal Government expanded its activity in direct provision of services in such fields as electric power and social insurance. The 1930's also saw the first legislation—in the Wool Labeling Act of 1939—of separate labeling provisions for particular types of products.

A third, less extensive, addition to Federal consumer legislation took place in the 1950's with the passage of the Celler-Kefauver Anti-Merger Act, the food additives amendment to the Food and Drug Law, and labeling laws for fur products, flammable fabrics, and textile fiber products.

Perhaps the most significant developments at the Federal level in the interest of consumers in the 1960's have been the reorganization and strengthening of several regulatory agencies and the passage of the Kefauver-Harris Drug Amendments of 1962. The latter instituted requirements for premarket testing of drugs for efficacy as well as safety and also directed that drug labels show the common or generic name for the drug. New steps have also been taken in such fields as the control of water and air pollution, recreation, transportation, communication, and public health.

As of 1963, Federal responsibility for promoting the consumer interest is well-grounded in the historically validated, commonly accepted principles reflected in President Kennedy's Consumer Message. By meeting this responsibility in the past the Federal Government has improved the quality of living. In cooperation with private producers, consumers, and State and local governments, it can further enhance consumer welfare in the future.

Protection of consumer rights

THE RIGHT TO SAFETY. The Federal Government acts to assure the consumer's right to safety by limiting the sale of goods, e.g., narcotics and meat from diseased animals, that are potentially harmful to the user. It acts—e.g., in its programs to eradicate animal diseases—to eliminate conditions giving rise to unsafe products or services. And it also acts—in the cases of highway safety and the protection of air-navigation radio channels, for example—to regulate the use of goods by consumers themselves in a way that limits the hazards they create for other consumers.

In the long history of government policy as to the consumer's right to safety there has been a shift in emphasis away from consumer responsibility, under the doctrine of *caveat emptor,* to seller responsibility for damages arising out of negligence or implied breach of warranty, and to government responsibility for prevention of damage. In the case of food and drugs, for example, government now has authority to seize and prevent the sale of products that are potentially harmful, without waiting for damages to be shown. In some cases, as with immunizing serums, there is authority to prevent the sale if the product is not efficacious. The 1962 Drug Amendments extended this principle to the full range of drugs.

With the advance of science and technology, consumer products have become highly complex, and the responsibility for the finished products has, in many instances, been widely dispersed among a range of producers and distributors. Consequently, it is difficult for the consumer to appraise his risk prospectively or fix responsibility for damages retrospectively. It is important, therefore that he be shielded against hazards to his health and safety by alert and efficient administration of those laws that have followed upon the Pure Food and Drug Act of 1906 and the Meat Inspection Act of 1907. At the Federal level this responsibility is centered in the Department of Health, Education, and Welfare and the Department of Agriculture. But it also extends, for example, to the Department of Interior's voluntary inspection of fish products and to the Treasury Department's regulation of narcotics and alcoholic beverages. Likewise, the Interstate Commerce Commission, the Federal Aviation Agency, and other specialized agencies promote safety in transportation.

Plainly, of course, passage of a law is only a first step in achieving consumer protection. Equally important is vigorous and imaginative enforcement by adequately staffed agencies.

Enforcement must be adjusted to take account of the growing population and the changing nature of products. President Kennedy pointed to this in his Consumer Message, saying—

> Thousands of common household items now available to consumers contain potentially harmful substances. Hundreds of new uses for such products as food additives, food colorings and pesticides are found every year, adding new potential hazards.

> As Americans make more use of highway and air transportation than any other nation, increased speed and congestion have required us to take special safety measures.

THE RIGHT TO BE INFORMED.   The right to be informed prompted the earliest Federal legislation concerned directly with the consumer, namely, the Mail Frauds Statute of 1872. Today implementation of this right extends from prevention of fraud and deception to government-sponsored and government-conducted research. Included within this range are the positive requirement of full disclosure (as in the case of issues of new securities), the establishment of standard weights and measures, performance testing (as in the case of drugs), grade labeling, standardization (a case of mandatory standards is that of bottle sizes for alcoholic beverages), and the provision of objective information on consumer problems.

The Wheeler-Lea Act of 1938 gave the Federal Trade Commission power to take action against false advertising, especially in the fields of foods, drugs, devices, and cosmetics. The Commission's authority extends to requiring affirmative disclosure in advertising or labeling when necessary to prevent consumer deception. An advertisement is considered false if it is "misleading in any particular," thus giving the Federal Trade Commission a broad area for enforcement.

The positive requirement of full disclosure has also been extended through the years to the labeling of many products. Disclosure of identity, composition, and quality, or the presence of harmful ingredients was required in the case of drugs in 1906, insecticides and fungicides in 1910, seeds in 1912, animal viruses, serums, and toxins in 1913, horse meat in 1919, caustic poisons in 1919, substandard canned goods in 1930, and alcoholic beverages in 1935. Requirements were broadened in the case of foods in 1938, wool products in 1939, human viruses, serums, and toxins in 1944, fur products in 1951, and textile fiber products in 1958. Requirements with respect to labeling vary from commodity to commodity. The Federal Trade Commission has issued guides or rules relating to labeling practices, deceptive practices, and advertising for approximately 175 industries. A recent example of this is a Guide for Shoe Content Labeling and Advertising.

Action has been taken to protect the individual as a purchaser of securities. This was done primarily through the Securities Act of 1933 and the Securities Exchange Act of 1934, which, with certain exceptions, required the registration of new issues. The 1934 Act established the Securities and Exchange Commission, and in 1962 legislation was passed providing for reorganization of the Commission. The Commission has completed a major investigation of the securities markets, which has already provided the basis for pending legislation, the Securities Acts Amendments of 1963 (S. 1624 and H.R. 6789), and administrative changes.

The Congress has assigned primary responsibility for the establishment of standard weights and measures to the National Bureau of Standards. Certain acts have been passed establishing standard size packaging for some products. Fruits and vegetables are covered to some extent by the Standard Container Acts of 1916 and 1928. Alcoholic beverages are covered under the Alcoholic Beverages Administration Act of 1936. Quality of product is identified for the consumer in certain cases through government inspection and grading—especially of food products. For example, some meats and eggs are sold according to governmentally established grades.

The idea of the government's providing objective information directly to the consumer is not new. The Bureau of Home Economics of the Department of Agriculture, now incorporated in the Division of Nutrition, Consumer, and Industrial Use Research, was created in 1923. Information is provided by direct contact between consumers and government representatives—particularly, the Food and Drug Administration's consumer consultants and the Cooperative Extension Service's home demonstration agents. Information is also provided by government reports addressed to the consumer.

The Federal Government also supports research of value to consumers in such agencies as the National Bureau of Standards, the Department of Agriculture, and the National Institutes of Health, as well as in universities and private nonprofit research organizations.

THE RIGHT TO CHOOSE.   The direction of the American economy depends heavily, as we have seen, on consumers' choices among products and among producers. In asserting the consumer's "right to choose," President Kennedy has implicitly indicated the importance of there being a number of alternative producers and of there being effective freedom for producers to enter new fields and offer new products and services. Thus, the consumer's right to choose and the maintenance of competition are intimately related. Promotion of competition, however, is a complex undertaking. In pursuing it the Federal Government has employed a series of legislative acts, some general in scope, some specific with regard to a type of practice or a particular industry.

Government intervention to ensure competition is older than the legislation in this field. Common law courts would not consider a contract binding if it was a clear case of conspiring to monopolize. However, the Government itself did not initiate action against any conspiracy or on behalf of third parties injured by conspiracies until passage of the Sherman Act of 1890. This committed the Government to active prevention and limitation of monopoly, and declared every contract, combination, or conspiracy in restraint of trade, or attempts at such restraint, to be illegal. Later antitrust acts were designed to modify the Sherman Act's coverage and to define more precisely actions considered harmful to competition. The Federal Trade Commission Act and the Clayton Act in 1914, the Robinson-Patman Act in 1936, the Wheeler-Lea Act of 1938, the Trade Mark Act of 1946, the McCarran Insurance Act of 1948, and the Celler-Kefauver Anti-Merger Act of 1950 are among the leading statutes indicating Congressional intent with respect to competition. Responsibility for enforcing these laws is vested primarily with the Antitrust Division of the Department of Justice and the Federal Trade Commission. In the administration of virtually every one of its economic programs the Government influences the structure and operation of commercial markets. In negotiating international trade agreements, in establishing agricultural, labor, or transportation policy, in procuring defense supplies, in setting directions for housing finance, in regulating securities markets, in making loans to small businesses, in providing marketing services and technical information to farm and business firms—in all these and in many other ways—the Government affects the consumer's right to choose.

In some industries, however, technical considerations do not allow the consumer to have a choice among the varying products of numerous producers. In such cases the government may, while leaving the producing firms in private hands, act as agent for the consumers, regulating the number of firms in the industry, maximum or minimum price, quality, and conditions of service. While the bulk of such detailed regulation is done at the State level in this country, the Federal Government has entered the field in a number of industries, beginning in railroading in 1887 with the establishment of the Interstate Commerce Commission, whose jurisdiction was extended to internal waterborne transport in 1920 and to interstate motor carriers in 1935. Other transportation rates and service are regulated by the Federal Maritime Commission and the Civil Aeronautics Board. Similarly, other specialized government agencies regulate interstate aspects of the telephone, telegraph, radio, and television industries; of banking and credit institutions; and of the electric power and natural gas industries.

In the case of electric power the Federal Government also serves the consumer directly through such public power suppliers as TVA and the Bonneville Power Administration. These have increased total power availability and afford "yardstick competition" to private suppliers.

In a dynamic economy not only do the problems facing regulators grow with the population and the size of business firms, but also they change with the demands of consumers and the technological frontiers within reach of the producers. Presently, for example, we face the mushrooming demands for improved urban transit, the exciting possibilities of transoceanic communication via satellites, and the economies promised by long-distance, extra-high-voltage transmission of electrical energy.

In order to play their intended role on behalf of consumers, the regulatory agencies must have clear rule-making authority, fair and efficient procedures, and adequate numbers of competent personnel.

THE RIGHT TO BE HEARD.   Besides promoting the consumer interest, the Federal Government also promotes the interests of producers. It may be said to seek the public interest partly through balancing the separate private interests of producers and consumers. Consumers, however, are not organized to the same degree as are producers for the purpose of influencing government policy, nor are they likely to be so organized in view of their scattered and varied interests. While seeking to learn the views of voluntary associations of consumers, therefore, government must remember that these views are not always expressed effectively enough to achieve a balance automatically in the array of private opinion being brought to bear on public policy issues.

To some degree the regulatory agencies are charged with representing the consumer interest. But at various times in the past it has seemed appropriate to provide within government more direct means for assuring the expression of the consumer viewpoint. The history of such "consumer representation" includes experiments in assigning the function to government as well as private individuals to serve in a consultative relationship to the government.

History of efforts from 1933 to 1962.   The first Federal attempts to provide for the expression and representation of the consumer interest were made in the New Deal period. The Office of Consumer Counsel in the Department of Agriculture, which was established in 1933, was first located in the Agricultural Adjustment Administration. This Office represented the consumer interest in the development of production control programs and in proceedings leading to marketing agreements, which were designed to further the interests of producers. The Consumer Counsel was charged with seeing that the agreements did not at the same time injure consumers. The office also gathered and published information on food prices. It often came into conflict with the interests of processor and agricultural groups, and its functions were gradually attenuated. After the AAA was held unconstitutional in 1936, the Counsel gave most of his attention to consumer education, with primary emphasis on the consumption of agricultural products. In 1941 some functions were transferred to other agencies, and in 1945 the office was terminated.

The Consumers' Advisory Board of the National Recovery Administration was also formed in 1933. It was charged with watching (according to an NRA release), "every agreement and every hearing [of the NRA] to see that nothing is done to impair the interest of those whose daily living may be affected by these agreements." Theoretically it had equal power with the Labor and Industry Advisory Boards. At one time the Consumers' Advisory Board had a sizable staff working on studies of industry structure and operation. Its representatives served with representatives of the Industry and Labor Advisory Boards on the NRA policy council and were making the Consumers' Advisory Board's views felt increasingly when the National Industrial Recovery Act was declared unconstitutional in 1935 and the whole advisory structure died.

Prior to that time, in order to cope with the lack of an organized consumer constituency, the Board had taken steps to organize local county consumer councils, using the mechanism of the National Emergency Council, which coordinated New Deal agencies in Washington and in the field. A Consumers' Division was established in the NEC to service these councils, of which some 150 came into existence at least nominally. A few of these local units outlasted their parent organization.

The Consumers' Counsel of the Bituminous Coal Commission, organized in 1937, was responsible for safeguarding the interests of coal consumers under legislation regulating coal prices and production. His functions were similar to those of the Consumers' Counsel under the Agricultural Adjustment Act. This was the first consumer representative established specifically by statute, and he was directly responsible to the Congress. The Counsel had the right to appear at Commission hearings and to exercise the power of subpoena; he also had access to information in the possession of the Commission. The law establishing the Commission and the Counsel expired during World War II.

During World War II the practice of consumer representation was continued, but was directed to a very different set of problems. The National Defense Advisory Commission (1940) included a Consumer Commissioner as one of seven Defense Commissioners. This office combined with the Office of the Price Commissioner to form the Office of Price Administration in 1941. Within OPA, the Consumer Division was particularly interested in the threat of rising prices at the retail level, in the dangers of quality deterioration as a concealed form of price increase, and in the problems of adequate housing and rent control. Its influence on OPA policy was short-lived. After 1941 it was made part of the information division, and its primary role was to explain the work of the OPA to the public and enlist consumer cooperation.

From 1944 to 1946, a Consumer Relations Adviser in the Office of the OPA Administrator acted as Staff for a Consumer Advisory Committee that brought the consumer viewpoint on specific aspects of the price control program to the attention of the commodity divisions and the Administrator. A similar National Consumer Advisory Committee to the Office of Price Stabilization was formed at the time of the Korean War. Some local consumer advisory committees were established in World War II and again in 1952.

Under the Employment Act of 1946, the Council of Economic Advisers invited consumer groups to form a Consumer Advisory Committee as a consultative body to the Council. It functioned continuously from 1947 to 1952, meeting with the Council two or three times a year. It had no staff, however, or means of carrying out the studies or other activities it proposed. The new CEA that took office in 1953 let this committee lapse. But the Council did hold meetings with consumer representatives from time to time.

During the 1950's, a large number of citizen advisory committees contributed to the work of various Federal agencies, though few were specifically designated to speak for the consumer interest. However, the Food and Drug Administration and, to some extent, the Housing and Home Finance Agency had formal arrangements for obtaining the views of consumers. One notable innovation was FDA's Consumer Consultant program, which was started in 1953.

Between 1946 and 1962, while the Federal Government did relatively little in the field of direct consumer representation, there was significant activity at the state level. In Connecticut, a State Department of Consumer Protection was created in 1959. To this Department were transferred the consumer services previously performed in a number of existing agencies. In 1955 the Office of Consumer Counsel was established in the Governor's office in New York. This office concerned itself with the development and support of legislative programs, development of information on consumer problems, dissemination of information to consumers, coordination and support of existing State consumer programs, and protection of consumer interests before State public utility and transportation regulatory agencies. The office was discontinued in 1958, and some of its functions were transferred to the attorney general's office.

In 1959 the California Legislature established a Consumer Counsel position in the Office of the Governor to: advise the Governor on all matters affecting the interest of the people as consumers; recommend to the Governor and to the Legislature the enactment of legislation deemed necessary to protect and promote the interests of the people as consumers; make such studies as are deemed necessary and render reports thereon to the people of the State; and appear before governmental commission departments, and agencies to represent and be heard on behalf of consumers' interests.

Certain States and the District of Columbia have arranged for the active presentation of consumers' viewpoints through people's counsels, appointed independently of the regulatory commissions, to serve as consumers' attorneys in commission proceedings. In a number of States, including Massachusetts, Michigan, Minnesota, and Washington, the consumer has been represented by an unpaid consumer advisory council. In some cases, these councils are attached to the attorney general's office.

Lessons from the past.   Past efforts to bring the consumer point of view into the Federal Government resulted in a series of expedients, each of which proved to be temporary. This history is sometimes cited as evidence of the unworkability of such representation. Several reasons have been offered to explain the succession of "failures." One is that historically "consumer advice" has been associated with depression, experiments with industrial cartelization, and wartime price control. In each case, consumer representation was part of an emergency plan, and hence disappeared when the emergency was over or the plan failed. A second reason offered is that the consumer counsels or advisers were unpopular with their parent organizations, sometimes because of a basic conflict of interest. In some cases the operating personnel felt that the principal function of their agency was to protect the consumer, and they saw little need for relatively uninformed advisers. A third reason points to the original argument for "official consumer representation," namely, the lack of an organized constituency and of a clear concept of the consumer interest as distinct from the public interest. The chairman of the 1963 Consumer Advisory Council attributed the weakness of some consumer organizations to the narrow scope of their activities. It was her belief that they have too often focused their attention on protective measures relating to such matters as mail fraud, mis-labeling, and food and drug abuses—issues with which most consumers identify themselves only when, individually, they have unpleasant experiences along these particular lines.

One lesson that may be learned from past experience in consumer representation in the Federal Government is that such representation, to be effective, must be permanent, well staffed, continuous, and at a high level. By facilitating direct contact between consumer spokesmen and the Executive Office of the President, the present Consumer Advisory Council plans to open a new way of giving attention to the consumer point of view that is quite different from anything hitherto attempted in the Federal Government. Council members themselves, without being involved in the operation of specific consumer protection and service programs, maintain high-level liaison with all departments and agencies responsible for such programs.

2. The Great American Gyp

Ralph Nader

Last January a confidential nationwide survey by the Opinion Research Corporation spread considerable alarm among its corporate subscribers. The poll concluded "that seven Americans in ten think present Federal legislation is inadequate to protect their health and safety. The majority also believe that more Federal laws are needed to give shoppers full value for their money." To many businessmen, this finding merely confirmed what speakers had been telling them at trade gatherings during the previous year—that consumers were beginning to fall prey to "consumerism."

"Consumerism" is a term given vogue recently by business spokesmen to describe what they believe is a concerted, disruptive ideology concocted by self-appointed bleeding hearts and politicians who find that it pays off to attack the corporations. "Consumerism," they say, undermines public confidence in the business system, deprives the consumer of freedom of choice, weakens state and local authority through Federal usurpation, bureaucratizes the marketplace, and stifles innovation. These complaints have all been made in speeches, in the trade press, and in Congressional testimony against such Federal bills as truth-in-lending, truth-in-packaging, gas pipeline safety, radiation protection, auto, tire, drug, and fire safety legislation, and meat and fish inspection.

Reprinted with permission from *The New York Review of Books,* Vol. 11 (November 21, 1968), 27–34. © 1968; The New York Review.

But what most troubles the corporations is the consumer movement's relentless documentation that consumers are being manipulated, defrauded, and injured not just by marginal businesses or fly-by-night hucksters, but by the U.S. blue-chip business firms whose practices are unchecked by the older regulatory agencies. Since the consumer movement can cite statistics showing that these practices have reduced real income and raised the rates of mortality and disease, it is not difficult to understand the growing corporate concern.

That the systematic disclosure of such malpractice has been so long delayed can be explained by the strength of the myths that the business establishment has used to hide its activities. The first is the myth of the omniscient consumer who is so discerning that he will be a brutal taskmaster for any firm entering the market. This approach was used repeatedly to delay, then weaken, the truth-in-packaging bill. Scott Paper Co. ran an advertising campaign hailing the American housewife as "The Original Computer": ". . . a strange change comes over a woman in the store. The soft glow in the eye is replaced by a steely financial glint; the graceful walk becomes a panther's stride among the bargains. A woman in a store is a mechanism, a prowling computer. . . . Jungle-trained, her bargain-hunter senses razor-sharp for the sound of a dropping price. . . ." John Floberg, Firestone's General Counsel, has been even more complimentary, arguing that consumers can easily discriminate among 1,000 different brands of tires.

However, when companies plan their advertising, they fail to take advantage of the supposed genius of the consumer. Potential car buyers are urged to purchase Pontiacs to experience an unexplained phenomenon called "wide-tracking before you're too old to know what it is all about." Sizable fees are paid to "motivation" experts like Ernest Dichter for such analysis as this: "Soup . . . is much more than a food. It is a potent magic that satisfies not only the hunger of the body but the yearnings of the soul. People speak of soup as a product of some mysterious alchemy, a symbol of love which satisfies mysterious gnawings. . . . The term 'pea soup'—mystery and magic— seem to go together with fog. At the same time we can almost say soup is orgiastic. Eating soup is a fulfillment."

A second myth is that most American businesses perform honorably but are subjected to underserved notoriety because of a few small, unscrupulous merchants and firms. This notion is peddled by so-called consumer protection agencies as well as by the business-dominated

Better Business Bureaus. But the detailed Congressional hearings on drug hazards, unsafe vehicles, vicious credit practices, restraints on medically useful or dollar-saving innovations, auto insurance abuses, cigarette-induced diseases, and price-fixing throughout the economy have made it clear that this argument will not hold up.

Most misleading of all is the myth that irresponsible sellers are adequately policed by local, state, and Federal regulatory agencies. Years ago, corporations learned how to handle these agencies, and they have now become apologists for business instead of protectors of the public.

First, the agencies are made to operate on a starvation budget. The combined annual budget of the Federal Trade Commission and the Antitrust Division of the Justice Department in 1968 was $23 million, the highest amount yet appropriated. With this sum, they were supposed to collect data, initiate investigations, and enforce the laws dealing with deceptive and anticompetitive practices of a $350 billion economy.

Secondly, political patronage has undermined local and state consumer protection agencies; it has, for example, helped to make the Federal Trade Commission as ineffectual as it is.

Thirdly, business lobbying—including campaign contributions, powerful law firms, trade associations, and public relations—works against vigorous enforcement.

Finally, so many regulatory officials resign to go into high-paying jobs in the industries they were once supposed to regulate that these government posts are viewed as on-the-job training by cynical appointees.[1] The Federal Aviation Agency, Interstate Commerce Commission and the Federal Communications Commission all carry on a tradition that inhibits officials from action and attracts appointees who are temperamentally reluctant to act.

The increasing irrelevance of these older agencies was made apparent by the unprecedented consumer legislation enacted under the Johnson Administration. After the dismal spectacle of the cigarette labeling act of 1964—which foreclosed action by the states and the FTC in return for a paltry warning on the package that could serve

---

[1] Two recent chairmen of the Interstate Commerce Commission later became President of the National Association of Motor Business Carriers and Vice-President of Penn-Central. Both industries are supposedly regulated by the ICC.

as a company's defense in liability suits—Congress passed a string of important bills and has other legislation near passage. A shift of responsibilities for consumer protection to the Federal government now seems to be taking place: state and local governments have for years defaulted on these obligations to the consumer.

In no other period of history have the safety and prices of marketed products and services received remotely comparable legislative treatment. Sensing this climate, President Johnson allowed his consumer adviser, Betty Furness, to speak openly to business groups. In 1964, her predecessor, Esther Peterson, could not get White House clearance even to make a public statement about rigged odometers which misled motorists about the accuracy of mileage traveled, enriched car rental companies to the amount of $4 million a year, and encouraged automobile sales. In 1968, Miss Furness was urging appliance manufacturers to tell their customers how long they can expect their products to last. In 1969, President Johnson established the post of Consumer Counsel in the Justice Department—a first small step toward the creation of a Federal office which would have powers to intervene in cases before the courts and regulatory agencies as the representative of consumer interests.[2] In July, 1969, Vice-President Humphrey said he favored enlarging the counsel's powers to include making complaints about dangers to public health. He also became the first government official to endorse public disclosure of information about consumer products now in the files of the General Services Administration and the Department of Defense. These agencies test hundreds of consumer products—from light bulbs and bed sheets to washing machines—in order to determine which have the best value. But they have refused thus far to release the data that would rank products by quality—a refusal naturally supported by the business community.

The business world, meanwhile, has become increasingly adept in dealing with the rising pressures for consumer legislation. Tutored by their well-connected Washington lawyers, the large corporations and their trade associations can sense the critical moment at which it is wise to stop opposing a bill and begin to cooperate wtih Congressional committees in order to shape legislation to their liking. For example, after opposing the passage of any auto safety bill whatever, the auto

---

[2] The first appointee to this job was Mr. Merle McCurdy who died in May, 1969.

manufacturers relented in the spring of 1966 and hired Lloyd Cutler, an experienced Washington lawyer, who succeeded in weakening the disclosure provisions of the bill and in eliminating all criminal penalties for willful and knowing violations of the law.

Although consumer measures may be weakened in this way, they do at least commit the government to the idea of consumer protection and they lay the groundwork for the stronger legislation that may be feasible should the consumer movement gain more strength. The attack on corporate irresponsibility which produced the recent flurry of legislation in Congress has not, it must be said, been the work of a broad movement but rather of tiny ad hoc coalitions of determined people in and out of government armed with little more than a great many shocking facts. They have gotten important support from Senator Warren Magnuson, Chairman of the Senate Commerce Committee, whose interest in consumer problems set in motion a little-noticed competition with the White House to promote legislation.

What has taken place during the last few years may be seen as an escalating series of disclosures. The charges made by independent Congressmen and people like myself almost always turn out to be understatements of the actual conditions in various industries when those industries are subsequently exposed in Congressional hearings and investigations. As these charges get attention, demands for new legislative action increase. This, at least, has been the case with the exposure of defects in vehicles, industrial and vehicle pollution, gas pipelines, overpriced or dangerous drugs, unfair credit, harmful pesticides, cigarettes, land frauds, electric power reliability, household improvement rackets, exploitation in slums, auto warranties, radiation, high-priced auto insurance, and boating hazards. How many people realized, for example, that faulty heating devices injure 125,000 Americans a year or that poorly designed stoves, power mowers, and washing machines cause substantial injury to 300,000 people annually? Or that, as Rep. Benjamin Rosenthal recently revealed, the food rejected by Federal agencies as contaminated or rotting is often rerouted for sale in the market? These abuses are now starting to be discussed in the press and in Congress.

One result of the detailed Congressional hearings has been a broader definition of legitimate consumer rights and interests. It is becoming clear that consumers must not only be protected from the dangers of voluntary use of a product, such as flammable material, but also from *involuntary* consumption of industrial by-products such as air and water pollutants, excessive pesticide and nitrate residues in foods, and antibiotics in meat. A more concrete idea of a just economy is thus beginning to emerge, while, at the same time, the assortment of groups that comprise the "consumer's movement" is moving in directions that seem to me quite different from the ones that similar groups have followed in the past. Their demands are ethical rather than ideological. Their principles and proposals are being derived from solid documentation of common abuses whose origins are being traced directly to the policies of powerful corporations.

This inquiry is extending beyond the question of legal control of corporations into the failure of business, labor, and voluntary organizations to check one another's abuses through competition and other private pressures. It is becoming apparent that the reform of consumer abuses and the reform of corporate power itself are different sides of the same coin and that new approaches to the enforcement of the rights of consumers are necessary. There are, I would suggest, at least ten major forces or techniques that now exist in some form but greatly need to be strengthened if we are to have a decent consumer society.

1. Rapid disclosure of the facts relating to the quantity, quality, and safety of a product is essential to a just marketplace. If companies know their products can quickly be compared with others, the laggard will be goaded to better performance and the innovator will know that buyers can promptly learn about his innovation. On the other hand, buyers must be able to compare products in order to reject the shoddy and reward the superior producer. This process is the great justification for a free market system. Manufacturers try to avoid giving out such information and instead rely on "packaging" or advertising. Auto companies refuse to tell the motorist the safety performances of his car's brakes and tires, and concentrate on brand-names—Cougar, Barracuda, Marauder—and vehicle "personality": "Mustang makes dull people interesting. . . ." From cosmetics to soaps and detergents, the differences emphasized are emotional and frivolous and have no relation to functions. This practice permits the producer with the largest advertising budget to make matters very difficult for a smaller competitor or potential entrant into the market who may have a superior product. The anti-competitive effects of such advertising led Donald F. Turner, the former head of the Anti-trust Division of the Justice Department, to suggest that the government subsidize independent sources of consumer information. Senator Philip Hart has gone a step further in proposing a National Consumer Service Foundation to pro-

vide product information to consumers at the place of purchase. Computers could help to assemble such information cheaply and quickly. One can, for instance, imagine machines dispensing data on individual products at shopping centers, a plan which Consumer's Union has begun to study.

2. The practices of refunding dollars to consumers who have been bilked and recalling defective products are finally becoming recognized as principles of deterrence and justice. More than six million automobiles have been recalled since September, 1966—the date of the auto safety law. The Food and Drug Administration now requires drug companies to issue "corrective letters" to all physicians if their original advertisements were found to be misleading. Nearly 30 such letters were sent out by drug companies during the first 20 months of FDA action. The threat of liability suits and the willingness of the press and television to mention brand and company names in reporting on defects are causing companies to recall products "voluntarily" even where no law or regulation exists. Earlier this year, for instance, Sears-Roebuck recalled some 6,000 gas heaters after public health officials warned of lethal carbon monoxide leakage. After similar warnings by U.S. Public Health officials and the threat of disclosure by a major newspaper, General Electric made changes in 150,000 color TV sets which had been found to be emitting excessive radiation. Some insurance companies are beginning to offer "defect recall" insurance.

The duty to refund remains even less well recognized than the duty to recall a product because of defects. Orders to "cease and desist," the usual decree of the Federal Trade Commission after it catches swindlers, at best stop the defrauder but do not require him to pay back the funds. Without this sanction, a major deterrent is lost. The mere order to "go and sin no more," which replaces it, is easily evaded.

The only enforcement action made by the FTC is pertinent here. For 30 years, the Holland Furnace Company used scare tactics and routinely deceived the public. Its salesmen were encouraged to pose as "safety inspectors" and were trained to be merciless: one elderly and ailing woman was sold nine new furnaces in six years, costing a total of $18,000. Following up on complaints beginning in the Thirties, the FTC secured a stipulation from the company that it would stop its misleading advertising. This had little if any effect. A cease and desist order was entered in 1958 but it was not until January, 1965, that the company was fined $100,000 for violating the order and an ex-president was sent to jail. At that point, the Holland Furnace Co. decided to file a petition for bankruptcy. But as Senator Warren Magnuson said: "In the meantime, Holland Furnace at the height of its business cost the American public $30 million a year." The FTC's ponderous procedures and anemic enforcement powers (it has no power of preliminary injunction, no criminal penalties, and no power of its own to fine, assess, or award damages) encourage the unscrupulous businessman to continue his abuses; if he is caught later on, he will merely be told to stop.

Two developments in recent years have strengthened private actions against malpractices by established corporations with large assets. The first is the growing practice of filing treble damage suits against violators of anti-trust laws. In the early Sixties, corporate and government customers of G.E., Westinghouse, and other large companies collected about $500 million in out-of-court settlements after these companies and their officers were convicted for carrying on a criminal antitrust price-fixing conspiracy. Although such punitive damage payments were tax-deductible as "ordinary and necessary business expenses," [3] the deterrent was an effective one. Cases brought by both private and government procurement agencies have multiplied in many other industries recently—from drugs to children's books—and these will increase, especially with tougher antitrust action by the Justice Department and by the states.

The second development is in the use of "class actions" in which suits are filed on behalf of large numbers of people who have been mistreated in the same way. In modern mass merchandising, fraud naturally takes the form of cheating a great many customers out of a few pennies or dollars: the bigger the store or chain of stores, the greater the gain from gypping tiny amounts from individuals who would not find it worthwhile to take formal action against the seller. Class actions solve this problem by turning the advantage of large volume against the seller that made predatory use of it in the first place. Poverty lawyers, supported by the U.S. Office of Economic Opportunity, are just beginning to use this important technique.

A case of great potential significance for developing broad civil deterrence has been brought in New York City against Coburn Corp., a sales finance company, by two customers who signed its retail installment contracts. They are being assisted by the NAACP Legal Defense

---

[3] Starting in 1970, only one-third of such damages are deductible.

and Educational Fund. The plaintiffs charge that Coburn violated Section 402 of the New York Personal Property Law by not printing its contracts in large type as specified by law. They are asking recovery of the credit service charge paid under the contracts for themselves and all other consumers similarly involved. If the plaintiffs win, consumers in New York will be able to bring class actions against any violations of law contained in any standard form contracts.

3. Disputes in courts and other judicial forums must be conducted under fairer ground rules and with adequate representation for buyers. Here the recent appearance of neighborhood legal service attorneys is a hopeful sign. These poverty lawyers—now numbering about 2,000 and paid by the Office of Economic Opportunity—are representing the poor against finance companies, landlords, auto dealers, and other sellers of goods and services. Because of their work, the law of debtors' remedies and defenses is catching up with the well-honed law of creditors' rights that generations of law students studied so rigorously. These lawyers are bringing test cases to court and winning them. They are gradually exposing the use by slum merchants of the courts as agents to collect from poor people who are uninformed or cannot leave their jobs to show up in court. For the first time, poverty lawyers are challenging the routine contract clauses that strip the buyers of their legal defenses in advance, as well as those involving illegal repossession, unreasonable garnishment, undisclosed credit, and financing terms, and a great many other victimizing practices.

But even many more poverty lawyers could handle only a few of the cases deserving their services. What is important is that recent cases are documenting a general pattern of abuses and injustices in the legal system itself. This is beginning to upset influential lawyers; it may prod law schools to more relevant teaching as well as guide legislatures and courts toward much-delayed reform of laws, court procedures, and remedies. At the same time, wholly new and more informed ways of resolving conflicts are being considered—such as neighborhood arbitration units which are open in the evenings when defendants need not be absent from their work. However, if such developments seem promising they must not obscure the persisting venality of the marketplace and the generally hopeless legal position of the consumer who is victimized by it.

4. The practice of setting government safety standards and periodically changing them to reflect new technology and uses is spreading, although it is still ineffective in many ways. Decades after banking

and securities services were brought under regulation, products such as automobiles (53,000 dead and 4½ million injured annually), washing machines and power lawn mowers (200,000 injuries annually), many chemicals, and all pipeline systems did not have to adhere to any standards of safety performance other than those set by the companies or industries themselves. With the passage of the auto safety law in 1966, other major products have been brought under Federal safety regulation. To avoid continuing a piecemeal approach, Congress in 1967 passed an act establishing the National Commission on Product Safety to investigate many household and related hazards, from appliances to household chemicals. Moreover, the Commission must recommend by this year a more detailed Federal, state, and local policy toward reducing or preventing deaths and injuries from these products.

The Commission's recommendations will probably go beyond household products to the problem of a safer man-made environment. So far, most state and Federal efforts to set meaningful safety standards and enforce then have failed miserably. The only organized and effective pressures on the agencies responsible for setting standards have come from the same economic interests that are supposed to be regulated. Two illustrations of this failure have been the Flammable Fabrics Act of 1953 and the Oil Pipeline Safety Act of 1965. In both cases, little has happened because the laws have not been administered. It took three-and-a-half years before the Federal government even proposed oil pipeline standards, and these were taken almost verbatim from the pipeline industry's own code. Similarly, when the General Accounting office recently reviewed the enforcement of the pesticide law by the Department of Agriculture it found that repeated mass violations of the laws between 1955 and 1965 were never reported to the Department for prosecution. This is a typical example of how consumers are deprived of legal protection in spite of a statute intended to protect them.

5. If the government is to impose effective standards, it must also be able to conduct or contract for its own research on both the safety of industrial products and possible methods of improving them. Without this power, the agencies will have to rely on what is revealed to them by industry, and their efforts will be crippled from the start. They will, for example, be unable to determine whether a better vehicle handling system is required or to detect promptly the hidden dangers in apparently harmless drugs. The government could also

bring strong pressures on business by using its own great purchasing power and by developing its own prototypes of safer products. The existing safety laws, however, do not even permit the government to find out quickly and accurately whether industry is complying with the law. The National Highway Safety Bureau, for example, had little idea whether or not the 1968 automobiles met all the safety standards since no Government testing facilities existed.

But full enforcement of the law also depends on the existence of effective penalties, and in this respect the recent safety laws are feeble, to say the least. There are no criminal penalties for willful and knowing violation of the auto safety, gas pipeline, radiation control, and similar laws. The civil fines are small when considered against the possibility of violations by huge industries producing millions of the same product. Of course, the Washington corporation lawyers who lobby to water down the penalties in these safety laws have no interest in the argument that stronger sanctions would not only act as a deterrent to industry but make enforcement itself cheaper.

6. In the ideology of American business, free competition and corporate "responsibility" are supposed to protect the consumer; in practice both have long been ignored. Price-fixing, either by conspiracy or by mutually understood cues, is rampant throughout the economy. This is partly revealed by the growing number of government and private antitrust actions. Donald Turner, the former head of the Antitrust Division, has despaired of effectively enforcing the law against price-fixing with the existing manpower in the Justice Department. Price-fixing, of course, means higher prices for consumers. For example, the electrical price-fixing conspiracy, broken by the Justice Department in 1960, involved not only G.E., Westinghouse, Allis Chalmers, but several small companies as well; the overcharge to the direct purchasers of generators and other heavy duty equipment was estimated at more than a billion dollars during the ten-year life of the conspiracy that sent several executives to short jail terms.

Even greater dangers arise when the failure of large industry to compete prevents the development of new products that might save or improve the lives of consumers. When such restraint is due to conspiracy or other kinds of collusion, it should be the task of antitrust enforcement to stop the practice of "product-fixing." Traditional antitrust enforcement has been slow to grasp the fact that the restraint of innovation is becoming far more important to big business than the control of prices. New inventions—steam or electric engines, longer lasting light bulbs and paints, and cheaper construction materials— can shake an industry to its most stagnant foundations. For 18 months the Justice Department presented to a Los Angeles grand jury its charges that the domestic auto companies conspired to restrain the development and marketing of vehicle exhaust control systems. When and if it files its complaint, a pioneering case of antitrust enforcement in a health and safety issue could reveal much about this as yet unused weapon for public protection.

Ideally, one of the most powerful forces for consumer justice would be the exercise of corporate responsibility or private "countervailing" and monitoring forces within the corporate world. Unfortunately for believers in a pluralist economic system, recent decades have shown that the economics of accommodation repeatedly overwhelms the economics of checks and balances.

The casualty insurance industry is a case in point. Logically it should have a strong interest in safer automobiles. In fact it has chosen to raise premiums instead of pressuring the auto industry to adopt safety measures that have been available for a long time. The casualty insurance industry has not demanded legislation to improve the design and inspection of motor vehicles; nor has it encouraged the rating of vehicles according to their safety. It has been equally indifferent to the need to reform methods of fire prevention (where the U.S. is far behind Japan and England) or standards of industrial safety and health. What the industry has done instead is to spend large sums on advertising assuring the public it is concerned about the consumer safety it has declined to pursue in practice.

7. Professional and technical societies may be sleeping giants where the protection of the consumer is concerned. Up to now, such groups as the American Society of Mechanical Engineers, the American Chemical Society, and the American Society of Safety Engineers have been little more than trade associations for the industries that employ their members. It is shocking, for example, that none of these technical societies has done much to work out public policies to deal with the polluted environment and with such new technological hazards as atomic energy plants and radioactive waste disposal. Except in a few cases, the independent professions of law and medicine have done little to fulfill their professional obligations to protect the public from victimization. They have done less to encourage their colleagues

in science and engineering to free themselves from subservience to corporate disciplines. Surely, for example, the supersonic transport program, with its huge government subsidies and intolerable sonic boom, should have been exposed to careful public scrutiny by engineers and scientists long before the government rather secretively allowed it to get under way.

The engineers and scientists, however, had no organization nor procedure for doing this. None of the professions will be able to meet its public responsibilities unless it is willing to undertake new roles and to create special independent organizations willing to gather facts and take action in the public interest. Such small but determined groups as the Committee for Environmental Information in St. Louis, headed by Professor Barry Commoner, and the Physicians for Automotive Safety in New Jersey have shown how people with tiny resources can accomplish much in public education and action. If such efforts are to be enlarged, however, the legal, medical, engineering, and scientific departments of universities must recognize the importance of preparing their graduates for full-time careers in organizations devoted to shaping public policy; for it is clear that professionals serving clients in private practice will not be adequate to this task. Had such organizations existed two or three decades ago, the hazards of the industrial age might have been foreseen, diagnosed, exposed, and to some extent prevented. During the recent controversy over auto safety I often speculated that the same kind of reform might have occurred 30 years ago had a handful of engineers and physicians made a dramatic effort to inform politicians about scandals that even then took more than 30,000 lives a year and caused several million injuries. Instead the doctors were busy treating broken bones and the engineers were following corporate orders, while their technical journals ignored a major challenge to their profession. For all the talk about "preventive medicine" and "remedial engineering," this is what is happening now.

8. During the past two decades, the courts have been making important if little noticed rulings that give injured people fairer chances of recovering damages. These include the elimination of "privity" or the need to prove a contractual relation with the person sued; the expansion of the "implied warranty" accompanying items purchased to include not only the "reasonable" functioning of those items but also the claims made in deceptive advertising of them; and the imposition

of "strict liability" which dispenses with the need to prove negligence if one has been injured through the use of a defective product. At the same time, the laws of evidence have been considerably liberalized. This reform of the common law of "bodily rights"—far in advance of other common-law nations such as Great Britain and Canada—has been followed by some spectacular jury verdicts and court decisions in favor of the injured. These are routinely cited by insurance companies as a rationale for increasing premiums. The fact is, however, that these victories still are rare exceptions, and for obvious reasons. Winning such cases requires a huge investment in time and money: the plaintiff's lawyers must collect the evidence and survive the long and expensive delays available to the corporation defendant with its far superior resources. But now the rules give the plaintiff at least a decent chance to recover his rights in court or by settlement. It remains for the legal profession to find ways to cut drastically the costs of litigation, especially in cases where a single product, such as a car or drug, has injured many people.

However, the law of torts (personal injuries) still does not protect the consumer against the pollution of the environment which indiscriminately injures everyone exposed to it. Pollution in Los Angeles is a serious health hazard, but how may the citizen of that besmogged metropolis sue? A group of eighty-eight residents of Martinez, California, is suing Shell Oil's petroleum refinery for air pollution and its "roaring noises, recurring vibrations and frightening lights." In an increasingly typical defense, Shell claims that it meets the state's mild pollution-control regulation. But such standards are largely the result of political pressures from corporations whose profits are at stake. Thus, increasingly, justice in the courts must be paralleled by justice in the legislatures. However, there are some signs that the courts are beginning to take account of the right to a decent environment in cases against industrial pollutants. In 1967, a lady in Pennsylvania recovered about $70,000 for injuries sustained from living near a beryllium plant which emitted toxic fumes daily. (The case was appealed.)

9. One of the more promising recent developments is the growing belief that new institutions are needed within the Government whose sole function would be to advocate consumer interests. As I have pointed out, the Johnson Administration has done no more than create in 1968 an Office of Consumer Counsel in the Justice Department. The Executive Branch has been hostile to a proposal by Congressman Rosenthal and others for a new Department of Consumer Affairs on

the Cabinet level. This proposal has been criticized by Federal officials on grounds that it would duplicate what government agencies are now doing. The fact is, however, that most of the government agencies that are supposed to be concerned with the health and safety of consumers are also promoting the interests of the industries that cause the consumer harm. The U.S. Department of Agriculture represents the farmers and processors first and the consumers second—whether in controversies over the price of milk or over the wholesomeness of meat and poultry. The regulatory agencies themselves at best merely act as referees and at worst represent business interests in government.

Clearly it would be useful if a new bureau within the Government itself could both expose these regulatory agencies and challenge them to take more vigorous action. Senator Lee Metcalf has introduced legislation to create an independent Office of Utility Consumer's Counsel to represent the public before regulatory agencies and courts. This approach is different from that of Congressman Rosenthal and it remains to be seen which scheme can best avoid the dangers of bureaucratization and atrophy. What is not generally appreciated however is that if they are to succeed, such new governmental units will badly need the vigorous support of organizations outside the government which would have similar concern for the consumer and would also be able to carry on their own research and planning.

10. I have already pointed out the need for independent organizations of professionals—engineers, lawyers, doctors, economists, scientists, and others—which could undertake work of this kind. But they do not as yet exist. Still, we can draw some idea of their potential from the example of people like Dr. Commoner and his associates who have managed to stir up strong public opposition to Government and private interests while working in their spare time. Similarly, other small groups of professionals have saved natural resources from destruction or pollution; they have stopped unjust increases in auto-insurance rates; they have defeated a plan for an atomic explosion to create a natural gas storage area under public land, showing that excessive safety risks were involved.

Is there reason to hope that the high energy physicists who lobbied successfully for hundreds of millions of dollars in public funds might be emulated by other professionals seeking to improve the quality of life in America? Certainly there is a clear case for setting up professional firms to act in the public interest at Federal and local levels. While thousands of engineers work for private industry, a few hundred should be working out the technical plans for obtaining clean air and water, and demanding that these plans be followed. While many thousands of lawyers serve private clients, several hundred should be working in public interest firms which would pursue legal actions and reforms of the kind I have outlined here. Support for such firms could come from foundations, private gifts, dues paid by consumers and the professions, or from government subsidies. There is already a precedent for the latter in the financing of the Neighborhood Legal Services, not to mention the billions of dollars in subsidies now awarded to commerce and industry. In addition, groups that now make up the consumers' movement badly need the services of professional economists, lawyers, engineers, and others if they are to develop local consumer service institutions that could handle complaints, dispense information, and work out strategies for public action.

Notwithstanding the recent alarm of industry and the surge of publicity about auto safety and other scandals, the consumer movement is still a feeble force in American power politics. The interests of consumers are low on the list of election issues; the government's expenditures to protect those interests are negligible. Some would argue that this situation will inevitably prevail in view of the overwhelming power of American corporations in and out of government. But, as I have tried to show, new approaches to judging and influencing corporate behavior have begun to emerge in the last few years. It seems possible that people may begin to react with greater anger to the enormity of their deprivation—each year consumers lose half a billion dollars in securities frauds and a billion dollars in home repair frauds, to name only two of thousands of ways in which their income is being milked. The current assault on the health and safety of the public from so many dangerous industrial products, by-products, and foods has resulted in violence that dwarfs the issue of crime in the streets. (In a recent three-year period, about 260 people died in riots in American cities; but every two days, 300 people are killed, and 20,000 injured, while driving on the highways.) What the consumer movement is beginning to say—and must say much more strongly if it is to grow— is that business crime and corporate intransigence are the really urgent menace to law and order in America.

3. The Dialogue That Never Happens

Raymond A. Bauer
and Stephen A. Greyser

In recent years, government and business spokesmen alike have advocated a "dialogue" between their two groups for the reduction of friction and the advancement of the general good. Yet, all too often, this is a dialogue that never happens. Rather, what passes for dialogue *in form* is often a sequence of monologues *in fact,* wherein each spokesman merely grants "equal time" to the other and pretends to listen while preparing his own next set of comments. Obviously, this is not always the case; and, if taken literally, it tends to minimize some real progress being made.

Our aim here is to try to facilitate and stimulate that progress by exploring what lies behind the dialogue that never happens and by suggesting what can be done—on both sides—to develop more meaningful and effective business-government interactions.

In this context, we link "government spokesmen" with "critics." Naturally, not all in government are critics of business, and vice versa. However, almost all critics seek redress of their grievances via government action and seek government spokesmen to present their views "in behalf of the public."

Our primary focus will be in the field of marketing—particularly

Reprinted from *Harvard Business Review* (January-February, 1969), 122–128.

selling and advertising—which is perhaps the most controversial and most frequently criticized single zone of business. Marketing seems to be the area where achieving true dialogue is most difficult and where business and government spokesmen most seem to talk past each other.

Before examining why this takes place, let us look at two comments on advertising that illustrate the lack of dialogue. The first comment is that of Donald F. Turner, former Assistant Attorney General in charge of the Antitrust Division of the Justice Department:

> "There are three steps to informed choice: (1) the consumer must know the product exists; (2) the consumer must know how the product performs; and (3) he must know how it performs compared to other products. If advertising only performs step one and appeals on other than a performance basis, informed choice cannot be made." [1]

The other comment is that of Charles L. Gould, Publisher, the San Francisco *Examiner:*

> "No government agency, no do-gooders in private life can possibly have as much interest in pleasing the consuming public as do . . . successful companies. For, in our economy, their lives literally depend on keeping their customers happy." [2]

Double Entendres

Why do business and government spokesmen talk past each other in discussing ostensibly the same marketplace? We think it is because each has a basically different model of the consumer world in which marketing operates. This misunderstanding grows from different perceptions about a number of key words.

The first word is *competition.* The critics of business think of competition tacitly as strictly price differentiation. Modern businessmen, however, as marketing experts frequently point out, think of competition primarily in terms of product differentiation, sometimes via phys-

---

[1] Statement made at the Ninth Annual American Federation of Advertising Conference on Government Relations held in Washington, D.C., February, 1967.

[2] *Ibid.*

ical product developments and sometimes via promotional themes. The important thing is that price competition plays a relatively minor role in today's marketplace.

Some of the perplexity between these two views of competition has to do with confusion over a second word, *product*. In the critic's view, a product is the notion of some entity which has a primary identifiable function only. For example, an automobile is a device for transporting bodies, animate or inanimate. It ordinarily has four wheels and a driver, and is powered by gasoline. There are variants on this formula (three-wheeled automobiles) which are legitimate, provided the variants serve the same function. Intuitively the businessman knows there is something wrong with this notion of the product because the product's secondary function may be his major means of providing differentiation (an auto's looks, horsepower, and so on).

Then there is the term *consumer needs,* which the business critic sees as corresponding to a product's primary function—for example, needs for transportation, nutrition, recreation (presumably for health purposes), and other things. The businessman, on the other hand, sees needs as virtually *any* consumer lever he can use to differentiate his product.

Next, there is the notion of *rationality.* The critic, with a fixed notion of "needs" and "product," sees any decision that results in an efficient matching of product to needs as rational. The businessman, taking no set position on what a person's needs should be, contends that any decision the customer makes to serve his own perceived self-interest is rational.

The last addition to our pro tem vocabulary is *information.* The critic fits information neatly into his view that a rational decision is one which matches product function and consumer needs, rather circularly defined as the individual's requirement for the function the product serves. Any information that serves that need is "good" information. To the businessman, information is basically any data or argument that will (truthfully) put forth the attractiveness of a product in the context of the consumer's own buying criteria.

Table 1 summaries our views of these two different models of the consumer world. We realize that we may have presented a somewhat exaggerated dichotomy. But we think the models are best demonstrated by this delineation of the pure views of contrasting positions, recognizing that both sides modify them to some extent.

Table 1. Two different models of the consumer world

Key words	Critic's view	Businessman's view
Competition	Price competition.	Product differentiation.
Product	Primary function only.	Differentiation through secondary function.
Consumer needs	Correspond point-for-point to primary functions.	Any customer desire on which the product can be differentiated.
Rationality	Efficient matching of product to customer needs.	Any customer decision that serves the customer's own perceived self-interest.
Information	Any data that facilitate the fit of a product's proper function with the customer's needs.	Any data that will (truthfully) put forth the attractiveness of the product in the eyes of the customer.

Views of Human Nature

A review of our "vocabulary with a double meaning" and the two models of the consumer world shows that the critic's view is based on a conviction that he knows what "should be." In contrast, the businessman's view is based on militant agnosticism with regard to "good" or "bad" value judgments which might be made (by anyone) about individual marketplace transactions.

The businessman's view of human nature may be the more flattering, perhaps excessively so. Certainly, the marketer's notion of "consumer sovereignty" compliments the consumer in attributing to him the capacity to decide what he needs and to make his choice competently even under exceedingly complex circumstances. It also sometimes challenges him to do so. This perhaps undeserved flattery glosses over some obvious flaws in the market mechanism. It is rooted in the belief that this mechanism, even though imperfect in specific instances, is better than administrative procedures for regulating the market.

The critic takes a far less optimistic view of human nature—both the consumer's and the seller's. He thinks that the seller often (sometimes intentionally) confuses consumers with a welter of one-sided argumentation. Such information, in the critic's eye, not only lacks impartiality, but usually focuses on secondary product functions and is not geared to consumer needs.

Both sets of assumptions are, we think, at least partially justified. Customers do have limited information and limited capacity to process it. This is the way of the world. Furthermore, there is no reason to believe that every seller has every customer's interest as his own primary concern in every transaction, even though in the long run it probably is in the seller's own best interest to serve every customer well.

All of this disagreement comes to focus on a point where both business and government are in agreement; namely, modern products are sufficiently complex that the individual consumer is in a rather poor position to judge their merits quickly and easily. The businessman says that the customer should be, and often is, guided in his judgment by knowledge of brand reputation and manufacturer integrity, both of which are enhanced by advertising. The critic argues that the customer should be, but too seldom is, aided by impartial information sources primarily evaluating product attributes.

These conflicting views of vocabulary and human nature are reflected in several specific topic areas.

Brands and Rating Services

One of these areas is the relationship of national branding to consumer rating services, the latter being a traditional source of "impartial information" for consumers. Somehow the crux of this relationship seems to have escaped most people's attention: consumer rating services are possible *only because of* the existence of a limited number of brands for a given product. In order for a rating to be meaningful, two conditions are necessary:

(1) *Identifiability*—the consumer must be able to recognize the products and brands rated.

(2) *Uniformity*—manufacturers must habitually produce products of sufficiently uniform quality that consumer and rating service alike can learn enough from a sample of the product to say or think something meaningful about another sample of the same product which may be bought in some other part of the country at some later time. This is a seldom-realized aspect of national branding.

It is generally assumed by both groups that the "consumer movement" is basically opposed to heavily advertised branded goods. The stereotype of *Consumer Reports* is that it regularly aims at shunting trade away from national brands to Sears, to Montgomery Ward, or to minor brands. Yet the one study made of this issue showed that, contrary to the stereotype, *Consumer Reports* had consistently given higher ratings to the heavily advertised national brands than to their competitors.[3]

Ideological blindness.   What we have here is an instance of the consumer movement and brand-name manufacturers being ideologically blinded by different models of the market world. The consumer movement concentrates on the notion of a product having a definable primary function that should take precedence over virtually all other attributes of the product. True, some concessions have recently been made to aesthetics. But, on the whole, the consumer movement is

---

[3] Eugene R. Beem and John S. Ewing, "Business Appraises Consumer Testing Agencies," *Harvard Business Review*, 32 (March-April 1954), 113–126, especially 121.

suspicious of the marketing world that strives to sell products on the basis of secondary attributes which the consumer movement itself regards with a jaundiced eye.

The evidence available to the consumer movement is that, in general, national advertising is *not* accompanied by poorer performance on primary criteria. But the consumer movement fails to realize that it *takes for granted* the central claim for advertised branded products— namely, that by being identifiable and uniform in quality, they offer the customer an opportunity to make his choice on the basis of his confidence in a particular manufacturer.

But the manufacturers of nationally branded products and their spokesmen have been equally blind. First of all, we know of none who has pointed out the extent to which any form of consumer rating must be based on the identifiability and uniformity of branded products. The only situation where this does not apply is when the rating service can instruct the consumer in how to evaluate the product—for example, looking for marbleizing in beef. However, this is limited to products of such a nature that the customer can, with but little help, evaluate them for himself; it cannot apply to products for which he has to rely on the technical services of an independent evaluator or on the reputation of the manufacturer.

Moreover, except for such big-ticket items as automobiles, consumer rating services usually test products only once in several years. In other words, they rate not only a *sample* of a manufacturer's products, but also a sample of his performance *over time*. Thus, if one "follows the ratings" and buys an air conditioner or a toaster this year, he may buy it on the rating of a product made one, two, or three years ago. Similarly, if one buys a new automobile, he depends in part on the repair record (reported by at least one rating service) for previous models of that brand.

In large part, then, consumer rating services are devices for rating *manufacturers!* This is not to say they do not rate specific products. Sometimes they even draw fine distinctions between different models from the same company. But in the course of rating products, they also rate manufacturers. What more could the manufacturer ask for? Is this not what he claims he strives for?

Basic dichotomy.   More to the point, what is it that has kept the consumer movement and brand-name manufacturers from paying attention to this area of shared overlapping interests? Neither will quarrel with the exposure either of factual deception or of product weaknesses on dimensions that both agree are essential to the product. This is not where the problem is. The problem is that the manufacturer *sells* one thing and the rating service *rates* another.

The concept of a "product" that dominates the thinking of rating services and the thought processes of those who suggest more "impartial evaluation information" for consumers (e.g., Donald Turner of the Department of Justice and Congressman Benjamin Rosenthal of New York) is that a product is an entity with a single, primary, specifiable function—or, in the case of some products such as food, perhaps a limited number of functions, e.g., being nutritious, tasty, and visually appealing. The specific goal of many proposed ratings—with their emphasis on the physical and technical characteristics of products—is to free the customer from the influence of many needs to which the marketer addresses himself, most particularly the desire for ego-enhancement, social acceptance, and status.

The marketer, oddly enough, tends to accept a little of the critic's view of what a product is. Marketing texts, too, speak of primary and secondary functions of a product as though it were self-evident that the aesthetic ego-gratifying, and status-enhancing aspects of the product were hung on as an afterthought. If this is true, why are Grecian vases preserved to be admired for their beauty? And why did nations of yore pass sumptuary laws to prevent people from wearing clothes inappropriate to their status?

We shall shortly explore what may lie behind this confusion about the nature of products. First, however, let us examine another topical area in which similar confusion exists.

"Materialist society"

The selling function in business is regularly evaluated by social commentators in relationship to the circumstance that ours is a "materialist society." We could say we do not understand what people are talking about when they refer to a materialist society, beyond the fact that our society does possess a lot of material goods. But, in point of fact, we think *they* do not understand what they are talking about. Let us elucidate.

At first hearing, one might conclude that criticism of a materialist society is a criticism of the extent to which people spend their resources of time, energy, and wealth on the acquisition of material things. One of the notions that gets expressed is that people should be more interested in pursuing nonmaterial goals.

The perplexing matter is, however, that the criticism becomes strongest on the circumstance that people *do* pursue nonmaterial goals —such as ego enhancement, psychic security, social status, and so on—but use material goods as a means of achieving them. Perhaps the distinctive feature of our society is the extent to which *material* goods are used to attain *nonmaterial* goals.

Now there are many ways in which societies satisfy such needs. For example, there are ways of attaining status that do not involve material goods of any substance. Most societies grant status to warriors and other heroes, to wise men who have served the society, and so on. Often the external manifestation of this status is rigidly prescribed and involves signs whose material worth is insignificant: a hero wears a medal, a ribbon in his lapel, or a certain type of headdress, or he may be addressed by an honorific title.

However, in societies that value economic performance, it is not uncommon for material goods to be used as status symbols. Indians of the Southwest, for example, favor sheep as a symbol even to the extent of overtaxing the grazing lands and lowering the economic status of the tribe. As a practical matter, this might be more damaging to the welfare of the Navaho than is the damage that many low-income Negroes do to their own individual welfares when, as research shows, they insist on serving a premium-priced brand of Scotch.

Many of the things about which there is complaint are not self-evidently bad. Art collecting is generally considered a "good thing." But take the worst instance of a person who neurotically seeks self-assurance by buying art objects. Clinically, one might argue that he would do himself a lot more long-run good with psychotherapy even though, when one considers the resale value of the art objects, he may have taken the more economical course of action. Similarly, it is not self-evident that the promotion of toiletries to the youth as a symbol of transition to manhood is inherently cruel—unless the commercials are especially bad! It is clear, however, that there is no societal consensus that the transition to manhood should be symbolized by the use of toiletries.

What seems to be the nub of the criticism of our society as a materialist one is that simultaneously a great number of nonmaterial goals are served by material goods, and there is no consensus that this should be so. Behind this is our old friend (or enemy): the concept of a product as serving solely a primary function. In the perspective of history and of other societies, this is a rather peculiar notion. Who in a primitive society would contend that a canoe paddle should not be carved artistically, or that a chief should not have a more elaborate paddle than a commoner?

Much of the confusion over the words on our list seems to be a residue of the early age of mass production. The production engineer, faced with the task of devising ways to turn out standardized products at low cost, had to ask himself, "What are the irreducible elements of this product?" This was probably best epitomized in Henry Ford's concept of the automobile, and his comment that people could have any color they wanted so long as it was black. Clearly, Ford thought it was immoral even to nourish the thought that a product ought to look good, let alone that it should serve various psychic and social functions.

But all this was closely related to the mass producer's effort to find the irreducible essence of what he manufactured. This effort broke up the natural organic integrity of products, which, at almost all times in all societies, have served multiple functions.

Many writers have called attention to the fact that in recent times our society has passed from the period of simpleminded mass production to that of product differentiation on attributes beyond the irreducible primary function. As yet, however, we do not think there is adequate appreciation of the impact of the residue of the early period of mass production on thinking about what a product is. In that period even very complex products were converted into commodities. Since each performed essentially the same primary function, the chief means of competition was pricing.

Products as commodities

At this point, we shall argue that the thinking of those who criticize the selling function is based on a model for the marketing of commodities. This factor does not exhaust the criticisms, but we believe it is at the core of present misunderstandings over the concepts on which we have focused our discussion.

On the one hand, to the extent that products are commodities, it is possible to specify the function or functions which all products in that category should serve. It follows that a person who buys and uses such a commodity for some purpose other than for what it was intended has indeed done something odd, although perhaps useful to him (for example, baseball catchers who use foam-rubber "falsies" to pad their mitts). In any event, it is possible both to specify the basis on which the commodity should be evaluated and the information a person is entitled to have in order to judge that product. A person searching for a commodity ought first to find out whether it serves this function and then to ask its price.

On the other hand, to the extent that products are *not* commodities, it is impossible to expect that price competition will necessarily be the main basis of competition. Likewise, it is impossible to specify what information is needed or what constitutes rational behavior. Is it rational for a person to buy toothpaste because its advertiser claims it has "sex appeal"? Presumably people would rather look at clean than dingy teeth, and presumably people also like to have sex appeal—at least up to the point where it gets to be a hazard or a nuisance.

But it does not follow, insofar as we can see, that ratings—or grade labeling—should discourage product differentiation or the promotion of products on a noncommodity basis. If the consumer were assured that all products in a given rating category performed their primary functions about equally well, could it not be argued that those attributes which differentiate the products on other functions would then become increasingly interesting and important? Or, to be more specific, what makes it possible for "instant-on" TV tuning to be promoted—other than a presumed agreement, by both manufacturer and consumers, that the TV set performs its primary function little better or worse than its competition?

This is a facet of competition not appreciated by the opponents of grade labeling, who have argued that it would reduce competition. Perhaps it would be more helpful if the opponents of grade labeling first gathered some evidence on what has actually happened to competition in countries where grade labeling has been introduced. (The head of one major relevant trade association recently told one of us that he knew of no such research.)

Toward more information

Readers will note that we have indulged in considerable speculation in this article. But most of the issues on which we have speculated are researchable. Relatively little, for example, is really known about how businesses actually see themselves carrying out "the practice of competition," or even about the actual competitive mechanisms of setting prices. Furthermore, in all of this, there is no mention of the *consumer's* view of these various concepts or of his model of the marketing process. To be sure, we can be reasonably certain of some things. For example, we know that consumers do regard products as serving needs beyond the bare essentials. Yet it would be helpful to know far more about their views of the overall marketing process.

What we propose as a worthwhile endeavor is an independent assessment of the consumer's view of the marketing process, focusing on information needs from his point of view. Thus, rather than businessmen lamenting the critics' proposals for product-rating systems and the critics bemoaning what seem to be obvious abuses of marketing tools, both sides ought to move toward proposing an information system for the consumer that takes into account *his* needs and *his* information-handling capacities while still adhering to the realities of the marketing process.

For those who have the reading habit, it will be obvious that this proposal is but an extension of the conclusions reached by members of the American Marketing Association's Task Force on "Basic Problems in Marketing" for the improvement of relations between marketing and government.[4] In brief, along with suggested studies on the influence of government policies and programs on corporate marketing decisions, a special study was recommended in the area of consumer-buyer decision making and behavior:

"It is of the highest importance to investigate the impacts of the host of governmental regulations, facilities, aids, and interventions upon the quality and efficiency of consumer-buyer decision making."[5]

The report went on to state that, particularly in light of the generally recognized drift from *caveat emptor* toward *caveat venditor,* "abundant basic research opportunities and needs exist" in the area of government impact and consumer-buyer behavior.

What can businessmen do?

Certainly there is a crying need for more information and, as we have tried to illustrate, for fresh analytic thinking on almost all of the issues

---

[4] See E. T. Grether and Robert J. Holloway, "Impact of Government upon the Market System," *Journal of Marketing,* April 1967, pp. 1–5; and Seymour Banks, "Commentary on 'Impact of Government upon the Market System,'" *ibid.,* pp. 5–7.

[5] Grether and Holloway, *ibid.,* p. 5.

on which government and business are butting heads. We have elaborated on the different models of how the marketplace does, and should, work because we think their existence explains the largest part of why marketers and their critics often talk past each other, even when they have the best intentions of engaging in a dialogue. The other part is explained by the relative absence of facts. As we have noted, the consumer's view of the market-advertising process and his informational needs represent an important (and relatively unprobed) research area.

Returning to the "dialogue," we should add a further problem beyond that of business and government spokesmen talking past one another. Inasmuch as many on both sides see themselves as representing their colleagues' views, partisanship becomes mixed with the aforementioned misunderstanding. Since such partisanship is likely to address itself to stereotyped views of "the other side," the comments become irrelevant. That many well-qualified first-hand commentators are regarded as self-serving by their critics is a point aptly made by Denis Thomas. Equally apt is his corollary observation that those "who view business . . . from a suitably hygienic distance lose no marks for partiality even if their facts are wrong." [6]

How then can effective interactions take place? Obviously, the key parts will be played by:

(1) Thoughtful business and government leaders.

(2) Marketers and their critics who take the time to consider and to understand (even if they do not agree with) each others' premises and assumptions.

(3) Those who engage in meaningful dialogue oriented to fact finding rather than fault finding.

(4) Those on both sides who address themselves to solving the problems of the real, rather than the presumed, public.

These constructive parts are not easy to play, but there are many who are trying, and succeeding, as these three examples illustrate:

(1) The Department of Commerce has taken a series of measures, including the formation of a National Marketing Com-

---

[6] *The Visible Persuaders* (London, Hutchinson & Co., 1967), p. 11.

mittee, to play a positive "activist" role in business-government relations; marketers are involved in what goes on rather
than, as has occurred in many previous government situations, being informed after the fact.

(2) William Colihan, Executive Vice President of Young & Rubi-
cam, Inc., proposed at the University of Missouri's Freedom
of Information Conference that marketing undertake a major
consumer education job to "make the marketing system benefit the nonaffluent, the undereducated." [7] This 20% of adult
consumers represents, he feels, both a public responsibility
and a marketing opportunity.

(3) John N. Milne of Toronto's MacLaren Advertising Company
Limited spelled out 11 specific major economic, social,
ethical, and communications research projects to provide a
"factual basis for an objective assessment of advertising, to
replace emotional pleas." Business, government, universities,
and projects in other nations would serve as sources and bene-
ficiaries of data "so that advertising's usefulness to all segments of society can be assessed and improved." [8]

Beyond the parts played by thoughtful business and government people, we see a distinctive role for schools of business in bringing about
meaningful interaction. Business schools are a unique resource both
in their understanding of the business system and in their capability to
conduct relevant research. Other faculties, at least equally competent
and objective in research, generally do not have the depth of understanding of why things are the way they are—a necessary precursor to
relevant study. We hasten to add that grasping how something *does*
operate implies no consent that this is how it *should* operate, now or
in the future.

Both in research and as participants (or moderators) in dialogue,
business school faculties can play a significant role.

Business and government should sponsor the necessary research.
The particular need for business is to recognize that the era of exclusively partisan pleading must end. In our judgment, the American

---

[7] *Freedom of Information in the Market Place* (FOI Center, Columbus,
Missouri, 1967), pp. 140–148.

[8] Speech given at the Annual Conference of the Federation of Canadian
Advertising and Sales Clubs, Montreal, June, 1967.

Association of Advertising Agencies' sponsorship of research on consumer reactions to advertising and advertisements is a splendid model.[9] The findings are by no means exclusively favorable to advertising. But they make more clear where problems do, and do not, lie. And academic "insurance" of the objective conduct of the research and presentation of findings should bring about a degree of governmental acceptance and set the standard for any subsequent research. We can use more of this, and more of it is beginning to take place. A dialogue is always most profitable when the parties have something to talk about.

[9] For a description of the research and a review of the major results, see Stephen A. Greyser, editor, *The AAAA Study on Consumer Judgment of Advertising—An Analysis of the Principal Findings* (New York, American Association of Advertising Agencies, 1965), and Opinion Research Corporation, *The AAAA Study on Consumer Judgment of Advertising* (Princeton, 1965), the findings and their interpretation are the subject of the authors' book, *Advertising in America: The Consumer View* (Boston, Division of Research, Harvard Business School), 1968.

4. Industry Still Has Something to Learn about Congress

Jeremy Main

For Senator Philip Hart, the gentlemanly Democrat from Michigan, it started at the breakfast table. The Harts and their eight children all like to eat Nabisco Shredded Wheat in the morning. But in 1961 they discovered that the old, familiar box had changed; it had become taller and narrower. Inside, there were still twelve biscuits, each apparently the same size as before. But a close reading of the new label indicated that here, too, something curious had happened. The net weight of the contents had been reduced from twelve ounces to ten and one-quarter. The Harts concluded that they were paying the same price for less cereal and more package.

The Harts didn't stop buying shredded wheat, but the incident helped convince the Senator that the shopper in an American supermarket doesn't always get what the package makes him think he is getting. Thereupon Hart set off on a minor crusade that ended, after five years of lobbying and legislating, with the passage of the Fair Packaging and Labeling Act, commonly called the "truth-in-packaging" law.

The law that finally emerged from Congress has not seriously disrupted industry. Many of its provisions were actually already contained

Reprinted by special permission from *Fortune Magazine* (February 1967), pp. 128–135. © 1967; Time Inc. Jeremy Main is an Associate Editor of *Fortune*.

in a series of food and drug laws enacted since the beginning of the century. But industry was concerned, for, as the National Association of Manufacturers Report put it, the law "gives the consumerists the start they need." Hart himself has stated, not entirely accurately, that "this is the first time Congress legislated to protect the economic— rather than the health or safety—interests of the consumer."

One alarmed food maker claimed "consumerism is rampant." And there is evidence to support his statement. There have been three presidential messages on consumer interests in recent years and, in 1964, President Johnson appointed Mrs. Esther Peterson, a persuasive lady of attractive Scandinavian wholesomeness, the nation's first Special Assistant to the President for Consumer Affairs. The Senate Commerce Committee created a subcommittee on consumer affairs, which will doubtless produce new consumer laws. A "truth-in-lending" bill has been enacted. Another bill regulating warranties and guarantees on consumer goods is a possibility. And the N.A.M. is warning its members to watch out for still other forms of consumer legislation that will affect manufacturers.

Relations between the consumer-products industry and the government are plainly entering a new phase. And the lobbying against the Hart bill—at first petulant and clumsy, later more skillful and to the point, but never really well organized—showed how much industry has to learn about the delicate art of dealing with Congress. The old kind of lobbying that gave the trade such a bad name never appeared during the truth-in-packaging battle. "There was no hanky-panky, no slush funds, no political contributions," claimed one of the lobbyists, and there's no evidence to the contrary in Congress. But the companies concerned were surprisingly backward in the more sophisticated kind of lobbying: presenting sound arguments attuned to political reality in all the right places.

"Too Busy or Too Tired or Too Harassed"

Industry's strategic mistake in battling truth in packaging was to adopt an attitude of intransigent opposition. The companies concerned denied any need for the bill, challenged the right of the Federal Government to interfere, and attempted to kill the legislation. They thereby lost a number of opportunities to come to terms with Congress on an early compromise. Five years of lengthy public hearings gave consumerists a public forum for publicizing their cause and complaints.

If "consumerism" really is "rampant," then the companies that stock the nation's supermarkets helped make it that way.

The long series of hearings held before Senate and House committees between 1961 and 1966 offered plenty of evidence that food and soap companies were, at times, guilty of deceptive packaging. Proponents of the bill exhibited "giant economy size" cans of coffee selling for more per ounce than the smaller jars; complained of "packaging to price" (reducing the contents of a package without reducing the price or package size); described "cents-off" sales that went on for years and, in fact, did not always represent a saving; and criticized the confusing proliferation of odd-sized packages of the same product. (Potato chips were being sold in 71 different-sized bags, boxes, and cans.) One Senate witness, magazine writer and critic Marya Mannes, summed up the frustrations of many consumers when she said, "Most of us are simply too busy or too tired or too harassed to take a computer, a slide rule, and an M.I.T. graduate to market and figure out what we're buying."

The companies concerned did a poor job of meeting such complaints. In most cases they talked in generalities and argued that the bill was an attack on free enterprise. The market, said industry witnesses, was self-policing: the housewife is smart enough not to buy a deceptively labeled item twice. But evidence disproved this. The industry also claimed that existing laws and regulations were adequate to deal with deception. The bill's supporters didn't agree. Moreover, the critics were no longer satisfied with case-by-case action against deception by the Federal Trade Commission and the Food and Drug Administration, which is what the existing laws allowed. They wanted the government to set standards for packaging and labeling so the housewife would know exactly what she was buying.

Pressuring the Press

At times, industry witnesses were inept as well as vague. D. Beryl Manischewitz, chairman of the N.A.M.'s marketing committee, rose to a high cumulus of nonsense when he tried to explain the need for fancy containers. "These examples of individual taste are difficult to explain," he said. "But no more difficult than why more than half a million persons gathered in the city of Washington recently to view the four-hundred-year-old masterpiece portrait, *Mona Lisa*. Those who cannot understand this will not be able to understand why millions of American women find an urn-shaped container of toiletry with a golden stopper more appealing than a standard jug or bottle." Senators were bored with the industry's witnesses. In fact, they were bored with the bill. During the five years that it dawdled in the Senate, only Hart himself and Oregon's Senator Maurine Neuberger consistently supported the bill. Industry, in turn, was offended by the Senate's lack of interest and apparent lack of understanding. Top executives were insulted when they traveled across the country and found themselves testifying before only one or two Senators (which is quite normal to those who know the Senate). Senators were put off by industry's refusal to consider any alternative to killing the bill. Lobbyists were disappointed when they found it difficult to see Senators (which is also normal) and then found it even harder to get them interested in the bill. "These were among the least constructive hearings in my experience," said one Senate staffer.

With the Senate unreceptive, industry turned to the press, a perfectly legitimate maneuver, but in this case badly handled. In 1962, Paul Willis, president of the Grocery Manufacturers of America, boasted in a speech to a television-industry group how he had enlisted the help of national magazines. "We suggested to the publishers that the day was here when their editorial department and business department might better understand their interdependency relationships as they affect the operating results of their company. . . . We invited them to consider publishing some favorable articles about the food industry instead of only singling out isolated cases of criticism." He pointed out that G.M.A.'s members were spending $1.2 billion on advertising that year and said threateningly, "We are not aware of any great amount of cooperation that television extended to us."

Willis' remarks set off protests in Congress and the press that delighted supporters of the Hart bill, but the speech apparently had some effect. Hart complained later that several TV appearances he had scheduled were canceled; he says, "I was told off the record that advertisers had objected." It isn't likely, however, that this crude pressure won the grocery manufacturers any close friends.

In any case, industry did not seem to have much to worry about until the beginning of 1965. The bill was blocked in the Senate Judiciary Committee. Although Esther Peterson had been traveling around the country arousing consumers, the Administration, which had never offered any truth-in-packaging bill of its own, gave the Hart bill only tepid support. But then Hart got his bill transferred to the more sympathetic Senate Commerce Committee. At first its chairman, Washington's Senator Warren Magnuson, was not convinced that there was enough support in Congress or the White House to carry the bill. However, in early 1966, President Johnson, having got approval for his priority Great Society legislation, turned to consumerism as a cause—because, say the cynics, he needed a new victory that wouldn't add to the budget. The President told Magnuson that he wanted the Hart law. In a message on consumer interests in March, 1966, the President asked Congress to pass a truth-in-packaging law because "there are instances of deception in labeling. Practices have arisen that cause confusion and conceal information even when there is no deliberate intention to deceive. The housewife often needs a scale, a yardstick, and a slide rule to make a rational choice."

By now it was clear that much of the bill was acceptable to a majority in the Senate committee. The acceptable parts included a ban on meaningless adjectives attached to statements of the quantity of contents such as "giant quart," the establishment of standards for the prominent statement of net quantity on packages, and a requirement that net weights in packages under four pounds be expressed either completely in ounces or in whole pounds.

However, a majority of Magnuson's committee—and all of the industry—were firmly opposed to a section of the bill giving the government the right to standardize package sizes and prohibit odd shapes. Opponents of the bill contended, with some reason, that setting such standards would put an end to competitive, attractive packaging; this section, they said, had to be amended if they were to vote the bill out of committee.

After beating off Republican attempts to strike the standardization section, Magnuson and Hart worked out a compromise that provided for a complicated way of establishing standards with industry participation. Basically, the government could still establish package size standards, but only after allowing industry 18 months to formulate voluntary standards. This compromise concluded an unusually long series of executive sessions (thirteen in all) and won over the doubtful members of the committee. The bill was reported out of committee 14 to 3 in May, 1966. After another unsuccessful Republican attempt on the floor to extract the standardization section, the Senate passed the bill 72 to nine.

The bill was weaker than Hart had intended it to be. But industry could take little credit for the change. Lobbyists did manage to get specific product exemptions written into the law's provisions. However, they had refused offers by Hart and others to discuss compromises on the main parts of the bill. Senate sources say that before the bill picked up political steam in the Senate, industry could have negotiated half of it away. Instead, the industry stuck to its determination to kill the bill outright in fear that if any of its representatives helped draft a truth-in-packaging law, they would be maneuvered into supporting it. As a result, the major surgery on the legislation was performed by the Senators with little industry guidance. And it was performed not to adjust the law to industry arguments, but as a maneuver to win the support of doubters in the Senate.

Industry continued intransigent until the end. However, by the time the House Interstate and Foreign Commerce Committee opened its hearings on truth in packaging in July, the lobbyists were far better organized than they had been in the early years of the battle.

Back in 1963, an *ad hoc* committee of some 50 companies and trade associations had been formed in Washington to oppose Hart's bill. The committee limited itself to arousing industry opposition and made no effort to direct lobbying. In early 1966, however, the most active members of the group formed an executive committee, consisting principally of representatives of Procter & Gamble, National Biscuit, the National Canners Association, the N.A.M., General Foods, the Soap and Detergent Association, Colgate-Palmolive, and Kellogg. The "excom" began coordinating lobbying chores so all of the key people on Capitol Hill would be plied with arguments.

The "excom" had a forceful ally: forty-year-old George Koch, the Sears, Roebuck representative in Washington, who had become president of the Grocery Manufacturers of America. Koch, who knows how to get people to listen to him on Capitol Hill, is credited with being the most effective industry lobbyist in the truth-in-packaging battle. "Who did I see?" Koch says. "Every living soul I could. It was important to get the facts across and important to do it person to person."

A Good Idea Backfires

Koch also helped to organize "district teams" of businessmen in the constituencies of the members of the House committee. The

idea that Congressmen would be more likely to listen to businessmen in their own districts than to lobbyists in Washington was a
sound one. In practice, it was only a partial success. The lobbyists discovered that it is difficult to arouse local businessmen except
with an issue that hits the current year's balance sheet. Congressmen were contacted at home only on a haphazard and occasional
basis.

One local effort backfired when the Staten Island Chamber of
Commerce passed out leaflets to ferryboat commuters asking them to
tell their Congressman, Democrat John Murphy, that they were against
the bill. Murphy got a lot of mail on truth in packaging—as much, he
says, as on the war in Vietnam—but it ran two to one in favor of the
bill. To the chamber's chagrin, many of the letters were written on the
back of its leaflets.

For the House hearings the industry selected its witnesses more
skillfully than it had during the Senate hearings. The executives who
testified had more facts and, especially on the question of standardization of packages, they had better arguments. Arthur Larkin, executive vice president of General Foods, for example, explained why his
company's 13 regular cake mixes come in different and odd sizes. The
mixes have different densities. But the housewife can take any one of
them, add two eggs, and produce a cake of a standard size. "If we
were bound by a standard requiring all cake mixes to have the same
net weight, conceivably the recipe might call for 1¾ eggs," Larkin
said. "Poor a cook as I am, I know that might be difficult to accomplish in the kitchen." With such arguments presented to attentive and
probing Congressmen, and with lukewarm testimony from government
witnesses, several of the House committee members became uneasy
about the bill.

At this point the bill's fate was focused by circumstances on a
freshman Congressman from Ohio, John Gilligan, 45. Gilligan was a
member of the committee; he represented Cincinnati, headquarters
for one of the biggest lobbyists against the bill, Procter & Gamble; and
he was engaged in a difficult campaign for re-election (which he
eventually lost).

As a liberal Democrat, Gilligan was expected to support the Hart
bill down the line. But he and four other Democrats on the thirty-three-
man committee were not convinced by the government witnesses, and
became the key swing group. Gilligan decided the government had not

made a good case for being given sweeping authority to standardize packages.

A Visit at Home

Before the hearings began, a delegation of about eight local business-men had called on Gilligan during one of his visits to Cincinnati. "They didn't know much about the legislation," says Gilligan, "but they knew what they were afraid of. When local people come to see you, you tend to give them more attention than you do the professional in Wash-ington." Then, just before Procter & Gamble was scheduled to testify, P. & G. Chairman Neil McElroy and Gilligan spent an hour chatting about the bill at McElroy's invitation. McElroy said he did not want a bill, but if there had to be one he felt something had to be done about the standardization section. Despite the "district team" idea, the two meetings were the only efforts to influence Gilligan in Cin-cinnati. But, in Washington, Gilligan—and the other swing men—were approached time and again by industry lobbyists as well as supporters of the bill, especially labor representatives.

When the hearings ended and the committee went into executive sessions, the problem facing Chairman Harley Staggers of West Vir-ginia was similar to the one faced by Magnuson and Hart in the Senate: a majority of the committee would oppose the bill unless the standardization section was weakened even more than it had been in the Senate.

By this time Gilligan had decided that a compromise was possible if standardization were made purely voluntary. While campaigning at home one weekend in mid-September, he got a call from Wilbur Cohen, then Under Secretary of Health, Education and Welfare. Cohen asked Gilligan why he couldn't support the bill. Gilligan ex-plained his doubts about standardization and proposed his compro-mise. Cohen talked to the other swing men, to the White House, and to the Commerce Department. Before the weekend was over, he called Gilligan back to tell him the Administration would back a compromise.

With the Administration and the swing men behind it, an amended bill was easily reported out of committee on September 22. Eleven days later, it passed the House by a vote of 300 to eight. That close to Election Day, only the most adamant opponents were willing to vote against a bill with the built-in voter appeal of "truth in packaging."

"Consumerism" Won't Go Away

Hart claims that 90 percent of his original bill is contained in the final act. Other "consumerists" say it was eviscerated when standardization of package sizes was made purely voluntary. Certainly industry was delighted to see this happen. The act says that when the Secretary of Commerce determines "there is undue proliferation of weights, measures, or quantities" that "impairs the reasonable ability of consumers to make value comparisons," then he can ask industry to develop voluntary standards. If industry fails to do so within a year, he can ask Congress for further legislation.

The rest of the act contains much of what Hart wanted—and much that the industry didn't want. The contents of a package, if it is less than four pounds or one gallon, must be stated in total ounces as well as pounds or quarts. Contents must be printed on the main display panel, in a color that contrasts with the background and in type sizes to be established by government agencies. When the number of servings is given, their size must be given. Exaggerations, such as "giant quart," are prohibited. Government can control "nonfunctional slack fill" and "cents-off" sales.

The law is one that industry can live with. It requires no more than changes in most labels, which are frequently revised in any case. But since much depends on future regulations and since Congress has invited future amendments, the battle over truth in packaging is not necessarily finished. Moreover, Congress will be considering other such laws.

In this time of "consumerism," the experience with truth in packaging offers some simple, important lessons: straight, factual testimony is more effective than oratory; the most telling lobbying begins at home, but an astute Washington representative is also a great asset to a company; cooperation among the companies concerned can be useful even if it is difficult and perhaps undesirable to present a united front that looks like a superlobby; legitimate complaints against industry cannot be shrugged off as attacks on free enterprise.

Most of all, the consumer-goods industry is going to have to face up to the fact that "consumerism" has become politically popular. As industry learned when it tried to kill truth in packaging, "consumerism" cannot be killed. It is part of the Democrats' legislative program; it is strongly supported by organized labor and other groups; and consumers themselves have become more aggressive and articulate.

Truth in packaging was signed into law by President Johnson in November, 1966. At the ceremony he handed out several hundred pens. With each was a statement that said, in part: "One of the pens used by the President in signing *S. 985,* An Act to regulate interstate and foreign commerce by preventing the use of unfair or deceptive methods of packaging and labeling." In fact, only a dozen or so of the pens had been used. It was a clear case of deceptive labeling.

5. Industrial Self-Regulation and the Public Interest

Harper W. Boyd, Jr.
and Henry J. Claycamp

The responsibility of business organizations to society has recently been the subject of increasing attention. Even though most American corporations have become substantially more enlightened about their responsibilities to the consumer, the feeling abounds in certain quarters that business performance in this respect is not always adequate—particularly with regard to protecting the consumer's health and safety. Current inquiries by the Federal Government into the safety of automobiles, cigarettes, and pharmaceuticals, for example, indicate that some influential persons believe that more governmental intervention on behalf of consumers is necessary. In the past, expanded governmental control has frequently resulted from the failure of private business to provide the kind of leadership that would have obviated federal intervention.

Historically, businessmen have argued that competition is the best protector of the consumer's interests. This assumption implies that the market place offers sufficient alternatives and that the consumer knows how to select those products and services which best meet his needs. Nevertheless, governmental and business leaders have demonstrated

Reprinted from *Michigan Law Review*, Vol. 64 (May, 1966), pp. 1239–1254.

a considerable amount of agreement with respect to the need of the consumer for assistance in improving his buying skills. Over the years, the number of business and governmental organizations designed to aid the American consumer has risen sharply; such organizations include, among others, better business bureaus, trade associations, product testing laboratories, consumer advisory councils, and state consumer fraud bureaus.

It is one thing to help the consumer make "better buys" in an economic sense, but it is quite another to help him safeguard his own life as well as the lives of others. Obviously the consequences in these two situations are very different. Typically, whenever threats to the consumer's health and safety have become obtrusively apparent, the Federal and state governments—in one way or another and with varying degrees of efficiency—have taken action. Responsibility for protecting consumers has devolved upon a large number of Federal agencies, such as the Federal Trade Commission, the Food and Drug Administration, the United States Department of Agriculture, the Interstate Commerce Commission, and the Federal Aviation Agency.

As the affluence of the American society grows, a concern about such matters as health, education, and welfare has also become more apparent. Some concern derives from technological breakthroughs which require control, such as the development of aircraft for mass transportation. In other cases, increased recognition of serious threats to public health and safety has led various groups of aroused citizens to advocate governmental control. Today, growing numbers of individuals and organizations believe that the consumer's health and safety are not being adequately protected.

The following discussion is directed to the vital issue of whether the automobile industry can voluntarily advance consumers' interests through the imposition of adequate safety standards, or whether widened Federal intercession is essential.

Automobiles

Automobile accidents account for about 50,000 deaths per year. In fact, such accidents constitute the fourth leading cause of death in the United States, and for people between the ages of five and 30, the automobile is the leading cause of death. In addition, several million persons sustain injuries each year from automobile mishaps. Nearly one out of every three persons admitted to hospitals is there because of a car accident, and one out of every four partial or complete paralysis cases caused by injury is due to the automobile.

In recent years, car accidents have cost the public tens of billions of dollars in property damage, lost wages, medical expense, and insurance premiums. Moreover, this large burden does not include such costs as those involving the police, the courts, emergency standby facilities, driver licensing, and automobile safety inspection. These add more billions of dollars to the annual cost.

The traditional attitude has been that although automobile accidents were recognized as a function of the environment in which the car operated (that is, the roads, the driver, and the automobile), it was felt that only the driver could be "controlled" to any great extent. Thus, past efforts to meet the problem have relied mainly on driver education. Without gainsaying the importance of drivers in the prevention of accidents, the belief has been growing that the vehicles themselves can be improved in ways which will significantly reduce deaths and accidents.

Misplaced emphasis by both designers and consumers

Automobiles are certainly a highly visible status symbol, and it is felt by some people that a car tells a lot about the owner, including his adventuresomeness, virility, wealth, and social class. Rarely is an automobile thought of as simply a vehicle for transportation. Certainly the several million people who flocked to the showrooms during the first few days after the introduction of the first Mustang were not just interested in a machine to convey them from one point to another.

As a consequence of the consumer's conception of the role of a car, the stylist has emerged as perhaps the most important man in the automobile industry. Manufacturers now cater to the public by offering, in the aggregate, hundreds of body styles and thousands of trim combinations. Annual style changes are surrounded by secrecy and are introduced with fanfare which costs tens of millions of dollars. It is quite clear that the large sums of money spent to create and introduce styling reduce the funds which might otherwise be devoted to engineering and safety.

The relative emphasis placed on style and safety features undoubtedly reflects the fact that the effect on consumer demand is unquestionable, whereas there is little evidence to suggest that consumers make brand choices on the basis of safety. For example, consider the elimination of door posts in many models and the continuation of fins for several years after reports that they contributed to serious accidents. The failure of consumers to give more weight to safety features when purchasing automobiles is due to many factors. As previously noted, most Americans place the blame for accidents on the drivers; seldom has anyone blamed the car, an inanimate object. Similarly, all safety campaigns are addressed to the driver, on the theory that he is the only one who can prevent an accident. In fact, accidents are recorded on the basis of driver fault, since most traffic laws have been set forth in a way which, if followed, would prevent accidents. If an accident occurs, a traffic regulation must have been violated. Such accidents are investigated almost exclusively by the police and by insurance companies. This process reinforces the law enforcement aspects of such inquiries, and only rarely is a question raised about the contribution of the car's design to the accident.

No national or state body that systematically investigates accidents has ever focused upon the design of the cars involved. The National Safety Council, which is primarily responsible for compiling and reporting traffic accident statistics, does not compile data dealing with the car makes and models involved in accidents or report on the effect of automobile design and performance on accident results. It was not until the early 1950's that vehicle design was evaluated in this connection, and then the study was made by a university under a grant from the Federal Government.[1]

Automotive design ignored by safety organizations

In his chapter entitled "The Traffic Safety Establishment," Ralph Nader discusses the bewildering array of organizations involved in automobile safety.[2] The number of these organizations and their interrelationships are substantial, which is to be expected in view of the great complexity of the passenger-car system. The system includes the automobile industry, the insurance industry, the Federal Government, state and local governments, and a variety of associations.[3]

Nader points out that safety has been largely delegated to a number of non-governmental organizations which are subsidized heavily

---

[1] The research was done at Cornell University. The initial grant of $54,000 was made in 1953.

[2] See Ralph Nader, *Unsafe at Any Speed,* New York: Pocket Books, 1966.

[3] Of course, advertising media and related industries are also mixed in the pattern in one way or another, but they are not discussed here in the interest of conserving space.

by the automobile and insurance industries. These groups include:

1. The National Committee on Uniform Traffic Laws and Ordinances, which periodically publishes a guide for state motor vehicle laws. The guide does not specify any features of vehicle design which have been related to injuries sustained from accidents. In dealing with vehicular inspection, it provides a check list which, if followed, will restore the inspected car to its original condition.

2. The Automobile Safety Foundation, which awards grants to a variety of groups (such as the American Bar Association, the International Association of Chiefs of Police, the National Safety Council, and the American Municipal Association) for support of traffic safety programs.

3. The Insurance Institute for Highway Safety, which operates much like the Automobile Safety Foundation.

4. The National Safety Council, which is heavily involved with safety programs. This organization does little or no research directed at accident prevention and has not made any statements about automobile designs.

5. The President's Committee for Traffic Safety, which is supported by private industry. The committee's work is largely that of distributing safety information materials to other organizations.

In addition to the above organizations, the American Automobile Association, while a powerful force at both the national and local level, has almost never become involved in a critical evaluation of automobile designs. Similarly, insurance companies have been reluctant to make open attacks on automobile designs, although Liberty Mutual did design several cars which incorporated a substantial number of tested safety features. This program was subsequently terminated.

The foregoing discussion is a great oversimplification of the problems associated with automobile safety, but it does indicate that no single agency has any real responsibility (or enforcement power) for setting safety standards related to vehicular design. It also indicates the preoccupation with driver performance. Nevertheless, what little research has been done in relating car design to accidents shows clearly that cars can be built which will drastically reduce injuries received under certain conditions. Without too much effort, most recommendations regarding visibility, glare, and penetrating steering wheel assemblies could be implemented.

Problems inherent in self-regulation

There are three main factors that affect the available solutions to the problem. They are: (1) the number of parties involved; (2) the solution is only a matter of degree (better safety design); and (3) the individual driver automatically involves other people (pedestrians, passengers, and other motorists) and their property in his actions.

One solution is to permit the automobile companies to respond to the problem on an individual basis and take whatever action they deem best. It seems evident, however, that, until consumers perceive safety features as an important consideration in the purchase of a specific make, hope for the achievement of significant results through action by individual firms must remain small. Incorporation of safety features as standard equipment results, for the most part, in higher costs. If consumers do not consider these features important, the company using them is placed at a competitive disadvantage. Recognizing this, automobile manufacturers have made many safety features optional equipment, but this approach does not meet head-on the problem of conflicts between style and safety. As long as relevant safety standards are not made obligatory for the entire industry, individual manufacturers are not likely to resolve such conflicts in favor of increased safety.

Individual manufacturers, however, can increase the importance of the safety appeal. Undoubtedly, all purchasers of automobiles possess at least a latent desire for safety. The literature on mass communications provides some evidence that repeated appeals to latent desires can increase their saliency and make them important variables in the decision process.[4] If a company were to embark on such a

---

[4] See Carl Hovland, Irving Janis & Harold H. Kelley, *Communication and Persuasion,* New Haven: Yale Univ. Press, 1953. If one wants to increase the saliency of the desire for safety, appeals must be used which allude to the physical danger which might occur as a result of failure to take action which would increase safety. See *id.,* ch. 3, for a summary of the literature relating to this communication situation and a discussion of the conditions under which such communication can be effective.

campaign, it would of course have to devote a significant amount of its promotion expenditures to safety appeals in order to prove that the need for safety was being met by its products.

Some of the major manufacturers apparently have made a start in this direction. For example, a few years ago, the Ford Motor Company undertook a significant promotion campaign in which the major theme was safety.[5] Although this undertaking represented only a small part of the company's promotional expenditures, and the majority of the advertising space was devoted to aspects of safety other than automobile design, considerable attention was given to the new safety features which were standard equipment on 1966 products of the Ford Motor Company. As might be expected, most of these features—seat belts, emergency flashers, and padded visors—were easily demonstrated to and recognized by the consumer. Nevertheless, if such promotions were carried out on a broad scale by the entire industry, it is possible that safety could become a more important dimension of competition, and the consumer would benefit.

A more pervasive solution would be for the industry to delegate complete responsibility for specifying and enforcing design standards to an autonomous agency. The agency could be either a new organization specifically established for this task or an existing but somewhat inactive body, such as the Automotive Safety Foundation, which could be revitalized. The functions of such a unit would include the collection and analysis of reports on accidents, research on the effect of alternative designs on safety under a variety of conditions, performance of the engineering required to translate the research results into product specifications, and control over the products manufactured by the automobile industry.

Such an agency would have to be an organization of considerable size and power. The need for highly qualified engineers and researchers (who would come from a variety of disciplines, including medicine and related areas) and the high cost of laboratory equipment would certainly indicate that such a center would be expensive to set up as

<hr/>

[5] Announcement of the promotion was reported in The Wall Street Journal, Dec. 27, 1965, p. 5, col. 4. The news story reported that the promotion would include a twelve-page insertion in Time Magazine and sixteen-page supplements in 25 Sunday newspapers. Included in the story was an announcement by the president of the University of Michigan that an institute to study and report on safety aspects of vehicles, drivers, roads, and traffic would be established at Ann Arbor with a $10 million grant from the four major automobile manufacturers.

well as to maintain. Some rough idea of possible costs can be obtained by looking at the funds spent by the Federal Government in its aviation safety work. In recent years, the annual expenditure has varied between approximately 35 and 60 million dollars. Even though airplanes are far more complicated than automobiles, there is no reason to believe that a passenger-car safety center would cost less to operate than the aviation safety program. Indeed, an automotive safety center might be substantially more expensive because of the difficulties of monitoring car accidents, working with engineers and designers from the various companies, and making certain that the minimum standards were effectively implemented in new cars. However, since the annual profits of the automobile manufacturers run into many hundreds of millions of dollars, the cost of such a center should not be regarded as the critical issue. It is also likely that the expense would eventually be passed on to the consumer.

A more serious question regarding the feasibility of such a center concerns its investigative powers and the legal consequences of its findings. Since automobile accidents involve local law enforcement authorities, local courts, and insurance companies, the question of how such a center could obtain cooperation arises. Would such persons permit their work to be scrutinized closely by an outsider? Some of the problems could undoubtedly be overcome by delegating the responsibility for data collection to a prestigious institution such as a university.

A related problem would arise from investigations that resulted in the center requiring a change in standards for one of the automobile manufacturers. It could be reasoned that the imposition of such a requirement was tantamount to a finding that the manufacturer had been guilty of faulty design. Moreover, if such an investigation were instituted as a result of a series of accidents, it is likely that representatives of the center could be forced to testify as expert witnesses regarding the institution's conclusions as to design safety. The consequences of such disclosures could be devastating to the industry.

The specter of collusion would also undoubtedly be raised if an effective safety center were established. It is possible that effective safety standards, when applied, would raise the cost of manufacturing automobiles, and prices would be increased to cover both increased costs and a profit on the safety features. Increased car prices would raise a hue and cry from the Government as well as from consumers. The car is not only a vital part of life for most Americans, but it is also one of the most expensive possessions of a consumer. Automobile manufacturers would be accused of using safety as a rationale for price escalation. Thus, it is likely that the industry would be forced to submit to costly harassment by the Government.

Another aspect of the "collusion" problem has to do with the impact of safety standards on design. It is possible that the current variability of styles and designs would be substantially reduced, resulting in increased similarity among makes and models. This effect would be quite obvious and would undoubtedly lead some people to conclude that a conspiracy was underway to reduce design costs and the number of real alternatives available to the consumer. The oligopolistic nature of the car industry would intensify this suspicion.

Finally, we are faced with the problem of who would control such a center. Because of the power which would be required for an effective safety center, it would need to be controlled in an unbiased way, but the size and scope of the automobile industry would make it hard to find a "disinterested" board of directors. In addition, would the Government tolerate such power in the hands of a single unit without governmental monitoring? On the other hand, would the automobile companies voluntarily delegate such a substantial part of their decision making to an outside agency over which they had no control? Given the expenses involved in such self-regulation and the inherent dangers of provoking governmental interference, this delegation is not likely to occur except in response to an imminent threat of governmental regulation.

The only effective solution

It thus appears unlikely that the industry can or will attempt self-regulation to any substantial extent. Because of this and the obvious problems of individual state regulation, it can be argued that if safety design standards are to be established and regulation undertaken, such action must be taken by the Federal Government. The Government has a successful prototype in the Federal Aviation Agency, which promulgates and enforces safety regulations applying to all civilian aircraft. The FAA inspects and licenses all such aircraft, and also licenses pilots and aviation mechanics. In addition, the Civil Aeronautics Board investigates all airplane accidents. If an investigation reveals that a carrier or airplane manufacturer was negligent in following prescribed rules or was guilty of substandard workmanship which was a causal factor in the accident, then the party or parties involved can be sued for damages.

Not all governmental agencies have been as successful as the FAA and the CAB. For example, throughout its history the Food and Drug Administration has suffered from the low pay and prestige accorded many of its Bureau of Medicine positions, pressures from politicians acting on incomplete scientific evidence, and the problems of cooperating with scientists employed by the pharmaceutical industry. The large amount of work thrown on the FDA by the 1962 drug reform legislation has made it difficult for the Agency to carry out its basic responsibilities.[6] Thus, the efficiency of a governmental agency is not by any means automatic. Unless Congress were to set up an agency with the proper authority and funds, the results would probably not be impressive. Apparently the Johnson Administration had reasoned along these lines; according to statements in the press, the President was considering proposing to Congress a five-year automobile safety program which would cost about five hundred million dollars. It was reported that the bill would empower the Secretary of Commerce to fix minimum safety requirements for all vehicles sold in the United States. Thus, the Johnson Administration appeared to be taking a stronger stand on the safety issue than that proposed by Senator Ribicoff in the National Highway Safety Bill. The major provisions in Senator Ribicoff's bill dealt with the consolidation of safety programs, driver education, and uniform inspection to eliminate defective automobiles. Whether either bill would meet the design safety problem sufficiently was not known.

[6] For a report on the problems facing the FDA's medical director, see Spivak, *Regulating Drugs,* The Wall Street Journal, Dec. 28, 1965, p. 8, col. 4.

6. Consumer Protection Via Increased Information

Louis L. Stern

What about consumer protection?

The great concern of businessmen about recent demands for consumer protection is indicated by the establishment of: (1) a consumer-information service by the National Association of Manufacturers, known as Techniques in Product Selection (TIPS); and (2) a program of cooperation between the Association of Better Business Bureaus and federal departments and agencies that affect consumer-business relationships.

Although the NAM and ABBB programs may be public-relations efforts to mollify demands for consumer protection, nevertheless their creation reflects businessmen's concern that "Unless business moves to organize some communication apparatus, it will soon be confronted with a benevolent, bureaucratic structure that will take over such functions." [1]

Nor is such concern unfounded. Consider recent proposals to establish an Office or Department of Consumers, and for the Federal Government to engage in "Consumers Union" types of product-evalu-

---

[1] "GF's Cleaves Calls for Food Industry Consumer Information Unit," *Advertising Age,* 36 (April 19, 1965), 16.

Reprinted from *Journal of Marketing,* Vol. 31 (April, 1967), pp. 48–52, published by The American Marketing Association.

ation and reporting. Is it madness to speculate that the precedents set by the Drug Amendments of 1962 and the "fair labeling and packaging" act might lead to proposals for a "fair advertising" law?

Probably no other Congress ever faced as many consumer-protection proposals as the 89th. Even the U.S. Supreme Court showed an interest in consumer protection, as evidenced by its handling of the Rapid Shave case.[2]

Other signs of increasing government interest in consumer protection include:

1. Completion by Congress, the Food and Drug Administration, the National Commission on Food Marketing, and the Consumer Advisory Council of voluminous reports relating to consumer protection

2. Establishment of a special division within the U.S. Department of Agriculture to handle the Department's labeling programs

3. Establishment by the Office of Economic Opportunity of an experimental program of consumer education

4. Within the Federal Trade Commission, setting up of a new office of Federal-state cooperation; new studies of consumer-goods marketing practices; and new trade-regulation guides and rules pertaining to the marketing of consumer goods.

But perhaps the best indication of the great amount of government interest in consumer protection is the statement of Charles Sweeny, Chief of the FTC's Bureau of Deceptive Practices: "The present Commission is more deeply determined to combat consumer deception than any Commission I have known in my 30 years of service." [3]

Why is there so much interest in consumer protection?

One reason is that rising incomes and a cornucopia of new products has multiplied the number, value, and variety of consumers' market transactions. Therefore, there are far more opportunities for consumer deception than ever before. Furthermore, the mounting variety of consumer products is increasing the competitiveness of our economic system. In turn, this may be leading to a deterioration of

---

[2] *Colgate Palmolive Co. v. FTC*, 85 S. Ct. 1035.

[3] "Druggist May Be Liable for Brand Copy in His Ads," *Advertising Age*, 36 (June 7, 1965), 1.

business ethics, thus giving rise to added interest in consumer protection.

Yet it is not at all clear that deception in the marketplace has, in fact, increased. What is clear is that the history of the United States is a record of accumulated social and technological efforts to protect the individual from adversity of every sort. The drive for consumer protection may be viewed as simply a continuation of those efforts.

The Need for Product Information

Do consumers have a right to be informed, as distinct from a right not to be deceived?

Our economic system is based on the belief that free and intelligent decisions in the marketplace, rather than by government fiat, will produce the most efficient allocation of resources toward the achievement of private and social goals. To exercise free and intelligent choices in the marketplace, consumers must have access to terms of sale and product information.

However, it is likely that the loss of personal relationships in the marketplace has reduced both the availability and the reliability of product information.

A second factor contributing to the problem is the rising level of technology. New materials, new operating principles, new functions, new designs, and new packaging have increased the difficulty of choosing one product or brand over another. The growing number of synthetic textiles and textile mixtures with varying prices and performance characteristics amply illustrates this situation.

Because of their usually greater complexity, durable products may reflect more advances in technology than nondurable products. Hence, the problem of adequacy and comprehension of product-performance information may be compounded in the case of durable goods. Furthermore, consumers are less capable of personally evaluating durable products because the long life and varied conditions under which these products are used cloud post-purchase brand comparisons. To make matters even more difficult, the reports of such organizations as *Consumers Union* are quickly rendered obsolete by model changes or model number changes.

A third factor contributing to the problem of adequacy of product information is the language of advertising. From Martineau to Weir, many advertisers and copywriters have preached the sermon of *image*.

In the words of Pierre Martineau, "It is generally insufficient to convince a person on intellectual grounds. His feelings must be involved. And this we achieve by affective or esthetic suggestion and imagery, by the meanings behind the words and pictures." [4]

Consider also the "heretical" words of William D. Tyler, *Advertising Age* columnist: "Most advertising down the years has done little more than say sweet nothings about a product . . . It has contained the least information, the fewest facts, of almost anything ever written. We have relied mainly on adjectives, on charm, on manner of presentation, coupled with unspecific, unsupported claims of superiority." [5]

The question is how greater disclosure of product and terms-of-sale information can be achieved. The difficulties of attempting to provide greater information to consumers are substantial. The problem of communicating technical information to a nontechnical audience, the time and space limitations of the vehicle of communication, and the cost of the time and space used must all be taken into account.

On the other hand, there is the question of *methods*. Will the methods of information be voluntary or compulsory? Will they involve standards, labeling requirements, consumer-advisory services, consumer-education programs, or some combination of these?

Voluntary Disclosure

Private industry has made great strides in attempting to provide information to consumers and to forestall government activity. Consider the following:

1. Formation over the years of codes of ethics by various associations in the packaging field.

2. Adoption by the 50th National Conference on Weights and Measures (June, 1965) of a standard for conspicuous labeling, as an amendment to the Model State Regulation Pertaining to Packages. (The new standard defined officially and nationally for the first time what constitutes a "clear and conspicuous" statement of net contents on package labels.)

---

[4] Pierre Martineau, *Motivation in Advertising,* New York: McGraw-Hill Book Co., 1957, p. 187.

[5] William D. Tyler, "Is Competitive Comparison Really Bad in Advertising? Reform With Care," *Advertising Age,* 37 (March 14, 1966), 61.

3. Adoption by the American Standards Association, the National Bureau of Standards, and many other groups of standards for the size, shape, or performance ratings (such as BTU output) of innumerable products and containers.

Government Intervention

Of course, government regulations are sometimes unduly rigid, and create legal hazards for even the conscientious corporate citizen. (For example, the present standard of identity for butter was formulated at the turn of the century and does not permit the addition of emulsifiers or preservatives to butter, an unconscionable shackle to the butter industry's competition with margarine. Neither does it provide for the addition of vitamins to butter or the continuous-process method of manufacturing butter, both of which are common today.) Nevertheless, even more regulations probably are in prospect.

Terms of sale

Aside from regulations pertaining to safety or gross misrepresentation, the greatest need for consumer protection is in regard to clarity of terms of sale. The least restrictive measure would require merely a statement of net contents on the package. However, mere knowledge of the weight or quantity of a product is an inadequate basis for intelligent choice; and if the statement of net contents is inconspicuous or the shopper unobservant, not even that much information will be known.

A further level of protection would be to provide for standardization of weights and quantities in which a consumer product may be distributed for retail sale. State laws already provide for standard package sizes for a few staple food products such as bread, butter, margarine, milk, cream, and flour.

Standardization of weights and quantities would provide informational gains to consumers. It would enable many shoppers to compare the price of equivalent amounts of alternative brands. In contrast, indications of price per ounce carried out to several decimal places would be no real improvement, and actually might distract consumers from making price comparisons of total amounts.

Standardization of weights and quantities would also call attention to price increases, which are otherwise hidden from some consumers in the form of a reduction in quantity.

It would be desirable, therefore, to establish standard weights or quantities in which selected consumer goods might be distributed. Provision for variations from these standards in multiples of 25% of the standard amounts would probably satisfy most consumer preferences for size of unit of purchase.

Establishment of standard weights and quantities might reduce the number of opportunities for using one size and style of container for packaging a variety of products as soup, cracker, and cereal companies now do. Considerable expense would also be involved in adjusting packaging machinery to the new weight or quantity standards. Nevertheless, the long-run advantages to consumers probably would exceed these disadvantages.

A still higher level of restriction, to regulate container sizes and shapes, is not only unnecessary but contrary to consumers' interests. It would severely inhibit package innovation. However, the International Organization for Standardization, whose standards may acquire the effect of law in over 50 member nations, has launched a program to develop retail package size standards that would affect *all* consumer products. Its program could, within a few years, force U.S. manufacturers to adopt similar standards for export purposes.

Standards and grade-labeling

Compulsory standards of minimum quality or performance can be a useful form of consumer protection where health or safety is involved. Minimum standards can also serve to prevent consumers from being sold grossly inferior products.

Product standards usually impose minimum product requirements. On the other hand, grade-labeling involves an attempt to communicate in one or more symbols the relative quality of a product as influenced by a variety of characteristics.

Because grade-labeling requires a high degree of agreement as to what constitutes the best combination of product characteristics, its utility is limited to simple products having few attributes. Yet these products tend to be those which consumers are most capable of evaluating themselves. And even for these products, the whirlwind pace of product and package innovation occurring today would present an enormous grade-labeling task.

Furthermore, the effects of grade-labeling upon product research and innovation must also be considered. Grade-labeling would reduce product differentiation and thereby tend to promote price competition.

As a result, smaller marketing margins would yield less research-and-development revenues.

CONSUMER ADVISORY SERVICES. As proposed by Donald Turner, then Chief of the U.S. Justice Department's Antitrust Division, another means of communicating more information to consumers would be for the Federal Government to evaluate products and publish its evaluations, or to subsidize organizations such as *Consumers Union*.[6] Such publications as *Consumers Bulletin* or *Consumer Reports* provide a source of clear and continuing product information; and their evaluations can be both capsulized and detailed.

On the other hand, their value is limited by their remoteness from the point of purchase. A more serious disadvantage, were they to achieve widespread consumer influence, would be the power they would come to possess over the economic fate of individual companies. If the majority of consumers followed their brand recommendations, producers of lower-rated brands would be strongly induced to imitate the preferred brand as closely as possible.

Accordingly, product differentiation might be expected to decrease, and this would be to consumers' disadvantage. Simultaneously, a loss of product differentiation might lead to a reduction in the number of producers, another undesirable effect.

Full Disclosure

"Full disclosure" has a variety of implications. Most commonly, it is assumed to imply disclosure of the dangerous nature of a product. Such laws as the Flammable Fabrics Act (1953), the Hazardous Substances Labeling Act (1960), the Drug Amendments of 1962, and the Cigarette Labeling Act (1965) already impose this level of meaning.

A second level of meaning would compel disclosure of component ingredients, net contents, and other terms-of-sale information, such as interest and related charges. Laws such as the Food, Drug and Cosmetics Act (1938), the Wool Products Labeling Act (1939), the Fur Products Labeling Act (1951), the Textile Fiber Products Identification Act (1958), and the Automobile Information Disclosure Act (1958) are intended to provide legislative mandate for this type of

---

[6] "Anti-Trust Chief Urges Alternative to Advertising," *Advertising Age,* 37 (June 6, 1966), 1 at 147.

disclosure. Disclosure of component ingredients is primarily useful in relation to determining the healthfulness, safety, value, or performance of a product. Over and above this, compulsion of such disclosure might be interpreted as protection for and responsiveness to the existence of individual preferences for certain products. The next higher level of disclosure is the revelation of a product's performance characteristics. To some extent this level of disclosure is implemented voluntarily by manufacturers of above-average quality products who employ rational selling appeals. Horsepower ratings, BTU ratings, and lumber ratings are familiar voluntary disclosures by manufacturers and distributors of performance characteristics. But unfortunately, many voluntary performance descriptions are meaningless or unreliable and sometimes refer to inputs rather than outputs.

Most manufacturers prefer to avoid direct performance statements in favor of evocative expressions or episodes. This is especially likely to be the case where no substantial differences in performance exist among rival brands, because for these products disclosure of meaningful performance information would tend to reduce the apparent differentiation among brands.

The Drug Amendments of 1962, although passed in the wake of the thalidomide scare and applying to a narrow and emotionally-charged area of consumption, provide a legislative precedent for regulatory agency concern with product performance *even where health or safety are not involved.* Witness the FDA's attempt to require vitamins to be labeled with the statement: ". . . Except for persons with special medical needs, there is no scientific basis for recommending routine use of dietary supplements." A likely outcome of regulations pertaining to *nonperformance* would be regulations pertaining to *degrees* of performance.

As to the question of consumers' abilities to understand performance information, this problem will diminish over time in response to rising levels of education, the enormous capacity of consumers to learn informally, the effectiveness of media in informing consumers, and, most importantly, the challenge to learn presented by the availability of such information.

A still higher level of disclosure pertains to potentially derogatory information unrelated to health, safety, terms of sale, or performance of a product—illustrated by the FTC requirement of disclosure, where applicable, of the foreign origin of a product or component part. Conceivably, the FTC requirement could be extended to include disclosure, where applicable, of ratings by such groups as *Consumers Union,* production by companies not subscribing to voluntary codes of advertising practice, or production by nonunionized labor, etc. The U.S. Supreme Court decision pertaining to disclosure of use of television mockups falls within this category of compulsory disclosure.[7] The Court took the extreme position that not only misrepresentations, but also deceptive presentations of valid claims, even if necessary to compensate for the technical deficiencies of communications media, are illegal.

Implementation

Note especially that the FTC may be capable of expanding its disclosure requirements without the aid of new legislation. FTC Commissioner Everette MacIntyre has been quite explicit on this matter.[8]

Furthermore, the position taken by the Commission is this: "The question . . . is not whether the Commission may declare substantive standards and principles, for it plainly may and must. The question is whether the Commission may . . . promulgate them only in the course of adjudication." [9]

In the Commission's opinion, it is also free to promulgate them in formal rule-making proceedings.

The issue is whether consumers have expectations of receiving some standard of product performance, say, average for that industry's product. If they do, then failure to disclose the fact that a particular brand is below that standard of expectation would appear to be deceptive. If, in addition, the performance factor in question is material to the consumer's purchase decision, its nondisclosure violates the FTC Act.

The principle that nondisclosure of material information constitutes a misrepresentation is well established in law.[10] Moreover, the U.S. Supreme Court made abundantly clear in the Rapid Shave case that reviewing courts should ordinarily accept the Commission's judgment as to what constitutes deception.[11] ". . . When the Commission

---

[7] *Colgate Palmolive Co., op. cit.*

[8] *The Packaging-Labeling Controls Bill* (Washington, D.C.: Chamber of Commerce of the United States, 1965), p. 14.

[9] *The Packaging-Labeling Controls Bill, op. cit.,* p. 18.

[10] *P. Lorillard Co. v. FTC,* 186 F.2d 52; *Raladam Co. v. FTC,* 283 U. S. 643. But see also *Alberty v. FTC,* 182 F.2d 36, Certiorari denied, 340 U. S. 818.

[11] *Colgate Palmolive Co., op. cit.,* p. 1043.

finds deception it is also authorized, within the bounds of reason, to infer that the deception will constitute a material factor in a purchaser's decision to buy." [12] Accordingly, the opportunity for the FTC to widen its requirements for full disclosure is clear.

The selection of what additional disclosures should be required is admittedly a difficult administrative decision, particularly so the more complex the product involved.

Nevertheless, a reasonable compromise could be reached whereby certain information would have to be provided with the product, and whereby other, more extensive, information would have to be made readily available on request. Nothing in this proposal would prevent a manufacturer from extolling additional characteristics of his products. Nor does this proposal imply that compulsory disclosures should be included in advertising or in promotion.

In short, this proposal would improve the functioning of the marketplace by increasing the amount of information therein. It would enable consumers to choose products rationally *if* they wished to do so.

Conclusion

The consumer-protection movement is definitely in the ascendancy. The issue is not whether consumers will be better protected, but what form the protection will take.

Better and more reliable product and terms-of-sale information on package labels is perhaps the most economical and least restrictive type of consumer protection. Moreover, *full disclosure* might help to dissuade current demands for additional restrictions on advertising.

---

[12] *Colgate Palmolive Co., op. cit.,* p. 1046.

Part Two
The Pre-Purchase Phase: The Availability and Quality of Information

Introduction

Before a purchase decision is made, a consumer usually consults or is exposed to several information sources. The resulting flow of information contributes to attitude formation and, ultimately, to decision. During this process, the consumer necessarily relies heavily upon sources which are impersonal and commercial in nature. It is important that these information sources be readily accessible and of adequate quality. The individual consumer lacks either the time, interest or capability to actively search out and evaluate relevant information for purchase decisions. As a result, a special burden falls upon those involved in media and point of sale communication and the governmental organizations which are representing the consumer's interest. This section will examine the size and nature of this burden.

It is natural to think of information in this context as a flow. Yet, it is also stored in some summary construct such as a brand

image which is indexed by a brand name. Without such con-
structs, the already difficult consumer information retrieval task
would become impossible, as all information would have only
temporary value. In Part One, Bauer and Greyser observed that
unless the manufacturer is motivated to support a brand, the
information provided by even an independent rating service has
little usefulness. On the other hand, it doesn't seem functional
to permit a brand image to substitute for performance or for
content. Levitt examines the delicate issues which are associated with brand names.

The most visible information source is advertising. Weiss
comments on a study of the consumer's view of advertising
and warns his colleagues in the advertising industry that they
have a real moral and practical responsibility to generate
public confidence in their advertising. Jentz describes Federal
regulation of advertising, its history and some colorful and
representative specifics. Cohen suggests that Federal regulation would have more impact if more complete and realistic
"models" of consumer behavior were used to motivate and
support actions.

Credit terms would seem to be a part of the actual purchase
transaction. Yet, the truth-in-lending section is included here
because its central thrust is in its disclosure sections. Kripke
takes a critical view of the first truth-in-lending legislation,
arguing that its provisions will have little effect in the poverty
sectors where the need for relief is greatest.

The package is a powerful communication vehicle. Birmingham
discusses the Fair Packaging and Labeling Act with economic
theory as a frame of reference. He finds that the availability of
information has a real effect on consumer welfare. Naylor
presents a study which supplies empirical evidence that is
directly relevant. The problem is that such studies are still only
too rare.

A. Branding

7. Branding on Trial

Theodore Levitt

Over the years American business has spent billions of dollars creating, developing, and sustaining trademarks and brand names. While there is a good deal of tired folklore about the virtues of brands in the great commercial scheme of American life, it takes either a resolutely closed or an extremely uninformed mind to doubt that they have played a highly important economic role. But, beyond that, this article will suggest that they have also played a highly useful and socially desirable role.

Yet there is increasing evidence that certain governmental actions and judicial rulings during recent years are moving implacably toward the possible destruction of brand-name marketing.

Current Attacks

The legitimacy of brands and trademarks has been under attack in recent years in a variety of ways which themselves often obscure the fact that an attack is occurring. This has been particularly true in court cases involving franchising and dealer territory issues.[1] While such issues do seem superficially to be concerned with franchising alone,

---

[1] *FTC* v. *Snap-On Tools Corp.*, 321 F.2d 825 (1963); *U.S.* v. *White Motor Co.*, 83 S. Ct. 696 (1963); *Susser* v. *Carvel*, 85 S. Ct. 1364 (1965).

Reprinted from *Harvard Business Review,* Vol. 44 (March-April 1966), 20–38, 171. © 1966; President and Fellows of Harvard College; all rights reserved.

they deal in a hidden but highly potent way with the question of what trademarks and brand names really should be, what their real value is, and what their holders' rights should be. Specifically, they deal with the total issue of trademarks and the brand holder's rights to determine the distributional and promotional practices for his brands all the way to the ultimate consumer.

To the untrained observer, this statement may sound somewhat alarming, if not fantastic. Yet by the time this article reaches its readers, the United States Supreme Court may have issued an opinion on a case, the results of which could vastly change brand-name marketing as we have known it for nearly a century. In its current session, one thing the Court is to consider is whether the Federal Trade Commission should be upheld in its contention that The Borden Company is engaged in illegal price discrimination (under Section 2a of the Robinson-Patman Act) when it sells its own branded evaporated milk at a higher price than it sells its physically identical but private branded evaporated milk without offering "the private brand . . . to all customers who want it, on terms that would make it actually available to them." [2]

What is significant in this issue is that the FTC contends that the two products are of like grade and quality—that a brand name attached to a product has no bearing on its value. Hence if Borden's selling of the private or unbranded product at a lower price than its branded product results in a tendency to lessen competition, the FTC contends that this difference in price should be held as discriminatory and therefore illegal.

If the Court upholds this contention, the FTC will undoubtedly be proved right retrospectively. Brands will have little or no value. (Even if the Court rules in Borden's favor in this one instance, the total issue of trademarks and brand names will be far from settled.) Moreover, if brand owners are in these circumstances prohibited from seeking a premium price over their unbranded products, and if the owners cannot in certain noncoercive ways protect their distribution channels, then brand names will indeed cease to have the economic value their owners now believe them to have.

The extraordinary irony of current attacks on brand-name marketing in the United States is that they are occurring precisely at the

---

[2] *FTC* v. *The Borden Co.,* U.S. Sup. Ct., Docket #106, "Brief for the Federal Trade Commission," November 1965, p. 21.

same time that brand-name marketing has begun to flourish in perhaps the world's most hostile ideological environment—the Soviet Union. As I will point out a little later, Soviet developments in this area are tremendously instructive and significant. The inescapable realities of mass technology and mass markets are driving the Russians to do something we now seem on the verge of perhaps accidentally undoing. Therefore, it seems appropriate at this time to review the situation and consider its implications—particularly in relation to effective business competition and public welfare.

A Brand's Reputation

A trademark or brand identifies a product and its source; but it does even more. Depending on how its owner has managed both the product and the trademark, the brand says something about the product's worth. If a retailer in some important way mishandles or mismanages a given brand, then the value of both that brand and the product it represents will somehow be diminished in the consumer's eyes.

American law now clearly recognizes this in respect to certain retail practices. Thus it gives to a brand-name owner a remedy against a retailer who purposely adulterates his product, let us say, by systematically and malevolently refusing to rotate the shelf stock of a perishable item, or against a distributor who jeopardizes the effective operation of a product by failing to exercise proper care in its installation in the consumer's home or plant. The manufacturer can legitimately refuse to sell to such dealers and distributors in order to protect the reputation of his product and the brand name under which it is sold.

There are many ways of building and keeping a brand reputation. Aside from the quality of the product, the most widely used methods involve advertising, packaging, pricing, and the conditions under which the brand is sold at retail.

Some brand owners, such as Magnavox (radio and television sets), carefully limit their distribution to highly reputable retailers who will not only add to the prestige of the Magnavox brand, but service it with the care that such prestige implies. Others, such as cosmetics companies, use a powerful combination of heavy prestige suggestive advertising, luxurious packaging, and demonstrators or leased-department operations in high-quality stores.

But not all promotional methods are available (much less *equally* available) to all trademark owners or product categories. A discussion of this is essential to a clear understanding of all the issues involved. Indeed, the issues and arguments are infinitely more complex and involuted than most people seem generally to think. The following brief analysis will help to make this clear—but, at the same time, the analysis may, to the casual reader, seem repetitious and unduly elaborate. Yet if the matter is to be given analytical attention equivalent to the complexity of the reality with which it is concerned, this is essential.

Small and new companies

One promotional method that is frequently unavailable for building a brand reputation is massive advertising. This is particularly true in the case of smaller consumer-goods producers, relatively new companies, and companies producing items for which the total demand is relatively low and the retail distributional outlets are limited.

Where both the markets and the competitors are large, the small or new company's typical and most important competitive disadvantage is not its failure to achieve parity in production costs or product quality, but rather its inability to match the giant competitors' advertising budgets. Hence it must seek other means of building and holding a brand reputation, and other means of getting and holding retail distribution and support. Whereas the large advertiser appeals directly to the consumer, the small or new company must first appeal to the distributor and retailer. It must find special ways of obtaining this direct cooperation so that its brand obtains reasonable shelf space, attractive display, and on-the-spot selling support.

In cases where the market is relatively small by today's standards, there are severe limits on how much advertising can be done in support of any brand, and on how effective such advertising can be. Consequently, building and holding a brand reputation in such a product category as lawn fertilizer, for example, and getting retail distribution for it requires exceptionally close work with distributors and retailers, and unusual cooperation and effort on the retailer's part. Moreover, a product whose total market size is small is usually purchased infrequently and irregularly, and is often a technical or highly specialized product. This means that keeping it on the shelf and well displayed calls for a degree of close cooperation between manufacturer and retailer that is not generally required in a high-traffic branded product, such as coffee, for example. The retailer needs special encouragement and incentive to maintain a good stock and good display conditions.

Furthermore, when a relatively low-volume product is also somewhat technical and specialized in nature, the retailer must be prepared to give considerable advice and help to the consumer. Thus the brand which succeeds in obtaining over a long period of time this kind of dealer support does more than merely outsell its competitors; it builds a reputation that in time produces the kind of consumer confidence which results in some measure of brand preference.

Therefore, the small producer, whether he is competing with giant competitors in a giant market, or competing with other small producers in a smaller market, is uniquely dependent on the retailer's special efforts in behalf of his brand. When the producer's strategy in part involves building and holding a brand reputation for his product, these efforts are doubly important.

Understandably, the retailer in some way must cover the costs of his supportive efforts if he is to survive. If, however, certain retailers sell a brand at promotional prices which attract customers away from the retailers who keep their prices of the trademarked product at a level which the brand owner believes necessary to provide retail margins sufficient to induce proper stocking and servicing of his brand, then some retailers will drop that product or cease to give it adequate support. The results will then be a reduction of the brand's retail availability, and a reduction of the sales and service support that the brand owner believes is necessary to give his customers full value.

The consequence will be a diminution of this trademarked product's competitive staying power and of its value to the brand owner. In the end it may mean the demise of the company in question.

In this sense, it is important to distinguish between short-term expediencies and long-term necessities. A retailer will seldom suffer from the death of any given brand. Yet any given retailer may greatly benefit from the process that destroys that brand. He can systematically loss-leader a brand, particularly one that has little or only modest advertising resources, in a way that builds short-run traffic for him but destroys the brand's reputation and the willingness of his competitors to carry it. The brand may die, while the offending retailer goes on to repeat the process with some other hapless supplier.

It seems neither fair nor sensible for the law to shackle the brand owner in such circumstances by prohibiting him from withdrawing his brand from retailers who in this way could destroy his business and, ultimately, the competitive vitality of the industry in question.

It is the recognition by the smaller brand holders of the necessity of retailer support, and adequate compensation to the retailer for his efforts, that today adds a new dimension to the so-called Colgate doctrine.[3] This, they contend, has long since given them the right to withhold at all times their trademarked products from distributors or sales outlets whose practices in relation to the brands in question would tend (in the owners' opinions) to harm the reputation and goodwill of their brands. These brand owners argue for the need, in certain instances, to keep their brands out of the hands of retailers who will not provide the requisite support, and who engage in pricing and distribution practices relative to the affected brands which discourage other retailers from carrying and supporting these brands.

Large companies

While it is primarily certain smaller brand holders who are involved today in attempting to obtain court and legislative reaffirmation of the Colgate doctrine, it is important to see that the issues involved are also of considerable concern to large brand holders. They, too, while they may have greater advertising power to reinforce their brand reputation and meaning, still require proper retailer support, especially when the trademarked product is complex and infrequently bought.

If some retailers who carry a large company's brand engage in arbitrary practices in connection with the brand that hurt the business of rivals who do not engage in such practices, the latter will be discouraged in ways that result in a general deterioration of the brand's effectiveness and reputation. They will reduce inventories and therefore the consumer's choices; they will cut service corners; they will reduce selling services. And, because of these consequences, the brand's reputation and perceived reliability will decline. Even massive advertising will not in such cases restore the brand's original value.

Soviet Experience

The reasons for the accelerating growth of branding in the Soviet Union are particularly relevant to the basic argument of this article.

---

[3] *United States* v. *Colgate,* 250 U.S. 300 (1919).

There is, I believe, more instructive value in a look at Soviet experience with branded products than in all the tangled rhetoric expounded by lawyers, economists, professors, businessmen, and politicians in recent years.

Nikita Khrushchev was always an enormously pragmatic commissar. When he saw Iowa corn growing taller and better than Soviet corn, he did not hesitate to replace the ideologically correct Lysenko approach with the ideologically neutral Roswell Garst approach. Similarly, and significantly, pragmatism has triumphed over historic Communist practices as they apply to the Soviet TV industry. Thus:

> A few years ago several Russian factories manufactured identical 17-inch TV sets. On more than one occasion, even though consumers were clamoring for more sets, many simply were not being bought. Inventories piled up. After a good deal of fruitless and wasteful searching for an explanation, the answer came. Because the public could not identify the factory source of any one 17-inch set, and one factory habitually produced "lemons," soon sales of all 17-inch TV sets fell. This refusal to buy was the public's only way to protect itself. But it threw the Soviet central economic plan badly out of kilter. Even worse, it caused a lot of public discontent with Soviet officials.

Factory marks

It was at this point that Soviet trademarks began to appear. At first, their function was little more than to identify (for the convenience of the authorities) the factory source, but the result was far more than the Russians bargained for. Here is what trademarking did:

(1) It enabled the consumer to choose the output of a plant with a good reputation, and to avoid the plant with a poor one.

(2) Though the sales of the factory with the poor reputation fell, and therefore it failed to meet its economic plan, this caused less economic dislocation than when the entire industry's sales had slumped previously.

(3) It resulted in consumer discontent being shifted from the political (Party) authorities to the trademarked plant with the poor quality.

(4) It created a form of consumer sovereignty—a way of giving the consumer the power to reward quality and punish shoddi-

ness—by enabling him to identify easily the source (trademark) of the output.

In sum, trademarking rewarded quality and efficiency, and punished shoddiness and waste, by making it easy for the quality producer to sell his product because the consumer had developed confidence in his trademark. From experience, the consumer had, in effect, learned that "You can be sure if it's Westinghouski."

Further developments

The Russians have, since this incident, expanded the practice of trademarking, or branding, the output of different plants. Soviet plant managers now guard the integrity and reputation of their trademarks with the vigor of Cossacks bearing down on revolutionaries. They safeguard the purity of their brands as sedulously as they watch their operating expenses. Their bonuses depend heavily on what happens to both of these.

Not surprisingly, consumer advertising has followed in close order. In spite of historic Soviet denunciations of advertising as a diabolical capitalist tool for the exploitation of the masses, there were at last count over 25 state-sponsored Soviet advertising agencies. Advertising courses are now offered in some Russian universities. What's more, both the Soviet press and Soviet literature have even begun making references to a bright, cheerful, and optimistic coterie of young Communist blades who sound extraordinarily like our own stereotype of the "Madison Avenue crowd."

Madison Avenue's own reaction to the rise of Soviet consumer advertising has been to suggest that not even the Russians could ignore forever the fact that America's economic growth and prosperity have been intimately linked with the magnitude and imaginativeness of its advertising activities. In their effort to catch up with us, it is therefore suggested, the Russians have been forced to copy us.

The truth is that the Russians have not adopted American trademarking and advertising practices because of what they have seen us do. The situation is much like that of a jockey on a racehorse coming up fast from way behind. He doesn't head for the inside rail because he believes this is what put the lead horse out in front, and he is imitating the leader. Rather he goes to the inside rail because that is obviously the shortest and most sensible path to the finish.

The fact that the Russians have adopted brand names and advertising simply reflects the fact that they are more responsive to the dictates of economics, technology, and good sense than to the muddled abstractions of obsolete philosophers. Moreover, the Russians have learned that with brand names, instead of economic planners having to establish arbitrary quality standards and hire engineers to enforce them, the sovereign consumer automatically establishes and enforces the high standards.

The moment trademarks were introduced in Russia, the consumer was presented with a choice as between suppliers. Given that sovereign choice, the question was no longer strictly whether a particular plant produced cheaply and abundantly, but how efficiently it utilized its resources relative to what the customer really wanted and valued. The governing standard for evaluating a plant then very properly became, in effect, "What is its return on investment?"

The net result was not only an almost automatic and continuing improvement in Soviet consumer-product quality and design, but also an accelerating tendency to use brand-name advertising as a means of reassuring consumers about the quality and desirability of particular brands and therefore raising their sales and profitabilities.

The Soviet experience clearly demonstrates that the consumer uses the brand as a means of protecting himself and of punishing the producer of trademarked products that do not meet consumer expectations. The invisible hand of Adam Smith, capitalism's patron saint, reached out to promote and protect the public welfare in a way that was no part of the Soviet officials' original intention. Brands became the means. More significantly, these brands were actually *created* by the consumers where none existed. The Russian consumer, in effect, "converted" the factory marks, whose purpose was to serve the commissars, into brands to serve themselves. These became measures of quality and integrity—a basis for recourse in the event of dissatisfaction—and identifiers of sources which had proved reliable and satisfying.

Brand-Name Protection

But in the Soviet Union, as in the United States, unless the image and reputation of brands and trademarks can be protected under the law by their owners, not only will they eventually cease to have any meaning for the consumer, but also they will cease to perform their obvious economic functions of facilitating trade and promoting efficiency.

Therefore, it seems in the public interest to give trademark holders those minimal powers needed to protect their brands and trademarks against adulteration by others.

We live in a world of increasing corporate bigness. The managers of the big corporations do not deny that they have certain advantages over smaller competing firms, and this is particularly so in branded consumer goods. The small and new firm has fewer means available to it with which to build and hold a brand reputation than does its larger counterpart.

What the smaller branded-product and specialty-product companies are today urging is not the old "fair-trade" right to compel retailers to sell at minimum stipulated prices. They want the much more substantive right to refuse to supply distributors or sales outlets whose practices in relation to their trademarked products are likely to be destructive of the kinds of reputations without which these brands cannot effectively compete.

What they seek is not price protection in the old "fair-trade" sense, but protection of brand reputation and consumer goodwill—the right to be selective in respect to retail practices that affect their brand reputations just as the larger companies are selective in respect to advertising practices that have similar effects. What they seek is not protection against the large advertisers, but the right to seek competitive equality by other means. The major objective that is at stake is the smaller companies' search for the right to protect their brand reputations by (1) withholding their trademarked products from distributors and retailers whose practices are viewed by the brand owners as potentially destructive of their reputation and goodwill, and by (2) maintaining the support of the distributors and retailers whose activities help sustain these perceived values.

The retail conditions surrounding the availability and sale of branded products have long been viewed by American companies as affecting the perceived value and goodwill of their brands. Just as people know that a great deal more goes into making their personal reputations than just their personalities and physiques, so companies know that much more goes into making their brand reputation than product quality alone. People understandably take considerable care in selecting the right dress, an appropriate hairdo, a suitable necktie, the neighborhood in which they live, the car they drive, and where they vacation. Appearances make a difference.

Similarly, companies know that, all other things being equal, the retail practices associated with their branded products also make a difference. Such differences can to a substantial extent be overcome by massive advertising in favor of a brand. But without this advertising power, the smaller company must have access to alternative means if competition is to be encouraged.

The small or new trademark owner cannot easily strive or survive in any battle that puts a premium on heavy advertising spending. Yet it is certainly both lawful and sensible for a manufacturer to spend great quantities of money on advertising and packaging in order t ; create a particular impression about his product in the eyes of the consumer. But if his strategies, or his resources, or market conditions —or any combination of these—result in his trying to create in a perfectly harmless fashion a particular product impression or competitive niche via the practice of surrounding his brand with appropriate retail practices, then it is reasonable to suggest that this should be equally lawful.

The mere fact that some people might deny that this is a sensible policy is scarcely any more reason for enjoining anybody from the practice than would be the conclusion that just because certain advertising may seem to be of doubtful utility, the advertiser ought to be denied the freedom to spend his money in such ways. Laws should not protect people from their own folly or delusions when the relative social cost of permitting such freedom is miniscule.

Exactly what the social cost amounts to in any of these cases is hard to tell. But it is not hard to tell that it is of a relatively modest order. Our society has, quite palpably, done well. It can take a good deal of sensible pride in having had a remarkably high tolerance of folly. It is only the compulsive perfectionist, or the intolerant elitist, who will not abide the ambiguity and messiness of a system of freedom. He would willingly sacrifice the freedom of others to his own notions of perfection. Of course, one man's freedom can be another man's confinement.

Equity and Law

What is it that is sacrificed in allowing a trademark owner to protect his business by withholding his brands from retailers whose practices are inconsistent with his policies?

Two things seem apparent:

(1) The retailer is denied the right to sell a brand he might wish to handle.

(2) In order to handle the brand, the retailer needs to fulfill conditions set by someone else. He has to structure at least some parts of his business regarding the branding to the requisites of a supplier who has no direct investment in his business.

Item one is self-evident and uncomplicated; yet the absence of a given brand in a retailer's store can hurt him. This is, of course, generally true only for a highly advertised brand. In such cases a retailer can be at the mercy of a supplier. Much the same is true of Item two. And since many suppliers are much larger than most retailers, the latter can conceivably be put into extremely disagreeable positions.

The question, therefore, is this: Does an attempt to protect the perceived value of a brand or trademark by withholding it from a distributor or retailer, whose action with respect to this brand does not meet the brand-name owner's minimum requirements, not deny these retailers the same rights as the trademark holder proposes for himself?

Reciprocal freedoms

The answer seems to be that in certain important respects there are no rights' infringements at all: it is simply a matter of reciprocal freedoms. The trademark holder should be no more compelled by law to make his brand available to a given retailer than should that retailer be compelled to stock and promote that particular brand.

What is proposed by the smaller companies today is the confirmation of this concept of reciprocal freedom—in their case, the freedom not to deliver their brands into situations that they believe might damage their goodwill and the continued support of cooperating distributors and retailers. Retailers perform a function for both consumers and suppliers. Yet retailers are not only the customers of their suppliers but also, in a vital and practical fashion, their partners. Both depend on, and survive by, the grace of the other. The job each tries to get done depends heavily on the performance of the other.

While mutuality and trust are essential ingredients of their partnership, so obviously is law. Each owes certain obligations to the other. If the *supplier* is to make his branded product available, and therefore expose his goodwill to possible damage, he must be allowed to choose those retailers whose actions do not tend to jeopardize *his* goodwill. In the same way, the *retailer* is not, and should not be, compelled to handle products and brands which he believes might tend to jeopardize *his* goodwill.

To argue that this comparison is uneven, owing to the fact that manufacturers are generally larger and more powerful than retailers, is neither generally true nor entirely relevant. Increasingly, retailing and wholesaling chains, and retailing and wholesaling cooperatives, are gaining size and power far beyond that of their suppliers. Moreover, it is a well-established legal doctrine that the brand belongs to the brand owner, even though the commodity to which it attaches changes ownership.[4] So the protection of the brand's goodwill remains the continuing and necessary concern of its owner.

As has been discussed, the supplier's right to insist on the proper conditions at point of sale as a condition of continuing to deal with a given retailer can be important for survival of the smaller manufacturer under today's competitive conditions. And in the end, even though this may at times result in higher short-term prices for the brand in question, this practice probably stimulates rather than retards competition. This is not because high prices protect inefficient manufacturers, but because such prices provide generous margins for retailers who will therefore give shelf space to lesser brands and thus expand consumer choices. It is then up to the consumer to decide which brand to buy. If he will not buy the higher priced brand, then it clearly will not survive. But the choice will have been made by the consumer—not by the law, the commissar, or the courts.

The courts have clearly held that in the case of a product whose ownership has been transferred to the retailer, the brand still belongs to the supplying brand owner. If the latter elects to use his brand reputation as a means both of attracting customers and obtaining the right kind of support from retailers, then it seems perfectly sensible, all other things being equal, for that brand holder to be able to choose which retailers can buy his branded product in the same way that retailers can choose which branded products to buy.

If the brand owner is compelled to sell to a retailer whose practices tend to adulterate his brand reputation or undermine his marketing

---

[4] *Old Dearborn Distributing Co.* v. *Seagram Distillers Corp.,* 299 U.S. 193, 194, 195 (1936).

relations with other retailers, this would put him in the anomalous position of participating in the destruction not just of his own trademarked product, but perhaps even of his entire business. No American custom or law has ever condoned, endorsed, or enforced commercial suicide, and there is no valid reason to change all that now.

Even in the Soviet Union, where the historic ideological disposition actually loads the dice against practices that would sustain and protect the purity of trademarks and brand names, the use, protection, promotion, and safeguarding of trademarks are becoming vital ingredients of commercial practice. The reason is that it makes economic sense, spurs competition and efficiency, and thus serves the public welfare.

Judicial confusion

There is considerable confusion in the judicial history of trademark cases regarding their meaning, and so also regarding the rights of trademark holders under important circumstances.

Back in 1936, Justice Sutherland, writing for a unanimous court, said:

> Goodwill is property in a very real sense, injury to which, like injury to any other species of property, is a proper subject for legislation. Goodwill is a valuable contributing aid to business— sometimes the most valuable contributing asset of the producer or distributor of commodities. And distinctive trademarks, labels, and brands are legitimate aids to the creation or enlargement of such goodwill. It is well settled that the proprietor of the goodwill is entitled to protection as against one who attempts to deprive him of the benefits resulting from the same.[5]

But in recent years, while the courts have not really disagreed with this view, neither have they found it useful. Thus the Oregon Supreme Court in a landmark decision in 1956 held it as not being relevant to the public welfare issues involved.[6] Having so ruled the court went on to explain part of its reasoning by referring to the following comment in a Michigan Supreme Court decision:

> The function of a trademark is *simply* to designate the goods as the product of a particular manufacturer or trader and to pro-

[5] *Old Dearborn Distributing Co., op. cit.*
[6] *General Electric Co.* v. *Wahle,* Trade Cases Para. 68, 333 (1956).

tect his goodwill against the sale of another's product as his; to prevent confusion of the public regarding the origins of goods of competing vendors.[7] [Emphasis added.]

The Soviet experience has indicated that the function of a trademark is far more than "simply" identifying the source and preventing confusion. In Russia economics told a compelling story. A great host of economic consequences followed from trademarking which showed that the prevention of "confusion of the public regarding the origins of goods of competing vendors" clearly served the public welfare. And it did so not just in one way, but in at least two ways. It served (1) to prevent wasteful consumer expenditures for shoddy products by improving national economic efficiency, and (2) in the long run, to benefit the whole economy. In the process, trademarks have gradually become almost as important to the Russians as they have to us.

Conclusion

The argument which has been reviewed in this article is far different from the traditional and tired fair-trade panegyric. It is in some respects its opposite, dealing with an entirely different dimension of the economic process. So-called fair-trade laws *force* the retailer to sell a given brand at a given price, provided he chooses to sell it at all. The argument of today's smaller trademark holders does not contend that the retailer should be forced to sell at a particular price, or indeed that he should be forced to sell or even to handle any particular product. But it does contend that neither should a brand holder be forced to sell *into* a situation which he believes (rightly or wrongly) would tend to be destructive to his own business. The argument is simply that the brand owner should be permitted, in effect, to be able to withhold his brand from distribution outlets whose practices he believes might compromise, diminish, or adulterate the reputation of his brand.

This is not to suggest that the right of refusal to deal is justifiable on simply *any* grounds, or on grounds contrary to certain antecedent national policies whose importance transcends economics. Refusal of a brand-name owner to deal on the narrow grounds, for example, that a retailer has certain racial, religious, or political policies would be contrary to established national policy on civil rights and would there-

[7] *Shakespeare Co.* v. *Lippman's Tool Shop Sporting Goods Co.,* 334 Mich. 109 (1952).

fore not be permitted. In short, arbitrary "cause" is *not* a justifiable stand for withdrawing or withholding a branded product from a retailer. But the protection of the goodwill of a brand or trademark *is* justifiable, and not only because this is consistent with historic U.S. practice. More importantly, it is because it tends to encourage effective competition and promote public welfare in today's complex industrial economies.

B. Misleading Advertising

8. Advertising's Crisis of Confidence

E. B. Weiss*

I am writing this on May 11, 1967. Why note the date? Because exactly three years ago—*to the day*—Clarence E. Eldridge (for years in charge of advertising at General Foods) delivered a talk before the Assn. of National Advertisers that was extraordinarily prophetic—indeed, so prophetic that his conclusions are remarkably relevant at this very moment.

Mr. Eldridge's talk was significantly entitled: "The Decline in the Influence of Advertising." It is one of the most disturbingly accurate portrayals of advertising's crisis of confidence ever painted (remember that the word "consumerism" had probably not even been coined three years ago—a striking commentary on the shocking speed with which Mr. Eldridge's gloomy forecasts came to be fact. Remember also that Mr. Eldridge invested hundreds of millions in advertising for General Foods—this is not an academician talking).

I wish space permitted reproducing it in its entirety. Since that is not feasible, here is the gist of Mr. Eldridge's frank analysis:

* E. B. Weiss is a regular columnist for *Advertising Age*.

Reprinted with permission from *Advertising Age* (June 26, 1967). © 1967 by Crain Communications, Inc.

It may seem paradoxical to imply that the influence of advertising is declining at a time when expenditures for advertising have reached an all-time high. Yet this very fact may reflect this declining influence. . . . It takes more dollars to accomplish a given result. . . . Erosion of the dollar . . . undoubtedly accounts, in substantial part, for the need for more dollars; but I think there are other reasons too.

. . . One of the chief purposes of advertising was to create, or strengthen, or to maintain brand loyalty. . . .

The result was a strong bond between consumers, and product. . . . The bond consisted not only of a brand-*preference,* but of a brand-*insistence*—which was relatively impervious to the siren-song of competitors, with their bargain prices and other inducements. . . .

There is alarming evidence that this situation does not exist today to the extent that it did. . . . With notable exceptions, consumer franchises are not as strong as they once were. . . .

Why Is Brand Switching So Prevalent?

If this were not so, why is brand-switching so prevalent these days? Why do manufacturers seem to have to rely so much more than formerly on "promotions"—consumer-lures of one kind or another: Off-label price deals, coupons, 2¢ sales, premiums and what-not? Why would so many consumers wait for "specials," and buy the brand that is being "specialed"—even though it is not their usual brand?

. . . What has brought this change about? . . . Here are some of the reasons:

1. With respect to a great many—not all—categories of products, there are no *substantial* differences between competitive products. . . . At best, the superiority of a product over competition is likely to be minuscule . . . hardly recognizable by the lay consumer. . . . That difference is less important to her than the pennies she can save by buying the product that is "on special."

2. The *believability* of advertising is being seriously jeopardized by the attempt to create "psychological differences," psychological superiorities, in products where no such differences or superiorities exist in fact.

This device may fool some of the people some of the time; but it certainly is not going to fool all the people all of the time. The educational level of consumers is rising. So is their sophistication. And, as that trend continues, they are becoming increasingly more discriminating, increasingly more difficult to bemuse with slogans, platitudes and irrelevancies—to say nothing of product claims which their own experience does not bear out.

It is not mere coincidence that it is the better educated, more sophisticated who are most skeptical of advertising claims, more prone to brand-switching, more susceptible to the price lure of private brands and the sales prices of advertised brands. . . .

I happen to believe that that point of diminishing returns has been reached—and passed. . . .

Note, for example, that consumers (in a 1964 AAAA study) "consciously react" . . . to a very small percentage (15%) of the ads they see. . . . This . . . means that 85% of your ads go through or over the heads of your audience without even hesitating —much less selling. . . .

But listen to this, if you will: Even of that 15% of the ads that evoke any conscious reaction, one-third are deemed especially annoying or offensive.

Is advertising creating ill will?

Again: It seems to have been interpreted (in this AAAA study) as cause for self congratulation that, of 78 classifications of advertising studied, only six—*only six*—produced more negative than positive reactions from consumers. The six were beer, liquor, dental supplies, soaps, underwear and cigarets.

Note that this does not say that only six categories produce negative reactions; but that, in the case of these six, they produced *more* negative than positive. Does this mean that with respect to these product categories their advertising is creating more *ill will* than *good will;* that it is doing the advertisers more harm than good? I wouldn't know.

Nor do I know what it signifies so far as the other 72 product categories are concerned. It may mean that their advertising produces *no* negative reactions; or it may mean merely that 51% of the reactions are positive, and only 49%—only 49%—are negative.

But whatever the fact may be, this kind of research finding, confirming as it does the opinion of many people seriously concerned with the image of advertising and the future of advertising, is not cause for complacency or self-congratulation—but, on the contrary, should be the cause for real concern and real soul-searching. . . .

Then there is the matter of believability. When every detergent gets clothes whiter, brighter, cleaner, sweeter-smelling than any other; when every brand of beer "brings a smile every time" (particularly if you're having more than one); when every toothpaste is better than every other in preventing tooth decay; when every gasoline makes your car run better than any other—what is the poor consumer to believe?

The claims can't all be true; so, in confusion, the consumer is likely to wind up believing none of them. "A plague on all your houses," she says, in effect. . . .

Without wishing to minimize the seriousness of the active negative reaction to so many ads, I think advertising has an even more destructive weapon: Apathy, boredom, indifference. . . .

Another thing: If 85% of the advertising messages are being ignored . . . and if another 5% are evoking negative reactions of some degree as being silly, irrelevant or unbelievable, there is grave danger that the image of *all* advertising will suffer; the believability and effectiveness of all advertising will be reduced, the innocent will suffer along with the guilty. . . .

If advertising wants to be believed and respected, it should treat the public as intelligent adults who will respond to a reasonable and believable presentation of the product's case. . . .

ADVERTISING HASN'T IMPROVED.   Has there been any improvement, on balance, in advertising during the intervening three years since Mr. Eldridge exposed advertising's clay feet? Surely that question is self-answering!

But those excerpts lead to another and totally different question, to wit: Isn't there a direct relationship between the economic doubts about advertising raised by Mr. Eldridge's statistics and the doubts raised by such critics of the economics of advertising as Donald F. Turner, assistant Attorney General?

Is any other function of business 85% wasteful? And can it be said of any other business function that, of the remaining 15%, no less than one-third is "especially annoying or offensive?"

And isn't it true that advertising that is "especially annoying or offensive" isn't merely wasteful of its own cost—but that *it must also depreciate results from other investments made by the advertiser* in areas other than advertising?

Yet *Advertising Age* for May 2, 1967 in an editorial correctly captioned with the questioning title, "Four A's More Sophisticated?", became much more—and I insist *unduly*—optimistic in the text that followed. Reported *Advertising Age:*

". . . what struck us was a new attitude of sophistication with regard to advertising's approach to government, and all the problems of advertising and business relationships with Washington.

"Instead of the ringing denunciations of federal bureaucracy and damning of the administration, which have served too long as a substitute for statesmanlike dialog at too many meetings, there was recognition of the fact that Washington simply will not go away; that advertising and business have a great stake in what is going on there, but that a greater degree of mutual understanding and confidence is essential; and that no one will get anywhere by simply denouncing every move made by any legislator or government official."

The Four A's Is Not "More Sophisticated"

I still remember the way Charles L. Gould, publisher of the *San Francisco Examiner,* "brought down the house" at the annual Advertising-Government Relations Conference with a ringing defense of "free enterprise" and a bitter attack on "bureaucracy."

I still remember how Herb Mayes "brought down the house" at the Harvard Business School Seminar on "Advertising—Bane or Benefit" with his Don Quixote attack on Esther Peterson.

My reports on that Four A's meeting indicate that the several speakers who suggested a more sophisticated response to our new social climate did not quite "bring down the house." And I venture to suggest that if Charles L. Gould of the *San Francisco Examiner* had repeated his talk before the Four A's, he would have scored another triumph!

No—I do not agree that the Four A's is more sophisticated (to answer the question in the title of the *Advertising Age* editorial). Neither do I believe that the AAAA has become more sophisticated— judging by a careful study of its recently published analysis of advertising by Jules Backman.

And, when I take note of the Magazine Publishers Assn.'s "Freedom of Choice" campaign, I am reminded of the American Medical Assn.'s "Freedom of Choice" campaign—as well as of the end result of that stalwart attack on our decline into "socialism."

If these represent the sum total of advertising's response to the deeply troublesome situation exposed by Mr. Eldridge, who invested hundreds of millions in advertising for General Foods (and, to date, that *is* precisely the sum total), then there is cause for concern about the future of advertising.

It may be argued, of course, that programs of advertising associations are simply reflecting the attitudes of their members. That is completely—*and unfortunately*—true.

Associations Must Lead Members

But it is now imperative that these associations *lead*—not follow—their members; that they lead their members into a statesmanlike response to the still mounting disenchantment with certain aspects of advertising of the most critical and influential segments of the public.

How much more encouraging it is to note that in Canada—where exactly the same trends are clearly evident, including deep studies by Parliament—the Institute of Canadian Advertising, representing 50 of the major advertising agencies in Canada, at the invitation of the special joint Senate-House of Commons committee on consumer credit (prices) presented quite a moderate brief on advertising, its contribution to economic growth and social welfare, and its effects on consumer satisfaction and prices.

In its conclusion, the brief recommended that *encouragement* be given to the consumer education movement, *offered its assistance* in this regard and said: "Our institute believes that consumer education can enhance materially the welfare of the people of this country. (Hear! Hear!) Consumer education will help homemakers formulate their buying decisions. This in turn would assist the business community, since a well-informed buying public facilitates communications and marketing . . . *In our view, consumer education is such a vital matter that it deserves encouragement from all sectors of the community including business, labor, the professions and government."*

Indicating that such education would deal with "the process of communicating information on family and personal budgeting, household economics *and general product information,"* the brief further recommended that (again, Hear! Hear!) consideration be given to establishing an advisory council on consumer affairs to study issues affecting consumer welfare and to advise government and the public on policy solutions!

The "Had Any Lately?" Age

How much reason is there to conclude that advertising is intelligently resolving its crisis of confidence when an experienced adman was recently moved to comment:

> Is the increasing use of the wink and the leer in advertising accepted by the public as a sign of the new sophistication or a

transparent outpouring of adolescent silliness? . . . The diction-
ary defines double entendre as "ambiguity of meaning," and it's
probably safe to say that quite a bit of ambiguous advertising is
making the rounds.

Another advertising man described advertising of 1967 as the
"had-any-lately?" age!

But these are lone voices—as is mine! Much more common is a
comment like this:

> Some people complain that advertising is repetitious. Others
> think it is often in bad taste. But the people spend thousands of
> hours reading and listening to advertising and buying billions of
> dollars of advertised products. They obviously don't disapprove
> of it.

Obviously, expanding public segments *do* disapprove—is any
more proof needed than that 85% figure quoted by Mr. Eldridge who
"don't note," "don't see," and the per cent he quoted who clearly
disapprove?

Certainly, Mr. Eldridge documented the conclusion—three years
ago—that there is an impermissibly high rate of economic waste in
advertising. And certainly a number of advertising's own practitioners
agree that too much advertising is indeed "socially immoral."

When a scientific study concludes, according to the *New York
Times,* that "one filtered cigaret—king-size Pall Mall—yielded *more*
tar and nicotine than the unfiltered king-size cigaret of the same brand"
—and when "in tests of Chesterfield, Lucky Strike and Camels, the
scientists found that the smoker gets as much or more tar and nicotine
from the filter cigarets as from the unfiltered, regular cigaret of the
same brand"—isn't this a bit "socially immoral"?

How much damage was done to the cause of advertising by the
expenditure of several hundred million dollars for advertising of filter
tip cigarets when scientific study proved that two of nine brands tested
let through more tars and nicotine than did unfiltered cigarets of the
same brand and that none was really protecting smokers?

The Credibility Gap Must Be Closed

Advertising has been under attack for years. But for years when advertising was criticized it was generally in terms of its "truthfulness."
Now, however, the attacks have broadened. Now critics are more often

raising fundamental questions about advertising's influence over the
structure of our economy, its social responsibilities, its ethics, its
morality, its esthetics.

How can advertising try on a halo for size when a slacks ad shows
the boss' wife with her foot on a young man's ankle (under the slacks)
while her husband dozes at the table; a swinger takes off his shirt for
a "final permanent press test" while, superimposed on the ad, an apparently naked girl waits expectantly; a man is urged to "come on
strong . . . go all the way" with a name brand sports coat while a
reclining girl with bared knee holds out her hand?

It is entirely probable that in the decade of the '70s, advertising
will come under more—and more intelligent—criticism than ever
before in its history. This means that advertising must close its credibility gap—and not through propaganda, but through more responsible leadership. *Without credibility there cannot be confidence.*

Ever since advertising assumed dimensions large enough to intrigue the public as a socio-economic force, it has been the butt of a
vast degree of reckless adverse comment. But now advertising will be
held up to public examination in a more discerningly critical way by
more intelligent observers presenting their observations to a more
sophisticated public. Half-truth rebuttal may have been an adequate
response when advertising was being attacked unintelligently. But it is
not wise to counter *intelligent* criticism *unintelligently!*

Advertisers will be hard pressed to match shopper sophistication
with equally sophisticated advertising programs—even if they are fully
aware of this remarkable change in our society. Where this awareness
does not exist, advertising sophistication will fall farther and farther
behind shopper sophistication—and that has been, is currently, and
will in future be damaging to advertising's status in our new society.

Even in our present-day remarkable era of high income for masses
of people, by far the lion's share of discretionary dollars are in the
hands of the smaller number of our families. These families are the
very ones whose members are rapidly becoming increasingly knowledgeable shoppers. The planning of too many advertising men shows
an unawareness of this fundamental fact.

There is frequent comment about the decline in brand loyalty.
There is little reason to question that brand loyalty is, at this very
moment, at an all-time low. Is this due to shopper ignorance—or to
shopper sophistication?

Clearly, the sophisticated shopper recognizes that there is too little difference between competing brands in too many merchandise classifications. So—since she is smart enough to comprehend this, she moves quite freely from one brand to another. Ignorant shoppers buy "chop" marks. Informed shoppers buy value.

It would be idiotic to take the position that all shoppers—or even a simple majority of all shoppers—are now highly cultured, highly knowledgeable, wise in shopper expertise. The three fundamental points I am making here are: 1. A substantial percentage of shoppers are much more intelligent shoppers than many in the world of advertising acknowledge; 2. It is these very shoppers who control the major part of this nation's total discretionary dollar; 3. These shoppers represent the articulate influentials.

Surely, if more manufacturers were keenly cognizant of the firm control on the discretionary dollar by sophisticated shoppers, we would not have so many advertising programs keyed to low intelligence levels.

Can the same old claims (including the balding "freedom of choice" theme) that advertising's defenders have been using for at least 30 years—with an obvious lack of success—mount an effective counterattack?

Can any counteroffensive, launched with the premise that any criticism of advertising is unjustified, possibly succeed?

Need for Public Meeting

Might it not be highly beneficial to advertising were the industry to arrange, at some time, a public forum at which the Turner, Schlesinger, Galbraith coterie, and a group of our more sophisticated advertising specialists (as differentiated from the fanatical, as well as the ultraconservative wing of advertising) could discuss their respective views?

Isn't it possible that these two coteries would find themselves separated by a much narrower gap than is commonly imagined by those in advertising who get nightmares when Turner *et al.* are merely mentioned?

Isn't it possible that these presumed opponents of advertising are really earnest critics who *correctly* deplore certain misuses of advertising such as exploitation of phony obsolescence, of unwarranted "status" prices for some presold brands, of the poor image some ads present to a world that is studying our image minutely?

If it has not been quite true in the past, it will be completely true in the future, that good taste is an essential ingredient in any formula for good business. Advertising never had the right to bore or irritate people. It will not be able to afford cynicism in the future—or flagrant disregard of public intelligence.

Advertising will be compelled to turn away from the ugly, the strident, the illiterate. This form of advertising will lose its sole presumed virtue—an ability to move merchandise in profitable volume.

Eliminate Advertising That Offends

Is advertising coming into the court of public opinion with even reasonably clean hands? And, if it is not, then will fanatical defense of the status quo fend off a political response to a mounting clamor from a sophisticated public? Advertising that deliberately seeks the lowest common denominator will, in the years ahead, be aiming too low and will invite still more government regulation.

Advertisers who employ "vulgarity, sex, deception and stupidity" can expect their products to "founder in a changing tide of public opinion." Who was the rabble-rouser who said that? None other than Ellen-Ann Dunham, vice-president of the General Foods Kitchens. Yet, vulgarity in advertising unquestionably achieved a peak in 1966 and shows no decline in 1967.

Instead of fanatical defense, instead of a self bestowed halo, advertising urgently needs self imposed higher standards of practice, greater self discipline and greater sensitivity concerning the outer boundaries of public tolerance. The advertising fraternity must accept responsibility for eliminating advertising that offends public taste, irritates sensibilities, intentionally misleads or denigrates a competitor.

There is one place, and only one place, to put the final responsibility for honest, tasteful advertising. That is with management—in industry, in media, in the advertising agency. If these three do not accept that responsibility—fully—government will make it legally compulsory.

9. Federal Regulation of Advertising

Gaylord A. Jentz

One of the most important and fundamental functions vital to the American economy is the mass distribution of goods. The complexities which surround this function have continued to increase as the sale and distribution have become more impersonal and competitive. Within this framework there has developed by all forms of mass communication media an unparalleled dissemination of a variety of information with which the manufacturer, processor, and seller in competition with each other have attempted to influence and affect the consumer's choice of products.

The producer with his technological know-how and engineering skill has found that the ability to produce a product in mass quantities is not his major problem. It is the consumer who decides by his selection what goods will be produced and in what quantities. Therefore the producer's life may well depend upon his getting the consumer acquainted with his product and how effective his persuasion is on the consumer to buy it.

Because of the pressure of competition, the vast means of media available to reach the consumer, and the gullible character of the consumer, truth in advertising, labeling, and packaging became a problem. The mere fact that the expression of words themselves blend so well to half-truths, implications, and double meaning invariably lead to

Reprinted with permission from *American Business Law Journal,* Vol. 6 (January, 1968), pp. 409–427, published by American Business Law Association.

various forms of deception which have as its prey the consumer. The majority of producers, and groups, whose specific trade is advertising (international groups as well), have embraced the concept of truth in advertising. The temptation, however, of a few to gain an advantage and the seemingly endless borderline cases in which one may or may not be engaged in deception have made self-regulation salutary, but obviously not effective in affording maximum protection to the consumer. The need for governmental regulation, particularly on the Federal level, became obvious. It is within the purview of this article to explore only a small segment of the deceptive practices in advertising under Federal regulation, with the full knowledge that on the State and Federal levels advertising is one of the most highly regulated activities in our nation.

History of Federal Regulation of Advertising

The first Federal legislation proposed could hardly be called legislation designed to handle the problem of false advertising. The initial proponents of early legislation were looking for the development of a Federal agency to bolster up the Sherman Act and help procure effective enforcement of these antitrust laws. In 1914, under the rigorous support of President Wilson, the Federal Trade Commission Act was passed.

The section of this Act which was of major importance was Section 54 which had the following prohibition: "Unfair methods of competition in commerce are hereby declared unlawful."

There is little doubt that the Commissioners themselves felt uneasy about the possible interpretation of their powers. By 1916, however, the Commissioners decided to extend their interpretation of the Act to false advertising and issued their first complaints against false advertising of selling mercerized cotton as "Sewing Silk," cotton goods as "Sun Fast Silks," and cotton thread as "Circle Cilk" and "Embroidery Floss." The first Supreme Court case upholding a cease and desist order against deceptive practices resulting in competitive injury came in 1922. This case involved the manufacturer selling underwear and other knit goods made partly of wool but largely of cotton, labeled as "natural merino," "natural worsted," or "natural wool." The Federal Trade Commission's cease and desist order was upheld. The labeling was held to be misleading to the public and an unfair method of competition as against manufacturers of like garments made of wool and cotton who branded their products truthfully.

In 1931, the Federal Trade Commission was faced with the issue of whether its jurisdiction extended to deceptive advertising which simply deceived the public but which had no adverse effect on *competition*. The case involved a manufacturer of an "obesity cure," through whose publications in newspapers, labels, and other printed matter indicated through scientific research a method of removing excess flesh of the human body in a safe and effective manner without danger to the health of the user. The Commission issued a cease and desist order and the decision was appealed. The Supreme Court held that jurisdiction of the Commission was dependent on three distinct prerequisites:

(1) Methods complained of are unfair.

(2) They are methods of competition in commerce.

(3) A proceeding by the Commission to prevent the use of the method appears to be in the interest of the public.

The Court, in ruling against the Commission's decision, could not find any present or potential competition to have been injured or threatened by the unfair methods complained of.

To some this was felt as a set-back for the Commission but as Weston writing in 24 Fed. B.J. 548, 550–551 (1964) stated, "But in retrospect this decision proves to be a blessing in disguise because it did not seriously handicap the FTC and it helped to furnish the stimulus for a major expansion of the Commission's jurisdiction in the Wheeler-Lea Amendment of 1938."

The Wheeler-Lea Amendment changed Section 5 of the Federal Trade Commission Act to read "Unfair methods of competition in commerce and unfair or deceptive acts or practices in commerce are hereby declared unlawful." The additional words alone gave the Commission authority to protect consumers against deceptive advertising without having to go through the disguise of protecting competitors. This interpretation was clearly brought out in a 1941 case. The case involved the deceptive use of the trade-name "Remington" for radio receiving sets. The Court held in referring to the Wheeler-Lea Amendment:

The failure to mention competition in the later phrase shows a legislative intent to remove the procedural requirement set up in the Raladam case and the Commission can now center its attention on the direct protection of the consumer where formerly it could protect him only indirectly through the protection of the competitor.

The Wheeler-Lea Amendment did more however. It brought false advertisements of food, drugs, medical and veterinary devices, or cosmetics within the meaning of Section 5 of the Federal Trade Commission Act, and generally enlarged the effectiveness of the Commission's decisions. For example, once a Commission order under Section 5 became final, a continued violation would allow a suit in a Federal district court with a civil penalty not to exceed more than $5,000 for each violation. Additional remedies were provided for dissemination of false advertisements of food, drugs, medical and veterinary devices, and cosmetics, such as the use of a temporary injunction pending final determination by the Commission. Criminal proceedings could be brought as a misdemeanor where the product was injurious to the health of the consumer or where there was an intent to defraud or mislead. Through the FTC's own policy statements, the use of these latter remedies have been seldom used but still appear effective deterrents.

In 1939, the Commission's powers were again enlarged with the passage of the Wool Products Labeling Act. Although the FTC already had the power and authority to control false advertising of wool products sold in interstate commerce, the Act extended this authority to include "informative labeling." The percentage of wool and other fibers, disclosure of use of reprocessed or reused wool, and registration number of the manufacturer, among others, were required to appear on the label. The label was required to be on the product until sold to the consumer. The Act was modeled in part after the Food, Drug, and Cosmetic Act and appears to have been effectively used by the Commission.

In 1950, Congress once again enlarged the powers of the FTC. In amending the Federal Trade Commission Act, it was provided that advertisements of oleomargarine or margarine shall be deemed misleading if such advertisement represents that such in any form of fashion is a dairy product. The Amendment also gave the Commission greater penalty power by providing that any violation of a final cease and desist order, *each day* would be considered a separate violation and the offender could be charged not more than $5,000 for each violation. As the Commission continued to gain more enforcement power, the courts also have placed on them more responsibility in the clearness of their order to avoid undue harshness in application of such penalties.

Since 1950, Congress has enacted numerous pieces of legislation designed to regulate false advertising, deceptive labeling, misbranding and deceptive packaging. In 1951, after obvious Commision success with the Wool Products Act, Congress enacted the Fur Products Labeling Act. The Act, as would be expected, closely followed the Wool Products Act as prohibiting false advertising plus requiring informative labeling such as the name of the animal that produced the fur as set forth in the Fur Products Name Guide. This Act provided the Commission with authority to provide guidelines to the fur industry, and set forth the first of a number of Acts calling for "informative advertising." Such advertising is deemed deceptive unless the advertising *includes* required information provided under the Act.

Closely following the passage of this legislation came the Flammable Fabrics Act of 1953, after considerable concern by Congress of serious injuries and death caused by igniting of highly inflammable wearing apparel. The Commission was given authority to establish standards of flammability of fabrics of wearing apparel and to prohibit the manufacture or sale of such that did not meet these standards. Although the standards have been amended, the use and enforcement by the Commission have been a substantial gain for the safety of the consumer.

In 1958, Congress again enacted legislation covering a specialized product area called the Textile Fiber Products Identification Act. This Act is one of the most comprehensive product acts ever written and covers prohibition against false advertising, as well as "informative labeling" *and* "informative advertising."

Congress continues to be active in its efforts to regulate the advertising and labeling of products. Two of their most recent efforts are found in the Cigarette Labeling and Advertising Act of 1965 and the Fair Packaging and Labeling Act of 1966. The labeling requirement of cigarettes has received a great deal of publicity and the requirement on each package, "Caution: Cigarette Smoking May Be Hazardous to Your Health," has been the subject of wide discussion. What is interesting is that no statement relating to smoking and health (informative advertising) is required in the advertising of any cigarettes whose packages contain the above label. The FTC is responsible for the regulation of this Act but this in no way effects their original authority under the Federal Trade Commission Act as amended over false or deceptive cigarette advertsing.

The Fair Packaging and Labeling Act, is not designed as an advertising regulation, but indirectly is effective as such. Labeling and packaging are as much a part of advertising as the direct persuasive use of television, radio, magazines, newspapers, and other forms of mass media. The purpose of this Act is "informative labeling and packaging," referred to as "Truth in Packaging." The Act sets up standards of informing the buying public as to the identity of the commodity, who manufactured or processed such, and sets standards of measurement of net quantities within the package. Any violation comes within Section 55 of the Federal Trade Commission Act as amended.

Perhaps one of the most important functions of the Federal Trade Commission in the controlling of unfair competition in advertising has been its authority to establish industry and general guidelines and regulations within which advertisements must fall. Examples of the above are "Guides Against Deceptive Pricing" and "Tire Advertising and Labeling Guides." Another function of the Commission gaining in popularity is the use of business advisory opinions which has proven effective in combating deceptive advertising practices before they reach the consumer.

The history of Federal regulation in advertising is still far from complete and there awaits in the wings more legislation and controls over the use of words as a means of unfair competition and deception to the consumer.

Patterns of Deception

What is deceptive and what is not deceptive, false, or misleading advertising is not easy to define or determine. The very general broad language of the statutes themselves gives flexibility to the Commission to establish guidelines and standards in their determination of what advertising is permissible and that which is not.

The basic rules which have been developed over the years by the Commission which govern all advertising are as follows:

(1) Proof of actual deception is not an essential prerequisite for the Commission to act, only the tendency to mislead or deceive.

(2) Knowledge of falsity and intent by an advertiser is immaterial as the businessmen acts at his own peril.

(3) Deception standards are based upon what would be deceiving to the public, which includes the ignorant, the unthinking and credulous. Whether one or more may not be mislead is not the issue as the Act is designed to protect the consumer and he comes with all sorts of degrees of understanding and intelligence. A phrase used by Judge Augustus Hand in the *General Motors* case and repeated by Judge Pope in the *Stauffer* case sums up this test as:

> If the Commission . . . thinks it best to insist upon a form of advertising clear enough so that, in the words of the prophet Isaiah, "wayfaring men, though fools, shall not err therein," it is not for the courts to revise its judgment.

(4) Even the truth may be misleading. Sometimes each segment of the advertisement taken separately may be true, but when the whole is viewed, the advertisement may be misleading. This can also be true when certain factors are omitted as well as the method within which the parts are put together.

(5) It is possible for the same advertisements to convey two meanings. Where such is the case if one such meaning would be false, misleading, or deceptive, to the public the advertisement is prohibited.

It is easy to see that these tests overlap each other and even with guidelines the Commission would have difficulty in applying these to all factual situations. The ingenuity of the advertising business in an atmosphere of strong competition is enough to test how close one can come to the edge of deception without dropping into the crevice.

Deception takes many forms. Among these are deceptive pricing, deception by nondisclosure, deceptive use of product or brand name simulation, deceptive disparagement of a competitor's products, deceptive testimonials or sponsorships, deceptive use of the word guarantee, deceptive representations of composition—character—or source of the product, and deceptive T.V. mock-ups. For each form numerous cases and rulings can be cited in determining when such an advertisement is deceptive. Time and space only permit a cursory glance at the latter two.

Areas of Deception

Numerous cases have been investigated and violations found where
there were representations of a product containing certain ingredients,
having a certain quality or composition, or coming from a certain
origin. Many of these representations were completely false; many
however deceive by inference.

Composition deception

Deception through false advertising or labeling of the composition of
a product has been strictly interpreted by the FTC. The problem becomes most difficult when it is the "brand name" of the product which
proves to be the deception in relation to the actual composition of the
product. The Commission's attitude is that full disclosure *possibly may*
remove the deception and thus the producer may preserve the use of
the brand name. The courts have attempted to uphold the findings of
the Commission as conclusive if supported at all by the evidence, but
also hold that complete excision of a trade name should never be
ordered if a less drastic means will accomplish the same result. Thus
the conflict becomes apparent.

An excellent illustration of this plight is found in the *Elliot Knitwear Case*. This case involved a label on sweaters containing the trade
name "Cashmora." On this label in large script-like letters was also a
designation of fiber content—"30% Angora—70% Lambs Wool."
The sweaters contained no cashmere and the FTC held that the name
"Cashmora" was thus deceptive *per se* and issued a cease and desist
order from using the trade name above.

The FTC relied heavily on a number of prior decisions, particularly those in which the courts have held qualifying words are really
contradictions and only tend to confuse the public. For example a
product was labeled "California White Pine," when in fact the product
was yellow pine. The Supreme Court upheld the FTC complete excision of the word "White" because a qualifying phrase such as "not
made of white pine" would be completely contradictory. Another
example involved goods sold by the Army & Navy Trading Company
when in fact few of the items sold in the store were army and navy
goods. The court held that the qualifying phrase "we do not deal in
army and navy goods" would have been contradictory and confused
the public.

The petitioners countered that the Commission had also held that qualifications would cure deception. Two cases were cited as being directly in point. The first is a Commission case involving the use of the trade name "Kashmoor" which contained no cashmere in it. The Commission itself stated:

> If the trade name were "Cashmere" itself, the absolute excision would appear to be inescapable. A complete contradiction of terms such as "Cashmere contains no cashmere" would not clarify the meaning, but would only tend to confuse. However, this is not true of the phrase "Kashmoor—contains no cashmere." While the trade name Kashmoor is a simulation of cashmere and while its use falsely implies a cashmere content in the garments so labeled, it is subject to clarification. An explanation that the garment so labeled is designed to imitate cashmere in appearance and softness, but does not contain any cashmere fibers, is not a flat contradiction of terms, but is a reasonable explanation which would recover the capacity and tendency toward deception inherent in the trade name Kashmoor used alone.

The second case relied on involved a fabric coat labeled "Alpacuna" which contained 50% alpaca, 20% mohair, and 30% wool *but* not vicuna. The Commission ordered the label completely excised. The Supreme Court reversed the Commission, upon learning that the petitioner's labels now read "Alpacuna Coat—contains no vicuna" and specified the fiber of the cloth, stating that nothing should prohibit the use of the trade name if in immediate conjunction there appears clearly a designation of the material of the fibers contained therein.

In reviewing these arguments the court relied heavily upon these last two decisions in holding that excision of the trade name was inappropriate as there was no basis for applying the contradiction doctrine to Cashmora. The court did leave open for the Commission the possible remedy of requiring the petitioner (if he wished to keep this trade name) of adding the phrase to the label—"contains no cashmere." Allowance for qualification to avoid deception is not new.

Character deception

Character deception, for our purposes, is misrepresentation or deceptive suggestions of what a product will do when such claims are in fact untrue. The closeness of the question of deception of composition and the variety of claims made, make this area a very broad one with numerous cases and decisions rendered. Since most of these cases follow a similar pattern, only a few are needed for illustrative purposes.

Two cases decided within two years of each other deal with claims of low calorie bread. One involved a bread called "Lite Diet" in which a typical advertisement would read "Who'd believe it could help you control your weight? So try it . . . Lite Diet . . . Lite Diet. . . ." The other case involved national advertisements of a bread called "Hollywood" bread. These advertisements often contained a picture of a beautiful motion picture star, in some instances in a "slender full length pose." The advertisements contained a picture of a loaf of bread bearing the label "Hollywood" and accompanied by such words as "reducing diets," "figure-wise mothers," "dieting," "panther slim," "tigress trim," "stay slender" and others. Practically all advertisements contained a legend stating there are "only about 46 calories in an 18 gram slice" of Hollywood bread. The Commission held that in both cases the inference was definitely that the eating of this bread would reduce weight because of lower calorie content. The truth showed that as compared to other bread, there was no basic difference in calorie content for the entire loaf, but the "Hollywood" and "Lite Diet" breads were cut into thinner slices. Thus, although it was true per slice there was a lower calorie content, the facts taken as a whole would be misleading as to the reduction of weight.

Another case involved the use of the trade-name "Goldtone Studios, Inc." and the advertising of "oil colored portraits" etc. It was discovered that the petitioner was in fact referring to "tinted" photographs as the "oil colored portraits" and was not engaged in using a goldtone process in its photographic reproduction process. The Court upheld the Commission's cease and desist order including the use of the tradename as having a tendency to deceive the public.

A more recent case dealt with a swimming aid device called "Swim-Ezy." The advertisements indicated that through its use the swimmer could become an expert or champion swimmer, and it would prevent the user from sinking. The facts showed some users did sink and when used the user would not look like a champion. The Court upheld the Commission's order.

Lastly, there are the cases that deceive the public into believing a product will measure up to a certain performance for a certain period of time, when in fact the performance will not last that long. A typical case involved "Continental Six Month Floor Wax," which by name and advertisement indicated that the wax would be an effective home floor covering for a period of six months. The evidence showed that the wax protection would not last that long and the Court upheld the Commission's order.

Deception as to source or origin

Another variety of similar deception deals with misleading the consumer as to where the product was manufactured or produced. There is always a certain intrigue and a definite selling point when the consumer believes a product is foreign made or has come from a location well known for its particular product. Again most cases of this nature follow a similar pattern.

To illustrate, one of the most frequently cited cases deals with boxes of cigars labeled as "Havana Counts." The Commission ruled that the use of the word "Havana" with tobacco products had acquired a special and significant meaning in that at least in part the cigar contained tobacco grown in Cuba. These cigars were made in the United States entirely of domestic grown tobacco. The Court upheld the Commission's ruling. A very similar case is found in which the Commission, upheld by the Court, prohibited the use of words "Grand Rapids" of a furniture manufacturing company, when in fact the furniture was not manufactured in Grand Rapids, Michigan.

Sometimes the Commission requires the source of origin to be stated to avoid deception. In a classic case, the FTC was concerned with labeling and advertising of wood from the Philippine Islands as "mahogany" when in fact such wood was not in the mahogany family. The Commission ruling that using the term "Philippine mahogany" was not deceptive was upheld by the Court.

Occasionally a source of origin acquires a secondary meaning which may be more important than the place of origin itself. A recent case deals with the manufacture and sale of hats under labels and advertisements as "Genuine Milan," "Genuine Imported Milan," and "Genuine Milan, Imported Handblocked." The problem arose in that the hats were not made from "wheat straw" from Italy but were made from Philippine hemp. In the testimony that followed, the word Milan was found to have perhaps two secondary meanings, i.e., hats made out of "wheat straw" (which was far more important as to where such wheat straw was grown), and perhaps connotates even a distinctive weave or braid, which would be more important than either where the product was grown or what it was made out of. Based on these possible interpretations, which could render the use of the name Milan as being non-deceptive, the Court returned the case to the Commission for further findings.

The troublesome problem of secondary meaning is not new to the Commission or the Courts. In 1929 the Court upheld a Commission's cease and desist order of prohibiting the Lighthouse Rug Company from using the word "lighthouse" and depicting a facsimile of the symbol of the Chicago Lighthouse for the Blind. The Court held that the word "lighthouse" had acquired a secondary meaning in a substantial part of the trade, i.e. the rugs were made by the blind in charitable or quasi charitable institutions called lighthouses.

Deceptive television demonstrations

In the 1950's, the T.V. industry blossomed into one of the leading entertainment industries in our nation. With it came new dimensions in the use of movement, voice, and eventually color which all were not found in any other media of advertising. The continued popularity of T.V. and the dimensions available in reaching a mass audience were naturals for the advertising industry. The ingenuity and imagination available in T.V. advertising soon brought a series of cases and F.T.C. decisions involving the use of deceptive T.V. advertising demonstrations.

The use of props and mock-ups as a means of T.V. demonstrations became a commonplace technique and often a necessity to simulate a real object. This has led to some inherent problems as pointed out in the *Carter Products, Inc.* case of 1963 by Circuit Judge Wisdom.

Everyone knows that on T.V. all that glistens is not gold. On a black and white screen, white looks grey and blue looks white: the lily must be painted. Coffee looks like mud. Real ice cream melts much more quickly than the firm but fake sundae. The plain fact is, except by props and mock-ups some objects cannot be shown on television as the viewer, in his mind's eye, knows the essence of the objects.

The technical limitations of television, driving product manufacturers to the substitution of a mock-up for the genuine article, if they wish to use what they may regard as perhaps their most effective advertising medium, often has resulted in a collision between truth and salesmanship. "What is truth?" has been asked before. On television truth is relative. Assuming that collisions between truth and salesmanship are avoidable, i.e., that mock-ups are not illegal per se, the basic problem this case presents is: What standards should the Federal Trade Commission and courts work out for television commercials so that advertisers will appear to be telling the truth, consistently with Section 5 of the Federal Trade Commission Act prohibiting unfair advertising practices.

There has been little hesitancy on the part of the Commission or the Courts to strike down mock-ups or props which create false and deceptive facts concerning the performance, quality, or comparative tests of the product. For example, the Commission prohibited the manufacturers of the household detergent "Lestoil" from showing a bottle of "Lestoil" near a burning candle or atop a stove as illustrating its non-combustible qualities, when in fact it possessed a very low flash point. The Commission prohibited the Colgate-Palmolive Company from using their "invisible shield" commercial. This commercial consisted of a transparent glass shield prop, against which a coconut, tennis ball, and the like were thrown with the announcer standing behind it. The object bounced off the shield without reaching the announcer. The Commission held that the advertising of Colgate Dental Cream with Gardol gave the false visual innuendo that decay cannot get to the teeth if brushed with this dentrifrice. The Commission also prohibited T.V. commercials of a toy set called "Giant Blue & Grey Battle Set" which pictorially showed the set included numerous trees and other scenery, components that produced smoke, and toy cannons that fired projectiles which exploded. The problem was that only three miniature trees were in the set and numerous other scenery illustrated did not come with the set. Also, there were no components that produced smoke nor did the toy cannon fire projectiles that exploded.

Other illustrations are the Commission's consent order against the manufacturers of "Blue Bonnet" oleomargarine to cease representing falsely on T.V. that moisture drops called "Flavor Gems" (actually magnified drops of a non-volatile liquid for the demonstration) caused Blue Bonnet oleomargarine to taste more like butter than competitive margarines. Another decision involved the use of a boxing glove on which the announcer (Bud Palmer) stroked a competitor's razor across the boxing glove cutting it, but when he repeated it with a "Schick" razor the glove was not cut. The Commission issued a consent order to cease this commercial as purporting to prove that the "Schick" razor was safer than other competitive razors and disparaging the competitors' razors by misrepresenting the harmful consequences of their use.

There are always those cases which involve, through props and mockups, deception by distortion of comparative results. One such decision involved a demonstration on T.V. involving the virtues of "New Super-Strength Alcoa Wrap." The demonstration showed two hams side by side, one wrapped in ordinary aluminum wrap, and the other in the Alcoa Product. The ordinary foil was shown battered and torn with the ham dried out. The "New Super-Strength" foil was not torn and the ham was fresh. The Commission in issuing its order found that the ordinary wrap was deliberately torn and that although a number of hams were purchased and aged the same period of time, the ham which appeared most fresh was then wrapped in the Alcoa foil while the one most dried out was then wrapped in the ordinary foil. Another example of distortion through comparative tests was the attempt by the Mennen Company to show the superiority of the consistency of "Mennen Sof' Stroke" over other competing brands. To show this, a skin diver with a heavy beard dived into six to eight feet of water. While underwater, he demonstrated how competing aerosol shaving creams rapidly dissipated in his hand before being applied to his beard. He then discharged the "Mennen Sof' Stroke" into his cupped hand, applied it to his face and began to shave. The Commission in issuing its order found that the demonstration was not a valid portrayal of the superiority of "Mennen Sof' Stroke" over competing brands because the diver cupped his hand at a sharp angle when using one shaving cream and not the other facilitating the result. Also, the so-called "Sof' Stroke" applied to the diver's beard was actually a mixture of shaving cream and tooth paste.

The crux of the problem came to a head in a classic case decision in 1963. Involved was a television commercial in which "Palmolive Rapid Shave" cream was applied to a piece of plexiglass covered with sand, which the announcer referred to as "sandpaper." The petitioner claimed that the mock-up was necessary because of the inherent difficulties of television in that real sandpaper cannot be distinguished from smooth colored paper. The actor after placing the shaving cream on the mock-up, in one stroke cleaned off the area path of the razor. The commercial continued claiming that "Rapid Shave" would shave the heaviest beards. The Commission held that even fine sandpaper could not be shaved immediately, and that coarse paper could not be shaved until "moisturized" for an hour, thus holding a clear misrepresentation through use of the demonstration. The Commission issued an order which in its initial and later stages was considered very broad as excluding the further undisclosed use of mock-ups. The Court of Appeals, First Circuit, felt that the order was in fact declaring the use of any prop or mock-up deceptive *per se* and in an opinion filled full of analogies entered a judgment setting aside the order of the Commission.

The Supreme Court granted a writ of certiorari and upheld the Commission's order that the mock-up was deceptive. The Court held that it was a material deceptive practice to convey to television viewers the false impression that they are seeing an actual test, experiment, or demonstration which proves a product's claims when they are not because of the undisclosed use of mock-ups. The Court did not conclude that the use of all props and mock-ups was deceptive. In distinguishing between a mashed potato prop as ice cream and the present case the Court held:

> In the ice cream case the mashed potato prop is not being used for additional proof of the product claim, while the purpose of the Rapid Shave commercial is to give the viewer objective proof of the claims made. If in the ice cream hypothetical, the focus of the commercial becomes the undisclosed potato prop and the viewer is invited, explicitly or by implication, to see for himself the truth of the claims about the ice cream's rich texture and full color, and perhaps compare it to a "rival product," then the commercial has become similar to the one now before us. Clearly, however, a commercial which depicts happy actors delightedly eating ice cream that in fact is mashed potatoes or drinking a product appearing to be coffee but which is in fact some other substance is not covered by the present order.

The conflict over the use of mock-ups and props is far from over. The *Carter Products, Inc.* case, from which Judge Wisdom stated the problem, involved a T.V. commercial comparing the virtues of "Rise" as a shaving cream that "Stays Moist and Creamy," while showing that the ordinary lather dried out. The only problem was the "ordinary lather" used in the commercial was not a lather but a mock-up consisting of 90% water and a foaming agent. The mock-up did not contain any soaps or fatty acid salts, which ingredients keep the shaving cream from breaking down. There was no doubt this mock-up was deceptive. A similar decision was reached involving T.V. commercials to show the superiority of Libbey-Owens-Ford safety glass used in all windows of GM cars over safety glass used in the side and rear windows of non-GM cars. The Commission found that the glass used in the side and rear windows of GM cars was not the same quality as used in the windshields and that in the use of undisclosed mock-ups and props, there was deception by use of different camera lenses, taking a photo through an open window when the viewer would believe it was taken through glass, and even the use of streaks of vaseline to add to the distortion.

These are only a few of the decisions involving T.V. demonstrations. One truth which seems inescapable is that the use of mock-ups and props will be carefully scrutinized by the Federal Trade Commission.

Conclusion

The bulk of Federal regulation of advertising is controlled by the FTC. In 1966, a 1,145 man staff with a budget of approximately thirteen and a half million dollars was needed to cover all of its activities. The complaints involving deceptive practices against consumers were up 45% from 1965. In 1965, 897,609 advertisements in T.V., radio, and newspapers and other media were examined of which 34,107 were set aside for further examination.

Statistics do not necessarily tell the complete story, but the power and authority of the FTC over advertising is continually having its effect. The extent of their power and the discretion of their decisions has been the subject of wide discussion and numerous articles. One of the most extensive treatises recently written on deceptive advertising is found in the 1967 March *Harvard Law Review*. The need for Federal regulation in advertising to avoid deception is beyond question. One course is evident, the competitive need for advertising and the ingenuity of the advertising industry will always be an interesting match for any Federal regulation imposed upon it.

10. The Federal Trade Commission and the Regulation of Advertising in the Consumer Interest

Dorothy Cohen

It is the purpose of this article to review the present means by which the Federal Trade Commission regulates advertising for the protection of the consumer, as well as the adequacy of the criteria which underlie the regulatory process. Further, it is suggested that additional measures be taken that would increase the effectiveness of the advertising regulatory process.

In implementing its responsibility to regulate advertising for the protection of consumers, the Federal Trade Commission has developed informal decision criteria. In broad terms, the Commission's judgments have been consistent with an "economic man" concept of consumer purchase behavior. It views the consumer as an informed, reasoning decision maker using objective values to maximize utilities. This is essentially a normative concept.

The basic assumptions of the Commission's regulatory design or criteria are maximization of the consumer's utilities and rational choice. A necessary ingredient to fulfill these assumptions is full, accurate information. The Commission, therefore, protects the consumer

Reprinted from *Journal of Marketing,* Vol. 33 (January, 1969), 40–44, published by The American Marketing Association.

by identifying and attacking information which is insufficient, false, or misleading. These deficiencies are uncovered by relating the objective characteristics of a product, as determined by the Commission, to its advertising representations.

The Commission, therefore, operates under the legally and economically acceptable premise that the consumer is to be assured full and accurate information which will permit him to make a reasoned choice in the marketplace. Nonetheless, examination of the results of the Commission's activities utilizing this concept reveals the existence of several gaps in its protection. For example, the poor are not always protected from excessive payments because of lack of information about true cost or true price. The health and safety of the consumer are not always assured, since information concerning the hazards of using particular products is not always available. The belief that added protection is needed was reinforced by a report of the Consumer Advisory Council to President Johnson which states "that although this is an era of abundance . . . there is also much confusion and ignorance, some deception and even fraud. . . ." [1]

The need for added protection does not necessarily suggest discarding the Commission's regulatory framework, because a more effective structure currently does not exist. The elimination of the present regulatory design would in fact create a void in the consumer protection network. It does suggest, however, that steps should be taken as a basis for stronger protection in the future. The current movement to improve regulation through stressing full disclosure, while serving to eliminate some deficiencies, is not sufficient.[2] The Consumer Advisory Council's report, for example, in summarizing the outlook for the future, observes:

> Technological change is so rapid that the consumer who bothers to learn about a commodity or a service soon finds his knowledge obsolete. In addition, many improvements in quality and performance are below the threshold of perception, and imaginative marketing often makes rational choice even more of a problem.[3]

---

[1] *Consumer Issues '66,* A Report Prepared by the Consumer Advisory Council, Washington, D.C.: U.S. Government Printing Office, 1966, p. 1.

[2] See *The J. B. Williams Co., Inc. and Parkson Advertising Agency, Inc. v. F.T.C., 5 Trade Regulation Reporter* ¶72,182 (Chicago, Ill.: Commerce Clearing House, Inc., August, 1967); and several aspects of truth-in-packaging and truth-in-lending legislation.

[3] *Consumer Issues' 66, op. cit.,* p. 6.

Full disclosure of pertinent facts is one step in improving the protection network. Additional steps are needed to assure that the consumer understands the significance of the facts. It has been noted, for example, that the consumer is selective in his acceptance of information offered. This selectivity is due, in part, to a difference between the objective environment in which the consumer "really" lives and the subjective environment he perceives and responds to.[4] The consumer reacts to information not only with his intelligence, but also with habits, traits, attitudes, and feelings. In addition, his decisions are influenced significantly by opinion leaders, reference groups, and so on. There are predispositions at work within the individual that determine what he is exposed to, what he perceives, what he remembers, and the effect of the communication upon him.[5]

It has been noted that appeal to fear (emphasizing the hazards of smoking or of borrowing money) may not deter the chronically anxious consumer, nor will it necessarily protect his health or pocketbook. Valid communications from a non-authoritative source may not be believed, whereas questionable communications from an authoritative source may be readily accepted. Thus, the extensive use of "sufficient" truth may take on an aura of non-believability and be rejected. Attempts to avoid conflicting evidence may result in ignoring the information completely.

The Commission's efforts to provide the consumer with economic information concerning value are not completely effective, since the consumer does not measure value in economic terms alone. Brand loyalties create values in the eyes of the consumer as does the influence of social groups and opinion leaders within these groups. His desire to attain certain levels of aspiration may lead the consumer to be a "satisficing animal . . . rather than a maximizing animal," [6] that is, one who chooses among values that may be currently suitable, rather than those which maximize utilities. In order for the Commission to improve the consumer protection network, it must reflect an understanding of the behavioral traits of consumers.

[4] Herbert A. Simon, "Economics and Psychology," in *Psychology: A Study of a Science,* Vol. 6, Simon Koch, editor. New York: McGraw-Hill Book Co., Inc., 1963, p. 710.
[5] Joseph T. Klapper, "The Social Effects of Mass Communication," in *The Source of Human Communication,* Wilbur Schramm, editor. New York: Basic Books, Inc., 1963, p. 67.
[6] Simon, *op. cit.,* p. 716.

Adapting the regulatory design to handle behavioral traits is no easy task. An examination of a behavioral model of consumer performance reveals the existence of many intervening variables, so that the creation of standards for this non-standardized consumer becomes exceedingly difficult. Moreover, current knowledge of the consumer as a behavioralist is far from complete. Indeed, the feasibility and success associated with the practical uses of this model are dependent upon future research.

It is, therefore, recommended that attention be directed toward current and future research in the behavioral sciences to devise means for amending the advertising regulatory framework. This would lead to improvements in the communication process and the elimination of protection gaps. The application of behavioral characteristics to the regulatory model is not intended as a panacea, but is a suggestion for improving some regulatory ailments. In broad policy terms the Commission can initially do little more than establish closer contact with the consumer and analyze behavioral data which may be relevant to the regulation of advertising. Suggestions for improved administrative procedures are limited to applications of current behavioral knowledge of the consumer. Future research may suggest more precise administrative action, for increased knowledge of the consumer's buying behavior should lead to the development of more effective mechanisms for his protection.

Recommendations

The following specific recommendations are suggested as guidelines for future governmental activities relative to consumer advertising.

Bureau of behavioral studies

A Bureau of Behavioral Studies should be established within the Federal Trade Commission (similar to the Commission's Bureau of Economics) whose function would be to gather and analyze data on consumer buying behavior relevant to the regulation of advertising in the consumer interest.

Consumer complaint offices

The Federal Trade Commission should establish "consumer complaint" offices throughout the United States. One method of gathering more information about the consumer is to provide closer contact between the Federal Trade Commission and the public. Complaints about advertising abuses may originate with consumers, but these have been at a minimum; and lately the Commission has accentuated its industry-wide approach to deceptive practices. Although the industry-wide approach is geared toward prevention and permits the FTC to deal with broad areas of deception, it minimizes the possibility of consumer contact with the Commission. In 1967, awareness of this fact resulted in an action in which the Commission's Bureau of Field Operations and its eleven field offices located in cities across the United States intensified its program of public education designed to give businessmen and consumers a better understanding of the work of the agency.[7]

If the Commission is to operate satisfactorily in the consumer interest, it must develop a closer relationship with consumers. Most consumers are still uncertain about the protection they are receiving, and the Federal Trade Commission appears to be an unapproachable body with little apparent contact with the "man-on-the-street."

Consumer complaint offices would identify the Federal Trade Commission's interest in the consumer and act as a clearing house for information. Consumers could be informed about steps to take if they believe they have been deceived, what recourse is open, and how to secure redress for grievances. The Commission could secure evidence about deception direct from consumers. Moreover, the complaints of these private individuals might be based on noneconomic factors, permitting clearer delineation of the behavioral man and the ways in which he might be protected.

Priority of protection

The Federal Trade Commission should establish a definitive policy of priority of protection based on the severity of the consequences of the advertising. While appropriations and manpower for the Federal Trade Commission have increased in recent years, they are still far from adequate to police all advertising. Therefore, the ability to protect is limited and selective. In a recent annual report the Commission did indicate, however, that it had established priorities:

> A high priority is accorded those matters which relate to the basic necessities of life, and to situations in which the impact of

[7] Federal Trade Commission, *Annual Report,* 1967, p. 67.

false and misleading advertising, or other unfair and receptive practices, falls with cruelest impact upon those least able to survive the consequences—the elderly and the poor.[8]

Nevertheless, in the same year the Commission reported that approximately 20% of the funds devoted to curtailing deceptive practices were expended on textile and fur enforcement (noting that the Bureau of Textiles and Furs made 12,679 inspections on the manufacturing, wholesaling, and retailing level).[9]

Priority may be established in two ways. First, it may be considered relative to the harmful consequences of deceptive advertising. This approach could suggest, for example, that the Federal Trade Commission devote more of its energies to examining conflicting claims in cigarette advertising than to examining conflicting claims in analgesic advertising (which seems to focus on the question of whether one pain reliever acts faster than the other). Exercising such priorities might accelerate the movement toward needed reforms (such as recent safety reforms in the automobile industry) by pinpointing the existence of inadequately protected consumer areas.

A second method of establishing priority could be to delineate the groups that are most susceptible to questionable advertising. This is where the behavioral model may play an important role. Sociologists are trying to discover common aspects of group behavior, and research has disclosed that each social class has its own language pattern.[10] Special meanings and symbols accentuate the differences between groups and increase social distance from outsiders.[11]

Disclosure of special facets of group behavior should be helpful to the Commission in designing a program of protection. As noted earlier, the poor cannot be adequately protected by the disclosure of true interest rates because their aspirations may provide a stronger motivating influence than the fear of excessive debt. Knowledge of the actual cost of borrowing would offer no protection to the low-income family which knows no sources of goods and credit available to it

---

[8] *Ibid.,* p. 17.

[9] *Ibid.,* pp. 30 and 81.

[10] Leonard Schatzman and Anselm Strauss, "Social Class and Modes of Communication," *American Journal of Sociology,* 60 (January, 1955), 329.

[11] Tamotsu Shibutani, "Reference Groups as Perspectives," *American Journal of Sociology,* 60 (May, 1955), 567.

other than costly ones. Nor would higher cost of borrowing deter the consumer who, concerned mostly with the amount of the monthly payment, may look at credit as a means of achieving his goals. In fact, the Federal Trade Commission concluded, in a recent economic report on installment sales and credit practices in the District of Columbia, that truth-in-lending, although needed, is not sufficient to solve the problem of excessive use of installment credit for those consumers who are considered poor credit risks and are unsophisticated buyers.[12]

The problems of the poor extend beyond the possible costs of credit. They include the hazards of repossession, the prices paid for items in addition to credit costs, and the possibility of assuming long-term debt under a contractual obligation not clear at the outset. It is possible that behavioral studies may disclose a communication system that would be a more effective deterrent to the misuse of credit than the disclosure of exorbitant interest rates. Until then, the Commission should give priority to investigations where the possibility of fraudulent claims, representations, and pricing accompany the offering of credit facilities to low-income groups. For example, advertisements of "three complete rooms of furniture for $199.00, easy payments" continue to appear despite the Commission's ruling that "bait and switch" tactics are unfair. Thus, the possibility exists that the low-income consumer may be "switched" to a much more expensive purchase whose costs become abnormally high due to the exorbitant interest rates included in the "easy payments." In its monitoring and review of advertising the Commission's staff should give precedence to investigations of such "bargain, easy payments" advertising, since much of it is especially designed to attract the low-income groups.

Improvement of the communication process

The consumer's cognitive capacity (the attitudes, perceptions, or beliefs about one's environment) and its effect on the communication process should be reflected in designing advertising controls so that the inefficient mechanisms can be improved or eliminated.

Currently the concept of full disclosure is being expanded as the major means of offering the consumer additional protection. This is particularly evident where the objective is to dissuade the consumer

---

[12] 5 *Trade Regulation Reporter* ¶50,205 (Chicago, Ill.: Commerce Clearing House, Inc., July, 1968).

from the use of or excessive use of a product or service. Little attention is paid, however, to determining whether the selective consumer is taking note of these disclosures.

An examination of behavioral man reveals that he is less "perfect" than economic man. His values are not based on objective realities alone, nor are his choices always what may be objectively considered as best among alternatives. In legislative design, the regulatory authorities should come to grips with the question of whether protection of the consumer includes "protection from himself." There are indications that the latter concept is considered a legitimate area for regulatory activities—as evidence in legislation affecting cigarette advertising and in some elements of the truth-in-lending and truth-in-packaging bills.

While questions may be raised about the legitimacy of interfering with the consumer's "freedom of choice," there is evidence that the methodology devised for this interference is deficient. In the current regulatory design, the proposed method of securing these different kinds of protection is the same, although the kinds of protection offered to the consumer may differ. For example, the consumer is currently protected against deceptive advertising by laws requiring that he be provided with truthful disclosure as to the product and its features. Where authorities believe that the advertising claims of certain products or services should be minimally used or completely avoided, the consumer is again protected by non-deceptive "full disclosure" as to the product and its features. Yet a quick review of consumer behavior and persuasibility reveals that a strategy designed to change or dissuade must, of necessity, differ from a strategy designed to reinforce. The consumer may be quite willing to accept information which supports his beliefs or preconceptions and yet be unwilling to accept evidence which refutes these same beliefs. Moreover, research has disclosed that adherence to recommended behavior is inversely related to the intensity of fear arousal. Intense fear appeal may be ineffective since it arouses anxiety within the subject which can be reduced by his hostility toward the communication and rejection of the message. It has also been noted that the tendency toward dissonance reduction can lead to failure to understand the information disclosed. Thus "full disclosure" cannot be a completely effective control mechanism when its main purpose is to protect the consumer from using a particular product or service, for the consumer may simply ignore these disclosures.

Based on current research, one approach the Commission might take toward an improved program of dissuasion would be to reinforce the negative information through an authoritative source, such as the Commission itself. Although the agency has a number of publications —*Annual Report, News Summary, Advertising Alert*—none of these is specifically geared to provide the consumer with information. A monthly report to consumers, initially available at "consumer complaint" offices, might serve as an effective mechanism for denoting the existence of hazardous products, excessive claims, questionable representations, and so forth. Specifically, this report could detail information of particular interest to consumers concerning advertising abuses that had been curtailed, cease and desist orders, questionable advertising practices currently under investigation, and so on. It is also suggested that this printed publication occasionally be supplemented by reports through a more pervasive medium—television.

It is not recommended that the Commission become a product-testing service, since the latter implies governmental control over competitive offerings and could place excessive restrictions on freedom of choice. Instead the report is to be considered a communication device, designed to insure that consumers take more note of available information on the premise that the information emanates from an authoritative governmental source.

Behavioral criteria

The Federal Trade Commission should use behavioral as well as economic criteria in evaluating consumer interest. Subjective as well as objective claims should be examined in determining whether a "tendency to deceive" exists. Due to insufficient knowledge of consumer behavior, an accurate blueprint for defining products in terms of consumer choice is not available. Future research may present more precise propositions about consumer behavior which would facilitate the development and implementation of behavioral criteria. However, currently, there are areas wherein the adaptation of behavioral factors in establishing criteria for advertising regulation may provide for more adequate protection in the consumer interest.

Assuming it were possible to provide the consumer with complete information based on economic criteria, the individual may still be unable to exercise informed choice. A report by the National Commission on Food Marketing stated: "Given complete price information, the help of computers and all the clerical help needed, it is impossible

to say which retailer in a particular community has lower prices." [13]
Moreover, as noted earlier, individuals do not choose on the basis of
price appeal alone.

Advertising today, to a great extent, stresses non-economic or promotional differences. Products are denoted as being preferred by
groups, individuals, society, motion picture stars, sports leaders, and
the average man. Since consumers may make their selections on the
basis of these promotional representations, adequate protection requires that advertisements be subject to as close an examination for
deceptive representation as they are for deceptive price claims.

Insufficient emphasis has been placed in the advertising regulatory
design on the importance of testimonials in influencing consumer
choice. In the examination of the selective consumer it has been noted
that his choice is influenced by a desire for group membership and by
the opinion of leaders within these groups. It has also been noted that
the consumer engages in selective exposure and selective perception,
suggesting that when the consumer finally does accept an "opinion
leader," the latter exerts significant pressure on the consumer's choice.

The use of testimonials in advertising takes account of this fact of
consumer behavior, but the regulatory design does not. Those who are
deemed to be opinion leaders and dominant members of groups are
selected and paid for their "testimonials." Moreover, where the selected figure does not perform well, for example, on television, an
actor is used to replace him. The consumer may be deceived into believing an "opinion leader" is evaluating a product or service. These
opinions may be used by the consumer to substantiate the suitability
of this particular item in his own value structure.

Currently, the basic legal requirement is that testimonials be truthful. However, if someone declares that he prefers "Brand X," valida-
tion of this statement is necessarily subjective. Adequate consumer
protection requires more stringent regulations which should extend
into evidence of truthfulness of this testimonial and disclosure as to the
way in which it was secured. It is suggested that in using a testimonial
no substitute attestors be allowed; and if payment has been made for
the endorsement, the advertisement should so state. If evidence is
available that the individual does not use the product (such as a cigar

---

[13] *Organization and Competition in Food Retailing, Technical Study No. 7,*
a report prepared by the National Commission on Food Marketing. Washington,
D.C.: U.S. Government Printing Office, 1966, p. 169.

recommendation by a non-cigar smoker), his testimonal should not be permitted.

Summary

In its efforts to protect the consumer against advertising abuse, the Federal Trade Commission has developed a protective network in the consumer interest primarily based on economic standards. There are gaps in this protection network, which result from the fact that the consumer does not appraise his interest solely in economic terms. Rather, the consumer develops patterns of buying behavior that reflect the influence of non-economic values and the individual's cognitive capacity. The Federal Trade Commission should take cognizance of this "behavioral" man in its consumer interest activities.

It is recommended that the Commission become more familiar with and establish closer contact with the consumer through a Bureau of Behavioral Research, consumer complaint offices, and through the distribution of consumer publications to disclose advertising irregularities. In addition, it is recommended that the Commission adapt regulatory criteria to current knowledge of the behavioral man in order to assure that Federal regulation of advertising is accurately functioning in the consumer interest.

C. Truth in Lending

11. Gesture and Reality in Consumer Credit Reform

Homer Kripke

Two major efforts toward reform of consumer credit by statute culminated in the summer of 1968. First, Congress passed the "Truth-in-Lending Bill" which had been pending before the Senate since 1961 and which was finally passed by nearly unanimous action by the Senate and then, with substantial additions, by the House. Second, the National Conference of Commissioners on Uniform State Laws (NCCUSL) promulgated, and the American Bar Association approved, the Uniform Consumer Credit Code (UCCC), for enactment by the states.

The Federal bill, by voluntarily renouncing the operative effect of its provisions in a state which has comparable provisions, has given a powerful impetus to the rapid enactment of state legislation in this field. Whether or not the states adopt the UCCC (and at this writing it is too early to tell), this code will remain the touchstone for consideration of all state legislation in the field for some years.

It is therefore appropriate and timely to consider what has been accomplished and what remains to be done. On this point the writer finds himself largely a dissenter from the received view that the Federal legislation is a great step forward. It accomplishes a little some-

Reprinted from *New York University Law Review,* Vol. 44 (March, 1969), 1–13, 51–52.

thing, but very little compared to what could have been done with the energy expended.

The "Put-On"

It is not too much to say that the strong support of witnesses, public officials, legal aid workers, and consumer representatives for the concept of full disclosure of the rate of finance charges and other aspects of a consumer credit transaction—as proposed to be required by the Senate bill during seven long years of hearings and legislative activity and by comparable "little Douglas bills" or truth-in-lending bills in the states—was a "put-on." Many of them knew that disclosure would have only a slight effect on the evils about which they were testifying and agitating; yet everyone acted as if disclosure bills would solve the problem.

It was not surprising that the vast discrepancy between the evils of deception and fraud, set forth in the testimony, and the disclosure remedy would escape the attention of popular writers who reasonably inferred that disclosure would remove the evils about which the witnesses were testifying. Such details as the fact that the widely-hailed Massachusetts Truth-in-Lending Bills had had very little impact failed to diminish the enthusiasm of the popular writers for the same thing on a national scale.

So far as the witnesses are concerned, the causes of the put-on are somewhat more difficult to understand. The writer does not, of course, mean to suggest that anyone was wilfully deceiving the congressional committees or the public. To understand why they deceived themselves is somewhat more complex. The reasons are a compound of superficial knowledge, concealing basic misunderstanding of the status of the instalment credit business, and a great deal of wishful thinking based on the unconscious hope that the simple disclosure solution would avoid the necessity of facing up to the hard and expensive decisions that would be necessary if one really wanted to attack the evils.

First, the spokesmen on the consumer side did not really understand the instalment credit business. The statistics that some of them used as to the size of "finance companies" lumped together the figures on consumer credit with those of commercial instalment sales and the quite different businesses of factoring, commercial receivables financing, etc. Second, and more importantly, they failed to distinguish in their minds the tremendous difference between instalment credit, as available in the purchase of new cars, high grade used cars, and appliances from reputable dealers in middle-class contexts and the totally different problem of instalment credit in the poverty areas, marked by ignorance on the part of the buyer, enticement, the bait of easy terms, fraudulent practices, shoddy merchandise, unreliable dealers, garnishment, and oppressive collection methods. While no sharp line between these areas could be drawn by a definition, there is in fact a significant distinction.

In the middle-class areas—where the consumer has mobility; some training in shopping; some experience in personal planning and, therefore, some restraint against impulse buying; some ability at price shopping; and occasionally some understanding of the amount of finance charges—disclosure in a prescribed form will undoubtedly do some good by making comparison easier. In a nation of 200 million people, there will certainly be some who will profit from standardized disclosure. But the writer has elsewhere argued that the amount of good to be accomplished will be relatively small and will by no means fulfill the high expectations, because the middle-class buyer has already learned where credit is cheapest. The writer there pointed out that statistical efforts to determine whether the consumer understood the cost of financing were merely unimpressive confirmation of the compelling economic fact visible to anyone who wanted to see: that the comparatively high-priced sales finance companies catering to middle-class buyers had lost position to banks providing financing at lower rates. Within six months after those views were expressed, they were amazingly confirmed by the fact that the three largest independent sales finance companies, which had been significant financial intermediaries between basic sources of savings and users of consumer credit for two generations, had lost or were on their way to losing their independent existence. The characteristic of these companies was that they showed low earnings growth potential despite earnest efforts to diversify into other financial and non-financial enterprises. It was the judgment of the financial community that their long-established borrowing power and existing long-term debt at favorable interest rates could be more advantageously used than in consumer credit.

Thus, for the middle-class consumer, the battle for competitive pricing of credit had been essentially won before it was aided by the disclosure statutes. In the poverty context, however, the problem as to disclosure was and is different. How much good will disclosure do in this context?

In the first place, the congressional hearings are full of stories of consumers who never understood even that they had to pay a finance charge, although the papers which they had signed showed a finance charge and a total cost far in excess of the cash price quoted to them. For this kind of consumer, it is unlikely that disclosure in writing, in a different prescribed form, is going to make any difference. Recognizing this fact, the Federal Trade Commission, although its officials have repetitiously been strong advocates of the disclosure statute, has gone so far as to require *oral* disclosure in an order in a fraud case in the light of its assertion that consumers do not understand written disclosure.

In the second place, there is much evidence that some consumers in the poverty areas understand very well that they are being bilked by high cash prices and high finance charges, even before the new legislation takes effect; but they also know that merchants or credit agencies with lower charges are not going to extend credit to them. A person who scarcely knows where the money for his next meal is coming from is not going to worry much about the risk involved in obtaining some needed goods when he does not know where next month's and next year's instalments are coming from.

A third reason that disclosure is a wholly inadequate solution in poverty areas is that, even when accompanied with rate regulation, it is concerned only with the admitted credit charges in a transaction. But a very substantial portion of all consumer credit is sale credit— *i.e.,* it consists of credit extended in the first instance by the seller or dealer, whether or not he subsequently transfers the credit obligation to a bank or finance company. The total profitability of a credit sale transaction depends on the combination of the merchandise profit and the financing profit. If a seller is restricted in the finance rate involved, either by maximum rate legislation or by a competitive desire to advertise "low finance rates" or "low bank rates," he can forego part of the possible finance profit, increase his cash selling price, and make the profit there. The forces of competition, of course, in some contexts, restrict the amount of cash selling price that may be quoted; but in the poverty areas, where the potentialities of abuse are greatest, the salutary effects of competition are the least effective. The ghetto shopper is not a comparison shopper and does not have access to the lowest prices. The Consumer Credit Protection Act (CCPA) totally failed to deal with this enormous loophole in the effect of disclosure and rate regulation. In contrast, the authors of the UCCC saw and expressed the problem clearly and dealt with it as best they could by a provision making it evidence of unconscionability to charge more than going prices to persons in like positions. This provision is all to the good, but it necessarily leaves open an enormous number of questions.

Even before the CCPA went into effect on July 1, 1969, it was already possible to forecast its effect from the experience of the widely-heralded Massachusetts Truth-in-Lending statues. The latter have had very little effect, and this was already clear before the CCPA was finally enacted. To the extent that they have had effect, the Massachusetts statutes seem to have been costly to the consumer by suppressing advertised rate competition and by causing finance charges to be buried in cash prices.

That the truth-in-lending provisions of the CCPA will have very little impact in the poverty areas as to which the most concern is expressed has been largely conceded by strong proponents of the legislation. The Chairman of the Federal Trade Commission had admitted this during Congressional hearings.

Mr. Dixon: [W]e found that in some instances retailers took all credit costs and put them in the asking price—just hid them, you see.

Now if we pass a truth-in-lending bill and this should be the development practice, truth in lending is not going to reach the problem in the ghetto.

Senator Sparkman: . . . A great many people seem to think the disclosure of finance charges will solve the problem. . . . But my thinking is that there are a lot of things involved not covered by disclosure.

Similar recognition has been shown by a professional staff member of the Senate committee which was the forum for the long drive to enact the Truth-in-Lending Bill and by the draftsmen of the UCCC. Yet neither the Federal Trade Commission nor the Senate committee ever took steps to have the bill amended to encompass credit abuses that could not be reached by disclosure, but which were before them not only in the drafts of the UCCC then in process but also in the Commission's own studies of the evils requiring remedy.

The writer recognizes, of course, that hearings on the Truth-in-Lending Bill served as a forum through which public interest in the problems of consumer credit was focused and accentuated for many years. In the long run, however, the Federal bill, even with some regulatory additions by the House, will prove to have been a minimal contribution to the overall problem. No doubt it was a necessary step, but it was far from being a sufficient step to meet the problems of consumer credit.

Beyond disclosure, there are many and more acute problems of fraud and deception even in middle-class contexts, notably in the field of "home improvement" (roofing, aluminum siding, aluminum windows, blacktopping, etc.), in other door-to-door sales, and even in store sales in poverty areas. Here is where our problem is, in an area untouched by the CCPA despite its broad pretensions and the abundant evidence in its legislative record.

In contrast with the CCPA, the UCCC deals with fraudulent and deceptive credit practices at all levels, it includes broad provisions on unconscionability, door-to-door sales, and the prohibition of certain clauses in agreements and certain remedies. The failure of the CCPA to go beyond its disclosure panacea in any rational fashion is its greatest failure. The entire course of enactment was the legislative process at its worst.

The Senate bill—to repeat—never, throughout the years, contained more than truth-in-lending provisions, although the hearings year after year demonstrated that the problem was largely one of fraud and deception, not merely non-disclosure and misunderstanding of the rate of credit charge. The House never took the matter seriously until it became likely that the bill, with administration support, would pass the Senate in 1967. The House, to its credit, immediately went beyond truth-in-lending, and its bill started with regulatory provisions.

The House committee reported on a bill which contained evidence of hasty drafting, and the committee report contains patchwork on the bill, as well as numerous dissents, separate statements, and promises of floor fights. The bill was in fact substantially amended on the floor, surely the worst possible place for legislative drafting. It was again significantly amended by the conference committee (notably by adding the curious provision against extortionate loans in Title II) and was then passed without debate by a Senate which in many years had never had before it anything but the truth-in-lending or disclosure provisions.

The CCPA ended with a useful restriction on garnishments, but not as good as the one that was available to Congress for consideration in the UCCC; a prohibition on discharge of an employee for one garnishment, though not as protective as the UCCC provision; a right of rescission on home mortgage and improvement transactions; and a title dealing with extortionate loans. It is a strange melange.

The most obvious problem of consumer credit is that on which a large part of the hearings was concentrated, downright consumer fraud: merchandise falsely described, merchandise switched or omitted in delivery, representations made orally but omitted in the written contracts, shoddy merchandise, etc. The CCPA, after all these hearings, fails totally to deal with these problems.

The Federal government has an agency, the Federal Trade Commission, which undertakes to deal with deceptive practices in the consumer field; but it complains bitterly of lack of funds and manpower and even questions its jurisdiction outside the District of Columbia. Why has no effort been made to beef up this agency and to give it the funds and the statutory tools with which to work? Why the put-on? The funds given it under the CCPA to enforce the disclosure requirements of that act could far better have been allocated for the Commission's use against deception and fraud.

One who, from an academic ivory tower, tries to guess what went on in Washington, is indeed reckless, but the background is known. One cannot doubt the genuineness of President Johnson's desire to make his mark in history through his Great Society, as expressed in his State of the Union Message of 1964, declaring "unconditional war on poverty," and leading to the Economic Opportunity Act of 1964; his moving messages in support of the Civil Rights Act of 1965; and his deep-felt speech at Howard University, June 4, 1965.

But, as Arthur Krock remarked in several columns in the *New York Times,* the Vietnam War was like the tar baby in the Uncle Remus story. The harder the President smote it, the harder he became stuck, and the unconditional war on poverty went by the board. As has been said by Daniel P. Moynihan, "[T]he address at Howard was in a sense his last peacetime speech" before he became mired in Vietnam. It is one reasonable reading of history that thereafter the war on poverty was unconditional only in so far as it did not substantially tax the Federal budget with expensive new programs.

Perhaps the tip-off occurred in 1967 with the President's appointment as Special Assistant for Consumer Affairs of Miss Betty Furness, who at the time of her appointment had no experience on the consumer side of sales and no discernible qualification for the job other than her photogenic qualities.

If we, unlike the celebrants of truth in lending, are not deceived as to the extent of the victory in truth in lending, we may pass to a consideration of the reality of the job remaining to be done. Matters of consumer protection other than consumer credit and prices are outside the scope of this article.

The writer suports the UCCC as a good bill and as a satisfactory compromise among the conflicting views that were represented in its drafting. Its academic draftsmen were consumer-minded, yet somewhat more realistically-minded than the one-sidedness of some consumer representatives; and I am pleased to see that both consumer spokesmen, like the National Legal Aid and Defenders Association, and Federal spokesmen have stopped sharpshooting at details of draftsmanship and have supported the UCCC.

Conclusion

The Federal effort in the field of consumer credit reform occupied most of the 1960's. This effort, however, will produce a bare minimum of benefit for the effort expended, because the proponents gave heed to nothing inconsistent with their preconceived notions; and their notions misconceived the problem. The House did not go beyond the Senate bill in any organized or comprehensive fashion, and the Senate bill was merely a more stringent version of the concept of disclosure already existent in numerous state statutes. The draftsmen of the UCCC understand the problem better: "The existing scheme of consumer-credit laws . . . is vulnerable to the criticism that it supplies largely middle-class solutions (e.g., rate ceilings, disclosure) to what has increasingly become a lower-class problem."

The Senate's professional staff member came to the same conclusion, but articulated it after the Federal statute was passed:

> Reform in the area of disclosure is certainly needed, but I think it will be the middle income consumer that will obtain the greatest benefit . . . now that we have largely solved the problems of middle class America (assuming the states will enact the Consumer Credit Code). I think we still have peculiar problems with low income consumers.

We are thus left with a Federal statute that does nothing to change the present picture of woefully weak state action against fraudulent retail practices victimizing low income consumers, and of total Federal non-action outside the District of Columbia.

It is interesting to note Miss Furness' remarks about flashy but superficial Federal programs in the consumer field:

> Some of the laws which have been enacted under promising consumer protection titles right up to this session of Congress come close to being name-only bills. Or the limited appropriation, limited administrative or enforcement staff provided tends to make them "name only." . . .
>
> Such laws deceive consumers into believing they have been given more protection than they actually have. The industry intended for regulation may have gained more protection than the consumer. *With a law on the books, there will be less public pressure on the Congress, and it will be quite some time before Congress can get up the steam to amend and strengthen the law.* [Emphasis added.]

One would think that Miss Furness had been talking about the Truth-in-Lending Title of the CCPA. Yet, the official Governmental position hailed that title as a great advance. Since her words are clearly appropriate to that act, it was an inadvertent moment of truth.

D. Packaging

12. The Consumer as King: The Economics of Precarious Sovereignty

Robert L. Birmingham

Recently the Magazine Publishers Association, an association of 365 leading United States magazines, sponsored a group of advertisements advertising advertising. One of the most popular of these, which appeared in many mass-consumption magazines in the spring and summer of 1967, was a Feiffer-like series of sketches set at a cocktail party.[1] A professorial and hence hardly virile-looking simpleton is depicted expounding his views on economic planning to a young woman obviously drawn to illustrate the ease of combining sexual attractiveness with the responsibilities of motherhood:

"Professor: Our economy is like a great complicated machine that has too many moving parts!
Matron: We used to have a car like that.
Professor: I say *simplify!* Give the public *one* good TV . . . *one* soap . . . just *one* brand of *everything.*
Matron: I do hope it's a pink soap or maybe a nice yellow or . . .

---

[1] *See, e.g., Newsweek,* April 10, 1967, at 101.

Reprinted from *Case Western Reserve Law Review,* Vol. 20 (1969), 354–367, 377.

Professor: *Think* what we'll *save* on promotion . . . advertising
. . . wasteful competition! The mind boggles.
Matron: When that happens to me, I take an aspirin or an "empirin"
or an "alka-seltzer." It depends.
Professor: Of course the *government* would see to it every product
met a certain *standard.*
Matron: And if they didn't, I'd simply switch to a better brand!
Professor: No, no!! Thousands of brands screaming to be bought is
a thing of the *past.* We must go *beyond* that.
Matron: You mean I couldn't choose things to buy the way I pick
a movie or a . . .
Professor: You wouldn't need to choose.
Matron: My husband and I passed through a *charming* little country
just like that.
Professor: Really, which one?
Matron: Albania."

Elaboration is provided in text at the bottom of the page, apparently to aid those missing the point but nevertheless literate:

> If you're laughing at that fellow up above, we've got news for
> you. He's serious!
> There actually are people—well-meaning people—in this coun-
> try today who think the government should regulate the number
> of brands on the market.
> Mrs. Smith is confused by all the varieties of soap on her super-
> market shelf, they say. It would simplify things if there were only
> four or five, they claim. Making shopping a whole lot quicker and
> easier.
> Of course, poor, little, mixed-up Mrs. Smith won't get to
> choose which soaps go and which soaps stay. Seventeen years of
> sharp-eyed, close-fisted comparison shopping and product testing
> apparently have left Mrs. Smith incapable of that judgment.
> So, now she'll have friends in high places to do her shopping
> for her. Lucky Mrs. Smith.
> Let's hope they know Mrs. Smith has a 12-year-old with dry
> skin. And a mauve bathroom.

Even disregarding the permissibility of travel through Albania at
the time of the trip, this advertisement raises interesting problems.
Our ideology asserts that maximization of satisfaction can best be
attained through vigilant protection preventing regulatory adulteration

of a largely mythical but nevertheless sacred market mechanism.[2] Consumer choice is held to be inviolable.[3] We blindly assume that each person is endowed with an immutable set of preferences dictating degrees of satisfaction associated with the acquisition and use of various combinations of goods. Since discovery of such pleasure schedules cannot be disassociated from individual selection among proffered bundles of products, interference with this selection is generally deemed to reduce community utility. Claims of efficacy, however, do not stop here: "[W]ithin the model of the free market lies one good chance of smoothing the frictions which develop between men on the score of religion, race, colour or social values. 'The market is a great civilizer.' "[4]

The increasing complexity of the modern market place has rendered the unaided individual almost defenseless against modern merchandising techniques. The head of a large department store has stated: "God created the masses of mankind to be exploited. I exploit them; I do his will."[5] In a message to Congress delivered February 5, 1964, President Johnson noted that "for far too long, the consumer has had too little voice and too little weight in government. As a worker, as a businessman, as a farmer, as a lawyer or doctor, the citizen has been well represented. But as a consumer, he has had to take a back seat."[6]

In spite of our ideological bias toward nonintervention, concern for consumer impotence has inspired recent legislation designed to

---

[2] "The ideology of laissez-faire outlived the structural reforms which changed uncontrolled market economy. Indeed, the discrepancy between what many think we ought to do—laissez-faire—and what we in fact are doing—creating a welfare state—has not yet entirely disappeared in the United States." Dalton, "Primitive, Archaic, and Modern Economies: Karl Polanyi's Contribution to Economic Anthropology and Comparative Economy," in *Essays in Economic Anthropology* 1, 9 (J. Helm ed. 1965).

[3] "It can . . . be affirmed that thanks to the nonintervention of the state in private affairs, wants and satisfactions would develop in their natural order. . . . Away, then, with the quacks and the planners! Away with their rings, their claims, their hooks, their pincers! Away with their artificial methods! . . . Let us cast out all artificial systems and give freedom a chance—freedom, which is an act of faith in God and in His handiwork." F. Bastiat, "The Law," in *Selected Essays on Political Economy* 51, 53, 96 (G. de Huszar ed. 1964).

[4] J. Jewkes, *Public and Private Enterprise* 71 (1965).

[5] Hamilton, "The Ancient Maxim Caveat Emptor," 40 *Yale L.J.* (1931), 1133, 1135 n.7.

[6] Address by President Johnson, H.R. Doc. No. 220, 88th Cong., 2d Sess. 1 (1964).

redress the imbalance of power. In this article, selected superstitions underlying our economic value judgments are briefly examined. Next, attention is focused on the Fair Packaging and Labeling Act. After briefly describing it I will attempt to evaluate its purpose and impact in the light of economic theory.

Equilibrium and Optimality

Pareto optimality—economic equilibrium such that with given community resources no person can be made better off without injury to another—will result if: perfect competition prevails; there are constant returns to scale; and there are no external economies or diseconomies with respect to production or consumption.[7] The Platonic ideal of a perfectly competitive commodity market requires that:

"**1.** firms produce a homogeneous commodity, and consumers are identical from the sellers' point of view, in that there are no advantages or disadvantages associated with selling to a particular consumer;

2. both firms and consumers are numerous, and the sales or purchases of each individual unit are small in relation to the aggregate volume of transactions;

3. both firms and consumers possess perfect information about the prevailing price and current bids, and they take advantage of every opportunity to increase profits and utility respectively;

4. entry into and exit from the market is free for both firms and consumers." [8]

Perfectly competitive factor markets must satisfy similarly rigorous conditions. All markets must be linked by perfect knowledge of the characteristics of their products or factors.

The basic assumptions of the model inherently connote a lack of realism. Not only are its requirements unattainable, but attempts to avoid unnecessary divergence from its norms cannot be justified without further detailed argument. If some aspects of a system are con-

[7] *See* P. Samuelson, "The Economic Role of Private Activity," in 2 *Collected Scientific Papers* 1419, 1422 (J. Stiglitz ed. 1966).
[8] J. Henderson & R. Quandt, *Microeconomic Theory* 86 (1958).

strained to non-maximizing levels, there is no a priori basis for asserting that satisfaction of other conditions of optimality will necessarily prove advantageous.[9]

The optimality of competitive equilibrium merely assures efficiency. In the general case welfare will not be maximized:

> Perfect competition represents a welfare optimum in the narrow sense of fulfilling the requirements of Pareto optimality. . . . An additional difficulty is introduced by the fact that the analysis of Pareto optimality accepts the prevailing income distribution. . . . The problem of finding an optimal income distribution is not considered. . . . The analysis of welfare in terms of Pareto optimality leaves a considerable amount of indeterminacy in the solution: there are an infinite number of points . . . which are Pareto-optimal. . . . In order to judge the relative social desirability of alternative points . . . society must make additional value judgments which state its preferences among alternative ways of allocating satisfaction to individuals. Value judgments are ethical beliefs and are not the subject of economic analysis.[10]

Our interest concentrates on the ability of the consumer, assuming satisfaction of other conditions necessary for optimization, to choose from the available goods that combination which, given his income, will yield him the most pleasure. Plot quantities of two desired goods, G_1 and G_2, along the horizontal and vertical axes of Figure 1. Then any point (for example, point A) within the quadrant will denote a unique combination of the two goods having a definite value to an individual. The individual, offered a choice between combinations of goods represented by any two points, will either prefer one to the other or be indifferent as to which he obtains. Ordinarily, we would expect a person to value the combination designated by point B more highly than that of point A, because the former contains more of each good. The locus of all combinations of goods from which the consumer derives equal satisfaction is called an indifference curve. Assuming infinite divisibility of both goods, each point along or between the axes will lie on some indifference curve. Three such curves, I_1, I_2, and I_3,

[9] Lipsey & Lancaster, "The General Theory of Second Best," 24 *Rev. Econ. Stud.* 11 (1956).

[10] J. Henderson & R. Quandt, *supra* note 8, at 208. *See also* P. Samuelson, "Modern Economic Realities and Individualism," in 2 *Collected Scientific Papers* 1407, 1410 (J. Stiglitz ed. 1966).

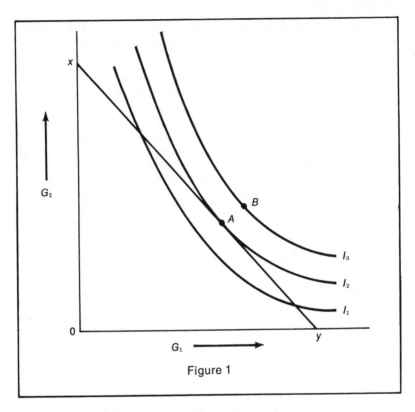

Figure 1

are drawn in Figure 1. The individual will prefer a position on I_3 to one on I_2, and would rather be on I_2 than on I_1.[11]

Limited resources normally prevent the consumer from obtaining satiating amounts of the goods in question. Combinations available to him will be limited to those on or below and to the left of a budget constraint, such as line xy in Figure 1. From the combinations which he can afford the individual will choose that usually unique one which will yield him the greatest satisfaction. If choice is unhampered, he will locate at point A, where budget constraint xy is tangent to indifference curve I_2, the highest indifference curve he can reach.

Since goods are valuable for the enjoyment they yield, it is possible to consider them merely combinations of qualities which themselves

[11] The curves are convex to the origin because acquisition of increasing quantities of a good will normally render it less valuable in terms of other goods possessed in unchanging amounts.

form more basic units of personal satisfaction. Consumer behavior, therefore, can be explained with reference to choice among combinations of these qualities in a manner paralleling our analysis of choice among combinations of goods. Thus we can measure quantities of two desired qualities rather than quantities of two desired goods along the horizontal and vertical axes of Figure 1. Assuming perfect information concerning the qualities associated with each good, unrestricted consumer choice will by a now familiar process again yield equilibrium at point A.[12]

Information

Legislation

The Fair Packaging and Labeling Act,[13] the product of partially abortive efforts by Michigan's Senator Hart and others to reduce consumer confusion caused by misleading marketing practices, became effective on July 1, 1967. Some indication of the anticipated impact of the regulations as originally formulated can be garnered from the ferocity of industry opposition to their enactment. The Michigan Chamber of Commerce stated:

> Inescapably, one concludes the Hart bill is not really aimed at consumer protection, for that's already available in existing law. The measure is little more than a federal grab for power to make decisions that heretofore have been made by consumers and by business—a power grab based on the fallacious concepts that the consumer is Casper Milquetoast, Business is Al Capone, and government is Superman.[14]

A representative of the National Association of Manufacturers argued that "[t]he inevitable effect of the bill will be to roll back the pack-

[12] *See* Fels, "Hedonistic Calculus as Seen from a Distance," 91 *Weltwirtschaftliches Archiv* 101, 108 (1963). "Instead of assuming that we have built-in schedules upon which all existing or potential objects are listed in order of preference, let us think of the individual having 'wants.' These 'wants' are not specific, but specific objects and services fulfill them to varying degrees." G. Tullock, *Toward a Mathematics of Politics* 7 (1967).
[13] 15 U.S.C. §§ 1451–61 (Supp. 1967).
[14] Michigan Chamber of Commerce, *Federal Legislation Report* 2 (1965). "What Salem did for its witches in 1692 may yet become a minute affair in comparison to the trial taking shape for the food industry." A. Mowbray, *The Thumb on the Scale: or the Supermarket Shell Game*. Philadelphia, Lippincott, 1967.

aging and marketing revolution of this generation. Had we lived in
recent years under such a law, we would not buy our products as fresh,
as clean, as unbroken or unspoiled, as accurately measured, as easily
handled or as cheaply as we do today." [15] Such resulting national disasters as a requirement that the holes in "Life Savers" be filled were
predicted.[16] A resolution against passage was adopted by the American
Bar Association, whose seven-man Advisory Committee of the Food,
Drug, and Cosmetic Division of the Corporation, Banking, and Business Section included several attorneys associated with the food industry.[17]

Section 1451 recites the sources of congressional inspiration:

> Informed consumers are essential to the fair and efficient function-
> ing of a free market economy. Packages and their labels should
> enable consumers to obtain accurate information as to the quan-
> tity of the contents and should facilitate value comparisons. There-
> fore, it is hereby declared to be the policy of the Congress to assist
> consumers and manufacturers in reaching these goals in the mar-
> keting of consumer goods.[18]

The means used to effectuate this policy, significantly less drastic
than those initially proposed,[19] seem hardly calculated to destroy even
those surviving fragments of our capitalistic system. The Act subjects

---

[15] Hearings on Packaging and Labeling Legislation Before the Senate Subcomm. on Antitrust and Monopoly, 88th Cong., 1st Sess., pt. 2, at 565 (1963).

[16] Hearings on Fair Packaging and Labeling Before the Senate Comm. on
Commerce, 89th Cong., 1st Sess. 639 (1965).

[17] Hart, *"Can Federal Legislation Affecting Consumers' Economic Interests
Be Enacted?"* 64 *Mich L. Rev.* 1255, 1266 (1966). The bill which became the
Food, Drug, and Cosmetic Act of 1938, 21 U.S.C. §§ 301–92 (1964), was subjected to vituperative attacks. A spokesman for the Proprietary Drug Association asserted: "The only manner in which the present bill could be properly
amended is to strike out all after the enacting clause. . . . I have never in my
life read a bill or heard of a bill so grotesque in terms, evil in its purposes and
vicious in its possible consequences as this bill would be if enacted." Hearings on
Food, Drugs, and Cosmetics Before a Subcomm. of the Senate Comm. on Commerce, 73d Cong., 2d Sess. 172 (1933). The Drug, Chemical, and Allied Trade
Section of the New York Board of Trade proclaimed: "The 'Tugwell' Food and
Drug Bill is anti-NRA. It will seriously affect employment and morale in the
industries indicated. It will put thousands of men and women out of work. It
will close dozens of manufacturing plants and hundreds of stores. It will hurt
thousands. It will help none." *Id.* at 471. *See* Hart, *supra* at 1264–65.

[18] 15 U.S.C. § 1451 (Supp. 1967).

[19] "[T]he battle ended in victory for the food manufacturers." A. Mowbray,
supra note 14, at 5.

to control "consumer commodities," broadly defined by Section 1459 to include:

> any food, drug, device, or cosmetic . . . and any other article, product, or commodity . . . customarily produced or distributed for sale through retail sales agencies or instrumentalities for consumption by individuals, or use by individuals for purposes of personal care or in the performance of services ordinarily rendered within the household, and which usually is consumed or expended in the course of such consumption or use. . . .[20]

Among goods specifically excluded from regulation are meat, poultry, tobacco products, and rat poison.

Section 1454 vests regulatory power in the Secretary of Health, Education, and Welfare, when the consumer commodity is a food, drug, device, or cosmetic, or the Federal Trade Commission, if it is not. These authorities are directed by Section 1453 to promulgate regulations providing that:

> **1.** The commodity shall bear a label specifying the identity of the commodity and the name and place of business of the manufacturer, packer, or distributor;
>
> **2.** The net quantity of contents (in terms of weight, measure, or numerical count) shall be separately and accurately stated in a uniform location upon the principal display panel of that label. . . .[21]

Additional paragraphs seek to avoid consumer confusion through establishing standards of clarity. Thus quantities contained "shall appear in conspicuous and easily legible type in distinct contrast . . . with other matter on the package," [22] and "shall be so placed that the lines of printed matter . . . are generally parallel to the base on which the package rests as it is designed to be displayed. . . ." [23] In some cases decimal fractions of a pound may not be carried out to more than two places.[24]

---

[20] 15 U.S.C. § 1459 (Supp. 1967).
[21] 15 U.S.C. § 1453(1)–(2) (Supp. 1967).
[22] *Id.* § 1453(3)(B).
[23] *Id.* § 1453(3)(D).
[24] "I remember telling [my mother's mother, Lady Stanley of Alderley] that I had grown 2½ inches in the last seven months, and that at that rate I should grow 4⅖ inches in a year. 'Don't you know,' she said, 'that you should never talk about any fractions except halves and quarters?—it is pedantic!' " B. Russell, *Autobiography* 33 (1967).

If compliance is impracticable or unnecessary, Section 1454 allows the authorities to exempt classes of commodities from requirements of Section 1453. Additional duties include prevention of "nonfunctional-slack-fill of packages" when "necessary to prevent the deception of consumers or to facilitate value comparisons as to any consumer commodity. . . ." A package is to be considered "nonfunctionally slack-filled" only "if it is filled to substantially less than its capacity for reasons other than (A) protection of the contents of such package or (B) the requirements of machines used for enclosing the contents in such package." [25]

Section 1454(d) states:

> Whenever the Secretary of Commerce determines that there is undue proliferation of the weights, measures, or quantities in which any consumer commodity or reasonably comparable consumer commodities are being distributed in packages for sale at retail and such undue proliferation impairs the reasonable ability of consumers to make value comparisons with respect to such consumer commodity or commodities, he shall request manufacturers, packers, and distributors of the commodity or commodities to participate in the development of a voluntary product standard for such commodity or commodities under the procedures for the development of voluntary products standards established by the Secretary. . . . Such procedures shall provide adequate manufacturer, packer, distributor, and consumer representation.[26]

The absence of penalties for noncompliance assures that standardization programs are truly voluntary:

> (e) If (1) after one year after the date on which the Secretary of Commerce first makes the request of manufacturers, packers, and distributors to participate in the development of a voluntary product standard . . . he determines that such a standard will not be published . . . or (2) if such a standard is published and the Secretary of Commerce determines that it has not been observed, he shall promptly report such determination to the Congress with a statement of the efforts that have been made under the voluntary standards program and his recommendation as to whether Congress should enact legislation providing regulatory authority to deal with the situation in question.[27]

[25] 15 U.S.C. § 1454(c) (Supp. 1967).
[26] *Id.* § 1454(d).
[27] *Id.* § 1454(e).

Judicial review of regulations issued pursuant to the Act is authorized in Section 1455. Section 1456 declares misbranded, within the meaning of the Federal Food, Drug, and Cosmetic Act, "[a]ny consumer commodity which is a food, drug, device, or cosmetic . . . introduced or delivered for introduction into commerce" in disregard of established standards. Similarly, nonconformity in the packaging of other consumer commodities is to be deemed "an unfair or deceptive act or practice in commerce" in violation of Section 5(a) of the Federal Trade Commission Act.[28]

Theory

Unfortunately equilibrium as depicted in Figure 1 is seldom achieved. Preference patterns which govern purchases are a combination of basic wants and beliefs concerning the characteristics of various products. Product purchases in turn are the means by which basic wants are satisfied. Selection of that combination of goods represented by point *A* in Figure 1 is axiomatic: argument for any alternative choice normally degenerates to an assertion that the relevant indifference curves should be differently drawn.[29] The problem is that point *A* generally

---

[28] 15 U.S.C. § 45(a).

[29] The problem is of course much more complex. *See, e.g.,* Richter, "Revealed Preference Theory," 34 *Econometrica* 635 (1966). Modern discussions of consumer behavior need not formulate a refutable concept of satisfaction:

> Neoclassical "utility" was a kind of economic ether: an element whose assumed existence was merely a convenient medium for the analytical transmission of the observable phenomena of consumer choice. Since other means have proved capable of yielding the same predictions of these phenomena, the assumption of its existence is simply not needed. To assert this is not to deny that operational theorems about consumer behavior can be obtained from the neoclassical theory, nor that they can be tested against reality. We may merely derive most of these theorems without this subjective ether.

R. Kuenne, *The Theory of General Economic Equilibrium* 54 (1963). Enjoyment as a goal is itself not unobjectionable:

> Suppose that it were discovered that a state of pleasure is always associated with a particular kind of space-time pattern of electromagnetic field, or other physical system, and that we were capable of producing such patterns in the laboratory. . . . Would we be justified in spending a large part of the world's resources in producing pleasure-fields of high intensity? . . . Should we breed billions of rats and supply them each with a pleasure-producing machine? Good, "A Problem for the Hedonist," in *The Scientist Speculates —An Anthology of Partly-Baked Ideas* 199, 200 (I. Good ed. 1962).

As an alternative to altruistic hedonism that author suggests as a possible goal "that we should maximise the chance that the human race should be immortal." *Id.* at 200.

does not represent an optimum with respect to the satisfaction of underlying desires.

The assumption of perfect information required by the competitive model is obviously unrealistic. In a recent test, 33 young married women with at least 1 year of college and 1 year of regular shopping experience were given nearly 2½ minutes per item to select 20 best buys among items typically stocked by supermarkets. They chose incorrectly 43 percent of the time, spending an average of almost 10 percent more than necessary. Nevertheless, "the average shopper sweeps past the 8,000 products found in the store and buys 32 items in 15 to 18 minutes. . . ." [30]

The merchant is of course more interested in selling his product than in creating a knowledgeable noncustomer. A. C. Fuller, founder of the Fuller Brush Company, stated:

> The American housewife is an intelligent buyer. . . . The greatest safeguard she has . . . is in shopping around from store to store. . . .
>
> This shopping impulse arises the moment she considers buying anything, and the house-to-house salesman *must stifle it,* if he can. He is giving his customer no opportunity to compare values or to postpone buying. "Do it now," he tells her, "I won't be back this way for a couple of months." She buys, when she buys, against

---

[30] 112 Cong. Rec. 11,507 (daily ed. June 2, 1966). *See id.* at 12,169–72. Potato chips may be purchased in packages of 71 different weights, all under 3½ pounds. Barber, "Government and the Consumer," 64 *Mich. L. Rev.* 1203, 1229 n.76 (1966). "A cursory review of packaged salted nuts in a neighborhood supermarket turned up two brands of different varieties, packed in net weights of 2⅛, 2¾, 3⅜, 4, 4¼, 5¼, 5⅜, 5½, 6, 6⅜, 7, 7½, 8, and 11 ounces, and all of them priced to end in 'nines'—at 29, 39, 49, or 59 cents a package." C. Bell, *Consumer Choice in the American Economy.* New York: Random House, 1967, p. 335.

Since inspection is normally cursory, advertisers frequently attempt to distinguish their product from those of competitors by stressing as implicitly unique qualities which all brands share.

"Platformate is the ingredient which Shell says puts more mileage into the gasoline gallon. What Shell did not say is that Platformate, or its equivalent, is present in virtually every gasoline refined. When we asked about this, Shell spokesman said only: 'We have never claimed that Platformate was an exclusive ingredient.' " Statement in Program on Gasoline Produced by National Educational Television, Dec. 1966, *quoted in* Sloane, *Advertising: Platformate Fuels German Tiff,* N.Y. *Times,* July 12, 1967, at 53, col. 3.

an inner voice of discretion which tells her to wait until she can compare values.[31]

Packaging is definitely an important instrument of persuasion: "I'm like a child. If you fix things up pretty, I'll buy them."[32] Opportunities for manipulation are not disregarded: "[T]hree motivating factors for a successful packaging program are consumer needs, desires and weaknesses. 'Consumer weakness includes the embellishments assigned to a package. . . . They add little or nothing to the functional aspects of the package, nothing to the product, but to a large measure they create the impulse for purchasing.' "[33]

Unwillingness to seek information before purchase often seems condemned as almost immoral indifference on the part of the individual.[34] A possible consequence of such an attitude is the assertion that if consumers are foolish enough to purchase blindly they do not deserve legislation which attempts to relieve them of the consequences of their stupidity. Such an approach advocates a needless sacrifice of welfare. Also, it frequently disregards the fact that information, an economic good like any other, can usually be acquired only through relinquishment of some alternative value. Information concerning the optimal level of information one should seek is likewise not costless.[35]

[31] Fuller, "Where Are We Headed in House-to-House Selling?," *Magazine of Bus.* 52 (1927), 703, 705, *quoted in* Note, "Consumer Legislation and the Poor," *Yale L.J.* 76 (1967) 45.

[32] Statement by a housewife, *quoted in* Nelson, "Seven Principles in Image Formation," 26 *J. Marketing* 67, 69 (1962), *reprinted in Consumer Behavior and the Behavioral Sciences* 365, 366 (S. Britt ed. 1966).

[33] *Printers' Ink,* Oct. 18, 1963, at 20.

[34] "If anyone is so foolish as to enter into an agreement such as this, I do not know that his case can be considered harsh." Statement by a British judge, *quoted in* M. Mayer, *The Lawyers* 283 (1967). Admittedly ignorance frequently appears unwarranted:
"Reporter: Twiggy, do you know what happened at Hiroshima?
Twiggy: Where's that?
Reporter: In Japan.
Twiggy: No. I've never heard of it. What happened there?
Reporter: A hundred thousand people died on the spot, all at the same time.
Twiggy: Oh, God! When did you say it happened? Where? Hiroshima? But that's ghastly. A hundred thousand dead? It's frightful. Men are mad."
"Seventh Annual Dubious Achievement Awards for 1967," *Esquire* (Jan., 1968), 49, 53.

[35] Pathetic examples of consumer inefficiency abound:
"Eight years ago, Mrs. Phillips sent a radio to be repaired. The bill came to $8.90. Mrs. Phillips refused to pay—she thought it was going to cost only $1. She sent her 20-year-old son to get the radio back. But John, an easy

Lack of full knowledge of product characteristics will normally
prevent a consumer from acquiring that combination of goods of greatest benefit to him. An error in estimating the characteristics of a
product will lead to preference patterns with respect to goods which
do not accurately reflect preferences as to qualities. In Figure 2 the
individual is shown initially to have achieved an equilibrium with
respect to goods identical to that of Figure 1. He has selected that
combination of products represented by point A, where indifference
curve I_2 is tangent to budget constraint xy. If he is only imperfectly
aware of the characteristics of the products, however, he will generally
not have succeeded in satisfying his more fundamental desires as fully
as his income permits.

The purpose of the Fair Packaging and Labeling Act and similar
statutes is to facilitate attainment of a higher level of consumer satisfaction. To accomplish this the government seeks to assure a supply
of information which permits an individual to evaluate more correctly
the goods available for purchase. Reduction of error in perceiving the
qualities associated with various products will transform the preference pattern depicted in Figure 2, resulting in a set of revised indifference curves including, say, I^R_1 and I^R_2. Point A, now situated on I^R_1,
is no longer an equilibrium position. Now the consumer will choose
that combination of goods represented by point B, where a higher indifference curve, I^R_2, is tangent to the budget constraint. The consumer's welfare has increased, since purchases now more nearly satisfy
his basic desires.

---

mark for a fast sales talk, came home with a new radio, for which he had
agreed to pay in $1.25 weekly installments. The radio-shop owner, chubby
A. M. Pearson, got Mrs. Phillips to sign the contract.

When Mrs. Phillips fell into arrears on her payments, Radioman Pearson
went to court and got a judgment which ordered her to give back the radio
and pay him $81.50 in court costs and collection fees.

Mrs. Phillips gave up the radio, but could not pay the rest. In August
1943, Pearson had the city marshall sell off Mrs. Phillips' assets—her house
and lot—to satisfy the court order. Pearson was the only bidder, and he
offered $26.50. A year later, as required by law, the marshall delivered the
deed to Pearson. During these twelve months, Mrs. Phillips could have kept
her home by paying the $26.50 plus a $25 marshall's fee. She says nobody
told her that.

Last week Pearson had the unrepaired radio, the "new" radio which he
sold her son, a still unsatisfied claim for $55, and the house and lot. (He
was willing to let Mrs. Phillips stay on—at $10 a week rent.)" *Time* (March
28, 1949), 23.
See also "Luck of Clarence Jackson," *Time* (Sept. 1, 1967), 64.

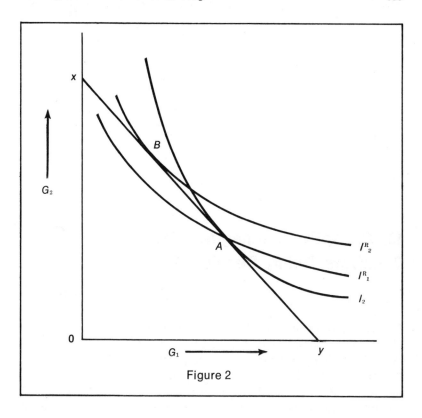

Figure 2

Conclusion

The Fair Packaging and Labeling Act is an attempt to increase the value of community consumption by restricting the freedom of the producer. As such it is based on reasoning antithetical to the principle of nonintervention of classical economic theory. In this article I have attempted to demonstrate that its effect will be not to impede attainment of ideal equilibrium but rather to increase welfare by tending to correct imperfections in the market mechanism. Thus, it correctly implements the overriding Smithian standard that "[c]onsumption is the sole end and purpose of all production; and the interest of the producer ought to be attended to, only so far as it may be necessary for promoting that of the consumer. The maxim is so perfectly self-evident, that it would be absurd to attempt to prove it." [36]

[36] Adam Smith, *An Inquiry into the Nature and Causes of the Wealth of Nations,* Modern Library, 1937, p. 625.

13. Deceptive Packaging: Are the Deceivers Being Deceived?

James C. Naylor [1]

The tremendous emphasis placed upon packaging as a wedge to success in the consumer market in recent years has resulted in certain packaging techniques which have been questioned on an ethical basis. The most outstanding of these is the practice known as "deceptive packaging." Briefly defined, deceptive packaging involves a deliberate attempt to mislead the consumer regarding some aspect of the product (usually quantity) by using packages specifically designed to convey a false impression concerning this product attribute (e.g., making the package oversize). The extent to which this practice has become prevalent is difficult to state, although the fact that a Senate subcommittee was formed to inquire solely into this particular problem would attest to its frequency of occurrence.

From the point of view of consumer psychology, the problem is not primarily one of ethics, but rather of determining what effect deceptive packaging has upon the consumer, per se. First, does he realize that he is being deceived? Second, what is the effect of the deception

[1] The author wishes to acknowledge the data collection efforts of G. Croft Henry, John Mitchell, and Don Shumaker, members of the research field team.

Reprinted from the *Journal of Applied Psychology*, Vol. 46 (December, 1962), 393–398. © 1962 by The American Psychological Association and reproduced by permission.

upon his perception of the product (a) if he feels he has been deceived, or (b) if he is not aware of any deception? The purpose of this study was to experimentally investigate a case of deliberate deceptive packing in an attempt to provide answers to some of these questions.

Method

The independent variable chosen for study was package quantity. Through the cooperation of a local potato chip manufacturer, it was possible to obtain 144 experimental twin packs which were filled to specified weight requirements. The normal contents of a regular twin pack in terms of weight was nine ounces. The experimental twin packs were of three weights: nine ounces (control packs), eight ounces, and seven ounces. The experimental packs were all filled with chips from the same batch in order to assure equal treatment. All were packaged in regular twin pack containers in a normal manner. The only difference between the experimental packs was in terms of quantity as determined by weight. Two retail outlets were selected for distribution: a medium-sized independent grocery located in a suburban area (Store A) and a large chain store market (Store B) in more metropolitan surroundings.

PROCEDURE. Because of possible ill feeling which might have been generated toward the donor company, it was not feasible to have the experimental packs actually purchased by the consumer. Thus, a procedure was adopted in which the experimental packs were given, free of charge, to any person willing to participate in the experiment. An observer was stationed with a supply of the seven-, eight-, and nine-ounce experimental packs within view of the normal store display. Any consumers who "purchased" (i.e., clearly selected from the display) a twin pack of the donor brand were approached by the observer and asked as to their willingness to cooperate in a university study of consumer preferences. They were told that they would receive a sample pack free of charge on the condition that they were to "compare the contents of the two packs (regular versus experimental) in terms of personal preference." This preference would be obtained by a follow-up ten-minute interview in their own home within three days.

If the customer was agreeable to this, he or she was then given one of the experimental packs as a gift (the three weights were distributed in random order) and a time and day for the subsequent interview were agreed upon.

A reminder slip with the time and date for the interview was made out and stapled to the sample (free) pack. This slip also served to provide the basis for differentiation between the sample and the regular pack.

Distribution of packs was done only between the hours of 4:00 P.M. and 9:00 P.M. on Thursdays, Fridays, and Saturdays. Twenty-four experimental packs were distributed every week—eight of each weight. This procedure was continued for a six-week period. To prevent staleness of the experimental chips, they were obtained from the donor once every two weeks in lots of 48 (16 of each weight). Thus, over the six-week period a total of 144 experimental packs was distributed—48 of each weight class. The first three weeks of distribution was in Store A, the remainder in Store B.

INTERVIEW.   The interview itself consisted of having the consumer fill out a short, nine-term questionnaire (see Table 1). The first five items were for the purpose of obtaining information desired by the donor company, and Questions six through nine were designed to obtain preference information as a function of perceived deception. Any requests for additional insight into the experiment on the part of the consumer at the time of the interview were refused. However, a promise to mail a short explanation at the conclusion of all interviews was made where desired. All such requests were subsequently honored.

INTERVIEWERS.   The distribution of packs and the subsequent interviewing of consumers were done by a three-man research team consisting of a senior psychology graduate student and two undergraduate psychology majors.

Results

Sample characteristics

Only six customers declined to participate in the survey when approached by the observer, making the total acceptances 144 out of 150. This represents a loss of only 4%. Out of the 144 customers who agreed to participate, however, 26 were lost during the interview phase—primarily due to absences as a function of summer vacation.

Table 1. Sample questionnaire used in the interview

AGE _____

                              SAMPLE _____

SEX _____

1. Was this the first time you have purchased this brand?   Yes ____ No ____
2. Do you usually purchase this brand?   Yes ____ No ____
3. Do you expect to purchase this brand again?   Yes ____ No ____
4. What did you like most about this brand? _____
5. What (if anything) did you like least about this brand? _____
6. Please circle the point on the scale that expresses your reaction to each pack.

    a. How well did you like the contents of the regular pack?

       1   2   3   4   5   6   7   8   9
      —|—|—|—|—|—|—|—|—
      terrible   poor   average   good   excellent

    b. How well did you like the contents of the sample pack?

       1   2   3   4   5   6   7   8   9
      —|—|—|—|—|—|—|—|—
      terrible   poor   average   good   excellent

7. If both were available for purchase the next time you went to the store, which would you buy?

    ____ sample pack
    ____ regular pack
    ____ either
    ____ neither

8. List three words that describe the two packs.
    a. Sample pack: _____
    b. Regular pack: _____

9. Which pack had the most in it?
    ____ regular pack
    ____ sample pack
    ____ same

Table 2. Breakdown of consumer sample in terms of age and sex

| Criterion | Experimental group | | | |
	9 ounces	8 ounces	7 ounces	Total
Age M	36.7	37.5	38.7	37.6
Age SD	10.7	12.3	7.7	10.2
Male	6	4	5	15
Female	35	31	33	99
N	41	35	38	114

Thus, the final data sample consisted of 118 consumers. Table 2 shows the age and sex characteristics for the 114 people who responded to these two interview questions.

As indicated in the table, the sample was predominantly female. A chi square test was performed on the sample frequencies to determine if the relative proportion of males and females differed for the three experimental groups. The results clearly indicated that they did not ($\chi^2 = .167$, $df = 2$, $p > .99$). In addition, a simple analysis of variance test was made to test for age differences. The mean ages for the three experimental groups were not significantly different ($F = .04$, $df = 2/113$).

In order to discuss the results of deceptive packaging, it was necessary to have some indication of the extent to which the weight shortages in the sample packs were perceived by the consumers. Table 3 shows the frequencies of the responses to the categories of Question nine on the questionnaire. Regardless of experimental pack weight,

Table 3. Frequency of people judging experimental or regular pack as heaviest as a function of experimental pack weight
($N = 118$)

| Weight of experimental pack | Pack judged heaviest | | |
	Experimental	Regular	Equal
9 ounces	9	4	30
8 ounces	5	8	22
7 ounces	7	8	25

Note. $-\chi^2 = 3.121$, $df = 4$, $p < .50$.

the majority of the responders indicated the two packs as being equal in contents. A chi square test of significance showed no significant shift in proportions as the contents of the experimental pack was decreased ($\chi^2 = 3.121$, $df = 4$, $p < .50$).

It was possible to obtain two judgment scores for each person—his judgment for the regular pack and his judgment for the experimental pack—from Question six. A difference score was then computed for each individual using the following formula: Experimental Pack Scale Value—Regular Pack Scale Value.

This resulted in a score indicating the degree to which the contents of the experimental pack were preferred over those of the regular pack. The mean of these scores was then computed for each group (see Figure 1). When the two packs were of equal weight a marked preference was indicated for the experimental pack. When the experimental pack was one ounce less, however, the preference for it was

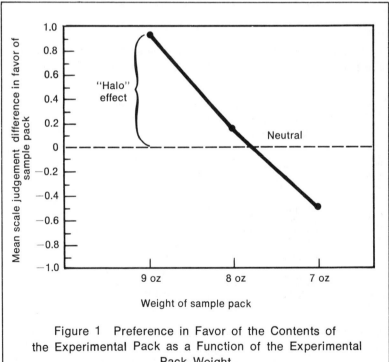

Figure 1   Preference in Favor of the Contents of the Experimental Pack as a Function of the Experimental Pack Weight

only slight, and when there was a two-ounce difference the regular pack was substantially preferred. An analysis of variance of these judgment differences (see Table 4) indicated that the decrease in preference for the experimental pack as a function of its weight was statistically significant at the .05 level ($F = 4.58$, $df = 2/115$).

Table 4. Analysis of variance of the differences in Thurstone judgments of preference between regular and experimental packs as a function of experimental pack weight

($N = 118$)

Source	df	MS	F
Weight	2	22.0	4.58*
Error	115	4.8	
Total	117		

* $p < .05$.

A second measure of the effect of weight on preference was obtained by analyzing the responses to Question seven. Table 5 shows

Table 5. Distribution of predicted next purchase choice as a function of experimental pack weight

($N = 118$)

Weight of sample	Predicted choice		
	Buy experimental	Buy either	Buy regular
9 ounces	22	2	11
8 ounces	13	12	6
7 ounces	12	8	15

Note. $-\chi^2 = 10.203$, $df = 4$, $p < .05$.

the distribution of responses to the alternatives presented by this question. The response alternative "neither" only attracted a total of four responses and was therefore eliminated in the analysis. When the packs were of equal weight, the majority of the consumers stated that, if given a choice, they would purchase the experimental chips. With a one-ounce weight differential the plurality response changed to "would buy either," and with a two-ounce difference the plurality response was in favor of the regular pack. A chi square test indicated that this change in preference was significant at the .05 level ($\chi^2 = 10.203$, $df = 4$).

A third analysis of package preference was obtained through the descriptive adjectives applied to each pack in Question eight. A total of 109 different adjectives or adjective phrases were used by the consumers in describing the two packs. These phrases were given to ten judges (psychology graduate students) who rated each of them for favorability on a five-point Thurstone rating scale. The phrases and their resulting mean scale values are shown in Table 6. The analysis of variance reliability for the ratings was .96, and the difference between rater zero points was significant at the .01 level ($F = 23.95$, $df = 108/792$).

Each person was then assigned two mean scores on the basis of the adjectives used to describe the regular and experimental packs using the favorability scale value for each adjective. The difference between these two means was then computed as follows: ($\overline{X}$ adjective scale value for experimental pack) $-$ ($\overline{X}$ adjective scale value for regular pack).

This resulted in an adjective preference score for the experimental pack for each person. The mean of these adjective preference scores was then computed for each group (see Figure 2). The same pattern of preference as a function of experimental pack weight was found with the adjective values as had been found previously with the Thurstone judgments. As the weight of the experimental pack contents was decreased, the preference for that pack was also decreased. The analysis of variance on the means in Figure 2 indicated that they were not significantly different from one another ($F = .34$), $df = 2/115$) even though the differences were in the expected direction.

Discussion

Deception in packaging can occur in two general ways. First, a consumer may be deceived at time of purchase and subsequently discover this deception at the time of product consumption. Such a case may be considered a "purchase deception." Second, a consumer may be deceived at time of purchase and not discover the deception at all.

Table 6. Scale values of descriptive adjectives used to describe sample and regular packs

Mean scale value	Words or phrases	Mean scale value	Words or phrases
4.6	Crispy, Delicious	3.0	Brown, Not burnt, Palatable, Salty, Smooth
4.5	Very tasty, Crisper		
4.4	Very very good, Very fresh, Excellent, Superb	2.9	More tender, Saltier, Shorter, Same
4.3	Scrumptious, Very good, Fresh	2.8	Not too oily, Brown edges
		2.7	Milder, Small, Not as large
4.2	Tastier, Crisp (as usual), Tasty	2.6	Not as thin, Unsized, Greasy but good, Less salty
4.1	Always good	2.5	Stronger taste, Average, Rough, Heavier, Too thin
4.0	Good taste, More crisp, Crisp, Full of goodness	2.4	Darker
3.9	Good color, Flavorful, Better flavor, Appetizing	2.3	Too well done, Ordinary, Thicker
3.8	Lighter, Good, Flavorsome, Good smell, Better taste	2.2	Not tender, Cheesy taste, Too brown
3.7	Better, Clean taste, Crunchier	2.1	Too small, Not enough shortening, Too salty
3.6	Wholesome, Satisfying, Good size, Richer, Crisp edges	2.0	Less flavorful, Heavy texture, Not very good, Not as crisp
3.5	(None)	1.9	Oily, Burnt, Green, Scanty amount
3.4	Good oil, Not greasy, Tangy, Not too salty	1.8	Hard, Not crisp, Unseasoned
3.3	Well done, Large, Thinner, Uniform size, Thin, Greaseless, Smooth texture	1.7	Flat
		1.6	A little greasy, Mealy
3.2	Digestible, Bigger, Lighter color	1.5	Greasy, Undesirable
		1.4	Slightly stale, Greasy taste
3.1	Done, Less oily, Dryer	1.3	Bitter, Limp, Tasteless, Too greasy

The latter may be considered a "consumption deception." Since the data from Question nine indicated that even following the actual consuming of the chips people were not aware of any shortages, the results of the study may be considered as applying to a consumption deception and not to a purchase deception.

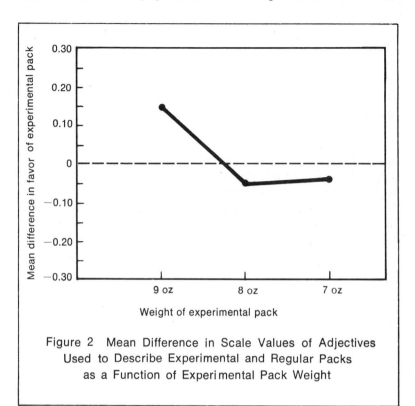

Figure 2   Mean Difference in Scale Values of Adjectives
Used to Describe Experimental and Regular Packs
as a Function of Experimental Pack Weight

From an ethical point of view the consumption deception is the most severe, since the consumer, unaware of anything amiss, will supposedly continue to be satisfied with his purchase. With a purchase deception, however, he is overtly aware of having been taken advantage of and is thus able to modify his subsequent buying behavior to avoid a repeat deception. The results of the several preference indices computed in this study, however, indicate that even in the case of a consumption deception there is created a dissatisfaction with the product, even though the source of dissatisfaction cannot be identified by the consumer! As the contents of the experimental pack were decreased, there was a related decrease in product preference for the experimental pack. This occurred for all three indices—significantly so for two of them. The nonsignificance in the third case may have been a function of limited variance due to the use of a five-point Thurstone scale in scaling the adjectives.

The fact that the experimental pack was markedly preferred with all indices when it was the same weight as the regular pack was probably a function of (*a*) the fact that it was free, and (*b*) an aura of "If it's something new, it must be better" surrounding the free pack. The end result was to produce a halo effect (see Figure 3) which accounted for the experimental pack preference.

If indeed the answers to Question seven were true predictors of future buying decisions, the fact that a consumption deception had occurred would result in a decrease in purchases for the pack having a weight shortage, and this decrease would be related to the degree of deception involved. While such extrapolation of buying behavior on the basis of questionnaire responses is sometimes dangerous, the implications should be obvious to those engaged or planning to engage in a program of package deception.

Part Three
The Purchase Transaction

Introduction

The consumer information-gathering and decision-making process culminates in a purchase transaction. The situation in which the transaction is imbedded can involve fraudulent manipulation and considerable pressure. In such situations, usually associated with major purchases, consumer decisions can be precipitated which are undesirable from the consumer's viewpoint and are soon regretted. In extreme cases, when consumers are overtly manipulated under pressure, it becomes clear that the freedom to choose is effectively non-existent. Magnuson and Carper graphically describe five major deceptive selling schemes. These are extreme deceptions that need to be controlled. Even when the case is clear, however, it is most difficult to generate and implement legal machinery for dealing with the problem as Magnuson and Carper illustrate.

Transaction specifics, such as price and the presence of promotions such as stamps and games, are another source of consumerism issues. When the purchase is minor or habitual, often these transaction details are not important enough to influence the decision process. In such cases, the consumer is particularly vulnerable.

Price is a central aspect of the transaction and is usually and ideally determined by competitive forces. Sometimes, however, there exist artificial barriers to price competition that unduly limit the range of choice of the consumer. Burack examines the price structure in the drug industry and finds that prices seem artificially high due to such barriers. He analyzes contributing factors and suggests possible corrective measures. It is often assumed that one can influence price by bargaining with a seller. The tough bargainers should get better prices. Jung subjects this idea to hard empirical analysis.

The use of promotions is also related to the consumer's freedom of choice. Is there a satisfactory alternative to participating in a promotion? Does the trading stamp saver have an adequate economic choice at the redemption center? Bell critically examines these questions and others, and Beem and Isaacson reply.

A. Selling Practices

14. Caveat Emptor

Senator Warren G. Magnuson
and Jean Carper

One evening, two men in a Cadillac paid a call on an elderly couple
in a small town in Arkansas. One of the men, a Mr. G., president of
the Superior Improvement Company in Little Rock, presented himself
to the couple as an important executive affiliated with Alcoa Aluminum Company. He told the couple that after a careful examination of
their house he had chosen it to be a model home as part of a new
advertising campaign to sell aluminum siding. Photographs, he said,
would be taken of the house "before" and "after" the siding was applied and would be featured in beautiful brochures. Salesmen would
bring prospective customers to view the house, and for every sale made
as a result, Mr. G. promised to give the couple a commission of $100.
When urged to sign an agreement, the couple protested that their
house was old and they were thinking of using their savings to rebuild.
But the promises of Mr. G. were irresistible. He asserted he was giving
them the siding at $1,000 below cost, cheaper than they could get it
anywhere, and that with the commissions their house would be trans-
formed into a showplace of beauty for virtually nothing. "Well, then,
he said one thing that kind of struck me," the homeowner later re-

Reprinted from the book "The Dark Side of the Marketplace" by Senator Warren G. Magnuson and Jean Carper. © 1968 by Warren G. Magnuson and Jean
Carper. Published by Prentice-Hall, Inc., Englewood Cliffs, New Jersey.

called. "He said to say a little prayer and pray to the Lord and let Him guide us as to whether to sign the contract." Touched by this display of humility, the man and woman signed a contract for $1,480 and gave Mr. G. a down-payment check for $200.

By the next morning, the couple was no longer so spellbound by Mr. G.'s promises. Skeptical, they checked around and discovered they could buy aluminum siding for much less than Mr. G.'s "bargain factory prices." The homeowner, realizing he had been fleeced, tried to stop payment on the check, but was told that one of Mr. G.'s representatives had been there that morning as the bank opened and cashed the check. Repeated attempts to reach Mr. G. by phone at his Little Rock office were futile. He was always "out," and, said the homeowner, "His secretary kind of laughed like it was a big joke." Finally, in desperation and worry over his wife's ill health, which had been aggravated by the transaction, the man borrowed money from a bank and paid off the bill in full. He was informed by a lawyer that if he refused to make payments, the finance company Mr. G. had sold the contract to could sue him—and collect. The workmen had already tacked up the siding, such as it was. And the contract he had signed was legally binding, regardless of the verbal misrepresentations.

Hundreds of persons in rural Arkansas, Tennessee and Kentucky, since 1960, have been seduced by Mr. G's prayers and phony promises into paying exorbitant prices for shoddy workmanship and poor quality materials. Mr. G. claimed his aluminum was manufactured by Alcoa, Kaiser or Reynolds Aluminum Co.; it was in truth an off-brand, most of it shipped from Illinois. He told customers that it would "never chip, crack, fade or soak up water, would never need paint and had a lifetime guarantee." To many a homeowner's dismay, the siding was not applied by "factory-trained personnel" as promised, but sometimes by local teenagers. It fell off; the caulking was not done properly; the upper layer of finish could be rubbed off with the sweep of a hand. Some homes were left unfinished, aluminum and trash piled high in the yard. One man's house was such a shambles within a year, pock-marked by the fallen siding, that he needed a completely new siding job. The only thing he had bought from Mr. G. was a $2,400 debt.

Mr. G. and his salesmen preyed shamelessly on the illiterate, the poor, the old and the guileless. One man said Mr. G.'s salesmen kept him up most of the night begging him to sign a note; weary and fatigued, he finally did. An elderly Negro was coerced into putting his

X mark on a contract. Many were induced to part with their pensions and Social Security checks. Others said they were tricked into signing mortgages on their homes, and one couple swore their names were forged to a promissory note. In this brutal marketplace, there was no compunction about tacking aluminum siding on a shack in the fork of a dust-covered road and proclaiming it a "showplace."

Many people understood that because of the $100 bonus, they would have to pay little or nothing for the siding. Instead, once their names were on the contract, few homeowners ever saw Mr. G. or any of his salesmen again. No one brought prospective customers to view the renovated house as the salesmen had promised. Some people waited and waited, actually stayed home for days on end, fearing to leave the house, waiting for the customers that never came, until their hope turned to anguish.

Many were left with disastrous debts. A young schoolteacher signed a contract with a total price of $3,650. By the time monthly payments were figured out—84 of them at $73.45 each—he discovered he had agreed to pay $6,132 over a period of seven years. Horrified, he borrowed money from his credit union and managed to persuade the finance company to let him pay off the debt; the company insisted, however, that he pay them more than $1,000 interest for use of the money for "less than a month."

Another couple signed a contract with Mr. G. for what they thought was about $2,000 and a mortgage on their house. Said a government lawyer: "When they sat down that night and in their sober judgment figured out what that was going to cost them over a period of 84 months—84 payments—they were not going to pay $2,000; it would be some $4,000 to $4,400. That fellow attempted to commit suicide." Another pensioned purchaser came home and found his elderly wife unconscious on the bed. She recovered but confessed she had been so worried over the transaction with Mr. G. and the prospect of losing their home that she drank Lysol.

Early in 1964, the Federal Trade Commission issued a complaint against Mr. G. and his company, charging him with a dozen "unfair and deceptive practices." After hearings, he was ordered by the FTC to stop using such sales practices in interstate commerce. Mr. G. chose to take his case through the courts, and finally in early 1967, when the Supreme Court refused to hear his case, he was forced to comply with the FTC ruling. (It is interesting to note that the primary basis for Mr. G.'s defense was not innocence of deceptive selling, for he admitted that he had promised bonuses to prospective buyers. His main contention was that he was not engaging in interstate commerce and that, therefore, the FTC had no jurisdiction over his actions. The FTC can intervene only when it can be proved that a misdoer is operating across state lines.)

It might appear that Mr. G. was forced by the FTC to stop using his lucrative, deceptive sales pitches (his annual volume of business was estimated at $400,000). On the contrary, Mr. G. shows every intention of carrying on. He mapped out for the FTC his blueprint for future business: he will not advertise in interstate newspapers or other media, will not use the mails to send out brochures and will not make sales to residents in other states. In other words, he pledges not to work his deceptive arts on anyone, except, of course, the unlucky prospects he may find within the borders of Arkansas.

At this writing, Mr. G. is still in business, his Superior Improvement Company still in existence. If complaints received by the Better Business Bureau of Little Rock are accurate, his salesmen are still active in Arkansas, using misrepresentations and "questionable advertising and selling practices" to unload shoddy jobs and merchandise at unconscionable prices. Who is to stop him?

Although the Federal Trade Commission may be reluctant to admit it for fear of seeming to condone deceptive practices, the sorry truth in this matter is that as long as Mr. G.'s corporation scrupulously avoids interstate commerce, it can operate with impunity, free from FTC jurisdiction or intervention, no matter how blatantly dishonest the sales practices or how appalling to human sensibilities the amount of human misery left in their wake.

It is certain that the authorities of Arkansas, when informed of this company's intention to hide behind state lines out of the reach of the FTC will *want* to take measures to protect the residents of Arkansas. But the question is: will they be able to? Do they have the authority under existing state law? Although it is impossible to predict the outcome of any legal action—and some states have achieved surprising victories with the imaginative use of seemingly inapplicable laws—legal authorities advise me that Arkansas probably does not have the legal machinery necessary to fight companies like Mr. G.'s. Arkansas does not have a comprehensive law covering deceptive selling. It has only a variety of laws forbidding the use of certain deceptive practices to sell specific products, but aluminum siding is not among them. It is true that Arkansas, like other states, has criminal fraud and false pretenses statutes, resulting in fines or imprisonment for those adjudged guilty. But these statutes are a poor vehicle for preventing deceptive selling. Indictments under the statutes are exceedingly rare and convictions even rarer. As far as we know, neither Federal, nor state, nor any other known authority can under present law take action to protect the citizens of Arkansas against the gouging of companies like Mr. G.'s.

Although the case of Mr. G. is one of the most dramatic on record of how deceptive sellers can operate outside the reach of the law, it would be a mistake to believe that Arkansas is like the old Oklahoma Strip of the 1880's: the only place where robbers could operate without interference from the law. On the contrary, although Arkansas is uncommonly hampered by weak consumer protection laws, it is hardly unique. Consumer deception flourishes nearly everywhere in the country, quite often unimpeded—and sometimes even abetted—by the law. As Helen Nelson, former consumer counsel for the governor of California, has said: "More money is being taken from Americans at penpoint than by gunpoint and the pen often makes it legal."

Deceptive selling by the unscrupulous few in the business underworld is, in fact, our most serious form of theft. It cheats Americans of several billion dollars yearly, more than is lost through robbery, burglary, larceny, auto theft, embezzlement and forgery combined. Unlike the con men of yesterday who were often so heavy-handed that they offended the law, today's modern bandits of the marketplace are the masters of the light touch. With their insidious misrepresentations, silver-tongued lies, half-truths and exaggerated promises, these men can reach even deeper into our pockets without producing a rustle to disturb the law, or often the victim himself. From coast to coast we are exposed to their Pandora's box of selling tricks—some old, but handily adapted to modern circumstances, and some new, carefully devised to outwit the law.

Although these schemes are staggering in scope and diverse in their nature (the Better Business Bureau has identified 800 different varieties), they invariably have several things in common: they are lucrative, they are subtle and their purveyors rarely come in conflict with the law. According to a nationwide survey for the President's Commission on Law Enforcement and Administration of Justice in 1966, nine out of every ten victims of consumer fraud do not even bother to report it to the police. Fifty percent of the victimized felt they had no right or duty to complain; 40% believed the authorities could not be effective or would not want to be bothered; 10% were confused about where to report.

It is startling to consider that the vast majority of Americans victimized by consumer fraud feel that the law can or will do nothing to help them; but it is even more startling to realize that in many instances those victims are absolutely correct. Our legal remedies against consumer deception and fraud, some of which were adequate 50, even 20, years ago, are now so outdated as to leave the consumer nearly helpless. Under our present laws, with rare exceptions, we neither give relief to the victimized consumer nor effectively halt the swindlers.

The scheme so successfully used by Mr. G. is but one of five major schemes on which today's pyramid of deceptive selling rests. Although Mr. G. combined several techniques, his primary deception consisted of convincing homeowners that by making their home a "model," he was giving them "a special low price." (The phony "special price" is also used to sell a variety of items, including encyclopedias, automobiles, carpeting, roofing and jewelry.) According to the Federal Trade Commission, the four other schemes that are currently most responsible for fleecing American consumers are *bait and switch advertising,* including "lo-balling," *chain-referral selling,* the *free gimmick* and the *fear-sell.*

Bait and Switch

Of these, the most troublesome to detect and curtail is bait and switch advertising, in which the merchant advertises goods *which he has no intention of selling* in order to switch the prospective buyer to another item, invariably higher priced and with a greater margin of profit. Not only is bait advertising perfectly legal in most states, but it is so subtle that most victims are never aware that they have been deceived. We all see bait advertising continually, but probably few of us are aware of its insidious calculated nature.

Typically, this is the way the scheme works. A housewife in Alexandria, Virginia, recently noticed this advertisement in the classified section of a newspaper:

SEW MACH.—1965 Singer
Touch and Sew * * *
Reposs. Balance, $86.40
New Mach. Guar. Dealer,
Credit Dept. * * *

When the salesman arrived at her home, following her telephone call to the company, she was appalled by the machine he carried. He set it down on the table and said: "Well, this is the machine." It was not the new one described in the ad. Rather, as the woman put it, it was "an old beaten-up Singer about 25 or 30 years old. . . . I'd seen machines in better shape at rummage sales." It was battered, scratched, and was a straight-stitch machine with no attachment. "I wouldn't have given more than $5 or $6 for it," she said. Noting her disappointment and admitting his "mistake," the salesman saved the day. He rushed to his car and brought in two sparkling, new, off-brand sewing machines priced at $289 and $365. The housewife chose the one for $289 and was given a discount because it was the "salesman's first day."

There were several glaring misrepresentations, designed to lure prospective customers, in this advertisement. The words "Reposs." (ostensibly standing for repossession) and "Balance" led the readers to believe the machines had been partially paid for by a previous purchaser and thus were being offered for a song. The signature "Credit Dept." created the same impression. In truth, the use of the Singer name was only a lure to support a full-time business of selling off-brand machines. This was proved by the fact that the dealer sold only two or three Singers a month, but spent $400 per month advertising them. Almost the total volume of his business was in the less well-known brand, the more expensive model to which customers were "switched."

Sometimes the salesman actually produced the advertised recent-model Singer, but then actively disparaged the "bait" by finding fault with it: "This machine is delicate and not functioning as it should." "We get a lot of complaints on these Singers." In most other instances, as in the case of the Alexandria housewife, the bait was so offensive that it had "built-in dissuaders," and prospects rejected it on sight. The way was then cleared for the salesman's pitch on the more profitable merchandise. In describing the subtlety of the approach, an FTC lawyer noted: "The prospective purchaser is led on without suspecting the insincerity of the salesman's presentation, and the switch is made to the higher-priced machine of a different make as though the transition were the suggestion of the prospect and not the salesman."

Lo-balling

A variation of bait advertising is lo-balling, and it is so new that the FTC used the term for the first time in 1967 in a case involving automobile transmissions. In lo-balling, the company advertises or promises a service at an outrageously low price and actually performs the work at the advertised price, but only as an enticement to get possession of the automobile (lo-balling to date has been almost exclusively associated with automobiles) so the company can gouge the owner for additional unneeded repairs.

The gist of the swindle is that customers are led to believe that by referring the names of acquaintances as prospective customers, they will have to pay nothing for a piece of merchandise, and very often will make money. For each friend who is sold, or who agrees to participate in the "advertising campaign," as it is invariably called, the victim is promised a commission. Salesmen frequently erase customers' doubts by telling them that 80% of those referred actually "participate" as proved by past experience. In truth, postal inspectors, by painstakingly searching through company records, have discovered that only about 5% of the referred actually sign up. And of course once they have sold the original customer, some companies don't bother to follow up the leads supplied, or to remit the commission if a referred friend does buy. This deceit is all the more cruel for it is being practiced on elderly people who find the lure of making a few pennies to augment their meager income irresistible.

Free Gimmick

Another pernicious type of selling which is sweeping the country is the "free gimmick," invariably accompanied by innumerable misrepresentations. It is doubtful that any American of any economic class is untouched by this scheme. A lawyer in New York whose wife was tricked into subscribing to three children's magazines under the impression that it was a "service" from the Board of Education recently wrote: "If wives of persons who are supposedly above average in education, sophistication, etc., and especially the wife of an attorney, can be so easily taken in, you can imagine what this person (a door-to-door saleswoman) must be able to do with less sophisticated persons."

The sales pitches are familiar: "This lovely x-cubic-foot freezer is yours absolutely free if you subscribe to our food-freezer plan." The food is usually low quality, overpriced, and the freezer is hardly free. The cost of the food more than covers the retail price of the freezer.

Fear-Sell

Perhaps no sales pitch has been around longer than the "fear-sell." Even the rulers of ancient countries were intimidated into buying amulets lest their souls be damned or they suffer a dreadful accident. In today's sophisticated marketplace, peddlers still make fortunes preying on people's fears. One woman wrote me she had four perfectly healthy maple trees felled by a wandering "tree surgeon," who told her they were rotten and could come crashing down on her house. Gangs of salesmen, according to the National Fire Protection Association, are scouring the country, displaying gruesome photographs of families burned to death in home fires. Their object is to sell home fire-alarm systems which are invariably outrageously priced and sometimes worthless.

Every spring, as regularly as the rain, reports the BBB, the phony chimney repairmen show up. They knock off a few bricks and claim the chimney is about to topple, or claim it is clogged and that the whole family is in imminent danger of dying from carbon monoxide poisoning. Some termite inspectors carry bugs which they plant in the wood, and then inform the alarmed homeowner that unless the "termites" are exterminated, the house will quickly deteriorate. Often the salesmen pose as government inspectors. That they extort millions of dollars from frightened Americans is well-documented.

A classic case is that of the Holland Furnace Company, which for thirty years conducted what Consumers Union branded "one of the most pernicious sales rackets in the country." Holland Furnace, based in Holland, Michigan, with 500 offices throughout the country and 5,000 employees, was the leading furnace-replacement firm in the nation. Through its "tear down and scare tactics" it victimized hundreds of thousands of Americans. Misrepresenting themselves as "furnace engineers" and "safety inspectors," the salesmen frequently dismantled a furnace, condemned it as hazardous and refused to reassemble it, stating they didn't want to be "accessories to murder." The salesmen were merciless. In New England, branch salesmen from one office sold an elderly infirm woman nine new furnaces in six years, for a total take of $18,000.

Defect in Our Laws

Why are we unable to control such deceptive practices and to prevent consumer exploitation? Primarily because our present laws are outmoded and inadequate to deal with the modern complexities of consumer fraud. Most of our laws on dishonest selling were designed long ago to catch and punish a few "hardened criminals" and not to cope with the vast web of subtle deceits and credit merchandising abuses that characterizes the businesses of today's "soft-sell" swindlers. Generally, our legal remedies have two defects: (1) they are ineffective in halting deceptive selling, and (2) they make virtually no provisions for redressing the wrong, whether by freeing the cheated consumer of a fraudulently induced debt or by reimbursing him.

The Federal Trade Commission, as the Federal agency primarily responsible for stopping deceptive selling on a national scale, has broad powers and has been effective in curtailing unscrupulous sellers in interstate commerce for half a century. Nevertheless, we cannot depend on the FTC alone to halt all deceptive selling nationwide. Even with an addition in personnel it would still be impossible for the FTC to stop all deceptive selling even within its interstate jurisdiction. And the FTC also has certain limitations in its powers to protect consumers.

As we have seen, the FTC cannot stop deceptive selling operations that limit their activities to intrastate commerce, staying within a state's borders, which is where most such selling occurs. Nor can the FTC in some cases move fast enough to halt the swindlers before they have victimized a number of consumers and accumulated a small fortune. Nor can the FTC act on behalf of an individual consumer; it can move only when a substantial number of Americans have been injured (enough to make an FTC action "in the public interest").

Then too, the FTC can only compel the offender to stop working his deceptive arts on future customers; it cannot order him to reimburse those whom he has already cheated or to cancel collection of their debts.

The Post Office Department, as the other Federal agency most responsible for halting fraudulent and deceptive schemes, also has been remarkably successful within their jurisdiction. But postal officials, too, are hampered in their efforts to control certain types of deceptive selling by mail. Under present law, they often cannot move fast enough to curtail mail-order schemes and sometimes cannot stop them at all. In testifying to this fact before a subcommittee of the House Committee on Post Office and Civil Service in April 1967, Henry B. Montague, chief postal inspector for the Post Office Department, illustrated the difficulty in halting mail-order land-fraud sales:

"The investigation of the Lake Mead Land & Water Company in Arizona began in 1962. Evidence that the desert property was not in fact 'an enchanted city in the making'; that the 'favorite swimming hole' pictured in the advertising brochure was in truth a cattle-watering pond not even located on the promoter's property; that various springs and wells depicted in the literature were also not located on the property, was not too difficult to ascertain. Proof of intent or personal knowledge on the part of the principal promoter, of course, required considerably more time.

"An indictment was returned in October 1963 and conviction resulted in June 1965. Three thousand home- or investment-seeking persons, many of the elderly class, lost an estimated one million dollars before the enterprise was finally stopped through conviction. The promoter continued to receive payments by mail up to the very end."

Even though a scheme is patently false and postal officials know it, they cannot always stop a perpetrator's inflow of mail containing the lucrative rewards of deceit. Postal authorities must stand helpless, witnessing the bilking of the elderly and the hopeful, until it can be proved that the purveyor of falsity *intended* to defraud, which as Mr. Montague pointed out, takes much longer than just proving untruth by comparing the brochures or advertisements with the lay of the land. Partially as a result of this time lag while investigators try to fathom the state of a man's mind, the 49 land-fraud swindlers finally brought to justice were able to accumulate, through a steady flow of mail payments, more than 50 million dollars from an unsuspecting public before they were convicted and their mail was marked "fraudulent; return to sender."

At the state level, officials who attempt to protect consumers are incredibly handicapped by inadequate laws. Although many states have recently passed effective laws and set up machinery to enforce them, the picture of state consumer legislation is, as a whole, dreary indeed. An informal survey by the FTC in June 1967 showed that only 19 states could be said to have "good" or "excellent" laws prohibiting deceptive selling practices. At least one-third of the states have pitifully weak laws. Effective consumer legislation is especially lacking in Alabama, Arkansas, Indiana, Mississippi, New Hampshire, North Carolina, Ohio, Oklahoma, South Carolina, South Dakota, Tennessee, Texas, Virginia, West Virginia and Wyoming.

In a few states legislation is simply nonexistent. Only a handful of states regulate correspondence schools, fraudulent selling of land or unsolicited merchandise sent through the mails. Only 20 states specifically outlaw bait advertising.

Absence of laws, however, is not the only problem in the states. For as the *Columbia Law Review* has noted, "The states have adopted a staggering number of statutes noteworthy for their ad hoc and piecemeal approach to the problems of advertising control and for the very slight degree to which they are enforced." In truth, all but three states —Arkansas, Delaware and New Mexico—have a "Printer's Ink" statute (named for the advertising magazine of the same name) making it a misdemeanor to make an "untrue, deceptive or misleading" statement with the intent to sell a product.

One would think this law so comprehensive that it would virtually wipe out deceptive advertising in the states. Such is not the case, for the law, broad as it is, contains an insurmountable flaw: it is a *criminal* statute, as are many of the other measures adopted by the states to halt deceptive selling. Under the criminal statute, conviction demands proof beyond a reasonable doubt, and carries with it fines, possible jail sentences and the stigma of being branded a criminal.

Since its adoption in 1911, the Printer's Ink statute may have deterred some sellers from deceptive practices, but the number of culprits it has actually brought to justice is infinitesimal. Law enforcement officials overwhelmingly consider the law so unrealistic that they don't attempt to enforce it. A survey by the *Columbia Law Review* in 1956 discovered that during nearly 50 years, only "a handful of prosecutions" had been brought under the Printer's Ink statutes throughout the country. Many attorneys general and county prosecutors freely admitted that they had never tried to enforce it. One reason is that local prosecutors are burdened with trying to halt major felonies such as murder, rape and robbery, and are disinclined to waste their time on such a relatively small "crime" as false advertising or selling. Another reason is that few prosecutors believe they will get a conviction. They have found that juries are hesitant to find a man guilty of a crime for what may merely be "overzealous salesmanship"; consequently, few public officials prosecute.

Two law students at the University of Pennsylvania, investigating the ineffectiveness of consumer legislation, recently found: "Even when a law enforcement official believes that a particular scheme has been made actionable by statute, he often does not prosecute because of a widely held belief that, except in the most egregious circumstances, fraudulent operators should not be treated like criminals. Lawyers, business leaders and prosecutors have stated that 'judges, juries and district attorneys do not like to put businessmen in jail.' One district attorney, when asked by the attorney general to prosecute an alleged fraudulent operator, retorted: 'I can't even get a conviction when they stick a gun in somebody's back; how can I get one when they just talk him out of his money?' "

Trying to completely control consumer fraud by proving criminality is an outmoded concept. But even if the criminal statutes could be enforced (and New York, for example, has achieved rare success in obtaining convictions), it is doubtful that society's purpose is best served by only putting a swindler behind bars. The sentence is usually short (in Pennsylvania one man who made $300,000 selling fake automobile parts was sentenced to a term of one year), after which the wrongdoer is set free to spend his ill-gotten money, and the cheated consumer, who understandably wants no justice so much as his money back, is left to suffer without restitution.

Additionally, the hit-and-miss proposition of locking up criminals who defraud the public is inefficient in halting consumer fraud on a broad scale. Only one operator can be put out of business at a time, after long, costly court proceedings, while thousands of other gypsters —perhaps associated with the same company or swindle—are allowed to flourish. And even after a short prison term, the ex-convict can start up a new racket, using the same fraudulent techniques, and rob Americans of a fortune, while local authorities once again gear up their machinery to start the slow, painful process of gathering evidence against him on the new charge.

The injured consumer can bring suit himself, but few do. They soon discover that lawyer's fees, court costs and time away from employment will cost more than they can possibly recover. A woman in Ohio, who hired an attorney to keep from losing her $15,000-house because of a home-improvement repairs bill of $7,200, had already paid a legal fee of $1,500 and still did not receive her house back. Under strict legal requirements in most states, the complainant must have an exceptionally good case in order to win; many times it is only his word against that of the shady seller.

Invariably, the victim has also unknowingly, by signing the contract, given away a number of rights of defense and agreed that nothing the seller told him, unless specifically stated in the contract, is binding. When a group of lawyers in Pennsylvania were asked in an informal survey what they would do with a client who had been gypped out of several hundred dollars for carpeting in a "bait and switch" scheme, they unanimously agreed: "Send him home."

Clearly, the weak, inappropriate, poorly enforced, hit-and-miss legislation that is the rule throughout the nation is quite undependable in combating the complexities and size of our present-day consumer deception. In this antiquated system of justice, the dishonest steal quietly off to count their loot, while the injured consumer is sacrificed on the altar of legislative short-sightedness.

B. Pricing

15. Price Policy and Discounts in the Medium- and High-Priced Car Market

Allen F. Jung

Medium- and high-priced cars have represented a sizable share of the automobile market for many years. The importance of this segment has declined somewhat in recent years, influenced partly by the down-grading of the automobile as an indicator of social status. However, although much has been written about this part of the automobile market, the type of people who purchase these cars, and their reasons for buying them, little evidence has been made public about the costs of such purchases.

This study of dealers of medium- and high-priced cars was conducted to gain information about their pricing policies and to learn how effective bargaining could be in purchasing high-priced cars. In addition, data were obtained regarding the cost of financing a car at the dealer and the selling methods of automobile salesmen.

Dealers in medium- and high-priced cars were found to offer substantial discounts from list price. High-priced car dealers further reduced their prices by more than 100 dollars, on the average, on the

Reprinted from the *Journal of Business,* Vol. 33 (October, 1960), 342–347, by permission of the University of Chicago Press. © 1960 by The University of Chicago.

basis of a brief standardized bargaining procedure. Price variations among dealers were large in every make studied. Finance charges also varied among dealers, with the average for all dealers in medium- and high-priced cars amounting to about 12% (calculated on a simple-interest basis from terms offered by the dealers). Salesmen for high-priced cars were found to use considerably more sales effort than did salesmen for medium-priced cars.

Method of Investigation

Prices were obtained from automobile dealers through personal shopping investigations. The same standardized shopping approach was employed on every buying contact. The interviewer posed as a knowledgeable person, well versed in car-purchasing procedure. He was definitely in the market for this new car at time of contact and was anxious to consummate the deal within a day or two. However, he was willing to wait for delivery of the exact car desired rather than accept a different model or one with different equipment from stock. Needless to say, every call was stated to be the first dealer contact, since it was felt that disclosing other dealers' prices might bias the salesman. The purchaser was buying the car "outright"; he did not have a car to trade in.

A short while after the salesman quoted a price, the shopper stated that this was more than he wished to pay. He further mentioned that he wanted to pay about X dollars.[1] No salesman was able to meet this suggested price, but many offered a lower price than originally quoted. A few dealers offered a third price. This third price was usually offered by another person, called "the boss," after the buyer had been lured into a "pressure chamber." The price originally offered and the final price after standardized bargaining were the two recorded.

Information was gained about finance charges. At the close of price negotiations the interviewer would take the difference between the lowest price the dealer offered and $2,000 and state that he thought he would make a down payment of about that much money. He then

[1] The offer was $3,000 for De Soto, $2,800 for Mercury, $2,900 for Oldsmobile, $4,200 for Cadillac, $4,200 for Imperial, and $4,200 for Lincoln. It was felt that these prices would be fairly close to dealer cost, not too unreasonable a price to suggest, and yet prices at which the dealers would refuse to sell the cars.

inquired about financing the $2,000 for the longest period of time possible. All dealers were willing to finance this amount for 36 months. The amounts of the equal monthly payments were recorded. An inquiry was made to determine whether the figure quoted included credit-life insurance.[2] Automobile insurance was to be placed privately, not through the dealer, because of a "family connection." The interviewer also recorded several items about sales behavior as soon as he left the showroom.

Sample

The sample was selected from new-car dealers in Chicago selling medium- and high-priced cars. One make was selected from each of the "Big Three" manufacturers in the medium- and high-priced field. The De Soto was selected from the offerings of Chrysler, the Mercury from those of Ford, and the Oldsmobile from those of General Motors in the medium-priced field. As each manufacturer produced only one make of high-priced (luxury) cars, the selection of Imperial, Lincoln, and Cadillac was predetermined. All factory-authorized dealers within the city limits of Chicago selling any of these cars were contacted.

When a dealer sold two of the makes, two contacts were necessary, since only one car was shopped at a given dealer at one time. All Lincoln dealers sold Mercury (although not vice versa), and one dealer sold both De Soto and Imperial. Half the Cadillac dealers in Chicago were factory-owned branches.

The four-door sedan in the middle-price series was selected for the medium-priced cars,[3] and the four-door hardtop in the lowest-price series for the high-priced cars. The De Soto Adventurer, the Mercury Montclair, the Oldsmobile Super 88, the Cadillac Sixty-Two, the Imperial Custom, and the Lincoln "Lincoln" series were priced with all the following equipment: automatic transmission, power steering, power brakes, radio, heater, white-wall tires, and windshield washers. Some cars included some additional minor accessories as standard equipment. All contacts were completed satisfactorily between June 10 and June 18.

---

[2] The interviewer did not mention the term "credit-life insurance" but referred to it in a less technical way.

[3] De Soto offered only two series; the more expensive one was chosen.

Findings

Medium-priced cars

There was considerable price variability among dealers for medium-priced cars (Table 1). The factory-suggested list prices were about $4,025 for the De Soto, $3,710 for the Mercury, and $3,855 for the Oldsmobile. Discounts ranged from $568 to $750 for De Soto and averaged $632 (15.7% of list price); Mercury dealers offered discounts from $317 to $650, averaging $532 (14.3%); and the dis-

Table 1. Prices quoted by Chicago dealers for medium-priced cars
(After Standardized Bargaining)

Dealer	De Soto	Mercury	Oldsmobile
1	$3,430	$3,075	$3,175
2	3,275	3,100	3,200
3	3,437	3,223	3,180
4	3,400	3,100	3,350
5	3,457	3,300	3,229
6	3,350	3,100	3,220
7	3,400	3,175	3,210
8	....	3,253	3,235
9	....	3,060	3,200
10	....	3,132	3,275
11	....	3,393	3,300
12	....	3,225	3,200
13	....	....	3,230
14	....	....	3,140
15	....	....	3,250
16	....	....	3,300
17	....	....	3,210
Mean	$3,393	$3,178	$3,230
Standard deviation	$ 62	$ 103	$ 53
Median	$3,400	$3,154	$3,220
Range	$3,275–$3,457	$3,060–$3,393	$3,140–$3,350

counts quoted by Oldsmobile dealers ranged for $505 to $715, averaging $625 (16.2%). The smaller discount offered by Mercury might be attributed to the success of Comet, their compact car. Their share of the total automobile market, when Comet is included, is above the 1959 figure. All medium-priced dealers, with the exception of one Mercury dealer, offered a discount of at least 11%. All prices shown for these cars were the prices obtained after the brief standardized bargaining.

For the first six months the share of the market for each of these three cars (and the three high-priced cars) has declined from the same period in 1959.[4] Despite this, the average discount for these cars was less than the discount granted by Ford and Chevrolet dealers in both February and August 1959.[5] The average discount for Ford was the same in both February and August, 17.1%; the February Chevrolet discount averaged 17.9% compared to 18.5% in August.

High-priced cars

There was also considerable variation in prices quoted by dealers of high-priced cars. Discounts offered by Cadillac dealers ranged from $658 to $865 and averaged $784 (14.3% of list price). Imperial dealers offered discounts from $855 to $1,155, averaging $979 (17.9%). Discounts ranged from $860 to $1,080 for Lincoln, with an average discount of $966 (17.6%). All three makes of cars listed at about $5,500 (Cadillac, $5,490; Imperial, $5,455; and Lincoln, $5,500).

The smallest discount offered by a Cadillac dealer, 12%, is especially noteworthy. Many consumers have the feeling that list prices for this automobile are fairly well maintained. The discounts offered by the four Cadillac factory branches, both before and after bargaining, were about the same as those quoted by the other four Cadillac dealers.

Average discounts as a percentage were smallest for the Cadillac and Mercury. Both sold more cars in the first six months of 1960 than in the same period in 1959. Imperial and Lincoln were more heavily discounted than were De Soto or Oldsmobile. Last year Ford and Chevrolet cars were discounted, on average, more heavily than either the medium- or the high-priced cars this year.

---

[4] *Automotive News,* August 8, 1960, p. 4.
[5] Allen F. Jung, "Price Variations among Automobile Dealers in Metropolitan Chicago," *Journal of Business,* January, 1960, p. 34.

Table 2. Prices quoted by Chicago dealers for high-priced cars

Dealer	Cadillac Before Bargaining	Cadillac After Bargaining	Imperial Before Bargaining	Imperial After Bargaining	Lincoln Before Bargaining	Lincoln After Bargaining
1	$4,740	$4,640	$4,550	$4,300	$4,550	$4,420
2	4,800	4,651	4,700	4,500	4,854	4,563
3	4,779	4,779	4,600	4,550	4,867	4,467
4	4,800	4,680	4,600	4,540	4,625	4,625
5	4,900	4,625	4,513	4,513	4,513	4,513
6	4,832	4,832	4,400	4,400	4,763	4,513
7	4,850	4,800	4,444	4,444	4,800	4,640
8	4,643	4,643	4,550	4,550	......	......
9	......	......	4,489	4,489	......	......
10	......	......	4,460	4,395	......	......
11	......	......	4,600	4,600	......	......
12	......	......	4,500	4,350	......	......
13	......	......	4,900	4,560	......	......
Mean	$4,793	$4,706	$4,562	$4,476	$4,710	$4,534
Standard deviation	$ 78	$ 83	$ 129	$ 91	$ 146	$ 85
Median	$4,800	$4,666	$4,550	$4,500	$4,763	$4,513
Range	$4,643– $4,900	$4,625– $4,832	$4,400– $4,900	$4,300– $4,600	$4,513– $4,867	$4,420– $4,640

Savings from bargaining

All prices shown above were prices obtained after a brief standardized form of bargaining. This was done because it was felt that most consumers undoubtedly engage in some form of bargaining when purchasing a new car. For the high-priced cars, the first price given by the salesman is shown in Table 2 as "prices before bargaining." Cadillac dealers, on average, lowered the price $87 after bargaining, Imperial dealers $86, and Lincoln dealers $176. Dealers in high-priced cars lowered the price an average of $108 as a result of bargaining, compared to an average of $63 for Ford dealers in February, 1959, and $44 in August, 1959, and $54 for Chevrolet dealers in February, and $30 in August of the same year.[6]

Savings from shopping additional dealers

The degree of variability in price offerings of different dealers for a particular make suggests that the consumer can benefit from shopping more than one dealer. In Table 3, average total savings to be ex-

Table 3. Average savings to be expected from shopping more than one dealer

No. of Dealers Shopped	De Soto	Mercury	Oldsmobile	Cadillac	Imperial	Lincoln
2	$34.87	$ 58.09	$29.89	$ 46.81	$ 51.32	$ 47.94
3	52.45	87.14	44.84	70.21	76.99	71.91
4	63.80	105.99	54.54	85.41	93.64	87.47
5	72.10	119.80	61.64	96.53	105.83	98.86
6	78.55	130.50	67.15	105.16	115.50	107.70
7	83.82	139.25	71.66	112.22	123.03	114.92

pected from shopping additional dealers for each make of car are given. The additional savings to be gained by shopping one more dealer can be calculated, of course, by finding the differences between successive dealers. The proximity of dealers, the value of one's time, and his general attitude toward automobile-shopping are important

[6] *Ibid.*

factors in determining the number of dealers an individual should visit. Based on the above information and the assumption that the dealers for a given make are located fairly close to each other, the average consumer would probably profit most from shopping a minimum of three to a maximum of five dealers.

Finance charges

There was some variation among the interest charges at dealers for a particular make and among the various dealers (Table 4). The deal-

Table 4. Finance rates charged by automobile dealers, expressed in simple annual interest

(Per Cent)

	Mean	Median	Range
Medium-priced cars:			
De Soto	12.5	11.7	11.1–16.5
Mercury	11.9	11.7	11.7–12.5
Oldsmobile	11.5	11.1	10.5–13.8
High-priced cars:			
Cadillac	11.6	11.7	11.3–11.7
Imperial	12.9	12.3	10.5–16.5
Lincoln	14.0	15.6	11.7–16.5

ers gave the prospective purchaser the information in terms of dollars per month for 36 equal monthly payments. The total interest was computed and reduced to simple annual rate of interest by formula.[7] Some of the dealers included credit life insurance in the terms quoted. Where this occurred, twenty-four dollars has been deducted from their total interest charges before computation.[8]

A large number of Oldsmobile and Cadillac dealers used the GMAC finance plan, which may explain the narrow range of their finance charges. The only unusual statistic is the higher rates charged

[7] $R = r(2n)/(n + 1)$; R = actual rate of interest; r = nominal rate of interest; n = number of equal monthly instalments.

[8] The cost of credit life insurance offered by GMAC is very close to this figure. Some banks in the United States make credit life insurance available to the consumer on automobile loans at this charge (40 cents per $100 per year on the net proceeds of the loan).

for Lincoln than for Mercury especially since the same Lincoln dealers were contacted for Mercury. Since discounts on Lincoln were higher than discounts on Mercury, perhaps the salesman was trying to recoup some of the markup in the form of higher finance charges.

Sales behavior

Dealer salesmen performed only about one-third (34.2%) of the things that might help to induce a sale (Table 5). Salesmen of high-priced cars exerted somewhat more effort (38.3%) than did their medium-priced counterparts (31.0%). Their sales managers would probably not be overjoyed with this performance.

Last year Ford and Chevrolet salesmen covered about 20% of the sales points included.[9] An unpublished study of Rambler, Lark, Renault, and Volkswagen dealers in August, 1959, showed results only slightly higher. Data on Falcon and Corvair salesmen taken early in the model year in three cities showed salesmen were covering about 37.1% of these points.[10] In light of these statistics, the performance of Cadillac and Lincoln salesmen seems outstanding by comparison.

Conclusions

The belief held by many that high-priced cars and, to some extent, medium-priced cars are not discounted heavily does not appear to be warranted. All makes of these cars were discounted substantially, and the average amount of discount in actual dollars was greater than the discount for low-priced cars. However, discounts from list price appear to be smaller on a percentage basis for high- and medium-priced cars than for low-priced cars.

The consumer can benefit from shopping additional dealers, and a simple bargaining procedure can evidently be used to advantage. Dealers in high-priced cars offered larger reductions, both in absolute and percentage terms, than did dealers in low-priced cars, when bargaining was employed. Even Cadillac dealers, whose first quotations were substantially below the list price, were ready to reduce them further when requested. Some Cadillac owners may be surprised (unpleasantly) by this statistic.

---

[9] Jung, *op. cit.,* p. 39.
[10] Allen F. Jung, "Prices of Falcon and Corvair Cars in Chicago and Selected Cities," *Journal of Business,* April, 1960, p. 125.

Table 5. Tabulation of questions concerning the actions of dealer salesmen by number of (per cent) "Yes" answers

	Medium-priced Cars			High-priced Cars		
	De Soto	Mercury	Oldsmobile	Cadillac	Imperial	Lincoln
Did the salesman offer a demonstration ride?	42.9	33.3	29.4	12.5	0.0	57.2
Did the salesman offer any literature?	14.3	8.3	23.5	62.5	30.8	42.9
Did the salesman try to sell you additional accessories?	42.9	25.0	23.5	37.5	38.5	28.6
Did the salesman mention any reason for buying his make of car?	42.9	58.3	23.5	87.5	15.4	57.2
Did the salesman mention any reason for buying the car from the dealer he represented?	14.3	41.7	11.8	75.0	7.7	71.5
Did the salesman take your address and/or phone number?	57.2	41.7	58.8	75.0	38.5	57.2
Did the salesman contact you after you left the showroom?	28.6	16.7	29.4	37.5	23.1	28.6
Average	34.7	32.2	28.6	55.4	22.0	49.0
Number of dealers	7	12	17	3	13	7

Since finance costs do vary among dealers for a given make, the finance rate offered by a dealer becomes an additional consideration for the credit purchaser looking for a low initial cost. Many consumers who have money available in savings accounts and think that it is better to purchase on time because savings are hard to replace may wish to revise their thinking in light of the interest charges. One's will power may be strengthened by the fact that car loans made by dealers cost about 12%, while banks savings and loan associations pay approximately 5%.

Salesmen for the medium- and high-priced cars exerted somewhat more selling effort than did those for low-priced cars. Apart from amount of selling effort, salesmen's behavior was very similar, regardless of the type of car sold. Generally, they would try to be certain that the prospect was in the market for a car before quoting a price and would try to sell a car from stock rather than order the desired car from the factory. A practice as pevalent among medium- and high-priced dealers as among low-priced dealers was the resort to calling in the "boss" and exerting pressure to get the order signed on the spot.

16. Introduction to the Handbook of Prescription Drugs

Richard Burack

The United States has reason for looking upon its medical profession with pride, for its medical schools and teaching hospitals have succeeded well in training doctors to make correct diagnoses and to perform proper surgery. Our level of medical practice is the envy of many nations because our practicing physicians and surgeons have managed, for the most part, to stay abreast of new, important developments in diagnostic and surgical techniques. That they have been able to do so is a tribute to the profession itself, which has taken the lead in encouraging their continuing education through the use of books, journals, postgraduate courses, lectures, and hospital staff conferences.

The great pity—bordering on scandal—is that too much responsibility for keeping doctors informed of developments in pharmacology has been forfeited to pharmaceutical manufacturers who have succeeded, through advertising, in influencing practicing doctors to write prescriptions for which the patient pays a maximum price. The immensity of this advertising effort is best appreciated by considering that it costs the drug industry at least $600,000,000 annually. Since there are approximately 200,000 prescribing doctors, the drug companies are spending more than 3,000 advertising dollars each year on each doctor!

Much of this advertising is misleading. According to Dr. Goddard, former Commissioner of the United States Food and Drug Administration, in 1965 "one third of the members of the Pharmaceutical Manufacturers Association had violated FDA agency regulations on fraudulent or misleading advertising." Clearly, a third and interested commercial party has inserted itself into the doctor-patient relationship, yet no clear warning voice has been raised against it from within the medical profession. As Dr. Goddard said, the American doctor is "frankly under siege."

Why should doctors, among the best trained of all professional cadres in this country, be susceptible to misleading advertising? As medical students were they not provided with adequate education about drugs? The answer is that the great majority have been given an excellent, modern laboratory and lecture course in pharmacology, but, with few exceptions, there has been little organized review or systematic presentation of such material after the student's second year of medical school. This is because those faculty members who teach pharmacology are only rarely practicing doctors (clinicians) as well as scientists. The scholarly, research-oriented pharmacologist has usually had little or no experience in the actual use in humans of the drugs which he knows so well in theory. He may have no interest in clinical medicine, and even if he does, he will probably not feel qualified to play a significant role in case discussions before members of the clinical faculty. Unfortunately, very few of the clinical faculty have much more than a superficial interest in pharmacology as such, for tradition has taught that the cornerstone of the best medical practice is learning to diagnose. It is commonplace to hear, "Drug therapy is easy; once the diagnosis has been made, all you have to do is look up the recommended drug and prescribe it." While this may once have been a useful view, rapid developments in pharmacology (not all of them beneficial) have rendered it obsolete and its persistence has led to an obvious result: the student ceases to continue to learn in depth about drugs, and while he receives first-rate instruction in pathological physiology, diagnosis, and surgical treatment, he frequently adopts sloppy habits with regard to the prescription of therapeutic agents.

This unhappy state of affairs is by no means unknown to responsible members of medical school faculties, and there have been moves here and there to institute courses dealing in pharmacology during the latter two years of medical school, the so-called "clinical" years. For the practicing doctor, similarly, there is no coherent plant for periodically updating his knowledge of drugs and their use. Into the breach has stepped the pharmaceutical industry to persuade, to cajole, and to "educate." To be sure, there is now available to all doctors and medical students a biweekly loose-leaf sheet called *The Medical Letter,* published by Drug and Therapeutic Information, Inc., a nonprofit organization which fearlessly dispenses objective criticism of drugs old and new, but it is not meant primarily to give comprehensive information on prices. Simply written and intelligently critical, *The Medical Letter* deserves the fuller support of the profession, for the struggle to control doctors' habits of therapeutic practice is a big stake and the giant pharmaceutical corporations can be expected to continue to promote, advertise, and "educate" at an increasing rate, one which even now far exceeds in cost the combined administrative and teaching budgets of all the nation's medical schools put together.[1]

Official and Unofficial Names of Drugs

The key to an understanding of why drugs often need not cost as much as they do is a knowledge of what is meant by the terms "official" and "unofficial" with respect to drug names.

New drugs and the processes by which they are made can be protected for 17 years under United States Patent Law. Every new drug approved for sale must be given an official name (also called "generic"[2] or "nonproprietary"), and it is by this label that it is known to pharmacologists and to the medical students whom they teach. A new drug which is developed by a drug company is also endowed with an unofficial (also called "brand," "trade," or "proprietary") name, and this is the label by which the drug is advertised to the profession. Until only recently these advertisements were not even required to include

[1] P. R. Garai, "The Pill the Doctor Must Swallow," *The Johns Hopkins Magazine,* Vol. XV, No. 7 (May, 1964), pp. 7–9, 21–23.

[2] Technically and correctly the term "generic" refers to classes or genera of drugs, but in common parlance it has come to be used interchangeably with "nonproprietary" and "official." To avoid confusion and pedantry, the *Handbook* adopts the popular usage.

a prominent display of the drug's generic name,[3] but now the law says that it must be included in letters at least one half as large as those used for the brand name. It is profoundly in the economic interest of the pharmaceutical manufacturer to "train" doctors and patients to use the brand name only, and the manufacturers have succeeded mightily in doing so. Approximately 90% of prescriptions in the mid-1960s were written using brand names.[4] Brand names are frequently easier to say, spell and remember than generic names because it has been common for manufacturers to make the latter chemical tongue-twisters, which discourages their use. Besides, brand names have often been designed so as to imply what the pharmacological action of a drug is advertised to be, an effective merchandising technique: e.g., the officially named chlordiazepoxide, a sedative, is almost universally known as "Librium." Since 1961, generic names have been subject to approval by a committee, the United States Adopted Names Council (USAN), which includes representatives of the United States Pharmacopeial Convention, the American Pharmaceutical Association, and the American Medical Association. Why "Adopted" rather than "Official"? And can any dignified official name compete with one designed to merchandise?

During the 17 years that a patent is in effect, the original developer of the drug is free to take advantage of his privileged position to recoup his investment and reap the reward of profit for his risk and enterprise. After 17 years, anyone else is free to help himself to the process described in the patent and to manufacture and market the drug on his own, *though he may not use the original brand name, which is limited by* trademark *law to the use of the original coiner.*

As an illustration, we can refer to the drug dextroamphetamine, widely used for its appetite-curbing properties. The substance was patented by Smith Kline & French Laboratories, who alone sold it in vast amounts for a 17-year period under the brand name Dexedrine. The patent has long since expired, and as of now, half a hundred companies are marketing dextroamphetamine, nearly all at lower prices than Smith Kline & French. But the many new producers of dextro-

---

[3] At one point during the Kefauver hearings the president of the Pharmaceutical Manufacturers Association, Dr. Austin Smith, found it impossible to locate the generic name on an advertisement until aided by a magnifying glass proffered by the Subcommittee counsel.

[4] *F-D-C Reports ("The Pink Sheet")*, Washington, September 5, 1966.

amphetamine may not advertise it as Dexedrine. If Dexedrine is the word the doctor writes on the prescription blank by force of habit, the druggist must by law in 39 states (except within institutions) dispense Dexedrine—and at its brand-name price. It must be pointed out, however, that even if the prescription read "dextroamphetamine," the druggist would be free to dispense Dexedrine at the higher price, and that is exactly what many of them do, since it is not yet common enough practice for drugstores to keep in stock the less expensive—but for practical purposes identical—dextroamphetamine tablets marketed by other companies without the trade name Dexedrine. Such less expensive, non-brand-name dextroamphetamine tablets are the "generic equivalents" of Dexedrine.

The Nature of Drug Promotion

Pharmaceutical companies influence doctors in several ways. For one thing, their salesmen, called "detail men," visit doctors' offices at frequent intervals to dispense samples, describe new products, remind the doctor of older ones, and sometimes to recite certain statements which the parent company considers of special importance and has ordered them to commit to memory. Many of these practices provide a service which the *Handbook* has no wish to denigrate. However, the major job of the detail man is to sell. Many doctors by now are aware that information obtained from the detail man must be examined critically, and that salesmen cannot be considered authoritative sources for continuing education about drugs. There is little chance to check on the accuracy of what the detail man tells the doctor in the privacy of his office, and there is plenty of opportunity for exaggeration, dissimulation, and outright concealment. During the course of the hearings on drugs conducted by the Kefauver Subcommittee it was reported that the National Research Council recommended to the FDA that a label be placed on chloramphenicol (Parke, Davis' Chloromycetin®) warning that it should "not be used indiscriminately or for minor infections" because serious blood disease had occasionally been found to occur with its use. The report of the hearings contains a copy of a Parke, Davis President's Letter telling the firm's detail men of the new warning label but prefacing the announcement with the statement that "Chloromycetin has been officially cleared by the FDA and the National Research Council with *no restrictions* on the number or the range of diseases for which Chloromycetin may be administered."

(Emphasis in original) Obviously, when the National Research Council recommended that chloramphenicol "not be used indiscriminately or for minor infections," it was proposing a restriction on the number and the range of diseases. The hearings report that in a Directors' Letter sent two months later to its detail men, Parke, Davis included "Planned Presentation 10," which contained arguments and figures designed to enable the detail man to allay apprehensions about the drug on the part of the physician. However, it is also reported that instructions accompanying the presentation carried this interesting admonition: "The special detail [Planned Presentation 10] should not be introduced unless the physician brings up the subject or unless you know that he has ceased prescribing Chloromycetin," a position hardly in keeping with the responsibility of drug manufacturers always to keep doctors fully informed on important matters.[5]

Thus, the detail man without realizing it himself can transmit information to doctors which is either misleading or false. In other cases he supplies misinformation for which the parent company cannot be blamed. As an example, a detail man recently tried to convince me that the United States Air Force had "three or four years ago" been "burnt" by the purchase of digoxin (the generic name for a commonly used heart drug) which turned out to be "only 47 percent of proper potency." It so happens that drugs used by the armed services are bought by generic name through secret bids and that all bidders must first pass inspection by the Defense Supply Agency; no delivery is accepted without check on identity, quality, purity, and potency of the material. It seemed, therefore, that either the detail man's story was incorrect or the Defense Supply Agency must have fallen down on the job. When I wrote to the man's company requesting more details, the vice president in charge of sales replied that the company was unaware of the incident. This points up the importance to the doctor of listening critically to the detail man. Drug corporations are aware that detail men may, by accident or design, transmit information which is not factual, and must guard against the possible repercussions of such practices by not supplying the men with stationery containing the company letterhead. Thus misinformation is unlikely to be put in writing.

[5] United States Senate, Committee on the Judiciary, Subcommittee on Antitrust and Monopoly, 87th Congress, 1st Session, S. Rep. No. 448, "Administered Prices: Drugs," pp. 192–96, and documentation in *Hearings on S. Res. 238,* Part 26, pp. 15945–15981.

Advertisements in medical journals represent a second method of influencing the doctor's prescribing habits. Advertisement of drugs is entirely proper and can undoubtedly be useful to the medical profession. However, as mentioned earlier, advertisements are too often characterized by misrepresentation or misleading captions, in spite of the supervision of journal editorial boards and scrutiny by the Food and Drug Administration. Examples would fill a book.

The Kefauver hearings contain documentary evidence of an advertisement for a steroid drug with X-ray pictures of the large bowel showing typical changes seen in ulcerative colitis. Although the first picture was not labeled "before," the second was labeled "Barium enema following successful therapy for ulcerative colitis." One physician wrote the company (Upjohn) to question whether the X-rays were of the same patient. By the time correspondence between the company's advertising manager, its medical director, and the physician had come to an end, it was clear that these X-rays were from two different patients each with different degrees of ulcerative colitis, and that in fact neither one had ever been treated with a steroid. The company, denying intent to mislead, expressed regrets over the incident; however, its advertising agency refused to admit to any impropriety.[6] The prescribing of drugs is too serious and potentially dangerous to be influenced by less than factual objective material. And if some advertisements are misleading, how does the doctor know which ones to trust?

The deluge of "junk mail" which descends upon doctors daily is by now common knowledge, and most physicians are either too busy or too wise to pay it much attention. However, the cost of this material is passed on to the consumer. And few members of the medical profession are likely to be aware that their names are obtained for mailing lists through the offices of the American Medical Association, the source from which the advertisers buy their names and addresses. This is an important source of AMA revenue: according to the general counsel to the AMA, accounting for about $1 million in income annually.[7]

Probably the shrewdest and most effective means by which the big pharmaceutical corporations perpetuate their hold over doctor and patients is through the book *Physicians' Desk Reference (PDR)*. Although some doctors may not think of it in these terms because its

---

[6] *Hearings on S. 1552*, Part 6, pp. 3084 *et seq.* and Part 7, pp. 3301–3310.
[7] *Hearings on S. 1552*, Part 1, p. 137.

format and veneer give it a cleverly noncommerical, authoritative appearance, *PDR* is in fact composed of advertising. The 1966 rate was $115 per column inch. With more than 15,000 column inches, the gross value of space in the 1966 *PDR* exceeded $1,725,000. The practitioner who habitually uses this volume to look up the names of drugs with which to treat his patients is unwittingly being influenced in his therapeutic practice by nonmedical commercial interests. His very freedom of therapeutic practice is at risk. Yet many if not most doctors are unaware of this; here the leaders of the profession must be blamed because they have remained silent, an ironic omission for a leadership which has in recent times spent millions of dollars to fight forces they accuse of meddling in the "sacred doctor-patient relationship." It is my belief that there is no force in American life today which more directly meddles in this relationship than that segment of the pharmaceutical industry which operates through the detail man, through advertising, and most boldly of all, through the *Physicians' Desk Reference.*

Annual publication of *PDR* is an enterprise of Medical Economics, Inc., which distributes it without charge to over 200,000 practicing "doctors of medicine and doctors of osteopathy." Until recently, it was also distributed free to "pharmacies and libraries of more than 5,000 hospitals," but now these institutions have been asked to purchase their copies at a nominal cost. Doubtless most of them have done so, for of all the reference books located on hospital floors for the use of doctors and nurses, the one most often used by far is the *PDR.*

The *PDR* states that its contents have been obtained with the "cooperation" of drug manufacturers, through whose "patronage" its publication is made possible. This is a euphemism. Drug houses *buy* space in the *PDR* and publish what they wish to publish. Even those unethical repackaging enterprises—"drug companies" owned and operated by physicians who buy up inexpensive generics, relabel them, and prescribe them under a special brand name at a higher price—are free to buy space. Since this is so, its contents can hardly be considered authoritative. *Precisely because it is an advertising catalogue, the PDR is incomplete; it gives prominent mention to too few generic names for widely consumed basic drugs.* The widespread use of this volume serves to conceal from practicing doctors the existence of numerous other manufacturers which very often can supply the same drugs at lower cost. There is a curious disclaimer in the foreword to *PDR* for 1960, the fourteenth annual edition: "It should be understood that in organizing the wealth of material in *PDR* the publisher is not advocating the use of any product listed by any manufacturer *nor attempting to influence the therapeutic practice of any physician.*" (My italics) In subsequent editions the italicized portion of the sentence was dropped.

The *Physicians' Desk Reference* has achieved its popularity not only by virtue of aggressive free distribution but also because the profession itself offers no good alternative reference volume. I hope that the *Handbook* will meet the need for a brief authoritative list of essential basic prescription drugs which can be purchased at minimum cost.

The Move to Promote Generic Prescribing

Many responsible members of our government are aware of the large savings to be made by buying generic rather than brand-name drugs where possible, and plans are under way to introduce legislation requiring the dispensing of generic preparations to patients whose drugs are being paid for under tax-supported Medicare. This comes as no surprise to those who know that all the military medical facilities buy and dispense only drugs which are bought by the Defense Supply Agency of the United States government under generic names from the lowest competitive bidders. Although many of the contract winners are small and middle-sized manufacturers (*institutional* buyers such as municipal hospitals are at present their major market), when the big corporations have entered into sealed bidding there have been some remarkable revelations. For example, CIBA, the enormous Switzerland-based company, offered to sell to the United States government for about 60 cents a quantity and quality of reserpine (1000 0.25 mgm tablets) for which the corner pharmacist must pay $39.50. The Government buys it as (generic name) "reserepine"; the corner pharmacist buys and dispenses it as (brand name) "Serpasil." There are no important differences between the two; only the name—and $39. Ironically, CIBA did not win the contract, for they were underbid by a company willing to sell the same drug for 51 cents.

In addition to Federal government institutions, state and municipal and many private nonprofit hospitals buy generics. Many have their own formulary, which restricts in-hospital usage to a list of selected basic generic drugs, the appropriate one being substituted for the expensive brand-name item wherever the institution's own committee on drugs (consisting of its own physicians and pharmacists) deems it appropriate and suitable. This meets with nearly unanimous acceptance on the part of the doctors, but is anathema to brand-name manufacturers. According to corporate thinking, the formulary restricts the doctor's freedom of choice. Therefore the National Pharmaceutical Council, Inc. (NPC), whose relatively few dues-paying members are exclusively heavily advertised brand-name drug manufacturers, is, according to its executive vice president, "particularly concerned with the practice known as substitution." He went on to say: ". . . a physician, in prescribing a particular brand of drug for a patient, may be doing so because that brand has characteristics which the physician wants his patient to have and which may not be present in other brands. The generic name does not indicate to the dispensing pharmacist what these characteristics are and he cannot necessarily tell from reading the prescription why the prescriber chose the brand he did. If the pharmacist is permitted to substitute the so-called generic equivalent, he *very likely* is not substituting a drug with equivalent characteristics and may be defeating the very purpose of the physician in selecting the brand of drug he chose." [8]

The statement is nonsense. In seventeen years of clinical experience, an instance where a prescription was written for a brand-name drug because of "characteristics" other than the identity of its major ingredient has never come to my attention. Furthermore, close physician colleagues I have questioned are unaware of any such instances. The representative of the National Pharmaceutical Council ended his prepared remarks by asserting: ". . . we insist that the medical profession be left free to prescribe exactly what it sees fit and that the public be assured that it gets what the doctor prescribed." [9] Any implication that the generically named drug does not contain what the doctor prescribed is false.

What About Research?

There is merit to the argument that some large pharmaceutical companies do important research and maintain facilities to provide a number of public services for which they are never adequately compensated in dollars. On the other hand, few manufacturers of generic

[8] *Hearings on S. Res. 238,* Part 21, pp. 11695, 11699.
[9] *Ibid.,* p. 11701.

drugs do research and none is equipped to provide an adequate supply, let us say, of rare antitoxins should need ever arise, whereas some of the big companies are in a position to do so. It has been pointed out, however, that the large corporations spend nearly four times as much for advertising and promotion as they do for research, and it has been said that much of the latter takes the form of "molecule-manipulating" attempts to produce a drug which will have the same pharmacological effect as an agent already patented and marketed by a competitor. Upon discovering such a compound the company may patent it, market it, and join in the competition even though it offers no substantial advantage over the older, better-known drug. It is the proliferation of such drugs, each with its own brand name, each launched with a giant promotional campaign, that has caused much of the confusion besetting the doctor. Activity of this sort could conceivably be beneficial by giving rise to price competition. Unfortunately, this rarely happens because the major manufacturers, with a few exceptions, peg their prices at practically the same, often identical figures.

However, while one can therefore legitimately question the value of introducing "copy-cat" drugs, it is not entirely fair to question the the kind of research (viz., molecule manipulating) which makes them available. Anyone aware of the nature of pharmacology knows it is impossible to predict when a small change in molecular structure is going to cause significant beneficial change in pharmacological effect or in toxicity. (A mere increase in potency is not beneficial, however, for it makes little difference to the patient whether he swallows a 10 or a 500 milligram tablet.) There is no doubt that the pharmaceutical industry has made many important research contributions.[10] Many conscientious physicians undoubtedly feel that this one factor alone justifies prescribing brand-name items even though the patents have expired and patients have to pay more than if generic equivalents are prescribed. There is something to be said for this view, *provided public money is not involved (as with welfare or Medicare patients) and that private patients who foot drug bills directly are agreeable. Patients (who are "captive consumers") have a right to know for what services they are paying.* Other equally conscientious physicians may take the view that the responsibility of the doctor is to his patient's immediate

---

[10] About two thirds of the *Handbook's* basic drugs were developed entirely or in part by the pharmaceutical industry, but the patents by now have expired on more than half of these.

welfare—including his pocketbook—and may not wish to allow an ideology of sorts to influence therapeutic practice.

Are Brand-Name Products Superior?

It is the contention of the *Handbook* that no one is in a position to make ironclad guarantees for any manufactured product, drugs included, and that there is no good reason to believe that brand-name drugs are necessarily more reliable than generics as to quality, purity, and potency. There is compelling evidence for this view in a study which presented unabridged details of all drug recalls [11] during a 33 month period ending June 30, 1965. This information was supplied by the Food and Drug Administration to a congressional committee. The facts speak for themselves: *nearly half of the recalls involved products of the largest and best-known corporations.* It is plain that a pharmaceutical manufacturer's reliability is not related either to size or to advertising budget. One wonders even whether physician, pharmacist, and patient have not been placing exaggerated confidence in certain well-known firms. It would be incorrect to infer that all large pharmaceutical manufacturers are not reliable in their over-all production, but the evidence does point up the injustice in wholesale condemnation of all smaller drug manufacturers.

Because 90% of the drugs currently sold in the United States are produced by about two dozen of the largest brand-name drug manufacturers, it is fair to ask whether the number of their substandard products, accounting for nearly half of the total, is nonetheless disproportionately smaller than would be expected. It is possible to provide a tentative answer, since the Kefauver Subcommittee did its work so thoroughly. In the hearings the then Commissioner of Food and Drugs, Mr. George Larrick, testified: "We confine sampling to drugs which we have reason to believe may be misbranded or adulterated." [12] Mr. Larrick provided data showing the number of samples taken per one-million-dollar volume of business in the cases of several large and several small companies during the decade 1950–1960. In the cases of Merck, CIBA, Schering, and Carter Products (Wallace Laboratories), one sample alone was taken per one million dollars of business;

[11] The removal from a pharmacy of drugs discovered not to meet *U.S.P.* standards or of drugs which are mislabeled.
[12] *Hearings on S. 1552,* Part 22, p. 12113.

for Smith Kline & French, Lederle, Pfizer, and Upjohn the range was from one to less than five per one million dollars. For small companies, however, the situation was strikingly different, for here the number of samples ranged around one hundred per one million dollars and in several instances was even more numerous! [13] This kind of sampling, in effect, spotlights the violations of the small companies, upon which the enforcement work is concentrated.

Furthermore, with respect to the activities of the major drug companies, Dr. Barbara Moulton, formerly an FDA staff member, testified: "Private conferences between representatives of industry and the Food and Drug Administration staff members are also the rule rather than the exception with respect to regulatory action under the law." Thus, when a large manufacturer was concerned, situations more commonly than not were rectified by informal rather than official agreement. Thus, damaging reports of official recall actions were often avoided, for the FDA records of such informal agreements were allegedly incomplete.[14]

Not least of the reasons forcing us to believe that brand-name drugs are not necessarily better than those sold by generic names is a finding made by the United States Food and Drug Administration. At the direction of its then new, no-nonsense Commissioner, Dr. James Goddard, the Agency sampled 4,600 drugs from 250 manufacturers. Quoting Mr. Winton B. Rankin, former Deputy Commissioner, as he addressed the American College of Apothecaries on October 15, 1966, in Boston, Massachusetts: "About 2600 of the drugs were sold by their generic name only and about 2,000 by brand name. They represented 20 of the most important groups of drugs used in medicine—antihypertensives, oral antidiabetics, anti-infectives, digitalis and digitalis-like preparations, for example. Antibiotics were not included because every lot of antibiotics for human use is checked by FDA before sale." Deputy Commissioner Rankin then went on to reveal to a hushed audience of pharmacists that "7.8 percent of the generic-named drugs were not of acceptable potency, 8.8 percent of the brand-named drugs were not of acceptable potency." Later, in reply to a question from the audience, the speaker made it clear that the difference between the 7.8 and 8.8 percent figures is not large enough to allow one to conclude that generic drugs are necessarily better than those sold by brand name.

[13] S. Rep. No. 448, p. 246.
[14] *Ibid.*

C. Trading Stamps

17. "Liberty and Property, and No Stamps" *

Carolyn Shaw Bell

The spectacular growth of trading stamps which began in the early 1950's evoked strong reactions from retailers (from "They're the finest thing that ever happened" [1] to "These stamps are a drag on civilization" [2]), led to a number of government investigations and efforts at restrictive legislation, and earned general condemnation from economists and consumer representatives. But so far, the competitive outcome has been as foretold by Kroger's President Joseph Hall, when he said, "Nobody loves stamps except the customers."

By the same token, the long-run position of trading stamps in retailing will depend on their continuing acceptability in the economy. Yet, as this paper shows, few analyses explain the basic functions of trading stamps or attempt to deal with the fundamental determinants of their acceptability. Many have prophesied the decline of stamps and the demise of the stamp companies, but with so little solid basis that one suspects the prophets of mere wishful thinking. This is true even though the last few years have seen a leveling of stamp company sales and the beginnings of what might be either an intermediate or a

---

* The title is a motto frequently used by colonial newspapers after the Stamp Act was passed in 1763.

[1] J. Reid Mercer, quoted in *Home Furnishings Daily,* May 2, 1957.

[2] Ralph W. Burger, president, A & P Company, at annual meeting, June, 1960.

Reprinted from the *Journal of Business,* Vol. 40 (April, 1967), 194–202, by permission of The University of Chicago Press. © 1967 by The University of Chicago.

major decline in a number of measures of consumer acceptance and retail use. For, without analysis, we still have only some short-run trends—the meaning of which is unclear—and the prophets, most of whom have an economic interest and/or a strong previous commitment to guide their forecast. This paper approaches prophecy through an effort to improve the analysis of trading stamps. The first part seeks to clarify the central issues of the use of stamps by retailers as a competitive weapon. The next part deals with stamps as currency and with redemption centers as stores.

Trading Stamps as Competition

Most investigators of trading stamps have asked whether or not they result in higher prices to consumers, and much persuasive theory and convincing data abound on both sides of the question. The approach suffers from its failure to analyze trading stamps in the wider context of retail competition: an area where there are many individual sellers and consumer-buyers who readily shift from one store to another.

Such markets correspond closely to those of the theory of monopolistic competition, for each seller exercises control over both "product" and prices, but what he sells bears close resemblance to the output of competing retailers. The struggle for consumer patronage involves many weapons of non-price competition, including trade stamps. But if trading stamps represent a form of non-price competition, it follows that calculating their effect on the level of prices is almost irrelevant. For if the stamps are used to differentiate the seller's output, they affect his costs but not necessarily prices; while if trading stamps are abandoned, they may be replaced by other ways of establishing the store's identity, including games, giveaways, increased advertising, or other promotional activity—and the effect on prices is equally unpredictable. This analysis can be illustrated by looking more closely at the retailers chiefly concerned.

Grocery stores

Most studies of the price effects of trading stamps have focused on food, presumably reflecting concern with the "necessities" of life and recognition of the importance of stamps in food retailing.[3] But how do

---

[3] See, for example, "Trading Stamps and Their Impact on Food Prices" (USDA Marketing Research Report No. 295, Washington, D.C., 1958); James

consumers buy, and how do sellers compete? Is the unit of purchase and sale of food plus or minus trading stamps? Clearly not. For any consumer, buying anything includes a number of processes: deciding what to buy and where to buy it, giving an order or making the selection known, receiving the purchase, and paying for it. What the consumer "buys" from a supermarket or corner store or food specialty shop—as from any other retailer—involves all these things—the shopping process as well as the commodity purchased. One store may display a wider range of choice, one may make the consumer's self-selection easier, one may have quicker checkout service and delivery to her car, one may impose unpleasant rules about cashing checks for payment. It is by varying these, and the myriad other conditions of shopping, that individual stores offer differentiated outputs. They compete by stocking different qualities and price lines of inventory, by arranging traffic patterns and shelf space, by providing flimsy or sturdy bags, by creating a friendly or efficient atmosphere. Price competition may be a part of the over-all marketing strategy, but the retailer and consumer both rely heavily on non-price considerations.

Studies abound which show the characteristics which influence a consumer's choice of store. The consensus is that in supermarkets consumers look for a "good" meat department, quality and freshness of meats and produce, cleanliness and orderly housekeeping arrangements, low prices, a convenient location, and courtesy. Shopping and switching are common; one study found that 71% of all the respondents shopped in more than one store, and 25% reported that the current "favorite" store where "most" food is purchased was chosen less than two years previously.[4] Other studies suggest that when a consumer quits a store her dissatisfaction stems from the quality of meats or produce, cluttered arrangements, or rude or unfriendly treatment by store personnel.

In such a situation, the individual food store seeks to increase sales primarily at the expense of its competitors. The store that can enhance its "image" in the eyes of the consumer attracts more new customers and may hang onto its steady customers for a longer period of

---

D. Bromley and William H. Wallace, "The Effect of Trading Stamps on Retail Food Prices" (Contribution No. 1091 of the R. I. Agricultural Experiment Station, Kingston, Rhode Island); and National Commission on Food Retailing, "Organization and Competition in Food Retailing" (June, 1966), chap. vii.

[4] *Food Topics,* January, 1965, 42.

time. And trading stamps, obviously, provide such a means of non-price competition. This is clear to the stamp companies; the president of the S & H Company has emphasized that stamps offer the consumer "an incentive to buy at a particular store," and give the retailer "what every competitor seeks to achieve—a way of making his store stand out." [5]

That trading stamps no longer serve to differentiate the individual seller when all stores offer stamps is the complaint of those who pose the question, "Who pays the costs of stamps when everyone is using them and there can be no gain in sales?" [6] Yet the retailer in a stamp-saturated market may differentiate not his store but his stamp plan from those offered by competing sellers. Hence double-stamp days, one hundred stamps on special items, and so on. Hence also the observation that trading stamps are not advertising but something to be advertised, or the advice by John Jacobszoon, customer relations manager for Orange Stamps, Inc.: "Trading stamps should be merchandised just like any other product, and every retailer should be able to play his own game as hard and as aggressively as he wishes," in an effort "to outsmart and outmaneuver the competition." [7]

Clearly, this analysis shows that no *a priori* conclusion about the effects of trading stamps on prices can be drawn.

That lower prices are not the only alternative to trading stamps appeared in an early study which questioned food and drug stores *not* offering trading stamps about how they competed.[8] Almost two-thirds of the drug stores and one-quarter of the food stores reported that they ignored the problem. Lower prices were mentioned by a minority of drug stores and only half the food stores; the remainder used one form or another of increased promotional activity. That removing stamps would not necessarily result in lower prices follows clearly from the suggestions made by a number of store operators who were asked what they would do with the cost saving from dropping

---

[5] William S. Beinecke, "Trading Stamps" (address for the Tobe Lecture Series, Harvard Graduate School of Business Administration, February 15, 1962).

[6] Similar complaints are often voiced by merchants who drop stamps; see the *Wall Street Journal*, September 17, 1963, p. 24, for a typical statement by a grocery chain manager.

[7] John Jacobszoon of Orange Stamps, Inc., quoted in *Supermarket Merchandising* (May, 1965), 10.

[8] *Status of Trading Stamps in Food and Drug Stores*, Selling Research, Inc., February 18, 1957.

stamps—estimated at $25,000 for a store with $1 million in sales.[9] An over-all price reduction of 2% was only one of the alternatives suggested; others included massive price reductions on a few items, adding more employees at the checkout stands, providing free delivery, or stepping up the store's program for renovation and replacement.

The analysis fits drug stores so easily that they need not be dealt with separately.

Gasoline stations

This third major category of stamp users resembles grocery stores in its reliance on non-price competition to confer distinctive appeal on what most consumers suspect is a fundamentally similar product. Gasoline stations have their own special characteristics, of course: their reliance on one brand and only a few closely related products, the fact that the shopper is most mobile just when he is ready to buy, and the frequent clustering of outlets at points of high vehicle traffic density. These and perhaps other characteristics of the product and industry cause many marketers to seek to avoid price competition, since price cuts will usually be so quickly and fully offset by the actions of so many close competitors.

Consequently, filling stations emphasize not simply the gasoline but also the station's combination of efficiency in filling a gas tank and cleaning windshields and headlights, or checking tires and oil, the attractiveness of its rest rooms, the personality of its servicemen, the availability of credit cards, and the general "image" of the dealer's business.

In this situation, trading stamps provide a new dimension of non-price competition for both buyers and sellers to explore. Although the stamps may look and sound like money, they are not so close to money as to provoke a price "war." This is because of the indefiniteness of their value and the fact that they must be accumulated and "spent" later—characteristics which will be discussed further in the next section.

Redemption Centers As Distributors

Although most analysis has centered on the cost of trading stamps to the retailer and whether these costs are passed on to the buyer in the

[9] *Progressive Grocer,* XLIV, No. 2 (February, 1965), 62.

form of higher prices, trading stamps are involved in still another transaction—that of the consumer in the redemption center where the
stamps are given up. These transactions and their costs have rarely
been mentioned and almost never analyzed in any careful way. Yet a
complete market structure has been developed by trading-stamp companies, a market with demand and supply and prices, with buyers and
sellers and a medium of exchange. In this market, trading-stamp companies are distributors, linking producers with consumers. It is this
market structure, its benefits and its costs, which deserves further investigation.

The notion that trading-stamp companies offer an additional system of distribution has been mentioned occasionally. *Consumer Reports* commented that "basically, a stamp redemption center is a
retailer." [10] An editorial in the *Nation* pointed out that the trading-
stamp companies have, in effect, erected a parallel system of retailing.[11] The S & H Company has even claimed that "trading stamps turn
out to be . . . a remarkably efficient way of distributing merchandise." [12] Nonetheless there has been little published analysis of this
claim of efficiency. The only data casting any light on the distribution
activities of trading-stamp companies concern the volume of merchandise handled by the companies, and most such estimates are necessarily
vulnerable.

The S & H Company states that the green-stamp book (containing
1,200 stamps) is worth an average of $3.00 in merchandise. Using
this value of $2.50 per thousand stamps, estimates of total merchan-
dise distributed by all companies showed a growth from $22 million in
1950 to $570 million in 1960. This method implies that merchandise
redeemed in 1964 amounted to slightly over $800 million.[13] But it is
an extremely crude estimate which makes no allowance for the type of
goods redeemed by consumers, or the alternatives available.

Frequent attempts have been made to derive the average value of
a book of stamps by comparing the prices of specific items shown in
catalogues or available at redemption centers to prices charged by
retail stores. One extensive study, by Bromley and Wallace, priced

---

[10] *Consumer Reports,* XXVII, No. 7 (October, 1962), 513.

[11] *Nation,* CCI, No. 10 (September 13, 1965), 130–31.

[12] *Progressive Grocer,* XLIV, No. 11 (November, 1965), 156, quoting
Eugene Beem, economist for the S & H company.

[13] The rate of redemption has, of course, not slackened off to the same extent as other indicators of trading-stamp usage.

"items in the stamp catalog . . . in several outlets, and an average value per book of stamps was computed to be $2.66. The range in value per book of stamps varied from $1.96 to $3.37 depending upon the item." [14] One of the most recent studies along these lines, and certainly the best, was reported by Vredenburg and Frisinger.[15] Their investigation, while confined to one type of stamp and to stores in Denver, sampled the items to be compared on the basis of actual redemptions by stamp savers, and obtained prices from different types of retail operations. Such detailed analysis calculated the purchasing power of a book of stamps to be a weighted average value of $3.11. Depending on the individual item selected, the book's value ranged from $2.00 to $5.88. When prices from discount stores only were used for calculation, the weighted average value for a single book was $2.82, compared to $3.21 on the basis of prices in "traditional" retail outlets.

All such studies, at best, provide more or less accurate estimates of the value of a book of stamps in one particular locality. But no such value can be blown up to estimate the total amount of merchandise distributed through redemption centers. To do this would require extensive sampling of consumer choices at redemption centers and of retail prices in stores surrounding these centers throughout the country. For one interesting fact about redemption centers as distribution channels is that the redemption experience of trading-stamp companies differs significantly. A survey of the ten largest trading-stamp companies shows, for example, that while soft goods lead in the type of merchandise redeemed, one company finds 12.8% of its redemptions call for such items, while another redeems 17.3% of its stamps with soft goods. Part of the variations in consumers' choice reflects regional differences: The widest range of redemption rates among companies occurs with outdoor accessories (from 2.3% to 10.4%) and tools (from 1.0% to 5.9%).[16] Part of the variation presumably reflects differences in family size and composition and income, just as dollar expenditures for consumer goods and services do. It is doubtful whether much of the variation reflects "price" differences—the number of books required for a specific item by different trading-stamp companies—if only because comparing the offerings of different stamp

---

[14] Bromley and Wallace, *op. cit.*, p. 8.
[15] Harvey L. Vredenburg and H. Howard Frisinger, "The Value of Trading Stamps as Measured by Retail Prices," *Journal of Retailing*, XLI, No. 3 (Fall, 1965), 28.
[16] *Premium Practice* (March 1964), pp. 46–48.

companies to calculate such differences is well-nigh impossible in most cases. But the variations do reflect the type of merchandise offered by the particular catalogue and redemption center and to some extent the availability, or lack of it, of similar items for sale at retail stores.[17] These circumstances would obviously differ in different localities.

For a useful appraisal of redemption centers, we need at least to consider some of the other aspects which are as important as the kinds and alternative prices of the merchandise that moves through them. Primarily, we must examine what the trading-stamp companies offer as a distinct type of shopping process, and their efficiency at satisfying consumers' preferences in this sphere, compared to that of retail stores. This can be done, from the consumer's point of view, by reviewing the steps in the shopping process. As posited earlier, any consumer must decide whether and what to buy and where to buy it, must give an order or make the decision known in some way, must take possession of the purchase and pay for it. How does the consumer fare in a redemption center?

The very act of collecting and redeeming stamps removes part of the first step: The consumer with S & H green stamps can obtain merchandise only in the S & H redemption center; the collector of Top Value stamps has no choice among retail outlets. While the individual centers operated by the same company may differ, the distances between them prevent the consumer's considering two Plaid stamp outlets competitors for her Plaid stamp patronage. Retail stores offer no real alternative, partly because of the difficulties of comparing price and product variation, but chiefly because the consumer has stamps to dispose of. While the notion of thrift and saving has often been associated with collecting stamps, and some consumers have said that any extra cost imposed by stamps is justified because stamps help them save up for discretionary purchases, it should be clear that for most consumers trading stamps do not force saving, but consumption.

The choice of what to buy is also sharply limited by the same circumstances. As of 1964, the S & H Company listed 1,742 items in its *Ideabook,* but any such number is subject to several adjustments. Most catalogues include more items than are found in the redemption centers, but groups can make special arrangements to buy such uncatalogued items as a school bus, a town ambulance, or a missionary tour.

---

[17] Vredenburg and Frisinger, *op. cit.,* sampled 100 items and found 26 of them unavailable in the Denver stores shopped.

For most consumers, the net effect is that the catalogue overstates the choices available at the redemption center.

The stamp companies' catalogue inventories consist largely of well-known branded items. Thus, in deciding what to "buy," the consumer can rely not only on the catalogue description but also on the manufacturer's advertising, product information from other retail outlets, and information from present owners of the product. To supplement these sources, the consumer can examine the product at the redemption center, if the item is in stock. One thing that is lacking is expert advice from a salesclerk; the thin coverage of any one merchandise line precludes the use of salespeople with special competence in particular lines.

It is generally true that the stamp catalogue represents only one manufacturer of a given product, although in some categories, noticeably household linens and some housewares, there may be more than one brand. Within a product line, the quality grades and brands offered are often, though not always, well below the top of the range.

All of the foregoing supports one solid conclusion about the merchandise offerings of redemption centers: Even though there may be two or three thousand items in the catalogue, the redemption centers impose a severe limitation on consumer choice.

Redemption centers force an entirely different pattern of choice on the consumer from that ordinarily encountered. Any buying decision involves opportunity costs. A decision to buy, for example, an electric blanket entails a cost represented by the other goods and services (including saving) which the consumer must do without. But the opportunity cost of a specific *style* and *brand* of blanket is merely the other, competing styles and brands of blankets. In the usual shopping process, the consumer weighs many different means of satisfying one want, for example, for an electric blanket. Opportunity costs in a redemption center are at once greater and less. The cost of an electric blanket shown in a stamp company's catalogue is not all other goods and services but only those offered in the catalogue. In some ways this might seem to ease the decision-making process for some consumers —those for whom stamp redemptions are their only way of acquiring "luxury" merchandise—but by the same token, it imposes a greater burden on consumers whose general level of living encompasses and exceeds the offerings of stamp companies. The second calculation of opportunity costs frequently does not exist. So the decision to "buy" a particular style and brand of electric blanket does not mean giving up other styles and brands of blankets, but giving up everything else in the catalogue. The consumer cannot weigh different means of satisfying one want, but must evaluate different products serving different desires. Trading-stamp companies, as distributors, limit consumer choice.

The shopping process continues when the consumer makes his wants known, and here the redemption center performs abysmally. Despite the convenience of catalogues for consumers to choose from, and despite the fact that the majority of consumers know what they want before going to a redemption center, the consumer must travel to the store, making an entire journey or "special trip" for stamp merchandise alone. Only if the redemption center is beyond a stated distance can the buyer order by mail, and again the decision of whether to shop by mail or in person is not the consumer's choice, but part of the stamp companies' regulations.

Once inside the redemption center, the process of ordering, getting the goods, and making payment ensues, with a glaring contrast to efficient retailing. The first move is to give an order, but frequently it involves a check with the clerk on price and a request to see a color or style not on display. "Upon entering the store, the consumer typically finds a line of people before him. In due time, it is his turn for service. If the customer finds something that suits him all he can do at this stage is to ask the price and permission to examine the goods. He then leaves the salesclerk (without the merchandise) and enters a new line in front of the cashier. . . . Here he pays the cashier the . . . amount . . . just quoted to him by the salesclerk, and, in return, receives a receipt. . . . With his receipt in hand, the shopper moves to a third line. After turning in his receipt . . . he finally receives his package." [18] Despite the aptness of the description, the quotations do not refer to the typical American trading-stamp store, but to a typical retail shop in the Soviet Union.

Like the managers of retail enterprises in the Soviet Union trading-stamp companies have made some endeavor to reduce the customer costs of this purchasing routine. In some redemption centers, the order clerk also takes stamp books in payment, reducing the number of queues. But if the clerk has to remove an item locked for protection in a cabinet, or bring a sample from the stockroom for inspection,

[18] Marshall I. Goldman, *Soviet Marketing* (New York: The Free Press, 1963), p. 17.

there is not always a saving of time. All too frequently the consumer finds that his choice, made from a catalogue, has been discontinued or is out of stock at the redemption center, so he must repeat the frustrating process of selection. Nor is the time and trouble imposed on the shopper compensated with service by the center—no interested salesperson makes an alternative suggestion, nor can the clerks provide the additional bit of technical information which might help the consumer arrive at a final choice. Some companies have been experimenting with self-service or drive-in centers, but these are few and far between.

Retailing in America has accustomed the shopper to the speed of self-selection and to service when the customer wants it. Queues in retail stores are so foreign to the typical shopper that those few outlets which experience temporary overcrowding use a number system to keep people in line, such devices are normal in stamp-redemption centers. Even where conditions are not crowded, the shopping process is a far cry from the efficient progress of the customer in a supermarket, self-service variety store, or discount outlet. Nor is the enforced leisure of the redemption-center shopper comparable to the time spent willingly in browsing through a department store or consulting with the knowledgeable sales force of a specialty shop. Again, the operative word is "enforced"—the consumer has no choice but to spend time and effort at the redemption center, which typically requires more of both than do competing retailers.

The development of American retailing shows an impressive pattern of innovation, adoption, reorganization, and innovation once again. Almost every form of retailing—mail-order houses, department stores, chain stores, supermarkets, discount houses, and shopping centers—prospered in the midst of opposition and fear on the part of "conventional" retailers. Each, in turn, appeared as a more or less dire threat which would wipe out established ways of doing business, but each has found some place in the present-day merchandising scene. It is exactly these innovations in retailing which make the theory of monopolistic competition so appropriate, enabling one store to differentiate its output from that of competing sellers. Does this point of view mean that trading-stamp companies represent one more development in the continually changing retail scene? They offer a slightly different shopping process: a smaller inventory composed of well-known brands of fast-selling items, relying on a considerable amount of preselling, catalogues rather than clerks to provide price and product information, and none of the frills of credit, telephone order, or delivery. Competition among different forms of retailing has proved healthy: Do trading-stamp companies provide another desirable element of competition as the stamp companies claim?

The analogy does not come off. No other form of retailing has a monopoly of the medium of exchange used in buying and selling. The consumer is free to choose among different forms of retailing (discount house or department store) or between different retailers (two department stores) because all the stores use money. The consumer tied to one store cannot threaten any loss of patronage or offer any opportunity to a competing seller. The impact on efficiency is clear: In the absence of competitive pressure, one of the greatest incentives to improve efficiency is lacking. Just this reasoning was of great concern in the United Kingdom during World War II, under a rationing scheme which required consumers to register with one retailer for certain scarce foods. To overcome some of the disadvantages of the situation, consumers were allowed to re-register periodically. Trading stamps tie consumers to a redemption center with no hope of escape. The S & H Company prides itself on redeeming green stamps that were issued before 1900.

Because trading stamps represent a special currency—a separate medium of exchange from that used for most consumer purchases—they inevitably distort the pattern of consumer choice. When all the stores in a locality give stamps, so that the consumer has no alternative but to take them, the evil is not that no opportunity exists for a store to recoup the cost of the stamps by increasing volume but that no opportunity exists for the consumer to spend his income freely. Some part of income must be spent on the goods provided in redemption centers and the shopping process there endured.

The significance of the separate medium of exchange goes beyond its diminution of retail competition and of consumer choice. Retailers and stamp companies incur costs in safeguarding and accounting for the medium of exchange; just as cash registers eased the problems of handling currency in retail stores, so various types of stamp-issuing machines assist in keeping track of stamps but represent an additional investment in equipment. Each stamp company incurs further costs in voiding or destroying the stamps redeemed; so far, trading stamps have not attained the stature of a circulating medium of exchange nor have they been serviced by the banking system which handled ration stamps during World War II. As a medium of exchange, therefore, stamps impose extra costs and inefficiencies.

The separate system of distribution developed by the trading-stamp industry, failing to compete with existing outlets and requiring an additional medium of exchange, imposes additional costs on consumers. They lie in a threefold limitation of consumer choice. First, trading stamps impose consumption; forms of saving are not readily available alternatives. Second, the goods which consumers are forced to acquire must be selected from a limited assortment. Finally, the consumer must participate in an unwieldy and burdensome shopping process.

The standard answer to all complaints about trading stamps is that the consumer wishing to avoid such costs can buy at stores which do not give trading stamps. Such reasoning requires the consumer to place more importance on the presence or absence of trading stamps than on any other aspect of retailing. As was made clear earlier, consumers (and retailers) consider a wealth of different characteristics in selecting a retailer, and there is no reason to ignore price, quality, service, location, and all the other forms of competition. Rather, those who support the process of competition find that the real question of acceptability has yet to be answered: Why, in the face of an efficient system of money and banking, with a network of retail enterprises which is constantly innovating to fulfill consumers' preferences, does the economy need another, separate system of distribution? Over the years each major innovation in retailing has had to offer the consumer something fundamental in order to survive. What, in the case of trading stamps, are these benefits which outweigh their costs?

18. Schizophrenia in Trading Stamp Analysis

E. Beem and L. Isaacson *

Professor Bell is at war with herself in her lively critique on trading stamps ["Liberty and Property, and No Stamps," see p. 235]. She starts out by placing trading stamps neatly into an analytical framework which is powerful in explaining non-price competition. In this framework, competition is the search for distinctiveness. Firms adopt non-price forms of rivalry because they find better opportunities there for effective differentiation than in price rivalry. Thus, Professor Bell properly identifies trading stamps not as a substitute for lower prices but as an alternative to other forms of non-price competition.

The Struggle

Having concluded that trading stamps are just one form of non-price competition, Bell proceeds to neglect this conclusion as she examines the efficiency of trading stamp *compared to money.* She summarizes her case against trading stamp companies when she states:

* Vice president corporate research, and economist, respectively, for the Sperry and Hutchinson Company.

Reprinted from the *Journal of Business,* Vol. 41 (July, 1968), 340–344, by permission of The University of Chicago Press. © 1968 by The University of Chicago.

[Trading stamps impose] a threefold limitation of consumer choice. First, trading stamps impose consumption. . . . Second, the goods which consumers are forced to acquire must be selected from a limited assortment. Finally, the consumer must participate in an unwieldy and burdensome shopping process.

How can trading stamps survive, she pleads, when they so obviously offer the consumer less choice than money?

Stamps Provide Wide Choice

Trading stamps admittedly offer less consumer choice than money. But they offer more than just about any other form of non-price competition. Paradoxically, what Bell has termed a limitation of the trading stamp may in fact be its greatest strength!

Consider, for example, some of the alternatives to stamps: giveaway promotions which involve dishes, or encyclopedias, or drawings for a brand new Cadillac. Where is the choice in these? Where is the choice for the consumer who rejects or neglects advertising, who walks to a store with a large parking lot, who couldn't care less about music while she shops? Most forms of non-price competition just give one, or a few, options. Stamps not only provide numerous choices but they provide a *range* of alternatives deliberately selected to appeal to the broadest possible audience.

Why stamps are used

Why do stores offer trading stamps, or other non-price promotions, when money—that is, price cuts—would seem so much more efficient? Bell developed a partial answer; but there is more worth saying:

1. As Bell indicates, in most retail markets "each seller exercises control over both 'product' and prices, but what he sells bears close resemblance to the output of competing retailers. The struggle for consumer patronage involves many weapons of non-price competition, including trading stamps. . . . What the consumer 'buys' from a supermarket . . . involves all these things—the shopping process as well as the commodity purchased. . . . It is by varying these . . . that individual stores offer differentiated outputs."

While price cutting is easily imitated, stamp use is typically on a franchised basis. Thus stamps provide distinctiveness. Other stores can use different stamps, but customer acceptance varies considerably among stamp brands, and the store with the best stamp and the best program for promoting its stamp has an edge.

2. There is also a threshold problem with price cutting. Reducing prices in a supermarket by the cost of stamps would mean an average reduction per item of one-half to three-fourths of a penny. Many customers would not perceive such a price cut. Others, who notice the change, may not respond. After all, in total, a 2% price cut amounts to only 10 or 12 cents on the average customer's transaction. But the same 2% means 50 or 60 stamps, which turns out to be a highly visible and dramatically attractive incentive for many shoppers.

Some retailers attempt to create the illusion of low over-all prices by using the same 2% to make large cuts in a few items. Results in the marketplace suggest that many customers recognize this tactic after a short while. Such stores tend to collect large numbers of bargain hunters—who buy only the bargains—and who display little store loyalty. Such retailers experience a constant need for new promotions to bring customers back. By contrast, the appeal of stamps continues unabated over long periods.

3. A third reason for stamp use is that most women (and even most men) like to save them. Most consumers think of stamps as discretionary spending power—a way to provide extras for the home—perhaps an easier way than putting aside nickels and dimes. Many consumers seem to prefer stamp saving to other promotional extras.

According to a survey by the Louis Harris organization, roughly a quarter of the men and women in America like stamps so well they say they would even prefer them to price cuts in supermarkets if such a choice were to be offered.[1] Had the Harris question specified that the price cuts equivalent to stamps would average just one-half to three-fourths of a penny per item, rather than leaving it to the imagination of the respondent, the vote for stamps would have been higher, as has been shown by other research.

So trading stamps continue to thrive in America not because they are generally more efficient than money but because they are more efficient in meeting the special competitive needs of some retailers and because they bring satisfactions to many customers that could not readily be realized in other ways.

Efficiency of the Stamp System

Moreover, simply as a way of using society's resources to move merchandise to customers, stamps are—Bell to the contrary—an efficient instrument of distribution.

[1] Louis Harris, *New York Post,* December 12, 1966, p. 17.

Let us examine Bell's specific charges. She states: "The separate system of distribution developed by the trading-stamp industry, failing to compete with existing outlets and requiring an additional medium of exchange, imposes additional costs on customers. . . . The impact on efficiency is clear: In the absence of competitive pressure, one of the greatest incentives to improve efficiency is lacking."

Bell suggests looking at the merchandise value customers get for their stamps versus the cost merchants pay for stamp service, as a way to judge efficiency. In a doctoral dissertation at Rutgers University, Dr. Harold Fox focused on just this issue.[2] What Fox found was that, taking S & H stamps as an example, customers received more in retail value than the retailer had paid! In other words, less resources are used up when goods move to consumers through trading stamp centers than when goods move to consumers through ordinary distribution channels.

In reaching this conclusion, Fox reviewed a number of previous value studies, including those cited by Bell, and he conducted new studies in discount and department stores in five cities. The average value for S & H stamps found by Fox was $2.88 per book for those items he located in discount stores and $3.29 per book in department stores.

Other studies of the value of trading stamps have reached similar conclusions, as Bell notes in her citation of the study by Vredenburg and Frisinger [3] which used similar methods. Despite numerous studies, it is not surprising that some public misunderstanding exists as to the value of a book of trading stamps. Fox found the average value in department stores to be 41 cents per book higher than in discount stores. Moreover, he found a wide range of values from stamp item to stamp item within each type of store. Thus a customer setting out to "price" a book of stamps might readily find a value ranging from below two dollars to above four dollars, depending on which items he chose to price and the store where he chose to do the pricing.

Moreover, different stamp companies offer different value levels; and stamp companies generally issue just one annual catalogue to serve a wide geographic area. The S & H Company, for example, issues

[2] Harold Fox, *The Economics of Distributing Merchandise Through the Trading Stamp Channel* (unpublished Ph.D. dissertation, Rutgers University, June, 1967).

[3] Harvey L. Vredenburg and H. Howard Frisinger, "The Value of Trading Stamps as Measured by Retail Prices," *Journal of Retailing,* XLI, No. 3 (Fall, 1965), 28.

32 million catalogues throughout the United States. Naturally, retail competition differs from city to city, and different items are on sale or used as price leaders. These specials vary from time to time. Types of items such as small appliances which are highly identifiable are often discounted routinely by regular stores as well as by discount centers. Thus, when only such items are used to evaluate a stamp book the resulting value is likely to be substantially lower than the average. Fox, for example, found an average value per collector book for S & H appliances of only $2.62—as compared with $3.95 for jewelry and clothing and $4.13 for silver, holloware, and flatware. *By using stamps selectively*—as with their cash purchases—consumers can increase their buying power.

The average cost to a supermarket for the S & H service is just under $2.50 per book of stamps issued. Other types of issuers, who buy in smaller quantities, pay somewhat more, bringing the S & H average income per book up to about $2.68.

Following procedures defined by Fox, Table 1 compares S & H operating data to those for department stores. In this table, S & H values are discounted for stamps that will not be redeemed, and regular store prices are adjusted to allow for average markdowns. Even after these allowances are made, the over-all performance of S & H is better than department stores. How can a trading stamp company, which must print stamps and catalogs and sell its stamp service to retailers, possibly provide consumers with more merchandise value than the stamp-using merchants have paid to the stamp company?

Stamp companies buy merchandise at low wholesale cost because item by item they are extremely large individual purchasers. Moreover, shipments come not to the stores but to warehouses, with attendant efficiency in shipping and processing orders. With limited and stable merchandise lines, stamp companies enjoy substantial economies in the warehousing function as compared to ordinary distribution channels and can employ a higher degree of automation. Moreover, they have virtually no selling costs within the distribution channel.

Even greater economies are realized in the operation of the redemption stores. Compared to department stores, for example, the S & H store expense is less than half because so many customers— roughly 85%—have preselected their choices from the catalog before coming to the store. In addition, the average value of a customer transaction is somewhat higher than for department stores.

Furthermore, the trading stamp company offers fewer in-store serv-

Table 1. Comparison of operating data for department stores and S & H
(Per book of 1,200 stamps)

	Department Stores [1]	S & H [2]
Prices as originally marked	$3.29	$2.83
Markdowns	0.21	0.01
Net selling price	3.08	2.82 [3]
Cost of goods at store door	1.98	1.79 [4]
Gross margin	1.10	1.03
Store expense	0.64	0.29
Administrative expense	0.17 [5]	0.17
Marketing expense	0.11 [6]	0.32
Total expense	0.92	0.80
Net operating income	0.18	0.23
Other income	(0.01)	0.06
Profit before taxes	0.17	0.29
Taxes	0.08	0.14
Profit after taxes	$0.09	$0.15

[1] *Financial and Operating Results of Department and Speciality Stores* (in 1966) (New York: Controllers Congress, National Retail Merchants Association, 1967). Operating data from the all-company summary on p. iv are applied to the $3.29 per book value found by Fox for items identical to the S & H line. This comparison assumes that costs for the entire department store are applicable to these items.
[2] The S & H Company 1966 operating data.
[3] Net income per 1,200 stamps issued: $2.68; allowance of unredeemed stamps (5%): $0.14; net income per 1,200 stamps redeemed: $2.82.
[4] The S & H Company operates its own central warehouses, while most department store firms do not. Therefore, S & H freight to warehouses and warehouse costs have been included in cost of goods.
[5] Fixed and policy expense.
[6] Sales promotion.

ices, such as credit and delivery, as Bell points out. Despite these limited services, typical consumer reaction to stamp redemption centers is predominantly positive, not typified by Bell's own personal response.

The Question of Choice

Bell voices her most strenuous objections to trading stamps when dealing with the problem of choice: "The redemption center performs abysmally. . . . All too frequently the consumer finds that his choice, made from a catalogue, has been discontinued or is out of stock at the redemption center . . . the consumer has no choice but to spend time and effort at the redemption center, which typically requires more of both than do competing retailers."

The results of recent research throw considerable light on the extent to which consumers are being satisfied. In a national survey, stamp savers were shown an extensive list of aspects of stamp saving. They were asked to classify them as "rather annoying or troublesome, a little annoying or troublesome, or not at all annoying or troublesome." On every aspect listed, the majority responded that stamp saving was "not at all annoying or troublesome."

Just 3% of all stamp savers questioned indicated they found it "rather annoying or troublesome" to "find something [they] really want in the stamp catalog," while an additional 9% reported "a little" difficulty.

Service at redemption centers also received significant endorsement from savers. In contrast to Bell's comments on redemption centers, a national sample [4] of recent redeemers responded: over-all rating: "poor," 2%; speed of service: "poor," 5%; courtesy and friendliness of clerks: "poor," 2%; quality of premiums: "poor," 1%.

Similar ratings for department stores are not available, so no direct comparison can be made. Perhaps consumer expectations concerning service are lower for trading stamp redemption centers than for regular stores. Nevertheless, these ratings are clear evidence that few consumers share Bell's critical opinion of the redemption process.

Conclusion

All of us are probably tempted to attribute to others our own subjective feelings. While Professor Bell has done an excellent job of placing stamps in a theoretical economic context, she has relied, in the absence of other information, on her own personal, subjective reactions to evaluate stamps from the standpoint of consumer welfare. As shown above, when stamps are compared to their most likely substitutes, they turn out to provide more choice, at good value to consumers, and in a manner which displeases few, while pleasing many.

[4] Benson & Benson, Inc. Princeton, New Jersey—*Nationwide Survey of Attitude toward and Familiarity with Trading Stamps* (Survey X), Princeton, N.J.: Benson & Benson, July, 1966.

Part Four
Post-Purchase Experience

Introduction

Research on the purchase decision process indicates that buyers who have made a significant purchase are likely to have negative post-decision feelings, or cognitive dissonance, about their purchase. Some of this dissonance is a residual of the doubts and anxieties generated by the painful process of choosing among many attractive alternatives. Unhappy post-purchase experiences are another source of dissonance. For example, the purchaser may hear information that reflects badly on his choice (imagine the feelings of the proud owner of a new television when he hears that it leaks dangerous radiation, or the distress occasioned by the recall of a new car to correct a potential brake defect). Performance may not match expectations or promises, and usage may be prone to unexpected failure. The effect is compounded when recourse to the manufacturer or retailer for service or replacement is unsatisfactory. The ultimate dissatisfaction comes from personal injury occasioned by proper use of the product.

255

Evidence is sparse, but it is hard to deny that post-purchase dissatisfaction and regret are at a high level in many product categories. Among the contributing factors that show no signs of abating are: (1) the flow of new durable goods which are often more complex and confusing to operate, and have greater potential for malfunction, (2) service facilities which are increasingly strained by the demands of these new products, and face severe cost and manpower pressures, (3) the remote and impersonal relationship between the buyer and the manufacturer, and (4) the fact that a growing number of channels of information are devoted to searching out and publicizing poor quality of manufacture and unsafe design and performance. The first three articles in this section, which deal with warranties, service, and safety issues are particularly helpful in explaining the nature and complexity of these problems. The articles are weaker when it comes to providing evidence on the scope of these problems, largely because good information is seldom available. Most designers and the manufacturer recognize their problems, and many are trying to cope responsibly with them. The article by Upton is a good illustration of such positive efforts. Nonetheless, it is clear from the articles by Bishop and Hubbard and by Southwick, that the courts and the legislators have a different view of both the problem and the likelihood that all manufacturers will act responsibly.

There has been sporadic demand for better safety legislation for over fifty years, with the urgency usually depending on the recency of the latest publicized disaster or the effectiveness of a campaign to arouse the public about a specific hazard. The principles behind much of the current legislation are that much of the danger is avoidable through better design standards, testing and performance disclosure, and that where danger is not avoidable (as with automobile collisions, for example) both manufacturers and consumers have a responsibility to reduce the adverse consequences. Many are of the opinion that the loss to innocent parties caused by automobile accidents is an external effect with the same justification for legislative action as attempts to control environmental pollution. Hence we see mandatory requirements for a wide range of safety equipment for cars.

In many respects the courts have anticipated the legislature by interpreting existing law in a manner that increasingly shifts the burden of risk from unsatisfactory or unsafe performance from the consumer to the manufacturers. The fourth article in this section, written by Southwick in 1963, accurately identified how the courts have moved to increase the liability of manufacturers by:

(1) Striking down attempts to limit liability through disclaimers in sales agreements and narrow express warranties. Now the manufacturer is obligated to satisfy reasonable performance and safety levels (including those implied by advertising).

(2) Weakening defenses based on lack of privity (or direct contractual relationship) between the manufacturer and the ultimate user.

(3) Moving toward adoption of the doctrine of strict liability in tort, which embodies a belief that the cost of accidents are best borne by the manufacturer who can pass these costs on to all customers in the form of higher prices.

Naturally, the manufacturer is uncomfortable with an imposition of liability that goes beyond his own negligence. The last two articles by Kolb and Schirmer demonstrate the nature of the conflict of points of view and the possible responses.

A. Warranties and Service

19. Report of the Task Force on Appliance Warranties and Service
Federal Trade Commission

This report is made up of three parts. The first covers the problems of the consumer. Next, the problems of the manufacturer are analyzed. Finally, the third part treats the problems of the retailer.

The Problems of the Consumer

The problems encountered by purchasers of major household appliances in obtaining the benefits of warranties and guarantees in those instances in which the appliances do not function satisfactorily or require repairs during the period they are supposedly covered by a manufacturer's warranty or guarantee are discussed in this part of the report.

The primary sources of the materials used in the preparation of this part were the files of complaint letters in the office of the Special Assistant to the President for Consumer Affairs and in the files of the Federal Trade Commission. There are certain inherent limitations in basing an analysis of these problems on this data. Primarily, the complaint letters give only one side of the story, and at least some of the

Reprinted from *Report of the Task Force on Appliance Warranties and Service* (Washington: Superintendent of Documents, January, 1968), 48–91.

problems may have been resolved after the letters were written. Further, there is no way of ascertaining the frequency of complaints with respect to the number of appliances sold. However, over 1,000 complaints have been examined and it can be stated that the tenor and apparent objectiveness of the overwhelming majority provide substantial evidence that many are justified and that the purchaser who attempts to exercise his rights under a warranty or guarantee may have considerable difficulty in obtaining satisfaction or redress.

The basic cause of consumer dissatisfaction with service provided under a guarantee or warranty is the failure of the manufacturer or the retailer, or both, to fulfill the obligations set forth in the guarantee to the extent and in the manner expected by the consumer. In some instances the cause of dissatisfaction may be based on a misunderstanding on the part of the consumer of the terms of the guarantee. In others it may result from the inability or refusal of the servicing organization to place the appliance in proper operating condition. However, the numerous facets of the problem should be itemized and discussed in order that they may be fully understood.

The unsuitable product

Many described the use of brittle plastic to fabricate moveable parts or parts subject to stresses or strains which resulted in repeated breakages and failures. The use of metal tubes, rather than plastic tubes which are immune to rust or chemical attack, was also identified as a fault of design. There are many others.

A recently purchased refrigerator began to "sweat" inside. Water accumulated on the sides and thoroughly soaked the contents. The owner was ultimately informed that the appliance was defective and that the only solution was to install an additional heater inside the box. The design made it impossible to correct the defect by other means. In one instance, the consumer was asked to pay for the installation of this heater.

Three complaints about the faulty design of television sets made by three large manufacturers are worthy of note. In each case numerous efforts to make the sets function properly were made by the local sellers and in two cases manufacturers' representatives attempted to make the necessary repairs. Despite these efforts none of the sets ever functioned properly. One purchaser was offered a $10 trade-in allowance on the set which he had owned for little more than a year.

Another was offered a trade-in allowance amounting to the original cost of the set less 15% on condition that he waive the warranty on the new set.

A casement air conditioner sustained repeated burn outs of the compressor and was repaired three times during the guaranteed period of one year. The owner ascertained that this model was peculiarly susceptible to this type of trouble. As the warranty did not authorize replacement of the appliance, an extended term for design defects, or money back, the owner expects to pay for these recurring failures in the future.

The lemon

It is somewhat difficult to determine whether a complaint is attributable to the faulty design of a product or to defects in certain parts and their assembly. Records of the manufacturers or a wide survey of dealers or servicemen might enable one to identify which products of the various manufacturers have design faults. The "lemon" or the machine which is the subject of various and numerous operative failures is constantly referred to in the complaints. Eventually, a number of these appliances are probably made to function properly. However, others continue to have a variety of troubles after the guarantee period has expired. The complaints indicate that there is a very great reluctance on the part of the dealers or manufacturers to replace the "lemon" with a new appliance or to refund the purchase price. While most guarantees contain undertakings to replace defective parts, one which provides for the replacement of a defective major appliance has not been seen.

Delay in making repairs

The files are replete with complaints regarding the failure of local service organizations to make the necessary repairs with reasonable promptness. Under this classification are situations in which those responsible for the repairs are apparently willing to make them but do so only after long delays. Such a delay can result in considerable costs to the owner, if for example, a freezer breaks down after it has been filled with food. In a number of instances the dealer or local service facility does not have the necessary parts; in others he does not have sufficient repairmen to schedule the service call without a delay of several weeks.

The unskilled and incompetent repairman is frequently designated as the source of many complaints. Undoubtedly there are many. However, their prevalence and actual role in the failure to perform obligations under a guarantee cannot be accurately assessed. A fully qualified and skilled mechanic cannot compensate for defective design or the improper assembly of products.

The orphan consumer

Most guarantees or warranties place the responsibility for actually making the repairs upon the selling dealer or upon a local service organization. Appliance owners have complained that frequently their warranties are valueless because the local dealer from whom they purchased the product has gone out of business or has stopped carrying the brand of appliance which he sold to them and will no longer repair the kind they purchased. Severance of the seller-customer relationship may also arise if the customer moves from the locality in which the appliance was purchased. In all of these situations the appliance owner may expect to encounter more than ordinary difficulty in obtaining the service authorized by his guarantee. His situation will be more serious if he lives in a small community where service facilities and competition are limited.

According to one complaint, a so-called orphaned consumer was given the option of shipping her appliance 150 miles to the nearest authorized service center or of paying for the repairs herself. In another instance, the original dealer had switched lines, and the consumer was referred to a competitor of the dealer. The competitor treated the consumer with contempt and rudeness and refused to provide the requested service. The factory representative located in a major city some miles distant referred the consumer to still another appliance dealer. This dealer attempted to repair the refrigerator and charged the owner $9.00 for labor and $36.00 for cartage. Almost immediately the refrigerator stopped running. A further appeal to the factory representative was unproductive so the consumer finally persuaded the selling dealer to make the repairs at a charge of $37.58 for "labor." Thus to have his refrigerator, which was still covered by a warranty, repaired the consumer expended $82.58 not counting the cost of the long distance telephone calls. He was also charged an additional $12.36 for a cold control unit which the original dealer advised the owner to purchase and install himself. As this part was covered by the warranty, it should have been provided without charge.

Excessive labor charges

Some guarantees provide that the customer must pay labor and other charges incident to the repairs. The amount and nature of these charges are often aggravating. In one instance the transmission of a washing machine which was covered by a warranty failed. The owner did not object to paying the $5.95 charge for a home call or the $10.95 labor charge but did object to a charge of $13.50 designated as shop labor. This was explained to her as the cost of repairing her old transmission in the shop so that it could be given to another customer whose transmission failed. Another appliance owner complained of a labor charge of $15.95 to replace a thermostat. He stated that it took the serviceman only 15 minutes to do the work and compensation at this rate would amount to over $60.00 an hour. Others complained of having to pay a stated amount ranging from $5.00 to $8.00 for the service call plus an additional amount for labor. These charges would then be repeated if the serviceman had to make another call because he did not have the proper part when he made the first call.

Failure to honor the guarantees

This leads to the discussion of the failure of a retailer or service organization to honor the provisions of the guarantee regarding the replacement of parts or labor without charge. Frequent examples of this failure of performance arise in those instances where the defect is of a nature which cannot be readily repaired by the dealer. In one instance a refrigerator was delivered with a chipped interior enamel. The seller disclaimed responsibility and refused to repair or replace the refrigerator for which the owner had unfortunately paid cash. After considerable correspondence between the owner and the manufacturer, the area distributor called and stated that they would arrange for a replacement. Subsequently an obviously reconditioned refrigerator was delivered. Renewed complaints to the retailer resulted in the offer of a refund of $25.00.

When the picture tube on a recently purchased color television set failed, the retailer stated that he could not replace it because he did not have one in stock. The unusually perceptive owner called the local distributor and found that a large stock of color tubes of the proper make and size was available. Shortly thereafter, the retailer called and stated that he had obtained from a named distributor a tube of another manufacturer which would be suitable if the owner agreed. Subsequently, the owner called the named distributor and learned that the retailer had not ordered a tube from him. It would appear that the retailer intended to install a rebuilt tube in the set.

The files contain many other examples of the failure of dealers to honor the terms of the guarantee by refusing to perform the necessary work, by performing the work in a slipshod manner, or by attempting to stall until the warranty period expires.

The disinterested manufacturer

When the owner of an appliance cannot obtain satisfaction from the dealer or local service organization, he turns to the manufacturer. The complaints establish that the results of such appeals are something less than happy. It is not uncommon for the manufacturer to ignore the appeal altogether and make no response. Some do respond and advise the consumer to contact the dealer about whose conduct she complained. Others recommend contact with a distributor or area service representative. This often leads to what is described as the "run around" with a considerable exchange of correspondence, broken appointments, and nothing being done, with the manufacturer, distributor, and retailer, all disclaiming any blame or ability to solve the problem.

The unscrupulous service operator

A number of consumers complained that they were treated unfairly by servicing agencies who performed in warranty service on their appliances. Some of these complaints can be attributed to incompetent servicemen. Others indicate a more basic dissatisfaction with the business practices of the servicing agency and with the failure of the manufacturer to take effective corrective action.

One independent service company in a major city was a factory authorized service center for a number of major appliance manufacturers. The Commission's files reflect that his activities resulted in over 100 complaints, of which a considerable number were brought to the attention of the manufacturers of the products involved. So far as we know, the company is still a representative for those manufacturers.

In response to a consumer complaint about the unfairness and inefficiency of an independent dealer service facility, the manufacturer replied that it had received many similar complaints about this particular dealer, and that it regretted that it could do nothing about it.

In response to another complaint about excessive labor charges, a manufacturer replied that it furnished its authorized repairmen with a list of suggested charges. However, it added that it could not force them to conform to these charges, and that it was expected that charges would vary in different parts of the country.

As one manufacturer frankly admitted, customers have no guidelines or means of judging or comparing the costs of product repairs. They may be victimized by the illegitimate unscrupulous service operators. There is at the moment no complete defense.

In conclusion it should be noted that the paucity of competent service facilities results in many manufacturers hesitating to give up an outlet in a particular area when there is no alternative available, particularly if such action would make him available to their competitors.

The illusive guarantee

An objective analysis of the warranties and guarantees used in the major appliance industry is set forth in a preceding section of this report. In this part, the views of consumers regarding these guarantees are described.

The failure of the guarantee to set forth clearly and in understandable language the nature and extent of the guarantee is a common complaint. A closely related complaint is that the guarantee contains conditions which are unfair and which frequently make the dealer or manufacturer the sole judge of whether a particular defect is covered by the guarantee.

According to consumers, the obligations of the purchaser which are prerequisite to the validity of the guarantee are not clearly disclosed or may be unreasonable. Thus the guarantee may be limited to the original purchaser, e.g., the builder of a new home and not to the purchaser of the home. There may be a requirement for presentation of the original sales slip, or evidence of registration of the sale with the manufacturer, or the purchaser may be required to remove and ship a part to the manufacturer, or to pay freight and other transportation costs. Sometimes the actual terms of the guarantee may differ from those advertised.

When unsuccessful efforts are made to repair a defective product during the guarantee period, further complaints regarding the same defect or condition made after the expiration of the guarantee period are answered with the announcement that nothing can be done as the warranty is no longer in effect. In one instance after a purchaser had finally prevailed upon the manufacturer to examine a color television set which had never worked properly, he was informed that the set was completely worn out, and that since the warranty had expired it would cost $300 to have it repaired.

Unreasonable conditions in the guarantee are also troublesome to the consumer. One small shop owner who purchased a window air conditioner was informed that the guarantee was limited so as not to apply if the product was installed in other than a single family home. Other provisions of guarantees limit the obligation to replace defective parts by use of such phrases as "which are found defective by us." All disclaim responsibility for consequential damages with a few exceptions such as loss of food in the case of a freezer failure.

Another complaint is that the duration of a warranty is unduly limited. Numerous expensive television sets carry warranties of only 90 days—this despite the manufacturers' claims that use of solid state circuitry has eliminated the factor (heat) which is responsible for the most trouble in television sets. The length of other warranties seem to have been carefully determined so that they lapse just before malfunctions may be expected to appear.

Lack of a forum

There is no readily available means or procedure by which a consumer can compel performance under a guarantee or be adequately compensated for its breach.

There is no question that the courts have long since departed from their previous policy of erecting protective barriers around the manufacturers and sellers of products. That policy was well described by a judge in these words:

> A wise and conservative public policy has impressed the courts with the view that there must be a fixed and definite limitation to the liability of a manufacturer and vendors in the construction and sale of complicated machines and structures which are to be operated or used by the intelligent and the ignorant, the skillful and the incompetent, the watchful and the careless, parties that cannot be known to the manufacturers or vendors, and who use the articles all over the country hundreds of miles distant from the place of their manufacturer or original sale.[1]

[1] *Huset* v. *J. I. Case Threshing Machine Company,* 120 F. 865, 870 (A-8, Minn., 1903).

However, for a variety of reasons the purchaser of an inoperable major home appliance is not inclined to seek redress in the courts for the failure of the manufacturer or seller to conform to the terms of the guarantee. The reasons why they fail to do so are legion—expense, delay, distrust of lawyers, and procedural problems, are perhaps the most common. Action has been taken by the Federal Trade Commission in a number of instances against manufacturers and appliance distributors or retailers who are in commerce and who have violated Section 5 of the Federal Trade Commission Act (15 U.S.C. 41), by deceptive acts and practices involving warranties and guarantees. However, the Commission does not have jurisdiction to reach appliance dealers or service agencies who are not engaged in interstate commerce, or to adjudicate disputes between the manufacturer and retailer on the one hand and the consumer on the other. Therefore the consumer does not really have, at least from a practical standpoint, a forum in which the justness of his claim can be established and which can direct that he be compensated for his damages. The recurring thought expressed in many letters is "I purchased an appliance made by _____ because I thought they were dependable. I was wrong! Where am I to turn?"

Problems of the Manufacturer

This part of the report is based primarily upon information submitted by industry members in response to the oral and written requests of Chairman Paul Rand Dixon. In these requests industry members were asked to describe the warranty service practices and policies of their respective companies, to list what they considered to be the major obstacles to improved warranty service, and to submit suggestions for remedying the problems associated with the warranty of their products. Knowledge of the manufacturers' practices and policies is a prerequisite to an understanding of the problems envisioned by them.

Manufacturers' arrangements for the provision of warranty service to purchasers of their products are not uniform, and many manufacturers employ more than one method. However, the basic arrangements may be categorized as follows:

(1) Service is provided through factory-owned service centers which are managed and staffed by employees of the manufacturers.

(2) Retailers who service as well as sell appliances. These are sometimes franchised.

(3) Factory authorized independent service companies provide service.

(4) Independent or franchised distributors may be responsible for providing service throughout the area in which they sell appliances.

The manufacturers used various means to ascertain whether the service organizations were performing at the required level of efficiency. These included customer sampling, review of invoices, inspections, and related procedures. Supervisory requirements were also imposed upon distributors to supplement the factory efforts, and several manufacturers stated that the distributors were required to assume responsibility for providing service if a dealer or independent servicing organization failed to do so.

Some manufacturers state that they do not prescribe standards for a servicing retailer or for an independent service agency. They point out that in some areas the paucity of really qualified service facilities gives them the choice of providing no service at all or of using a firm which they do not consider qualified. In those areas in which utilities provide service, manufacturers indicated a preference for them, because of the quality of service personnel these organizations employ. It was also pointed out that the conditions throughout the country varied so much that it was difficult to establish uniform standards on a nation-wide basis.

Where the community provided a choice of service representatives, manufacturers reported that they attempted to verify the reputation, credit rating, and adequacy of the manpower and equipment of the agency, as well as its willingness to purchase the necessary tools and maintain an adequate technical library.

Several manufacturers now require that distributors, or independent servicing agencies under contract, provide warranty service to purchasers who move in the area with an appliance purchased in another locality. However, others do not and seemingly have made no provision for providing warranty service to such orphaned consumers.

The methods used to determine the amount of compensation to be paid to servicing dealers or agencies for warranty work on appliances are subject to many variables and complexities. One of the simplest, and perhaps the most satisfactory from the standpoint of the consumer, is for the servicing agency to bill the manufacturer for the cost of parts and service at the same rates he would use for his other customers. In fact one manufacturer stated that he expected the amount of this billing to include a reasonable profit for the servicer.

One of the more common practices is for the manufacturer not to pay direct compensation for warranty work because its obligation is restricted to the replacement of any parts used in effecting the repairs. Compensation for the work, i.e., the labor and service charge, is thus dependent upon an agreement between the retailer and the consumer. The dealer may agree to provide warranty service without charge; he may sell the consumer a warranty service policy; or the consumer may pay the labor and service charges on a per call basis.

Those manufacturers which undertake to pay for warranty labor and service may agree to do so at the prevailing rates charged other consumers by the servicing agency, with the understanding that they will only replace the parts the agency used in making the repairs.

Many manufacturers have established detailed schedules showing the amounts they will pay for time spent in diagnosing and repairing various defects in appliances. These schedules will vary from one part of the country to the other because of differences in wage rates and costs. In compiling these schedules, information is obtained from the servicing agencies, who of course must agree to them, and factors such as the anticipated time necessary to make the repairs, the charges made by the agency for its non-warranty work, and the rates paid by other manufacturers are considered. The amount and method of making compensation will be set forth in the agreement between the manufacturer, distributor, or the retailer and the agency which will actually do the work. In some instances a flat rate based on the number of appliances sold in the area will determine the amount of compensation to be paid.

Manufacturers which expect retailers to provide warranty service on a non-reimbursable basis frequently use a method known as "in-boarding." Under this method a specific amount for each model of appliance is "paid" to a retailer who has agreed to perform in-warranty service. This payment is made by means of a deduction from the product price charged to him which is intended to cover the labor costs of the servicing dealer in doing warranty work. Manufacturers favor this arrangement because they believe that it gives the retailer an incentive to avoid unnecessary repairs and at the same time makes it unnecessary for the manufacturer to charge higher prices to cover the cost of factory provided service. If the appliance is sold to a non-servicing dealer, the payment is actually made to a service operator in that locality—this is his flat rate which was mentioned above. Under one variation of the in-boarding arrangement the dealer is simply expected to provide for warranty labor costs out of his margin of profit on the sale of the appliance to the purchaser.

Upon receipt of information that an appliance had a serious defect in its design or manufacture, most industry members stated that they would endeavor to locate all such products and repair them at no cost to the purchaser. Sale of the defective units would also be halted until the necessary modifications could be made. Several manufacturers indicated that such defects would be corrected free of charge, even though the warranty period might have expired. Others stated that they had handled those matters in the past as normal warranty type work, with the attendant division of costs between the manufacturer, the retailer, and the consumer. With respect to one defective product the warranty period was extended for an additional year.

More positive action was taken in the case of defects which might result in danger to life or property. In one instance a particular model of appliance was recalled and replaced with another, even though a number had been installed in purchasers' homes. The cost and difficulty involved in locating such units were reported as being of considerable magnitude.

The feasibility of simplifying the language used in appliance warranties was the subject of another question addressed to manufacturers. A surprising number, including some which had the most complex warranty certificates examined, responded that their warranties were written in clear concise language which was perfectly understandable, and that it would not be possible to improve or simplify the terminology used. They also stated that they had received no complaints regarding the clarity of their warranties. Some expressed the fear that simplification or increased brevity would subject them to unjustified claims by consumers. Others noted that as a result of the activities of the President's Committee on Consumer Interests they had undertaken to redraft, shorten, and otherwise simplify the warranties in use. Those who had done so stated that use of the revised warranties had not caused them any additional problems and that, on the contrary, use of the revisions had resulted in a more attractive package for the prospective purchaser. Several responses indicated a growing awareness that use of the numerous exceptions was not required and a willingness to go along with industry-wide efforts toward simplification.

Industry members were asked to state what they considered to be the major obstacles to improving the warranty service on their respective products. Their replies give an excellent picture of the problems from the viewpoint of the manufacturer.

All of the replies indicated that one of the greatest problems was a shortage of qualified technicians to repair and service appliances. This shortage is aggravated, as one manufacturer put it, by a tremendous expansion of product offerings and an explosive increase in the number of major appliances in use. The increasing demands on the technical abilities of servicemen because of the greater electro-mechanical complexity of appliances necessitate longer and more comprehensive training programs to qualify persons for entry into this field. The failure of many servicing dealers to take advantage of the manufacturers' training programs was noted. The image of the serviceman has not grown in proportion to the knowledge and qualifications which he must have. As a result some customers do not trust a serviceman and are inclined to view his comments and recommendations with suspicion. The demand for service on such products as air conditioners is seasonal. Sufficient personnel to handle promptly service calls at the peak of the season cannot be gainfully employed for the balance of the year. This necessitates some degree of compromise which will result in some consumer dissatisfaction.

The consumers themselves are said to be a major source of difficulties. While they insist on elaborate design and selective operational characteristics, they are unwilling to read and to follow the instructions which outline procedures requisite to the proper functioning of the product. Sometimes this results in damage or malfunctioning for which they blame the manufacturer. Frequently a serviceman is summoned and finds that he need only explain to the consumer how to operate the product. This entails a high cost to the manufacturer or servicing agent and makes it impossible for them to provide services which are justified within reasonable time limits. Consumers have on occasion been unreasonable in their demands for service. One manufacturer reported repeated calls for such services as cleaning a range within the warranty period.

Consumers sometimes attempt to make repairs on appliances and subsequently attribute their lack of success to a defective part or to a serviceman. This results in a number of false claims. A somewhat similar situation arises when a consumer permits an unauthorized service agency to undertake the repairs.

Many dealers will carry more than one line of appliances. This results in several problems for the manufacturer. First, the proliferation of lines makes it impracticable for the retailer to carry an adequate stockage of spare parts. Secondly, the salesmen on his floor generally have difficulty in giving an adequate explanation of the differing features of several lines and in giving competent instructions on how the appliances should be operated. Further this may also result in a misunderstanding on the part of the consumer of the provisions of the guarantee, for the salesman may confuse the guarantee of one manufacturer with that of another. Manufacturers point out that they are unable to exercise effective control over retailers who sell their products. Unjustified promises made by the retailer or his employees are presented to the manufacturer with the expectation that he will fulfill them.

Cost is considered to be a fundamental obstacle to the improvement of warranty service. The shortage of servicemen is said to be symptomatic of this obstacle. Because of the intense competition he faces, the dealer questions his ability to support an adequate service department. Some manufacturers have recognized and accepted the weakness of the retailers and have provided more financial support in the form of increased payments to service agencies which are doing the work. However, other manufacturers do not believe that they can go further than they already have. As one stated,

> If we were to offer labor and transportation for replacement parts and service then it would surely mean that we would be called upon to make simple, routine adjustments and to replace parts which were no longer serviceable because of abuse. No one could accurately determine the cost of providing such service, but it is hardly debatable that the cost would be tremendous. In the long run this would mean that people who use their appliances with proper care would be penalized by having to pay many dollars more in purchase price. This would be necessary to enable us to provide service for the less careful users of our appliances.

The varying length of warranty periods also serves to confuse the consumer. When components of a product are warranted against failure for different lengths of time, consumers who do not carefully read the warranty will often misunderstand what is and what is not covered for the extended period.

Another complaint of the manufacturer relates to the difficulty they have, particularly in rural areas, of locating a qualified service agency. This problem is more acute for the small manufacturer who cannot afford to establish a network of factory owned facilities.

The final complaint of the manufacturers is that intense competition has made it necessary for them to design appliances having new and complicated features and to offer them for sale at lower and lower prices. This has made it difficult for them to maintain quality control and set aside sufficient reserves to pay for the warranty service costs.

Problems of the Retailer

In this section of the report, the warranty problems of the servicing dealer and the independent repairman are discussed. The diverse nature of these establishments with respect to size and type makes it difficult to ascribe a common set of problems to them. In addition, the severity of a problem may vary considerably with the relative size of a business. Nevertheless, most retailers apparently share the belief that the major obstacle to providing better warranty service is the shortage of trained technicians to do the warranty work on appliances. Although a detailed consideration of the causes of this shortage is beyond the scope of this report, the more important of the reasons given by the retailers themselves are mentioned in the interest of completeness.

An appliance repairman, and particularly one who works for an independent service organization or for a servicing retailer who handles more than one line of appliances, must be completely familiar with the technical characteristics of a whole range of products. He must be a skilled diagnostician or trouble shooter, who is able to evaluate the symptoms reported by the owner of the appliance, and to ascertain the probable nature of the malfunction by a series of simple tests. After he has found the trouble, he must repair it using the tools carried from job to job, and the limited stock of spare parts carried on his truck. A competent repairman must have all of these abilities and more, for his skills must be developed and enhanced to enable him to keep pace with the demands presented by the novel and more complex appliances which come off the production lines each year.

The conditions under which the appliance repairman works are not among the best. He must ply his trade in the basements and utility rooms of private homes, and work on appliances which have been installed with no thought that access to them should be provided for the repairman. His frequent contact with dissatisfied consumers who complain of delays and question his ability to repair the appliance add to his woes. Finally, he must attempt to collect the charges due upon completion of his work and fill out various forms and repair tickets.

Many retailers recognize that a skilled repairman does not have too much inducement to enter or remain in the field of appliance repair, for the compensation is not particularly good, and in some cases seasonal demand may even put him out of work during slack periods. The proprietors of service establishments contend that their margin of profit on the sale of appliances and the financial support provided by manufacturers do not enable them to pay compensation sufficient to overcome the disadvantages of this work. They point out that job opportunities in factories and shops where the technician will enjoy the benefits of good working conditions, union membership, and better salaries are simply too much for them to overcome.

Some retailers recognize that the real core of the problem is inadequate salaries. However, many of these state that they cannot afford to pay more and must rely on the repetitive training of a rapidly changing work force which does not remain in position long enough to learn to give satisfactory service.

Retailers join with manufacturers in urging Federal and state governments to sponsor training programs in the high schools and vocational schools for appliance servicemen. However, it should be recalled that the manufacturers complained that the retailers do not fully utilize the manufacturer sponsored programs. Several proprietors of private technical schools have also alleged that the manufacturers were reluctant to provide them with training manuals, models, and other forms of assistance in the training of service technicians. Certainly it would appear that more cooperation by all concerned would result in the better utilization of existing training facilities and perhaps make government support unnecessary.

A lack of a readily available source of supply of spare parts is a complaint of a number of retailers. Some have reported that parts orders for even "likely to fail parts" have been delayed for weeks and even months by some manufacturers. Other retailers state that the manufacturers expect them to carry a relatively large inventory of parts on hand, to do warranty as well as ordinary repair work, and that they are financially unable to tie up their limited capital for this purpose. They complain that the manufacturers themselves have displayed the same unwillingness to maintain an adequate stockage of parts, yet since they do not deal directly with the irate consumer, the local repairman receives the blame.

Another of their problems, which the retailers lay at the door of the manufacturer, is poor and insufficient quality control. The retailers point out that major appliances are assembled on a production line and that defects can be eliminated much more cheaply in a factory than they can in a consumer's kitchen or in a neighborhood repair shop. They say it is uneconomical to expect them to correct factory mistakes and shortcomings under the much higher cost conditions that prevail in their part of the industry. Retailers also say that in production and design, ease of servicing should be given more consideration. Access should be provided to facilitate replacement or repair of likely to fail parts. Parts should be marked to permit their ready identification by the repairman.

Unreasonable and unpleasant consumers are also designated as a serious problem for the retailer. They report numerous service calls which result in the skilled repairman merely having to explain to the consumer how to operate the appliance and to repeat information contained in the manual which accompanied the appliance when it was sold. One retailer said that the purchaser who found he could not make timely payments on the appliance was the most difficult to deal with as such a purchaser would falsely allege that his appliance did not work properly. Abuse and discourtesy to servicemen and a failure to keep appointments for service were also noted.

The consumer who attempts to repair or modify his appliance and follows up his failure to do so with a claim that he is entitled to warranty service also presents problems for the retailer. In a somewhat similar category are the consumers who abuse their appliances. While the serviceman can ordinarily detect that such occurrences are the probable cause of the product failure, it is difficult to prove and the retailer feels that in case of doubt he should go ahead and provide service under the warranty with attendant increase in costs.

While many retailers agree that the warranties and guarantees used by major appliance manufacturers are sufficiently clear to be understood by most consumers, they state that a simplification program would be of considerable benefit to the retailer in enabling him to avoid misunderstandings with his customers.

The most serious problem for the retailer, and the smaller he is the more acute it becomes, is the matter of compensation for the warranty service he is called upon to provide. The various methods used by manufacturers to compensate retailers for warranty service were fully described in the section of the report which dealt with the problems of the manufacturers and will not be repeated here. However, under many of those methods the retailer is required to bear a very considerable part of the cost of correcting factory defects. The greater the burden imposed on the retailer, the greater the likelihood that the warranty service he provides will be totally inadequate by any standards.

It is the view of the retailers that they should be paid for warranty service work at the same rates they charge for ordinary service and that such arrangements could be coupled with provisions to provide the manufacturer with protection against exaggerated claims without undue difficulty. Further they believe that the manufacturers should incorporate in the price of their products a sufficient amount to permit the provision of adequate warranty service under the full reimbursement scheme.

The retailers report that no one seems to understand why the cost of servicing appliances is so high. They point out that the standard wage for service technicians is on the order of $4.00 or more dollars per hour. A firm must charge two and one half to three times this rate for service to pay overhead and provide a reasonable profit, and when this is coupled with the cost of providing a repair truck, stocking it with parts, and getting it from point to point the seemingly exorbitant repair charges become more credible. They recognize that steps should be taken to bring these facts to the attention of the consuming public but believe that the ultimate solution rests within the power of the manufacurer to pay all of these expenses.

20. The Use of Product Warranties and Guarantees as a Marketing Tool

Stephen E. Upton

Historically, Whirlpool warranties have resembled all other warranties. They were written by lawyers for the express purpose of protecting the manufacturer against unreasonable product claims from the consumer. Warranties, as you may well be aware, are drafted not so much to protect the consumer against the possibility of receiving a defective product, as to limit the duration of the manufacturer's express responsibility for that product. The courts have ruled that in cases where a product is sold without formal warranty accompaniment, an implied warranty exists that, in most cases, is as strong or stronger than the most liberal of the product manufacturer's warranties. It was for this reason that major manufacturers soon recognized the importance of providing a specific warranty coverage listing all exclusions and disclaimers so that their extent of liability would be minimized, while at the same time affording an equitable degree of protection to their ultimate customers.

And then came consumerism, and with it a new set of guidelines. Consumer advocates in high offices of our government such as Betty Furness expressed public dissatisfaction with the complexities and legalese of most major appliance warranties. She stated, and with some

Reprinted from an address by S. E. Upton, Vice President of Whirlpool Corporation, to the American Marketing Association in Cleveland, Ohio, on December 11, 1969. Used by permission.

justification, that although the product might have a most liberal warranty accompanying it, consumers often failed to understand the degree or duration of the protection to which they are entitled. She said the manufacturer that can take out the "to wits," and "wherefores," and minimize the "parties of the first parts," would win her good favor. Coincidentally, we at this time, had already begun work to simplify our warranties and make them easier to understand. Recognizing an opportunity to incorporate a marketing plus, with a realistic manufacturing refinement, we took one additional step and radically revised our warranty from the conventional certificate format to a friendly letter style. Our advertising department grabbed this idea and through the cooperation of our agency in New York, drafted an open letter to Betty Furness, in which we expressed our mutual support of her objective and had taken a positive step in providing simplified warranty protection to the nation's consumers. Betty Furness lent additional support to this early effort—heralding it as one manufacturer's cooperation in providing improved consumer protection. Naturally recognizing that we were on target with a good marketing tool, we placed full page ads in *Life, Look,* and *The Wall Street Journal* as well as leading newspapers across the country, announcing our conversion to the friendly letter warranty. Our dealers got behind this promotion at the local level and we feel that our product acceptance across the nation was enhanced by this small but timely refinement. At this time we have letter warranties for all of our products with the exception of our commercial business equipment. It is our opinion at this time that the people buying this equipment differ from the average housewife in that they can understand the to-wits and whereas's, and actually prefer a more legal looking and sounding certificate. [See Figure 1.]

The consumer responds to various stimuli when engaged in a customer-salesman relationship. Professional sales people are well aware of the many signals transmitted by a customer during this confrontation. They are quick to recognize reluctance to sign an order blank. They can sense when a customer is looking at a product which he or she cannot afford to buy. A good salesman can quickly win the customer's confidence by responding to these signals at the right time in the right way. Until recently a salesman carefully avoided any reference to service or to warranties, recognizing that these words resulted in a poor response from the customer. They were interested in the glitter and gloss of a new product. They envisioned this machine performing a valuable service for them and responded negatively to the

Whirlpool
CORPORATION

Administrative Center

BENTON HARBOR, MICHIGAN 49022 • AREA CODE 616 925-0651

Dear Customer:

Good performance. That's what this letter is all about.

We know that you expect good performance from your Whirlpool dryer, and we aim to see that you get it. Here's how its performance is protected.

YOUR WARRANTY

During your first year of ownership, all parts of the appliance (except light bulbs) which we find are defective in materials or workmanship will be repaired or replaced by Whirlpool free of charge, and we will pay any labor charges.

During the second year, we will continue to assume the same responsibility as stated above, except you pay any labor charges.

This protection is yours as the original purchaser for your home use, and requires that all service be performed by a service organization authorized to service Whirlpool products. Naturally, it doesn't cover damage by accident, misuse, fire, flood or acts of God. But it does cover you wherever you live in the United States. . .even if you move.

Now about servicing. Let's face it. Sometimes even the best products need service. So, if that's ever true of your Whirlpool dryer, there is a way to get action fast. Just call your servicing Whirlpool dealer or a Whirlpool Tech-Care agent. He is trained to make whatever's wrong right. We do not pay for service calls that only involve instructing you on how to use your new Whirlpool appliance.

On the other hand, we do offer a unique telephone information and assistance service. If you have any questions about operating, maintaining or servicing any Whirlpool appliance, just dial (800) 253-1301*. Free. From anywhere in the continental United States. We'll give you, day or night, the name and number of the authorized Whirlpool Tech-Care serviceman nearest your home.

We suggest you keep this letter with your sales slip and Operating Instructions. It's nice to know you'll have protection, even though you may never need it.

Sincerely,

WHIRLPOOL CORPORATION

* In Michigan (800) 632-2243
AD

Figure 1   Sample Warranty Letter

thought that it might possibly break down and even cost additional money to maintain this new product in proper operating condition. Today's consumer, we are told, and believe, has been educated to accept the fact that a product is a machine, and as such, is subject to mechanical failure and a need for occasional maintenance. Because of the attention focused on service and warranties from the various governmental offices, today's consumer is quick to ask the salesman, if he doesn't volunteer it, the extent, duration, etc., of the warranty on a given product. Of course, conveying a warranty on a piece of paper and fulfilling that warranty to the customer's total satisfaction are two different things. Not too long ago in Detroit, the decision was made by a major auto manufacturer to offer a five year or 50,000 mile warranty on various functional parts of their automobiles. The manufacturer had perfected the engine and gear train of his cars to the point where he could offer this warranty with confidence that not too many would fail during this period and that the cost for repairing those that did fail would not seriously affect his profits. As a marketing tool, this was probably quite effective; however, two or three years subsequent to this decision, as cars which normally would have been well out of the warranty period began showing up in dealer's service departments for free warranty adjustment, it became apparent that service facilities were being seriously overloaded. Service departments were physically unable to live up to a warranty provided by the product manufacturer. The problem was magnified in that it was not necessary for the selling dealer to provide this service, and dealers were being asked to provide warranty service at fixed rates way below what they would charge for retail service even though they had not made the original profit on the sale of the car. This is an example of the marketing strategy backfiring because sufficient consideration had not been given to the ability of the person responsible for fulfilling that warranty to be physically capable of fulfilling it. Automotive extended warranties lurched forward for about three years, plateaued, and have since regressed to a point where warranty fulfillment is once again possible.

Many products offer lifetime warranties and it has been found that many people immediately lose confidence in a product expressing such a warranty. Most people feel that there is a catch to this type of warranty and there usually is. Lifetime warranties are often misunderstood that the lifetime involved is that of the product rather than that of the product owner and in nearly all cases, a lifetime warranty is nontransferable. Even 20- and 30-year warranties on some products have a negative effect because consumers are not used to accepting the responsibility for anything for that length of time. What we have done as an appliance manufacturer is to aim for a warranty period which will protect the consumer during the initial period of ownership when most product defects occur and then drop that portion of the warranty protection which covers all parts and continue to protect the major cost items within the product. Two examples of this would be our automatic washers which have full parts and labor coverage for one year, with the parts warranty extending through the first two years, and the warranty on the transmission parts extending through the first five years of ownership. All of our products which incorporate sealed refrigeration systems such as refrigerators, freezers, air conditioners, etc., are protected against manufacturing defects in material and/or workmanship for a period of one year during which time all parts and labor are provided at no cost. For four additional years we offer free parts and labor on the compressor, condenser, evaporator and tubing, which comprise the sealed system. These components seldom fail, but when they do, generate a considerable expense to repair. With minor exceptions this is the warranty protection which we have had on our products for more than the last decade, and most appliance manufacturers afford a similar protection.

In her capacity as the president's special assistant for consumer affairs, Virginia Knauer expressed a sincere concern over product warranties which she feels should be looked into in depth by all manufacturers immediately. Washington wants to know how manufacturers will fulfill their warranties. With this focus, it is apparent that there will be quite a few changes forthcoming in the extent, duration and format of the warranties by all manufacturers. It is quite obvious then, that the manufacturers who can take this almost forced action and turn it into a powerful sales advantage will be in a better position to merchandise his products than those who comply to the minimum request from our government. A product revision can be promoted through the retail structure as a merchandising and marketing aid and I'm sure that the creative departments in your respective corporations are, at this time, moving for innovative ways to accomplish this.

To further support our warranty, we have expanded our field force to place more men in direct contact with our dealers and customers who have service questions and problems. We have accepted full responsibility for all service labor claims during the duration of the warranty contract. Any dealer, anywhere, can bill Whirlpool direct for warranty labor which makes our warranty valid any place the customer may move with the product. We call this warranty service central and it has proven to be a valuable asset to our customer satisfaction objective. We have identified our best service outlets across the country and labeled them Tech Care so that we can franchise these dealers and agents and promote their identifying Tech Care symbol nationally. Our most recent effort to close the gap between manufacturers and consumer has been to establish what we call the "cool line." This is a network of phone lines over which we will locate a customer's nearest service source, or provide any technical information she may request, or send literature, etc. If she has a serious service problem, we'll send our field representative to assist her. We are not totally philanthropic concerning all these service satisfaction programs, but we are genuinely sincere and we feel that in today's consumerism oriented society, there is no better marketing strategy than to "join em."

B. Product Safety

21. Danger

James W. Bishop, Jr.
and Henry W. Hubbard

For decades, most American consumers have blithely assumed that the undiminished array of products, gadgets and gimcracks flooding into the marketplace furnished quality, utility, safety and a touch of status and fashion to boot. No one seriously questioned the right of industry to make a profit, for profit is the fuel of progress, but industry put gratification of the consumer's needs first. Didn't advertisements constantly reinforce that soothing assumption?

Unhappily for the housewife's idealized concept of corporate motives, fed by a potpouri of puffery from women's magazines, that assessment, while still intact, is now tattered and no longer can be left totally unchallenged; evidence that shakes a once sacrosanct presumption is too overwhelming.

Describing the scene in a 1966 report, the White House Consumer Advisory Council arrived at the conclusion that the marketplace is marked by "much confusion, ignorance, some deception and even fraud, where in fact, understanding and honesty ideally should prevail."

In the next two years, the most vigorous consumer protection period in congressional history, a rich vein of unacceptably grim detail

Reprinted from "Danger," Chapter 7 in *Let the Seller Beware*, © 1969 by James W. Bishop and Henry W. Hubbard, Washington National Press, Inc.

was unearthed in such established industries as meat, tires, appliances, gas pipelines, drugs, fish and poultry. Surveying the arena in 1968, a high White House official added another dimension to the 1966 report: "There is a great deal of danger, too."

By 1969 some 2.5 billion potentially hazardous consumer products were present on the market, an average of 45 per household. The dangers they represented exclude the health hazards that exist in too many drugs and a surprising amount of meat. Moreover, the National Safety Council predicted that at least 60,000 Americans will be killed in 1968 in nonhighway accidents; another ten million will suffer disabling injuries. Products, to be sure, are not always the killers but in far too many cases they are, consumer leaders assert. The fact remains that despite such health problems as cancer and heart disease, the major cause of death for people between one and 36 years old is an accident.

Upon signing the Flammable Fabrics Act in 1967, President Johnson told an audience in the East Room: "Our society is more prosperous and it's more complex than any the world has ever known. It has not altogether eliminated some of these avoidable dangers." Lyndon Johnson was not known for his understatements but he made one there.

In 1967, Senator Warren Magnuson and his energetic Commerce Committee together with Consumers Union assembled a ten-year glossary of dangerous and hazardous products. For those who want to remain confident of U.S. industry's innovative abilities, the results were not very reassuring. Some radio and television sets were so shoddily assembled that enough current escaped to give the viewer a jolting shock. Dangerously exposed electrical terminals were found to exist on large numbers of kitchen ranges, broilers, portable heaters and dehumidifiers. Other dangers existed, the study determined, in such common products of the good life as garbage disposals, garden sprayers, travel irons and children's toys with metal edges sharp enough to cut. Consumers Union's conclusion: 376 products were rated not acceptable for use. But for many the real shocker was delivered by Senator Magnuson when he said after the study that "these products were not confined to fly-by-night firms; some came from the most reputable manufacturers in the country."

No one is precisely certain of the number of hazardous products marketed every year, but there is ample evidence nevertheless of Magnuson's thesis—and the heart of Ralph Nader's consumer doctrine—

that fly-by-night practices exist at the very core of the U.S. corporate community.

As television set manufacturers prepared for the coming color boom in 1966 quality control slipped badly. One result: General Electric built and sold at least 90,000 large screen sets which emitted excessive x-rays through the bottoms of the sets. Some of the sets, before they were recalled, discharged 50,000 milliroentgens an hour, 100,000 times the level determined as safe by the National Council on Radiation Protection.

One sensitive outpost of danger prevention is Underwriters Laboratories in Chicago. Many large companies submit their products for testing before they are sold, but since U.L. flunks 50% of the candidates, many others don't bother. They market them anyway. "Hardly a day goes by," reports Senator Magnuson, "when I and my staff do not hear of a new hazardous product."

If there is any single reason why Senators and Representatives have moved toward support of consumer legislation it is that the gap between appearance and reality in the marketplace, as personified by dangerous products, is wide enough to embarrass them into action. It is a picture contrary to the image of America they like and few of them are anxious to appear in the role of widening that gap through inaction.

If the consumerists are correct then the real world, as Ralph Nader insists, is one in which "people are being killed, injured and inconvenienced by the products and processes of technology." Nader, for his part, carries that assessment to the extreme. "As long as there is undue and parochial attention paid to the short range economic utility of product and process at the same time that the short and long range biological consequences are treated with indifference or contempt, our society is going to plunge into deeper collective cruelties."

Nader is not exaggerating. Acknowledging that human error and carelessness are involved, the scene is nevertheless grotesque, and much of it is avoidable. According to the National Safety Council, at least 175,000 people are mangled yearly by power lawn mowers; faulty electronic products electrocute 1,000 others; at least 175,000 suffer severe burns, and 12,000 die from incendiary clothing and upholstery. As shocking as any of that may be, 2,000 people are accidently poisoned every year, 25% under five years old because of improper labeling or nonlabeling. The killers are common, everyday household products, from soap to aspirin and insecticide to detergent. And, the consumerists ask, how is it that American industry, which has the expertise and finesse to send a high-performance, microminia-turized space ship to Mars, can't master the technology of constructing glass doors that don't maim or kill 100,000 people a year?

The picture, however, is not entirely depressing. The future is, in fact, hopeful now that the bodily rights of consumers are being recognized. A fundamental, qualitative change is needed, proclaim the consumerists, not just in the quality control of products but in the attitude of the manufacturers. Though they were unnecessarily contentious at times, the auto safety hearings and the meat debates did serve another purpose, besides insuring that consumers would be better protected: they illuminated the little known fact that not only do small, disreputable companies occasionally work against the consumer's interests but so do powerful, well known blue chip companies, such as Armour, Swift, and General Motors. Exposure and the resulting embarrassment, in short, were needed.

Among the most notable efforts bringing on a change is the White House Commission on Product Safety, authorized by President Johnson in 1967. It is conducting a two-year study of the categories of household products which present an unreasonable risk of injury to the consuming public. It will also determine the extent to which industry self-regulation, judicial decisions on product liability, and local, state and Federal statutes are adequate to protect buyers against dangerous products. In Johnson's words, the Commission's purpose was to "stop tragedy before tragedy strikes." Later, while rallying a small group of Congressmen at the White House to support his bills, he warned: "You better get with it. People are tired of meat with worms in it, blouses that burn and pipelines that blow up under their homes."

They are and that fact, along with pressure from the White House to respond with reform, has not been lost on Washington lobbyists. In their weekly intelligence cables, they've been warning their board chairmen that the new climate is: seller beware.

Consider, for example, the radical shift in viewpoint within just one company, Bristol-Myers, a leading pharmaceutical house. Back in 1940, when the consumer protectionists of the New Deal years were breathing their last, company president William Bristol told an industry audience: "I don't know how many of you are aware of the so-called consumer movement. There are 27 publications and organizations such as Consumers Research and Consumers Union feeding John Henry Public a lot of unsubstantiated and unsubstantiable so-called facts. It's grand reading, good fiction and unfortunately it is growing and undermining our industry. Courses are given in schools and universities along the same line. It's a constant gunfire on our business, on our jobs. . . . I don't think we can fight it singlehanded, but I do think we can do our share."

For more than 20 years he did, at least until his brother Lee, a vice-president, offered an entirely different appraisal of the consumer scene in a speech to New York's Sales Executive Club: "The great American ailment is manifest on all sides by a deepening shade in our ethics (both business and social), a sloppiness in our services, a mediocrity in our manufacture and a growing distrust and even anger in the public's mind."

These days the first Bristol would have trouble scaring up an audience, at least one composed of anyone who has read congressional testimony in the past few years. Congressmen and consumerists alike now trumpet a new theme, and businessmen are beginning to pick up the tempo. The time has arrived in America to deal with the social costs of private enterprise, which by definition means reducing the painful, dangerous by-products of great engineering accomplishments, whether air and water pollution, contamination of soil and food or the hazards of autos, drugs and appliances. And now is also the time to deal with what Ralph Nader terms, "the attitudes, conditions and disincentives which have prevented a comprehensive development of remedial engineering to reduce markedly the social costs of private enterprise." There is nothing inevitable, for example, about highway accidents, as the nation has discovered since the safety law went on the books.

Detroit and Safety

Wheeling down a Michigan road in early 1968, a 55-year-old man driving a 1967 model car collided with another car, head on at 50 miles per hour. Not only did the man survive an apparently unsurvivable crash, but he escaped with relatively minor injuries: bruised legs and stomach and a broken nose. If he's been driving a model built before 1967, before the Federal Traffic Safety Act, the chances would have been better than even that he would have been killed. The difference: an energy absorbing steering column which, despite the big four's early opposition, is now required on all cars built in and after 1967.

In another example, the driver of a pre-safety bill compact car, who wasn't wearing a seat belt, suffered severe neck and chin cuts, a number of broken ribs, internal injuries and a broken leg when his car smashed into a 1967 model at 35 miles per hour. Seven months after the accident, the imprint of the horn button was still visible on his chest. The driver of the other car? He suffered minor injuries but was not hospitalized. His steering column had compressed more than four inches.

After decades of assigning highway deaths to the classic "nut behind the wheel" both industry and the government have begun to construct a far more rigorous framework of responsibility for reducing, if not ending, highway casualties which kill more people than all wars combined. "Fundamental to the emergence of this national policy on motor vehicle safety," says archcritic Nader, "is the recognition of a value and a capability." The value is the right of people not to have their physical integrity violated by hazardous autos—whether by product design or by construction. The capability, of course, is an engineering one, the capability to invent the technological future once the nation decides that it wants the rich benefits of such a future.

If there was an impetus for auto safety reform, apart from the General Motors private detective affair, it was the result of a powerful meshing of deeply felt values and eminently graspable remedies. So much of the carnage is avoidable if products can be made to forgive the way a 2,000 miles per hour fighter plane or a space ship does. The difference, of course, is that in the companies which make space ships and secret reconnaissance aircraft, engineers and safety experts don't wallow in the middle-management mud, playing third alto to higher-ranking stylists and marketing men.

The shift in the Federal government's approach to highway safety and the impact that approach is having has rarely been illustrated better than by Federal Highway Administrator Lowell Bridwell during his department's appropriation hearings on Capitol Hill in April 1968.

While being questioned by Representative Charles Jonas of North Carolina, the following exchange occurred.

Jonas: I don't see how you can justify any expanded safety program unless you know where your problem is. Shouldn't the first step be to identify the cause of these accidents and see what the point is at which we should be directing our attention. . . ?

Bridwell: Mr. Jonas, I agree that that is a correct point of view . . . our problem in highway safety in general is that the cause of accidents has been very largely in the past left to the police investigation and their investigations have concentrated almost entirely upon pinpointing the so-called guilty party and don't get to the cause, but only at the problem of liabiltiy.

Jonas: From your investigations and the study you have given to the subject, would you agree that it is a fair statement that by far the greater number of accidents, the greatest cause of accidents is reckless and careless driving by individuals?

Bridwell: I don't believe I could make that statement, Mr. Jonas.

Speed and careless drivers cause accidents, of that there is no question. But cars kill. As government research is now beginning to show, spectacular accidents get the widest, splashiest publicity but they account for only a small minority of the 53,000 highway deaths a year. A study made in California in 1967, for example, revealed that after a large sampling of accident wreckage was sifted and examined, mechanical failure was a direct cause in 20% of the crashes. It's no wonder that between 1966 when the Traffic Safety Bill passed and December 1967, the big four manufacturers pulled back five million cars to check for possible mechanical defects, one half of the total production run that year.

Until a few years ago traffic safety beliefs have been based on little more than a consensus of subjective judgments, according to Dr. William Haddon, Highway Safety Bureau Director, who has led government programs into new areas of crash prevention, crash survival, and post-crash salvage of the injured and dying. To date, Haddon has issued 30 new safety standards covering 100 specific aspects of vehicle and tire safety performance; 40 others are in preparation in Haddon's office.

Some of the standards include better lighting, defrosting and defogging equipment and better tire performance; standards requiring energy-absorbing steering assemblies that act as a fire net for the driver's chest rather than as a spear, and laminated windshield glass that reduces the severity of injuries; a standard limiting fuel tank rupture and fuel spillage that increases the chance for escape and removal of the injured after an accident.

One of Haddon's most interesting developments is an anti-theft device for all cars by 1970. A system is being developed whereby the steering mechanism and the transmission can be locked, reducing the possibility of theft to zero. This is important because at least 100,000 stolen cars crash every year, a rate 200 times that of other cars.

Haddon's research for future standards includes better windshield mounting to prevent crash dislodgment; strengthening the side structure of cars to reduce frequent deaths and injuries happening daily in intersection and other lateral impacts. A well placed company executive admitted to him a few months ago: "We were appalled when we tested our own cars to discover they gave us no protection from side impact." Fresh from that shock, the industry is now driving ahead of the Government safety group, developing lifesaving side structure supports for future model runs, even before Dr. Haddon has proposed a standard. If other industry leaders begin reacting with such progressive programs, Ralph Nader will be out of work. The companies in Detroit, whatever their motives, were plainly horrified at the road tests. For even at low speeds, around 30 miles per hour, the impacting car penetrates as far as the steering wheel on current models; in a right side collision, the right side often will be pushed as far as the driver, crushing all the passengers.

Some Congressmen can contest the cost of the Government's traffic safety program but at $25,000 per standard, the investment is a remarkably good one. Any effort, in fact, which offers potential for reducing the incredible economic damage of highway accidents ($30 million a day) and human loss is worth the cost. Each week 70,000 Americans are injured and 1,000 killed. On an annual basis that equals the total American battle losses in the three years of the Korean War.

Budgetary arguments are inevitable, but already Dr. Haddon has reported a payoff in human lives. Highway injuries decreased 400,000 in the first year of the safety program, a dramatic 10% drop despite a rise in auto registrations.

Safe Tires

For all the soothing advertising about safety rushing from the nation's major tire manufacturers, investigations by Senator Gaylord Nelson and the Federal Trade Commission indicate that the tires on many new autos are inadequate to handle maximum loads. What's more, some original equipment tires can't be operated safely at the speeds the vehicles are capable of achieving. In fact, the consumer is provided precious little information about some very vital criteria, including a tire's impact resistance, endurance, traction, and mileage.

In the spring of 1968, Nelson's senate office was inundated with complaints from buyers about Firestone Wide Oval Tires. The tires not only showed unusually rapid tread wear, the complaints said, but the sidewalls had cracked and split.

Nelson set his staff to work. "I was shocked to discover how readily tire industry sources confirmed these reports," he said later, "about trouble with the Wide Oval. These people I talked with were well aware of the splitting and cracking as well as the unusually rapid tread wear and some other deficiencies."

Only after he was sure that Firestore hadn't ordered the defective tires recalled, did he confront the company. Privately, officials conceded that the letter writers had scored a point. There were problems with the Wide Ovals. Nelson found it astonishing that a large, respected company "privately concedes that it had produced a defective product, yet refuses publicly to take responsibility for the recall of that product."

Unquestionably, Firestone drew much of the fire down on its own position. The Nelson episode occurred amidst the company's spring advertising campaign. Its theme: "When you buy a Firestone tire no matter how much or how little you pay, you get a safe tire."

To one California tire dealer, who trafficked in Firestone products, that ad was the limit. "I am prepared to testify under oath," he wrote Nelson, "that I have seen many, many Firestone Wide Ovals with both small and large separations and cracks. These were all defects of a very serious nature . . . all the tire dealers I know have had similar experiences with Wide Ovals." When the time-consuming fracas was over, Firestone recalled the defective tires and made the necessary changes in the manufacturing process.

Complaints from consumers about poor quality and deceptive pricing had been gathering moss in Washington for years, until this decade when the Federal Trade Commission and Congress decided to investigate their merits, despite some strong words of discouragement from tire industry officials. "It wasn't pretty," a key Senator recalls. Apart from the incredible number and variety of brands available, at least 1,100 from coast to coast, the probers found that consumers basically had no way of determining for themselves what such words as "deluxe," "first line," "premium" and "super deluxe" meant to them. As consumer expert Sidney Margolius has written, "each manufacturer could call a tire anything he wanted to, and apparently did. Sometimes a manufacturer would call a mediocre grade 'super,' and a second grade, 'deluxe'."

The industry's first line of defense was to press for a system of voluntary standards. That was hardly a breakthrough since the common denominator was so low that most, if not, all, tires could meet the standards. Subsequently, Congress authorized the Commerce Department to establish a series of safety and grading standards, the first Government-developed guidelines for product quality outside the food area. When the grading standards are implemented, the consumer will know what he is buying to a degree as yet unequalled. If he doesn't care much about quality, which has been the argument industries have frequently used to head off standards and consumer protection regulation, that's his privilege. But many consumers do care, if the thousands of letters cascading into Washington are any guide, and it is to end the tire-buying nightmare that the Commerce Department has taken action.

The Federal Trade Commission, for its part, has promulgated some effective tire advertising guides. Under a 1967 ruling, tire manufacturers were obligated to provide buyers with information that enables him to match the weight of his car with the performance of the hundreds of possible choices available. The consumer leaders, however, haven't hung their lances on the wall; much more disclosure should be made mandatory, they say, before the tire buyer and the tire seller can meet on a level that even approaches equal terms.

Industry critics direct their fiercest tirade at the suppression of innovation within the industry, the reluctance to advance the state of the art for the buyer's benefit. Ted Rowse, editor of Washington's best consumer newsletter, *U.S. Consumer,* insists that back in 1957, Firestone developed but never marketed a tubeless tire equipped with a special valve for receiving injections of linseed oil. Oxygen is a natural enemy of tire life because it damages rubber. Linseed oil nearly eliminates the oxidation process by absorbing oxygen, leaving only nitrogen inside the tire. Manufacturers have long known that nitrogen can lengthen a tire's life but for one reason or another, few consumers have enjoyed the benefits of the breakthrough.

There has been a breakthrough, however, as research by one Texas company, Three-T-Fleet of El Paso, reveals. Tire life was increased at least 25% and as much as 50% after extensive nitrogen treatment. Such advantages are not available to the consumer, unless he wants to do it himself, and yet the manufacturers' band plays on about quality control excellence and innovation.

Consumer Reports in 1968 summed up the conditions in the rubber jungle, through which the buyer must hack his way if he wants a safe, fairly priced tire: "You can't consistently count on any single type of tire or material to give better performance than another." Moreover, while the buyer waits for reform he must make his decision from the broadest spectrum imaginable, tread life ranging from 15,000 to 40,000 miles, costs of $40 to $130 per 10,000 miles of driving on a full set.

If the industry can't produce safe tires the consumerists petition for the next best break. The industry advertising should be toned down so that buyers aren't misled into believing they are driving on miracle tires.

There has been movement toward reform, but, unhappily, the conclusions of the Consumer Advisory Council are nearly as relevant today as they were in 1966. "It is a sad commentary that, as a cost-cutting device, inferior grades of tires are provided on many new cars. There is no defense for an automaker equipping new cars with tires that are not capable of safely carrying a full load of passengers under all conditions commonly encountered . . . even the one point about which the consumer feels sure, the size of the tire he needs, presents an element of uncertainty: whether in fact he gets that size . . . a serious hazard results when the consumer calculates the load capacity of his car on the basis of the tire size he requested but is riding on a smaller tire."

Dangerous Drugs

In few other areas of the U.S. marketplace is the consumer as un-informed as he is when he buys drugs prescribed for him by his doctors, or for that matter, when he buys any kind of health remedies. Americans, the most health conscious population in history, consume mountains of pills, bromides, drugs and palliatives on doctors' orders. The doctors' information to a large extent comes from the drug industry's detail men, a euphemism for salesmen. Standing between them and millions of Americans is the Food and Drug Administration, whose vigilance varies. At the very least, the Consumer Advisory Council study warned, "the patient who receives a prescription from his physician should have reasonable confidence and expectation that the drug is truly needed."

The Kefauver drug hearings of the early 1960s provided new insights for those consumers who may have wanted to know more about the behind-the-scenes operations of the drugmakers. What was revealed was a picture of internal struggling between research men anxious to conduct thorough tests and the marketing men, whose eyes were trained on the sales and profit charts.

The hearings produced enough evidence to warrant new Congressional authority over the industry, including stiffer testing programs for industry before a drug could be approved by the FDA for sale. A host of questionable drugs have been held off the market until their efficacy has been established thanks to Senator Kefauver's efforts.

There were other new requirements established by Kefauver's bill, such as a review of 3,600 pharmaceutical products marketed between 1938 and 1962. Designated to conduct the review was a team of professionals from the National Academy of Sciences—National Research Council. The conclusions reportedly reached by the review team are guaranteed to place the drugmakers on the defensive more than Kefauver ever did, if that is possible. Only about 10% of the drug products marketed between 1938 and 1962 wholly measure up to the claims made for them; at least another 10% should be thrown off the market because they have no value one way or another.

Whether these findings will have an impact on the industry is dubious, the consumer leaders reason. If the new Kefauver amendments are a guide, however, the economic impact will be hardly noticeable. Though the drugmakers complained that the 1962 amendments would disrupt the inexorably rising profit and sales indicators, the industry's rate of return on net worth, 18%, still leads all U.S. industries while profit return on sales has actually increased since the new legislation, from 9.8% to 10.7%, according to *Fortune* magazine.

Then as now, the consumer suffers not only from physical malady but also from a woeful lack of relevant information about the drugs he takes. His only sources currently are exchanges between his doctor and the drugmakers' detail men who daily bombard doctors and druggists with new pills and antibiotics, accompanied by extravagant claims as to their potency and utility. Rarely, if ever, does news of a particular drug's disadvantages filter through that maze of overstatements.

The consumerists are fond of tracing the case of Chloromycetin, a broad spectrum antibiotic which was introduced by Parke, Davis in 1949, as an illustration of the occasional imbalances between sales and safety. If the drug business is a delicate balancing act between costs, profits and benefits to the patients, most consumerists believe that in the case of Chloromycetin, the scale tipped too far toward sales.

Soon after Parke, Davis had begun selling the drug, evidence cropped up that serious side-effects sometimes accompanied the cure. A sample: blood poisoning and aplastic anemia. It was held that the antibiotic was appropriate for typhoid conditions and for patients with Rocky Mountain spotted fever but wider use for such common ailments as respiratory infections and colds was risky. Looking on with dismay as four million people in 1960 alone were given Chloromycetin, such watchdogs as Senator Gaylord Nelson and Morton Mintz of *The Washington Post* shuddered. In their view, only a few thousand people who were down with typhoid should be treated with the prescription. Meanwhile, reports of fatalities and severe side effects grew in number.

When Parke, Davis' patent for Chloromycetin expired in 1966 (generic name, chloramphenicol), a half-dozen of the competitors rushed in with their own brands. Rugged though the new competition has been, Parke, Davis still draws a third of its sales and a third of its earnings from Chloromycetin.

Critics of the consumer movement object to excessive emphasis of the case because the pattern is not often repeated. On the other hand, much can be learned from it, not only because so many large, well known firms have been involved; new insights are provided into the world of the detail men.

In the 1950s, James Watkins, 10, of La Canada, California, came down with a urinary tract infection. His harried father, Dr. Albe Watkins, searched the family medicine chest for a cure. He recalled that Parke, Davis detail men, during one of their calls to his office, had touted Chloromycetin as being "perfectly safe." He gave it to his son. Three months later the boy died of aplastic anemia, in agony. "I might have done better," his father told a Senate committee later, "had I taken a gun and shot him."

Regrettably, there are hundreds of recorded cases like that one, even thousands, the morbid result of doctors treating patients for colds and other minor ailments, when other drugs would be demonstrably safer. "Using Chloromycetin for everyday ailments is like shooting a chicken with a bazooka," a government official confided recently. The company, no doubt, has been aware of dangers. Because it is required to, the company has published warnings in American medical journals. And yet, when it advertises in foreign medical journals, where there is no requirement, it doesn't.

During one recent Congressional airing of the drug industry's safety problems, some illuminating testimony was given by Dr. William Hewson of West Chester, Pennsylvania. A few months before while

wearing his other hat as a lawyer, he won a $215,000 jury award for
the estate of Mary Ann Incollinge, a child who died under the same
circumstances James Watkins had.

"The great disservice of the detail men is not their exaggeration of
a drug's beneficial uses," Dr. Hewson explained, "but in their approach
to its toxic effects. Commonly the toxicity is not discussed thoroughly,
is played down, and is not even broached. The otherwise informed
physician is thereby grossly misled."

As a practicing physician, Dr. Hewson said he didn't recall "the
Parke, Davis detail men ever discussing the relationship between
administration of the drug and the development of blood dyscrasias.
. . . Of the many physicians I have talked to with regard to these
detailing methods, not one has stated that the Parke, Davis men
voluntarily brought the toxicity to the physicians' attention."

Hammering first at high prices, Senator Kefauver in 1962 dug into
the allegation that there was profit for drugmakers who could deceive
physicians. He must have found evidence, for one of the amendments
in the 1962 legislative package included one which requires that "all
advertisements and other descriptive matter must carry a true statement in brief summary of efficacy, side effects," and conditions in
which the drug should not be used. The FDA was given right of review.

Under that stronger umbrella of prevention, the FDA took over
33 formal actions against 26 well known manufacturers, with Abbott
Laboratories and Upjohn Company cited at least three times each.
Under pressure from FDA administrator James Goddard, who resigned
for a job in private industry July 1, 1968, drug companies have allowed
a beam of light to penetrate its interiors. Despite their self-righteous
facade, drugmakers do make mistakes. In a recent two-year period,
21 companies mailed 23 letters correcting overstatements and soften-
ing claims to more than 280,000 doctors across the nation.

The era of "seller beware" has not yet arrived for the drugmakers,
but it is coming. No drug company deliberately plans to use drug
consumers as guinea pigs but in Washington there exists a strong feeling
that the consequences are the same as if they did. Extensive testing
before marketing is a small price to pay for health and safety, particularly when the industry has the resources. Furthermore, exploitation is no longer a tolerable condition in 20th century America. What
separates the drug issue from others in the consumer arena and renders
drug consumers more silent is the fact that even though they buy, it is

the physicians who order. And so when drug reform is set in motion in Congress, the fullest measure of responsibility rests upon the shoulders of the FDA; the real voice of the drug consumer seldom filters through because he doesn't know what to do. How much of a voice do consumers have? "Very little," commissioner Goddard said when he was sworn in, "unless it is ours."

In the final analysis, the consumers must rely on the drugmakers' social consciousness. "Thalidomide taught us," Morton Mintz wrote in 1967, "that the unborn child may have the most vital concern with the chemicals ingested by its mother. Yet a fetus is hardly in the best position to file a legal brief with the FDA in hopes of assuring that an advertisement will not mislead a physician into prescribing a needlessly dangerous drug that will cross the placental barrier."

Cleaner Meat, Fish and Chicken

When President Theodore Roosevelt led the first major, successful drive for pure food and drug laws, he was fought at every turn by the food and drug industry. The slaughterhouse conditions might have been abominable, but the companies fought to preserve the right of free choice for themselves and for the consumers' right to be wrong, which in those days included food poisoning. During the height of the hearings in 1906, which were triggered by Upton Sinclair's exposé, *The Evening Post* published a rhyme describing the conditions.

> "Mary had a little lamb
> And when she saw it sicken
> She shipped it off to Packington
> And now it's labeled 'chicken'."

A wave of indignation swept the country again in 1967 when meat plant conditions were publicized. To advocates of reform of the 1960s, the *Evening Post* rhyme was regrettably germane. The 1906 act, by exempting intrastate plants from inspection, had left a loophole wide enough for hundreds of impure meat merchants to drive their trucks through. Before the 1967 meat bill, fully one-quarter of the 50 billion pounds of meat processed in the U.S. was inspected only by the states, whose programs, Congressional testimony established, were tantamount to no inspection at all. Conditions in the poultry industry, if possible, represented even greater health dangers to the consumer. If consumers knew about the conditions, Senator Joseph Montoya of New Mexico told the Senate in August 1968, "they would never pick up another piece of poultry again, except to chuck it out the back door for the vultures." An estimated 11.5 billion pounds of poultry products are produced annually, of which at least 1.5 billion pounds are inspected solely by the states. Only five states have had active inspection programs.

Pressing for a legislative program similar to the meat bill, Senator Montoya cited an Agriculture Department survey made in January 1968, of 97 plants which were not subject to Federal inspection. The plants were in Alabama, California, Mississippi, Florida, Ohio, Texas, South and North Carolina, Missouri, and Tennessee. Some poultry and poultry products, said the report, are processed in "repulsive . . . primitive conditions," including fly and rodent infestation and "unbelievably filthy and stinking" picking rooms and equipment.

Once again, horrible revelations were needed to prod Congress into action. Far more than mere political demagoguery was the lever that propelled new inspection bills through: at least 2 million Americans contract such diseases as botulism and salmonellosis a year from inadequate, diseased food, mostly meat and poultry.

Such consumerists as Senator Walter Mondale and Ralph Nader jolted millions of consumers and Congressmen from their reverie with reports of intolerable processing conditions. A glance at the seamy underside of the free enterprise system was provided by Senator Mondale during the meat debates. There were some 15,000 meat packing plants dealing in meats sold only within states, subject to state and county and municipal laws. "A number of these were generally defective or not enforced for the protection of consumers," he said, while the plants were deliberately established "out of reach of Federal inspection" to effect savings "by passing the sick meat to consumers" and by using "additives not permitted under Federal regulation."

For the first time, consumers were allowed into the world of the "cripple buyers," who deal in "4-D" meat, dead, dying, disabled or diseased animals. Not only were those dealers out of reach of Federal inspectors but state inspectors rarely ventured near them. Reports of bribery were widespread.

Several times during the meat and poultry hearings in 1967 and

1968, meat inspectors were asked whether they would buy such meat for their own families. The answer was always no. Why should anyone else, either? Ultimately, Congressional consciences became so aroused that reform legislation was passed, but only with daily pressure from Betty Furness and the White House.

If these bills are properly financed with appropriations so that enough new Federal inspectors can be hired, the consumer will be much less likely to buy dangerous meat and poultry in the future. Top executives in both industries have come to realize the hard way that strict regulation is good business; if consumers have confidence, they'll buy more. As a measure of the consumer movement, the poultry interests recognized the need for reform in 1968 and supported the bill from the beginning. The year before, the meat interests reluctantly came around under pressure from all sides.

The lesson doesn't always get through, however. About six months after President Johnson signed the meat bill, a speech was delivered by William Heimlich, a vice-president of the Association of Better Business Bureaus International. His topic was consumerism. "We cannot quarrel with the thesis that the government has a right and the duty to protect the health and safety of the consumer. But we have every right to debate the question of whether the government can protect the consumer from his own bad judgment. Freedom of choice is a precious right and much of the unrest in those countries where government rules the marketplace with an iron hand is directly traceable to the demands of the people for the right of free choice." Mr. Heimlich evidently missed the message of the meat bill. Free choice of rotten meat and poultry is no longer tolerated by the leaders of the consumer movement and their followers.

The disclosures jarred enough Americans so that they took refuge in eating fish; all food wasn't hazardous, was it? There is no industry, with the exception of lumbering that has been on the American scene longer than fishing. But there is strong evidence that as in the meat and poultry industries, there is as much money to be made in the commercial market with bad fish as with good fish. "Many ships in the commercial fleet are old and unsanitary," Ralph Nader has written in the *New Republic*. "But even the more modern portions of the domestic fishing fleet have yet to surmount the long time that elapses between the fish catch and its processing. Dead fish often rest 5 to 14 days in the hold pens with ice piled on top of them. The unique odors attendant upon decomposition aboard ship proliferate here. Deficient temperature control is the most serious problem. Storage at temperatures above the level of 0° F bring deteriorating havoc on this highly perishable commodity."

A Consumers Union study revealed the dangerous whirlwind the housewife can reap from fish products: 85% of 646 cans of salmon (51 brands) were on the verge of discoloration and mushiness; 98 samples of 120 samples of frozen raw breaded shrimp tested contained coagulase positive staphylococci; 55 samples of 120 samples of cod, haddock and ocean perch fillets were of substandard quality.

There is ample evidence that housewives didn't need such disclosures to warn them of the possible hazards of bad fish, imported or domestic. Fish sales have not grown at all in the last 20 years and per capita consumption, 11 pounds a year, is approximately the same as it was in 1948.

All the housewife needs is to hear more reports of poisoning and she'll switch to another menu. Tuna sales, for example, dropped sharply in May 1966 after 400 cases of salmonella poisoning in New York City were tracked to smoked fish processed in substandard plants. Three years earlier, nine people died from botulism poisoning after eating canned tuna.

The FDA has sought to pressure the industry to take remedial steps. But the industry is shunning the warnings so far. They think disclosures such as Nader's are bad for business, and they are correct.

Early in 1968, W. B. Rankin, a deputy commissioner of the FDA, was scheduled to address a group of fishing industry executives. But at the last minute, his appearance was cancelled. A copy of his speech had fallen into outside hands. Part of it described the results of FDA surveys conducted at several processing plants:

"The fish were hung on wooden sticks for the processing operation. The sticks were encrusted with rotten fish scales and particles from previous batches. Debris from previous batches of fish was trapped in the nicked table top since no attempt was made to clean and sanitize the table between operations. These residues served to contaminate all batches of fish that passed over the table. No attempt was made to clean the rusty wire dip nets that were used to remove the fish from the thawing and brining casks. The nets had buildups of bits of rotten fish flesh and entrails . . . a rusty perforated metal scoop was generally used to mix the brine solutions. In one instance, an employee picked a stick off the floor and used it to mix the brine . . . after smoking, the fish was allowed to stand at room temperature for approximately 4½ hours before they were placed in a refrigerator."

Dangers in the marketplace are proving more extensive than housewives—or their husbands—realize. Unlike air and water pollution, however, remedies for removing them are clearly within reach. There has been a reawakening at Federal, state and local levels; almost daily U.S. industry is being reminded that what is good for the public is also good for business. If some businessmen remain unconvinced, the chances are better than they've ever been in the nation's history that the long arm of consumerism will reach out and remind them of their forgotten responsibilities. Not just the meat, drug, poultry and auto makers have learned that the hard way. So have the men who operate natural gas pipelines, sell medical devices and cosmetics, or pump undue amounts of powerful pesticides into the land and rivers. "To view past, present and future actions as 'anti-business' or as a 'bleeding hearts campaign,' " Betty Furness has said, "is to miss the whole point—we have a consumer revolution on our hands—as dynamic a force as the emerging labor movement of the 1930s."

It is, after all, not the consumer who fixes prices or processes diseased meat. Nor is it the consumer, Betty Furness explained to a meeting of the American Trial Lawyers Association in July 1968, who seeks "to undermine business or destroy competition. He is only guilty of the desire to buy wisely and the desire to be assisted through some pertinent information about his purchase . . . he also harbors the not unreasonable desire for some kind of standards and quality controls so that he can compare products wisely. These goals we want to achieve are as American as the 4th of July."

Achieving these goals is no longer a fit subject for academic discussion or abstract postulation, not when the national Commission on Product Safety is running out of file space because so many cases are coming to its attention. Here are some sample cases:

(1) A 16-month-old boy took the legs off a doll, exposing three-inch spikes, described by his mother as a "lethal weapon."

(2) A 13-month-old boy hanged himself in his crib with the string of a musical toy designed to entertain babies.

(3) A woman in New York City wrote, "The plastic lid of my gift coffeemaker caught fire . . . the flame reached almost to the ceiling."

(4) "For the third time this year my son has had a severe fall from his swing set," wrote a woman from Garland, Texas, "all because the hooks attached to the swing seats last only five days and chains last only about six months."

(5) A 62-year-old woman in California was standing in a puddle when her electric edger clipped its cord. She was electrocuted.

While not a landmark on the order of the auto safety or meat bill, the 1967 amendments to the Flammable Fabrics Act, nevertheless, extended new protection to buyers of carpets, drapes, hats, gloves and upholstery fabrics. It took 14 years for the bill's basic loophole to be closed; only with wearing apparel did the Government have the right to set limits of flammability. A disproportionate number of victims of such perilous products are children or the aged; 1,500 people die from clothing burns annually, another 100,000 are injured.

There is action on many other fronts, as well, protecting consumers against dangerous x-ray machines, toxic food additives, unsafe cosmetics and even sun tan lotion.

Some experts believe that less danger exists in the marketplace today than was present 50 years ago, although the majority view holds that there is substantially more now than ever before. The consumer's sense of rising expectations is demanding that industry do better because it knows how, if it chooses. Should reform not come from within, then the Government will be forced to take even more action, a confrontation no one wants, especially understaffed Government agencies who already have their hands full.

There are many optimistic indications that business will heed the new watchwords. Furthermore, attacks on the consumer movement are dwindling. There are few, if any, concurring voices when Dr. Oscar Sussman, a vice president of the New Jersey Public Health Association, wrote in the May 1968 issue of *Nation's Business* that the Wholesale Meat Act of 1967 was a "fraud," or that Betty Furness and Ralph Nader were "two self-styled protectors of the public weal (who) are the best known on the bandwagon of mob psychologists and public relations experts who clobbered the meat industry."

What the consumer really wants these days is assurance that the product he buys has integrity. Industry's opposition to such desires accomplishes nothing more than confirming the consumer's worst fears: dangerous imperfections are present in the marketplace.

C. Opinions on Liability

22. Mass Marketing and Warranty Liability

Arthur F. Southwick, Jr.

On May 7, 1955, Claus Henningsen purchased a new Plymouth automobile from Bloomfield Motors, Inc., in Bloomfield, New Jersey, an authorized dealer of Chrysler Corporation. Twelve days later, on May 19, Helen Henningsen, Claus's wife, drove the car to Asbury Park. On the return trip Mrs. Henningsen suddenly heard a loud noise "from the bottom, by the hood." She later testified in court that it "felt as if something cracked," that the steering wheel spun, and that the car veered to the right and hit a brick wall.

A bus driver proceeding in the opposite direction had observed the Henningsen car approach in a normal manner; he stated that "all of a sudden (it) veered at 90 degrees—and right into this wall."

Prior to the accident, the car had performed normally. The highway was smooth, the weather clear, and Mrs. Henningsen's speed at the time of the mishap was 20 to 22 miles per hour. The automobile odometer read 468 miles.

An inspector and appraiser for the insurance carrier stated that in his opinion something went "wrong from the steering wheel down to the front wheels"; that "something down there had to drop off or

Reprinted from *Journal of Marketing,* Vol. 27 (April, 1963), 9–14, published by The American Marketing Association.

break loose to cause the car" to act as it did; and that the accident must have been due to a mechanical defect or failure.

Mrs. Henningsen sued both the dealer and the manufacturer for her personal injuries. Mr. Henningsen claimed damages for the total loss of his automobile, for medical and hospital expenses, and for loss of his wife's society and services.

The plaintiffs' first argument was based upon the law of negligence. The Trial Court swiftly dismissed these claims against both defendants, for the reason that the evidence was insufficient to show lack of proper care in the manufacture, distribution, and sale of the automobile. However, the plaintiffs' complaint was also based upon breach of express and implied warranties. The jury gave verdicts to both plaintiffs against both defendants. In May, 1960, the Supreme Court of New Jersey affirmed the verdicts.[1] How and why was the court able to reach this decision?

Henningsen may well become a landmark decision. The case further expands the law governing liability for harm caused by defective products.

Legal concepts and the rules of law which govern the rights and duties of individuals and corporations develop and expand as business practices change. Modern advertising, mass marketing, and other activities of manufacturers designed to stimulate consumer demand have significantly influenced recent court decisions; and these influences will be examined in this review of the law of products liability.

Theories of Products Liability

When a disappointed buyer or consumer has allegedly been financially or physically injured as a result of a defective product, he has several possible legal theories upon which to base his claim for redress.

Negligence

The first is the theory of negligence—the failure to exercise reasonable care. Of course, when a plaintiff bases his cause of action on negligence, he must establish that the defendant was under the obligation to exercise care; that the obligation was not fulfilled, thereby producing harmful or defective merchandise; and that an injury was caused by the defective goods.

---

[1] *Henningsen v. Bloomfield Motors, Inc.,* 32 N.J. 358 (1960).

In appropriate cases where proof is available, it is possible to succeed in a negligence suit against a manufacturer. However, retailers, wholesalers, and jobbers who merely handle the goods are seldom in fact negligent; and usually a suit against a nonmanufacturer based upon lack of care is futile. Nevertheless, the law of practically all jurisdictions is well settled to the effect that most manufacturers, suppliers, and sellers of merchandise for a consideration owe the duty to all probable users of exercising reasonable care in the preparation and the furnishing of a product for market.

The law of negligence has not always been so clear, however. Over 120 years ago it was decided in a famous English case that a manufacturer had no legal responsibility for harm caused a consumer, even if the manufacturer had failed to exercise care in manufacture, unless the person injured had actually purchased the item directly from the manufacturer.[2] In short, a manufacturer or seller owed no legal duty to anyone except those with whom the defendant had a contractual relationship. Lack of privity of contract was a valid defense.

The courts soon recognized exceptions. The first exception to the *Winterbottom* doctrine was a situation where the defendant, not in privity of contract with the injured plaintiff, negligently mislabeled a bottle of poison.[3] By 1903, it was generally recognized that a manufacturer or seller owed a duty of reasonable care to make all "imminently" or "inherently" dangerous products safe for use by anyone who might be expected to use or consume the product.[4] Poisons, explosives, and things used for preserving or destroying life and health were within the definition of "imminently" or "inherently" dangerous items. Moreover, food products were recognized as an exception to the general notion that there was no liability for negligent manufacture unless there was privity of contract. Thirteen years later the New York court significantly extended the duty to exercise care, by including all products which were dangerous if defectively made, even if the product was not dangerous by its very nature.[5] In this

---

[2] *Winterbottom v. Wright,* 152 Eng. Rep. 402 (1842).

[3] *Thomas v. Winchester,* 6 N.Y. 397 (1852).

[4] *Huset v. Case Threshing Machine Co.,* 120 F. 865 (1903) (threshing rig); *Devlin v. Smith,* 89 N.Y. 470 (1882) (scaffold); *Statler v. Ray Manufacturing Co.* 195 N.Y. 478 (1909) (coffee urn).

[5] *MacPherson v. Buick Motor Co.,* 217 N.Y. 382 (1916).

MacPherson case, the Buick Motor Company was held liable to a consumer for injuries suffered, following retail purchase of an automobile that had a defective wheel.

The result is that the exceptions to the original rule of negligence law have become larger than the rule, and the vast majority of states have now reversed *Winterbottom v. Wright,* so that lack of privity of contract is not a valid defense to a cause of action based on negligence. This development would seem to be justified, since negligence is a tort, a wrong; and certainly the recognition of a duty to exercise reasonable care in the manufacture or furnishing of a product for sale should not be dependent upon the existence of a contractual relationship between the parties.

Warranties of quality

Products liability based upon warranty law must be carefully distinguished from the law of negligence. Warranty is strict or absolute liability. Failure on the part of the defendant to exercise care is not relevant; and to succeed in a claim the plaintiff need not establish that the defendant was at fault in causing the injury. Warranty liability is liability without fault. To succeed, the plaintiff needs only to establish the existence of a warranty, the breach thereof, and the resulting injury.

A warranty is a promise, either express or implied. An express warranty is usually, although not always, in the form of words, written or oral, which affirm a fact or make a promise relating to the goods. The affirmation of fact or promise must be relied upon by the buyer or be the basis of the purchase. Sometimes it is difficult to distinguish between an express warranty and sales puffing. An implied warranty is a promise that results from operation of law, and hence its existence does not depend upon the words or the actions of the seller.

The statutory Uniform Sales Act and the newer Uniform Commercial Code provide for several implied warranties. The Sales Act is in effect in approximately one-half of the states. The Code is a revision and modernization of all previously existing statutory law governing commercial transactions, and hence replaces the Sales Act in those states where enacted. By 1963, the legislatures of one-third of the states had adopted the Code.

Under both the Sales Act and the Code, manufacturers and all other sellers who deal in the kind of merchandise sold impliedly warrant that the goods sold shall be of merchantable quality. It is settled that this means that the goods shall be suitable for their usual purpose. Moreover, both statutes provide that there shall be an implied warranty that the goods sold will be fit for a particular purpose, if the seller knows that the buyer is purchasing the goods for a particular or specific purpose and if the buyer relies on the skill and judgment of the seller to furnish suitable goods. Both of these implied warranties exist by operation of law as a part of the sales transaction, unless the parties have entered an express warranty to the contrary or unless the warranties have been effectively disclaimed.

The Privity Rule

Since warranty is a promise, the liability for breach of warranty has frequently been defined or thought of as contractual in nature and not a tort. It has often been said that there can be no warranty of any kind unless a contractual relationship exists between the parties. It follows, therefore, that lack of privity of contract has generally been a valid defense to any cause of action based upon alleged breach of warranty.

Some legal historians have pointed out that this privity rule was all a mistake and a historical, legal accident. In their view "warranty" was actually a part of or an extension of the very early Common Law action of deceit, a tort action. It has always been recognized that intentional fraud or deceit will create liability, even in the absence of a contractual relationship between the parties.

Historical accident or not, it has been the general rule for many decades that an ultimate consumer has no cause of action against a remote manufacturer for breach of warranty. Lack of privity of contract is a good defense. Any warranty made by a manufacturer to his buyer or implied in their transaction by operation of law does not usually "run with the goods" or otherwise inure to the benefit of the consumer.

Similarly, any express or implied warranty existing between a retailer and his buyer cannot be the basis of a suit by a member of the buyer's family or other ultimate user of the merchandise. These principles are the logical result of the concept that warranties are contractual in nature. With one exception in the Uniform Commercial Code, neither the Uniform Sales Act nor the Code specifically mentions this privity rule. (The Uniform Commercial Code extends a retailer's warranties, express or implied, to the buyer's family, members of his household, and his guests.) [6] The rule was developed by the courts; and so, in the absence of express statutory provisions, the rule is subject to judge-made exceptions and even complete reversal.

The privity rule, even though conceptually logical, leads to some unjustified and seemingly uneconomical results. If a manufacturer produces a defective product capable of causing harm and sells the product to a wholesaler who in turn sells to the retailer, the ultimate consumer-purchaser is barred from seeking his damages from anyone in the chain of production and distribution except the retailer.

However, the purchaser can bring a succssful suit against the retailer on implied warranty or on any express warranty that the retailer may have made to the buyer. In turn, the retailer can recover from the wholesaler, and the wholesaler from the manufacturer. Hence, the eventual loss falls on the manufacturer, even though the privity rule prevents the consumer from suing and recovering directly from the manufacturer. This produces multiple lawsuits where one suit would have "done the job," and thus appears wasteful.

Of course, if the retailer was financially insolvent or out of business at the time of plaintiff's suit, then the privity rule, as a practical matter, has the result of denying the injured consumer compensation for his injury. To many, this appears socially unjustified. Moreover, under a strict application of the privity rule, if someone purchases a defective product which causes injury to some other member of his family, the injured person has no warranty course of action against anybody.

The human-consumption exception

Because of these and other apparent hardships, it is not surprising that various courts have from time to time created exceptions to the privity rule. In fact, the *Henningsen* case and other decisions raise the question of whether or not the courts are ready to completely abandon the rule. If so, warranty liability has departed from the realm of contract and entered the area of tort.

Where the privity rule has been eliminated, products liability based upon warranty has become a social duty imposed upon all manufacturers, distributors, and retailers. This is a strict and absolute duty to manufacture, distribute, and sell products fit for normal and customary use. Any harm caused by an unfit product must be compensated for by the payment of money for damages, even if the defendant

---

[6] Section 2-318.

used all possible care in the manufacture and/or distribution of the product. It is liability without fault and practically without defense.

The argument against multiple lawsuits, concepts of justice, and public policy has contributed to the creation of judicial exceptions to the privity rule, and in a sense forecast the rule's complete demise. But what are "justice" and "public policy"? In writing judicial opinions supposedly consistent with justice and public policy, judges look to the facts and the realities of modern business methods, to what appears "best" for society as a whole, and to their evaluation of society's expectations.

The most widely recognized exception to the privity rule relates to food products, drugs, and cosmetics. Presumably these are items which carry a high risk of personal injury to the consumer if they prove to be unfit for normal use, that is, either internal or external human consumption. Hence, courts in the vast majority of states now hold that lack of privity of contract is not a valid defense to a warranty cause of action where the harmful product is intended for consumption. Most often this result is reached simply on the grounds of "public policy" to protect the consumer.

In food cases, some courts have gone so far as to say that a sale is not necessary to support a warranty action. Hence, even though a restaurant may only "serve" food rather than "sell" a product, the restaurant nevertheless impliedly warrants that the food served is fit for consumption. (The Uniform Commercial Code provides expressly that a restaurant sells food; hence, it is clear that a restaurant impliedly warrants its food to be fit for human consumption.) [7]

The most noteworthy recent decisions applying the exception to the privity rule are certain polio vaccine cases against Cutter Laboratories in California.[8] Even though Cutter followed all governmental regulations and used all reasonable care in the production of its vaccine, there was implied warranty liability upon proof that live virus in the vaccine caused polio. The victims were not in privity of contract with the defendant manufacturer. The same result was seen in a Kansas hair-dye case, and an Ohio home-permanent wave case.[9]

---

[7] Section 2-314.

[8] *Gottsdanker v. Cutter Laboratories, Phipps v. Cutter Laboratories,* 6 Cal. Rep. 320 (1960).

[9] *Graham v. Bottenfield's, Inc.* 176 Kan. 68 (1954) (defendant distributor liable even though he neither manufactured nor packaged the hair dye); *Markovich v. McKesson and Robbins, Inc.* 156 Ohio App 265, at 275 (1958).

Will the well-recognized food, drug, and cosmetic exception to the privity rule be extended to more and more products? High risk of personal injury is not, of course, confined to products intended for human consumption. If unfit for its intended use, an automobile or an electric blanket might cause far more serious personal injuries than a mouse in a bottle of Coca-Cola.

Accordingly, the degree of risk of personal injury is not a satisfactory basis for the human consumption exception to the privity rule, or a satisfactory explanation of "public policy."

Pull-through selling

The elimination of the privity rule is largely due to the fundamental changes that have occurred in recent years in consumer advertising, marketing practices, and the realities of the modern economy. The manufacturer frequently directs his sales message to the ultimate consumer—thus, it is the manufacturer who stimulates demand, and who is in fact the true seller of the merchandise with respect to the nature and quality of the goods. In many instances, the retailer has become a conduit or distribution point through whom goods pass to the consumer—often he is a mere physical link in "pull-through" selling. In other words, the consumer relies more often upon the manufacturer than he does upon the retailer as to the nature and quality of the goods; and this fact has strongly influenced courts in warranty cases.

Printed matter furnished by manufacturers and the advertising conducted by manufacturers aimed at the consumer can constitute express warranties. Hence, many courts now recognize that lack of privity of contract is not a good defense when the plaintiff proves the breach of an express warranty contained in an advertisement, in a printed booklet accompanying the merchandise, or on a product label.[10]

A more enticing and alluring legal theory, however, for the plaintiff is the implied warranty of merchantable quality. It is in connection

---

[10] For example: *Rogers v. Toni Home Permanent Co.*, 167 Ohio St. 244 (1958) (manufacturer advertised product as safe and harmless; product labeled "very gentle."); *Lane v. Swanson & Sons*, 130 Cal. App 2d 210 (1955) (manufacturer's label read "Boned Chicken" and advertisement described contents of can as: "All luscious white and dark meat. No bones. No waste."); *Randy Knitwear v. American Cyanamid Co.*, 226 N.Y.S. 2d 363 (1962) (manufacturer's label read: "A Cyana-Finish. This fabric treated for shrinkage control. Will not shrink or stretch out of fit.").

with this theory that stimulation of consumer demand by the manufacturer is likely to have the greatest influence in court decisions. In short, the realities of modern marketing practices will lead the courts further along the path of requiring the manufacturer to respond directly to the consumer if the product proves unfit for its intended use.

The *Henningsen* case in New Jersey did exactly this. The decision held unequivocally that a contractual relationship is not necessary to create liability for breach of an implied warranty of quality. In reaching this conclusion, the court relied heavily on the fact that the privity rule developed at a time when marketing was relatively unsophisticated, when the buyer and the seller met face to face, when the buyer and the seller were on relatively equal bargaining terms, when the buyer had an opportunity to inspect the merchandise, and when the primary demand for goods was created by the retailer-seller rather than the manufacturer.

The New Jersey judge quoted from decisions in Texas and Washington, which in essence argued that it was "unjust" for a manufacturer to put merchandise into the stream of commerce, to create a demand for his product, and then to permit the creator of the demand to avoid warranty liability simply on the basis of lack of privity of contract. Noting that many previous decisions had abandoned the privity rule in the food cases, the court commented: "We see no rational doctrinal basis for differentiating between a fly in a bottle of beverage and a defective automobile." [11]

Yet *Henningsen* was not the first case to hold that a manufacturer not in privity of contract was absolutely responsible on the ground of implied warranty for the quality of his nonfood product. Several decisions preceded the New Jersey litigation, including important cases in Michigan, Florida, and Kansas.[12] Most cases to date have involved personal injury, although the doctrine is clearly applicable as well to cases involving only property loss.[13] However, *Henningsen* is the most unequivocal and dramatic case to date, and it is likely to become

[11] 32 N.J. at 383.

[12] *Spence v. Three Rivers Builders and Masonry Supply, Inc.,* 353 Mich. 120 (1958) (cement blocks); *Continental Copper & Steel Industries v. Cornelius, Inc.,* 104 So. 2d 40, (Florida App. Court, 1958) (electric cable); *Goodrich v. Hammond,* 269 F. 2d 501 (CA-10, purporting to apply Kansas law, 1959) (automobile tire).

[13] The *Spence* case did not involve personal injury. Neither did *State Farm Mutual Automobile Insurance Co. v. Anderson-Weber, Inc. and Ford Motor Co.,* 110 N.W. 2d 449, (Iowa, 1961), a case which follows *Henningsen.*

the landmark decision in this field of law and the guidepost for the future.

Connecticut and Iowa have followed the lead of New Jersey. In *Harmon v. Digliani, et al.,* a consumer was injured while using Lestoil, an all-purpose household detergent.[14] In ruling that a manufacturer should be held to warrant impliedly to the consumer that his product is reasonably fit for the intended use and that the plaintiff's allegations of breach of warranty could proceed to trial, Associate Justice Murphy of the Supreme Court of Errors reasoned:

"The neighborhood storekeeper who called all of his customers by their first names and measured or weighed out the desired amount of the commodity ordered before packaging it has practically disappeared from the commercial world. Where one occasionally survives, his method of displaying and dispensing his wares has radically changed. The shelves and showcases in his store contain for the most part packages and containers which have been packed and sealed by the manufacturer or by a producer who puts out as his own the products made by another. Neither the retailer nor the consumer can sample or otherwise examine the product. The maxim 'caveat emptor' has become a millstone around the necks of dealer and customer. While the customer may maintain an action under the Sales Act against the retailer for breach of implied warranty, the dealer in turn must sue his supplier to recoup his damages and costs where the customer prevails. Eventually, after several separate and distinct pieces of costly litigation by those in the chain of title, the manufacturer is finally obliged to shoulder the responsibility which should have been his in the first instance.

"The supermarkets and other retail outlets of our day dispense with the need for clerks behind counters to wait on customers. The goods are displayed on shelves and counters lining the aisles, and the customer, as he searches for a product, is bewitched, bewildered, and bedeviled by the glittering packaging in riotous color and the alluring enticement of the products' qualities as depicted on labels. The item selected is apt to be the one which was so glowingly described by a glamorous television artist on the housewife's favorite program, just preceding the shopping trip. Or the media of advertising might have been radio, magazine, billboard, or newspaper. All are widely used

[14] 174 A. 2d 294 (Connecticut, 1961).

in the appeal directed to the ultimate consumer. There appears to be no sound reason for depriving a plaintiff of the right to maintain an action against the manufacturer where the plaintiff alleges that he was induced to purchase the product by the representations in the manufacturer's advertising and that he sustained harm when the product failed to measure up to the express or implied representations." [15]

The result is that advertising is not solely an express warranty on the proper facts, but also (even in the absence of a finding of express warranty) greatly facilitates and encourages the abandonment of the privity rule in implied warranty claims.

In an implied warranty action, the plaintiff must establish that an injury was caused by a defective product and that the defect existed when the product was released from defendant's control. How are these matters of proof resolved? If the plaintiff shows sufficient evidence regarding breach of warranty to permit reasonable men to conclude that the product was in fact not of merchantable quality and that it was the cause of plaintiff's injury, then the plaintiff is entitled to have his case resolved by the jury. So it was in the *Henningsen* decision.

Disclaimer of Implied Warranty

One other significant legal and business issue in the *Henningsen* case remains for consideration. Both the Uniform Sales Act and the Uniform Commercial Code recognize that the parties to a sales contract may agree to disclaim and negate implied warranties.[16] Certainly this is a logical conclusion if warranty is in the nature of a contract or agreement.

When he purchased his car, Mr. Henningsen signed an agreement which recited the then standard automobile warranty suggested by the Automobile Manufacturers Association. This express warranty promised the original purchaser that the vehicle would be free from defects in material and workmanship but that the obligation was limited to

[15] *Ibid.*, p. 297.
[16] Uniform Sales Act, Section 71. Uniform Commercial Code, Section 2-316. The latter provides that the contract excluding the implied warranty of fitness for usual purpose must mention "merchantability" and, if written, the disclaimer must be "conspicuous."

replacing defective parts within 90 days, or 4,000 miles, whichever should first occur. Moreover, the manufacturer chose quite precise and unambiguous language to disclaim all other obligations with the provision: ". . . This warranty being expressly in lieu of all other warranties, expressed or implied, and all other obligations or liabilities . . ."

At delivery of the car, the buyer received the customary owner's Service Policy. The warranty provisions were identical with those recited on the purchase order, with the additional statement that the dealer extended the manufacturer's warranty to the purchaser.

It is clear that the actions of the plaintiffs against the dealer and manufacturer would have failed if the disclaimer was a valid contract. For years courts have construed disclaimers strictly and have never extended contractual language by implication beyond the precise words chosen. Furthermore, courts have frequently refused to enforce disclaimer clauses when they are in "small print" and are not adequately called to the buyer's attention at the time of purchase. The courts have stressed that valid disclaimer is a matter of knowledgeable agreement in a society encouraging freedom of contract. On the other hand, a purchaser is generally bound by a signed written contract, even though he failed to read the contract's provisions. Past cases have found it necessary to strike a balance between these two rules of law.

However, the *Henningsen* decision struck no such balance. It went considerably further by simply declaring the disclaimer void as a matter of law. The court observed that "the terms of the warranty are a sad commentary upon the automobile manufacturers' marketing practices." [17] After reading the express warranty, Justice Francis and his fellow Judges were left with the impression that the ". . . motive was to avoid warranty obligations which are normally incidental to sales. The language gave little and withdrew much." [18] Also: ". . . Courts must examine purchase agreements closely to see if consumer and public interests are treated fairly." [19]

Is this decision promoting or retreating from the long-standing and fundamental concept of freedom of contract? In one sense, the decision is certainly a retreat for the reason that the manufacturer,

[17] 32 N.J. at 375.
[18] 32 N.J. at 388.
[19] 32 N.J. at 387.

Chrysler Corporation, and the dealer are now told that the contract of warranty disclaimer is simply void and meaningless. In another sense, however, it can be argued that the very fact that the standardized warranty was used by all domestic automobile manufacturers prevented the true freedom of contract and, therefore, that the decision is consistent with fundamental legal doctrine.

The court stressed that the ability to disclaim implied warranties presupposes relative equality of bargaining power and hence true agreement. In the marketing of automobiles with the use of the standardized warranty, the buyer and seller do not meet on equal terms. The buyer has no choice or bargaining power with respect to the warranty except to refrain altogether from the purchase of an automobile. He takes the warranty offered by the seller or none at all. For these reasons the New Jersey court invalidated the disclaimer clause. It remains to be seen whether courts in future cases will take a similar position. The arguments pro and con will be heard for many years." [20]

Implications

There is no evidence suggesting that expanding concepts of the products liability law will result in an uncontrollable flood of claims. Nevertheless, these expanding concepts undoubtedly increase the direct and indirect costs of defending and responding to claims. More suits against manufacturers are likely. Paying for personal injuries is more expensive than repair or replacement of defective parts. Defense attorneys will be more likely to negotiate and settle claims; they will be less inclined to try cases in the courtroom because the opportunities in a jury trial for a successful defense are fewer in a warranty cause of action than in a cause of action based upon negligence. All these factors add to costs. Moreover, liability without fault, even in the absence of privity of contract, encourages attorneys for the plaintiff to

---

[20] Both *General Motors Corporation v. Dodson*, 47 Tenn App 438, (1960) and *State Farm Mutual Automobile Insurance Co. v. Anderson-Weber, Inc. and Ford Motor Co.*, 110 N.W. 2d 449, (Iowa, 1961) reach the same conclusions as the *Henningsen* case. They rule that lack of privity of contract does not bar a suit on implied warranty. Moreover, these cases apparently hold that the attempted contractual disclaimer and limitation of liability to the value of the defective part is void. In contrast, *Payne v. Valley Motor Sales, Inc.*, 124 S.E. 2d 622 (Supreme Court of Appeals of West Virginia, 1962) rejects the *Henningsen* view and holds that the express contractual language excluding implied warranties is an enforceable contract.

look more often to wholesalers and other middlemen as prospective defendants.

The ruling of the New Jersey court that the disclaimer of implied warranty liability is void as a matter of public policy is potentially more serious than the ruling that lack of privity of contract is not a defense to an implied warranty claim. If this is to be the law, warranty has been removed completely from the area of contract and has become a broad, absolute, social duty imposed upon sellers to answer for the consumer's personal injuries allegedly caused by harmful products.

Inability contractually to disclaim implied warranty liability limits the freedom of management in a free enterprise economy to determine the conditions under which merchandise is marketed. At this point of time in the development of the law, the moral of the *Henningsen* case would appear to be that management of individual companies should avoid standardized, industry-wide express warranties. If each manufacturing company within an industry develops its own individualized express warranty, and couples it with a precise, unambiguous disclaimer of implied warranty, the prospects of legal validity are enhanced.

The risk of products liability can be insured. However, insurance premiums add to costs. Furthermore, there will always be some cases where liability exceeds insurance coverage. The costs can be passed on to the consumer, it is sometimes argued. It is said that the risk can thus be spread throughout all of society. Nevertheless, as is always true, marginal producers may find it difficult to pass costs to their customers.

Will increasing costs of products liability deter producers from marketing new products? Such a result is not likely if other factors forecast the success of a newly developed product.

However, it would appear only prudent to withhold new and untried products from the market until the safety of the product is reasonably certain. If, after introduction to the market, unexpected results occur, the marketing manager should take prompt action to withhold further distribution, to recall units currently in the channels of distribution, and to warn consumers.

Courts are increasingly concerned with public health and safety; and the best defense against liability claims is for business management to be similarly concerned.

23. The Price of Faulty Design Gets Steeper Every Day

John Kolb

You can't make an omelet without breaking eggs, the old saying goes. It is probably also true that it was impossible to design, manufacture, and operate the machines of the Industrial Revolution without killing or injuring people.

"But that was a hundred years ago," points out Craig Spangenberg, Cleveland attorney. "Now American industry is good enough to send a rocket to the moon or to Mars, and get back information. So it should know how to make products of a quality at least as good as the advertising says it is."

Another attorney, Harry M. Philo of Detroit, believes the law and the courts are only now beginning to catch up with the fearful rate of accidental death and injury caused by manufactured products. Now this "growing, maturing social instrument," he says, is going to make it possible for victims "to obtain redress for their wrongs."

These two men, Philo and Spangenberg, are among the leading attorneys in the fastest-growing field of litigation: product design liability. All across the country they and their colleagues are causing more and more manufacturers and engineers to be called into court

Reprinted from *Product Engineering* (August 1, 1966), 34–43. © 1966; McGraw-Hill, Inc. Used in abstract by permission of *Product Engineering*.

to answer for faulty designs. Such suits usually allege negligence, in that design defects caused preventable death, injury, or property loss. When plaintiffs win—and more and more of them do—settlements and awards can run from the tens of thousands of dollars to the millions.

Engineer's Viewpoint

What should be the design engineer's attitude toward this mounting pressure? Can he shrug it all off as merely a spreading campaign for a fast buck by avaricious lawyers and clients? Or is it a signal, warning the engineer of a coming stage in his long search for professional status, wherein he will be expected to learn how to measure up to his awful power as the creator of machines that can kill and maim, even as they provide the very basis for our technological society?

Unfortunately, the engineer is at a loss to determine the strength of the signal. Reliable data on the incidence of personal injuries and property losses traceable to defective design are nonexistent. Even the National Safety Council has no such information and only lately has decided to start developing it. On the other hand, there is no difficulty determining the all-inclusive scope of product litigation, ranging as it does from heavy-duty industrial machinery through automobiles to many types of consumer products, including a number of the seemingly simple ones.

The engineer who prides himself on using his skills and training to make a meaningful contribution will carefully examine at least the more significant product-liability cases of which a sampling is included in this article. Perhaps he will be struck with the realization that here is that ultimate lever with which he can move his management in the direction of needed changes and improvements in design for human use, both generally and in relation to particular products. He may even find that product litigation will give the engineer a more powerful voice in arguing against the often exaggerated claims of sales and advertising.

But to achieve this stature and this leverage, the engineer will need to know how and why American industry is caught in this new legal thicket. Even more, he will have to find lasting ways to keep product designs out of litigation in the future. That is what this article is about.

Landmark Case

When a wheel collapsed on a new automobile he purchased not long before World War I, a Mr. MacPherson sued the manufacturer, Buick, and proved that the component had been made of defective materials. MacPherson's legal victory set the precedent for today's flood of product liability decisions favoring injured parties. Yet you can't really blame manufacturers for not heeding this early warning, for the precedent was long obscured by many adverse decisions.

As Harry H. Lipsig, New York attorney who recalls that he pleaded his first product case in the 1930s, says: "The accident and the injuries and losses caused by a defective product had to be cataclysmic in scale before a judge would even consider hearing a case, let alone find a manufacturer liable."

One reason for this, according to attorney Harry M. Philo, is that judges in the 1920s and 1930s were selected and appointed under a system that tended to favor the corporate side of product cases. The wave of social legislation beginning in the late 1930s and continuing through the present Congress, has brought judges to the bench by new routes and with new backgrounds. Today, Philo notes, "It is much easier to get a hearing for the individual who has suffered injury, loss of life, or property damage."

New Climate

"Still," Philo continues, "it was impossible for this to have happened until the legal myth that the manufacturer's responsibility ended when he sold his products to a distributor or retailer had been destroyed. Even though mass-circulation newspapers and magazines, together with coast-to-coast radio, had helped, the biggest single factor in changing this was television.

"Television put the manufacturers themselves—of everything from toothpaste to automobiles and office copying machines—right in the customer's living room—and even his bedroom. Express representations as to product superiority, safety, and other such benefits were made directly to the consumer. In the eyes of the law, such direct contact constituted a promise by the manufacturer of what we term the 'merchantability' of his product."

But most such cases were concerned with faulty manufacturing or such legalistic questions as express or implied warranty. A good number even turned solely on whether the manufacturer had sufficiently warned users of the potentially dangerous aspects of his product.

It was to be expected that attorneys, their clients, and the courts themselves would begin to look further for grounds on which to base new cases and on which to argue and decide them. They soon realized that behind most product defects stands an engineer, more or less to blame personally. Why personally? Because it is the engineering designer who is expected to keep defects out of the marketed product.

Even more important, if it could be proved that a defect was inherent in the design of a product, it was easier to prove negligence— in fact, it makes the negligence itself more meaningful. A manufacturing defect may affect a small number of the total output; a design defect presumably involves all or almost all of the units of a given product.

Thus it is easy to see why more and more engineers and other technically qualified persons are finding themselves on the witness stand—either trying to defend designs alleged to have caused injury, death, or loss, or acting as expert witnesses attempting to prove such liability.

This is a relatively new situation, and one that is still developing. For example, it is only in the last few years that the courts have begun to spell out the designer's and the manufacturer's responsibilities and liabilities in product design. These are the responsibilities:

(1) To know and understand the circumstances in which a product is used and to design it so that it will be reasonably safe for such use. This implies performing sufficient research, testing, and selecting adequate materials for applications intended. The designer and manufacturer must also anticipate and allow for the effects of reasonable wear and tear, and must warn of the hazards of use after excessive wear.

(2) To manufacture the product by the techniques and processes required to assure good workmanship.

(3) To keep up with advances in science, design methods, standards, manufacturing techniques, components and materials, and safety requirements.

(4) To apply the inspection and testing procedures necessary to assure a product "fit for use" by the ultimate user.

(5) To warn the user of hazards in either the use or the foreseeable misuse of the product.

Although these responsibilities are primarily those of the manufacturer and his engineering and manufacturing staffs, legally speaking
they have already provided grounds for successful suits against wholesalers and retailers, too. Moreover, the manufacturer can no longer
expect always to escape responsibility by claiming that the defect
arose from a dealer's failure to perform a required inspection after
selling a product, or from a dealer's inadequate servicing. Suits involving a distributing or servicing agent often name such parties as
defendants as well as the product manufacturer.

This is one reason why the manufacturer himself is no longer a
safe shield for the supplier of a component or a material proved to
have been among the root causes of a product defect. And whereas,
in the past, the courts usually limited judgments for injury or loss in
such circumstances to the manufacturer of the product containing
the faulty part, there now are decisions extending liability and payment to the injured party to both types of defendants.

In the past, the manufacturer could hope to recover from his supplier the costs of a suit over a defective product. He still may, but the
prospect is for more multiple suits, based on the same product—and
the same instance of injury or loss!

No longer is it only the purchaser of a product who can institute a
liability suit and collect. In most states, anyone in the household of
the injured party—even a guest or employee—can sue the manufacturer. It follows then that a claimant can sue when a spouse, child,
or other person of a significant relationship has been killed or injured,
and an award has even been made to an innocent bystander. In this
latter case, a person watching target practice was injured when a
defective shotgun shell caused a gun barrel to explode. Fragments of
the barrel struck this spectator and injured him, although he had been
standing in what would ordinarily have been considered a safe position. The bystander was not related to or otherwise connected with
the person whose gun exploded.

A case only recently settled, involves injury of an employee by
a metal-cutting machine already delivered and in use in the customer's
plant. In a similar case, a court made an award to an employee who
was injured by an industrial truck that was on loan to a prospective

customer for demonstration. The list of parties successfully sued is still growing.

Revolutionary Change

Harry Lipsig calls these developments "a revolution in the field of products."

What kinds of people have been waging this revolution? The prime movers are a small group of lawyers including, surprisingly—along with those who specialize in representing injured parties—some attorneys who defend the manufacturers and other parties that are being sued.

If this small group of colorful men can be said to share any one characteristic, it is the way they talk about the victims of product-caused accidents. As Lipsig expresses this attitude: "It is impossible to obtain money enough to pay for the human costs of those injuries which leave the victims confined to a wheelchair or a bed for the rest of their lives—or, worse, which leave their children to grow up without a parent or even a home. Such 'sentences' are worse than that of any criminal, who can at least pace his cell and dream of eventually rejoining his loved ones."

Does this sound like an emotional pitch by an opportunistic lawyer looking for the fast and easy buck for himself and his client? No engineering designer should entertain such a notion. Most of the attorneys who have specialized in this field are too informed about design for that. Also, they have prestigious professional support, including some of the ablest judges, scholars in leading law schools, and the American Law Institute.

Pinning the Blame

Another thing, most lawyers do not hold engineers directly or entirely responsible for the "wanton injuries and slaughter" caused by product defects. Philo, for example, believes that the principle of product responsibility is just now catching up with the manufacturers.

"We are in a period which is seeing the adoption of a number of kinds of social legislation," says Philo. "These are really evidence of society's attempts to improve the relationships between people, as well as with the economic, political, and other forces which make up our technological society. It is to be expected that in such a humanitarian era, society will use one of its instruments—the courts—to correct abuses of negligent manufacturers."

Esentially, George Bushnell, Detroit attorney who numbers US Steel Corp among his clients, agrees with Philo. "Industry must realize two things," he says. "First, our culture is dominated by a sense of fair play. Second, you do not, must not try to defend a product on the technicalities of the law. You are bound to lose, because these days it is pretty difficult to persuade a jury that a major manufacturing company is right and some guy who has lost an arm is wrong."

Speaking specifically of the engineer's role, Bushnell continues: "Judges and juries must act in accordance with the technological, sociological, and ideological advances of our times. This means that if you as a designer do not do the best possible job, if you knew or should have known that your design could cause someone to be hurt, then, by all reasonable standards—including common sense—you are liable."

Spangenberg, who has the reputation of being the most "engineering-minded" of all the lawyers who specialize in product-design cases, places responsibility for safe, reliable design squarely on the engineer and his employer, the manufacturer. "There is no essential difference between the careless driver and the careless designer or manufacturer," he says. "In fact, I feel more strongly about the carelessly developed product, because the driver may have been only momentarily negligent. There is never any such excuse for the engineering designer."

Spangenberg cities an example: "There is no excuse for a lawnmower with a casing that cannot contain the stones or other debris that everyone knows are in every lawn. With what we know about metallurgy today, we can tailor an alloy specifically for such an application. There is tooling available to hold precise tolerances. We can inspect by X-rays, sound waves, or other methods. Just about any kind of testing or analysis can be had."

Spangenberg and Philo both emphasize that they have never seen a product liability case in which there was any mystery about why the design failed or did not protect the user. Spangenberg points out: "In most machines, the engineering staff can determine which parts are most likely to create dangerous circumstances when they fail or wear out. In fact, in many such cases, the designers can even forecast how failure will occur and approximately when. Such components can and should be designed to fail safely."

Spangenberg is concerned about the fact that the people who buy manufactured products trust American industry. They believe that if a product has been put on the market it is safe to use, that it will not "take off a hand, tear out an eye, or kill." This means that a poorly designed product betrays the customer's trust. Even worse, it leaves him completely unprepared for that crucial moment when something does go wrong.

Spangenberg is aware that engineers are not responsible for the "decades" of intensive advertising that have created the customer's trust in the product. "In fact, I know that in most companies there is no meaningful communication between the engineers and the men who write advertising copy. And, in my opinion, these advertising people don't really care whether what they claim is true or not."

Perhaps Thomas F. Lambert, Jr. best described the present special position of the engineering designer. Lambert is a widely respected scholar of the law and is editor of the journal and newsletter of the American Trial Lawyers Assn, Boston.

"The law presumes every man to know the nature of what he creates," says Lambert. "This is why it is no longer enough for the designer to claim that he meant no harm, that he did not foresee that his design could cause difficulties. He can no longer plead his soul is white when his brain is gray enough to have created a hazardous design."

If Lambert is right, the question naturally arises: "Will the engineering designer in the future be personally liable for a design that causes injury or loss?" Some authorities, including some insurance companies, think this is a possibility. At least one company thinks it will be writing malpractice insurance for engineers, including those employed by manufacturers, in the foreseeable future.

Unfortunately, there is no reason to think that such policyholders can expect to receive much design guidance from the insurance carriers. Hartford Accident & Indemnity Co says it plans to apply present safety engineering approachs to product design, possibly after "refining practices" a little. It is not uncommon now for Liberty Mutual to be asked to evaluate a product in the prototype or working model stage as a means of preventing losses through subsequent claims cases. Most such evaluations, however, seldom go beyond an inspection to see if the given product meets applicable standards.

On the other hand, one authority in the field predicts that at least some insurers will soon be inserting clauses in product liability policies that eliminate coverage of product design itself.

Paul D. Rheingold, New York attorney, wrote in the *New York Law Journal* last February: "As applied by the courts, the concept of 'design' can have a number of meanings. One is the pure design problem where the drawing board specifications [contain] . . . a built-in flaw. Another . . . is a plan calling for construction . . . of unsafe materials. Failure to set up an adequate inspection program at the end of the production line is also regarded as a design fault . . . separate and apart from negligence in production or construction."

As the engineer assesses these disturbing developments in his technological world, he must not confuse the charge of defective design with a charge of moral fault. This view has been stressed again and again in current legal literature, by such authorities as the editorial staff of the *Harvard Law Review,* Assoc. Justice John J. Francis of the New Jersey Supreme Court in his landmark decision in the *Santor v. A. & M. Karagheusian Inc.* case, and Thomas F. Lambert, Jr. of ATLA.

It may help the engineer to understand his true role in this great wave of litigation if he paraphrases the question Harry Philo asks himself in every new product-liability case: "How could due care in the design and manufacturing of this product have avoided injury to my client?"

More and more, the courts are applying this sort of question in considering and deciding product-design liability cases. And more and more judges and juries are applying a legal concept known as "strict liability." Justice Francis has formulated the most-used wording: "If the article is defective, and the defect is chargeable to the manufacturer, his must be the responsibility for the consequent damage or injury."

To some, including an insurance executive and the general counsel of a cosmetics company, this concept simply means that a way has been found to make the parties with the most money—large manufacturing companies rather than small, independent retailers—pay for "innocently shed blood." As others see it, payment for losses incurred because of product defects should be considered a normal cost of doing business.

The decision in the famous *Greenman v. Yuba Power Products, Inc,* case in California put it this way: "The costs of injuries resulting from defective products . . . [should be] borne by the manufacturers that put such products on the market, rather than by the injured persons who are powerless to protect themselves." In commenting on this decision, the *Harvard Law Review* pointed out that the court in adopting this view was really saying ". . . that the business that makes a profit while harming someone should sustain the costs of his victims' injuries."

Lipsig predicts that product liability cases are going to become as common as automobile accident liability cases. He agrees with other predictions that such a vast wave of litigation may create demands for a kind of product compensation system modeled on current workmen's compensation legislation. If this comes, Lipsig says, it will be "a miscarriage of justice" engineered by corporate attorneys attempting to achieve lower overall settlement costs for product cases, although the ostensible reason will be to clear overcrowded court calendars.

Obviously, such trends present the engineering designer with one of the most powerful arguments for raising the overall standards for product design throughout his company's operations. The argument is money. If product litigation reaches only half the volume predicted, defective designs will prove so costly that it will be unfeasible for a manufacturer to do anything but eliminate such weaknesses.

[*Editors note:* The remainder of the article describes specific programs of user safety standards, reliability evaluation, and methods of design analysis to reduce the incidence of product liability.]

24. Products Liability and Reliability: The View from the President's Office

Walter E. Schirmer *

One of the most remarkable attributes of American industry is its capability for successfully responding to challenges. It is also remarkable how many of these challenges have been created, at least immediately, by law. This is, I suppose, partly because of the American tendency to try to solve every problem by passing a law. This indicates, in turn, our impatience with other and slower solutions to problems. One result is that we have much bad law. I think we are going to have a great deal of bad products liability law if we do not give the matter more attention. I am pleased, therefore, that the problem of products liability is now going to receive the attention of MAPI.

Boxing the Compass of Products Liability

Today engineers, production people, lawyers, and insurance men represent all the skills and talents which, as I will try to persuade you,

* Walter E. Schirmer is President of Clark Equipment Corporation.

Reprinted from "Products Liability and Reliability: The View from the President's Office" (Washington: Machinery and Allied Products Institute, 1967), 1–11.

will be needed if we are to have a good result. Although the lawyers may have been the first to alert us to this problem, they serve a limited function and the ultimate response must be made by the total organization. With all deference to my brothers in the law, the problem must be tackled on a broader front. I am sure they agree with me.

To make an effective response, we have to know something about the sources and causes of the problems. For, although the challenge has been created most immediately by new concepts in our legal thinking, the law is merely reflecting new and changing social, political, and economic concepts. Law is merely the most obvious manifestation of these changes.

As one author has observed, "Every rule of law, whether founded on a statute, on a code, on a decision of a court or on the edict of an administrative authority, has some immediate or historic relation to social policy." [1]

We have become familiar with the trend in modern society to spread risks, to remove from the individual the burden of personal catastrophe, whatever the reason, and to shift the loss to society as a whole. In the United States we have been fortunate that this has been accomplished so far without serious damage to our basic institutions. Mostly it has been accomplished by legislation but often, and this is certainly the case in the products liability area, the courts have been the chief actors. The layman's idea that the law consists of an immutable set of principles to be applied to a set of facts is simply not so— the law is not a "brooding omnipresence in the sky." In Justice Holmes' famous phrase, "The life of the law has not been logic; it has been experience." If this is true, then clearly a merely legal response will not be sufficient if we are to avoid becoming, in practical effect, insurers of our products with all that that entails.

Sources of Liability

Although others will discuss the legal and related problems in more detail, I think it is necessary to sketch very briefly and broadly the specific legal changes to which I have referred to show why everyone in each of your organizations is necessarily involved in products liability problems.

The liability of a manufacturer to consumers of his products may

---

[1] Maxwell Cohen, "The Role of Law and Lawyers in Industrial Relations," *Labor Law Journal*, Vol. 1, No. 4 (April, 1952), 276.

originate in a number of ways. Basically, there are two sources: (1) negligence in the design or manufacture of a product and (2) warranty. Traditionally, negligence law connotes some degree of "fault"; warranty liability represents some degree of false representation.

In contrast to these concepts, which involve culpability of some kind, is the view recently adopted by a few courts imposing liability *irrespective of fault.*

Nobody is going to argue that we should be insulated by technical legal theories from liability. If we make mistakes—if we fail to heat treat a king pin in an axle of one of our lift trucks and it fails and injures someone—we should be liable. If our advertising department tells the public that a 2,000-pound-capacity lift truck can lift 10,000 pounds and it does not and someone relies on that information and gets hurt, then we should be liable. But we do not expect to be held liable simply because we can afford it.

The proponents of the strict liability theory, however, would hold us liable without proof of negligence and without any culpability on our part. One of the leading proponents of this view argues that there are two principal reasons for adopting this theory—or for adopting it more widely, I should say, because it has already found its way into the case law of several states: first, the manufacturer is said to be in a more strategic position to promote safety and will thus be encouraged to do so and, second, the manufacturer is often dominant in the chain of distribution.

Others, less enamored with this method of creating a system of social insurance, point out that mechanical products are generally designed for use over a period of time during which their characteristics may be studied and safe operating procedures installed. A machine in use is not under the control of its manufacturer, and instructions and warnings—even the simplest precautions—may be disregarded. Furthermore, the manufacturer is not in the best position to insure safe use. Nor is it as difficult, if there are defects, to prove them as some of the strict liability theorists may claim. After all, the allegedly defective product is in the hands of the plaintiff.

These matters are illustrative of the broader arguments involved that may be overlooked because we may have placed an undue emphasis on technical defenses.

"Deterioration" in the Law

In a few jurisdictions (which we must assume may represent the wave of the future) some or all of the following changes have caused what may be described as, at least from the manufacturer's point of view, a deterioration in the law. A few examples follow:

(1) The erosion of the privity concept, first in negligence cases and later in warranty cases. This is the ancient rule of law which held that a manufacturer was liable only to those who were parties to a transaction. Incidentally, one author has enumerated 29 fictions, subterfuges, and theories by which courts have avoided the effect of the privity rule in order to extend liability to persons not a party to a transaction.[2]

(2) The development of the concept of strict liability without fault.

(3) The disposition of the courts to enlarge the scope of the jury's responsibility for deciding questions of "fact." As a lawyer I believe in the jury system, but as an engineer I sometimes wonder about the so-called questions of "fact" about which the juries are now being permitted to speculate.

(4) An increase in the size of verdicts.

(5) An increase in claims consciousness.

(6) The ineffectiveness of disclaimers and "hold harmless" agreements to limit liability. In his book *Products Liability in the Automobile Industry,* published in 1960, Professor Gillam noted that the standard warranty had never been used to disclaim liability for a defective condition.[3] He suggested that this was probably because of a fear of legislative control of disclaimer but pointed out that there was no reason why, if a disclaimer was otherwise effective in limiting liability in matters of commercial warranty, it should not be effective against "all . . . liabilities." The answer came the same year in *Henningsen* v. *Bloomfield Motors, Inc.* (32 N.J. 358). This case, decided by the Supreme Court of New Jersey, is regarded by some as the most important products liability case since *MacPherson* v. *Buick Motor Co.* (217 N.Y. 382) in 1916 which extended liability to third persons in claims based on negligence. In the *Henningsen* case the court held

---

[2] Cornelius W. Gillam, *Products Liability in the Automobile Industry,* University of Minnesota Press, 1960, 59.
[3] *Ibid.,* p. 176.

ultimately that it would be "unconscionable" to permit a manufacturer of a defective product to escape liability because of a standard clause in a contract used by all competing manufacturers and not really subject to negotiation between buyer and seller.

(7) The promulgation of safety laws and codes that are not based on the state of the art or that are unrealistic.

(8) Faulty design in contrast to faulty manufacture as a basis for liability. The idea of juries' second-guessing design decisions is a little frightening. This is particularly true when the fact of an accident itself is taken as evidence of a design failure. Will an automobile manufacturer sometime be held liable because a driver was trapped by seat belts even though there was no fault in the design in the belts?

Total Corporate Involvement

Although changing law has been most immediate in creating new problems in products liability for manufacturers, the response can certainly not be limited to legal responses. The response will have to be made by every department of our industrial and business organizations: engineering, manufacturing, advertising, sales—and law. This means to me that a united effort must be made to create an awareness of the problem and its causes and cures. Everyone in the organization is involved, and everyone in the organization must lend his efforts to the response.

Briefly, to be more specific, I mean this:

(1) Engineers and designers must be made aware of the problem. This means that the engineer approaches his problem with a balanced attitude. He must keep in mind not only that the device must work well and must be economically feasible, but he also must take account of the human beings with whom it will come in contact. The one quality that makes a successful man in any enterprise is judgement. The optimum solution to engineering problems must include the factor of safety. This calls for the visualization of almost every contingency which may occur in the operation of the device—no matter how simple.

(2) Production people must continue to emphasize quality. It is impossible to make a quality product with defective materials and slipshod workmanship. I once heard a story that one of our Allies during World War II finally determined how large a bomb load should be carried in a particular bomber by measuring the crash rate on takeoff against the bomb load. True or not, it represents the exact opposite of what our approach must be. We cannot measure quality only by our warranty costs; the measure must be absolute —even ideal. The basic key to accomplishing this is not mere exhortation of our machine operators to do good work. This will not be enough, and besides exhortation does not work very well. The key, it seems to me, is to devise systems and procedures, with the help of our industrial engineers, that do not permit faults to exist. This sounds idealistic, but let me remind you that we are improving every year.

(3) Advertisers have to be enlisted in efforts to educate users. The advertising fraternity seems to have more than its share of creative and talented people. They have done an exceptional job of selling products. Why can they not be enlisted in other areas to instruct and train buyers and users in the product? A simple example is the safety film. Let them help motivate people in this area, too. On the other hand, I urge that our lawyers scrutinize our advertisements before publication. Sometimes our advertising people are a little too exuberant in describing our products. Most of these people have had to learn something about trademarks to know how to protect these valuable assets. We may now have to impress our advertisers with the importance of products liability. It seems to me, as a simple example, that it is just as effective to say that a Cortez motor home will operate at highway speeds as to say it will go 70 miles an hour, and we have not encouraged users to be careless.

(4) The salesmen's natural enthusiasm should be directed toward user training programs.

(5) The service organization spends more time than any of the manufacturer's personnel in the customer's plants. They are

in a peculiarly good position to observe how the products are used and, if there are accidents, what the cause was. They should be encouraged to do so.

(6) Managers must be persuaded to support broad industry efforts. Remember that some of the pressures behind the new legal theories are extralegal. Statements in the press that a particular vehicle has an unsafe design is an example of an extralegal pressure, and they may evidence themselves in the reaction of the public—the people who will sit on juries. When the arena of public discussion is reached, a managerial response—not an engineering, legal, or some other response, but a managerial response—is called for.

(7) The tremendous story of labor-saving devices—and therefore accident-saving devices—must be told.

(8) We must realize our interdependence. Under our adversary system, bad law resulting from a poorly investigated and poorly defended case applies to everyone in the jurisdiction —not just the defendant in that case.

(9) The insurance industry can do much more, it seems to me, to aid us in bringing proper safety methods directly to the employee users.

(10) We are not only makers; we are users of each other's equipment. Top management must accelerate its efforts to create safe conditions of work. Many companies do an excellent job now; this effort must be emulated by all manufacturers.

Therefore, it is perfectly clear to me that a successful response to the challenge presented by these new ideas in products liability necessarily demands the combined efforts of everyone in the organization. We will not obtain the combined efforts of our people, however, if top management does not concern itself with the problem and lend its encouragement and support to the personnel directly responsible for the results we want. This is so obvious that it is sometimes ignored because of our American tendency to ignore the obvious and enjoy the complicated.

Capital Goods Industries' Safety Contribution

While the essence of my message is expressed above, I should like to make another observation. Conceding that statistical data in regard to products liability accidents is not available in any refined form, I nevertheless believe that industry has by and large done a good job and that it will continue to do so.

The National Safety Council (NSC) reported in 1964 that in the category most directly related to the products liability problem, described by the NSC as "Work—Non-Motor Vehicle," there were 11% fewer accidents than ten years ago. As to motor vehicles, Professors Harper and James, whose work *The Law of Torts* is a leading authority on the side of the strict liability theory, point out that in only 3% of the motor vehicle accidents is there a defect and in only one-quarter of 1% of the cases is the defect related to the cause of the accident.[4] They do not say, incidentally, whether even these defects were the responsibility of the manufacturers.

We should not, therefore, permit ourselves to be pictured as mere callous profit seekers by persons who would benefit from prejudicing us in the eyes of the public. We should insist, too, that whatever developments occur in our legal system, ideas of fairness should not be ignored to impose on us the idea that social justice will be accomplished merely by imposing liability on those who can afford it. Considerations of fairness and responsibility should be given the weight that our legal system recognizes in other areas.

As manufacturers we have reason to be proud of the hundreds of labor-saving devices we have created. Whatever our motives—and I will not concede that they are merely selfish—the result has been the saving of untold lives and injuries. The National Safety Council reports, as an example, that the manual handling of objects is the chief source of compensable work injuries. Nearly one accident in five results in this way. Consider what this rate would be without conveyors, cranes and hoists, lift trucks, straddle carriers, and the multitude of handling devices that have been developed. Other examples can easily be thought of.

Let us tell this story, too.

[4] Fowler V. Harper and Fleming James, Jr., *The Law of Torts* (Little, Brown and Company, 1956), vol. 2, p. 735.

Part Five:

Discrimination Between Segments: The Case of the Ghetto Consumer

Introduction

No two buyers will follow the same decision process, or encounter the same problems while they are buying or using a product or service. Consequently, all buyers have different needs for information and guidance, for protection, for reassurance and so forth. Since it is usually impractical to treat all buyers as different, the solution is to identify a few groups or segments, where the differences between groups are great and differences within groups are small. On virtually any criteria that relate to issues of consumerism there are only two important segments; low income ghetto consumers and all others.

As Schnapper and Caplovitz illustrate in the first two articles in this section, ghetto consumers differ from other consumers in many ways. They lack knowledge and skills essential to effective buying, opportunity to search for "best buys," and an appreciation of their legal rights. Consequently, they have little motivation to improve their situation. These shortcomings are magnified by the "deviant" and atomistic nature of the marketplace they patronize.

337

Among the many barriers to the elimination of these problems is a lack of full understanding of the scope of the problems. The selection from the Report of the National Commission on Civil Disorders illustrates the depth and bitterness of the abuses. This report identified "discriminatory consumer and credit practices" as one of the 12 major grievances underlying the 1967 riots. The research reports by the Federal Trade Commission and Burton Marcus provide a useful follow-up by providing measures of the extent of discrimination against ghetto consumers, and the role of the ghetto marketplace in fostering this discrimination.

The article by Sturdivant effectively completes this section and the book, by reviewing some of the most serious points of conflict in the ghetto marketplace: inflated prices and credit charges, lack of refurbishing and maintenance of stores, and the lack of courtesy toward customers. He suggests that consumer education programs or protection against unethical merchandising will not by themselves provide an adequate solution. Dramatic relief will require a new, highly developed, and efficient retail system fully comparable to the rest of the country.

A. The Problem from Two Perspectives

25. Consumer Legislation and the Poor

Eric Schnapper

A family's standard of living is a function of both the size of its income and the way in which that income is spent. It is an error in theory but easy in practice to conclude that low income alone causes poverty—tacitly assuming that the poor allocate their money in the same way, and pay the same prices at the same sorts of stores, as would a middle class consumer whose income was suddenly reduced. In reality, the poor buy different goods and services at different stores for different prices, and this has a profound effect on their standard of living—compounding, preserving and deepening their poverty.

Both national and local anti-poverty efforts have been largely concerned with increasing income. Of the total OEO budget for fiscal 1966 of $1.5 billion, only $1.4 million has been allocated to consumer programs—less than one tenth of one per cent. This concentration on what the poor earn rather than on how they spend their money has been and remains a serious mistake:

Reprinted from *The Yale Law Journal*, Vol. 76 (1967), 745–768, by permission of The Yale Law Journal Company and Fred B. Rothman & Company.

(1) Often it is less expensive to help a family save a given amount
     of money than to help them achieve an equal increase in in-
     come. This is especially true of a family which is and will
     remain on welfare.

(2) Many of the people not reached by the major income increas-
     ing efforts such as the Job Corps and the campaign for equal
     opportunity in employment could be helped by a consumer
     program.

(3) A serious number of those low income consumers who do
     have employment continue to lose it because their wages are
     garnished and their employers refuse to do the necessary
     bookkeeping.

(4) The benefits of increased income may be dissipated through
     poor spending habits.

(5) The riots in Harlem, Watts and Philadelphia resulted in part
     from the exploitation of the poor consumer; the arson and
     looting was directed almost exclusively at those businesses
     associated with sharp selling practices, excessive prices, ex-
     orbitant credit charges, or poor quality merchandise and
     service.

Thus, anti-poverty efforts must not only aim at raising the income of
the target population, but also at increasing the amount and quality
of the goods and service which that income provides.

New Legislation and Old Realities

Recent years have witnessed a marked growth in national and local
concern with consumer problems. President Johnson appointed a Special Assistant for consumer affairs and a number of consumer advisory groups. Several states, most notably New York and Massachusetts,
have appointed or designated special government officials to deal with
consumer problems. Both Federal and state officials have expressed
interest in the problems of the poor consumer.

The most significant new legislation proposals have been informational. The Truth-in-Lending Act requires that the cost of credit, either
in dollars, simple annual interest or both, be revealed to the con-

sumer. Truth-in-Packaging proposals would provide additional information on labels and packages of consumer goods. These proposals are adapted to deal with a special problem in a highly specific model.

Generally, the law presupposes a consumer equipped to deal with the business community on at least equal terms. This consumer has three essential characteristics:

(1) He knows that he should and wants to shop around for best buys when purchasing goods and services.

(2) He is competent to decide which product offers the greatest value for the least money.

(3) He knows his legal rights (and liabilities) in the event of a post-sale legal conflict with the seller, and is prepared to use all available tools in such a conflict.

Only such consumers can avoid repeated "bad buys" and insure the competition among businessmen which keeps prices at a reasonable level while assuring continued high quality.

Informational legislation does not question the general accuracy of this model, but assumes a very particular sort of deviation: the absence of a specific sort of knowledge needed to make "best buys." Once provided, that information will by itself return consumers to their rightful place as all-powerful sovereigns of the retail market and restore (if it was ever really absent) vigorous competition.

Whatever its validity for the middle class, this model is almost always inapplicable to the purchases of the poor. Low income consumers normally lack all the model characteristics:

Belief in comparative shopping

Low income consumers are often not aware that they could get more for their money by visiting a number of stores, particularly those outside their immediate neighborhood. Those who are may still not be inclined to shop around for good values; they search, if at all, for other things. (A) Low income consumers usually shop primarily for credit. This is particularly true for purchases of expensive durables, and for purchases by welfare recipients during the last few days before the arrival of a new check, when they have run out of cash and must rely on credit from the local grocery store if they are to eat. (B) Low income consumers are frequently concerned to satisfy non-material

needs by their purchases: status-seeking and escapism heavily influence their buying patterns. And unlike more affluent consumers, the
poor cannot satisfy such needs without neglecting essential goods and
services. (C) Many of the poor are shy and unwilling to deal with
strangers, preferring instead to trade with local people whom they
already know, and who are more likely to be personable and speak
their language. Thus the tradition of comparative shopping, accepted
in theory and at times in practice by the middle class, is largely unknown among low income consumers; frequently the poor purchase
food or durables without even inquiring as to their price.

Ability to pick out the best buy

Low income consumers generally lack the technical knowledge needed
to choose among consumer durables such as appliances or cars; they
are usually less educated, less likely to read publications such as
Consumer Reports, and generally less able to make rational choices
among products than their middle income counterparts. In addition
these consumers are often unable to recognize even poor quality food
and clothing—largely because that is the only quality that they have
ever had.

Freedom to engage in comparative shopping

Those low income consumers aware that they should engage in comparative shopping and able to make an intelligent choice among a
number of goods or services may nevertheless fail to do so. They feel,
usually correctly, that they cannot get the credit they need outside of
their own neighborhood, and, in some cases (such as buying food on
credit) that they cannot get it from anyone other than the local retailer
with whom they are already well acquainted. This pressure to shop
within the local business community is compounded by shyness, the
need to care for children, and the inconvenience of a time-consuming
trip to a more affluent area. Thus local merchants have an essentially
captive market, and experience no meaningful competition with businesses in middle and upper income areas. An ability and willingness to
shop outside of the local neighborhood is of great importance because
of the differences in area price levels.

Knowledge of legal rights and liabilities

Most laymen lack more than a superficial knowledge of their rights
and liabilities in a post-sale legal conflict, and rely on professional help

when conflicts arise. Many low income consumers lack even this superficial knowledge, and of the substantial number who feel that they have at one time or another been cheated by a merchant, few have ever sought professional aid—only 9% in a recent survey. When asked where they would go for help if they were being cheated by a merchant or salesman, almost two thirds of the low income consumers interviewed replied that they did not know. Only 10% mentioned the most significant sources of help: private lawyers, legal aid and small claims court. More than half of those who knew of any source of help mentioned only the Better Business Bureau, which does not engage in litigation and is generally unable to offer much aid. Thus the consumers with the greatest need for knowledge of their legal rights are the consumers with the greatest lack thereof.

Motivation

A low income consumer is profoundly different from a middle income consumer who awoke one day ill-housed, ill-clothed, ill-fed and ill-informed. Underlying his problems and essential to any discussion of remedies is a crucial lack of motivation. Many of the poor who do have a conscious desire to get more goods and services for their money have failed so often in attempting to do so that they no longer regard the attempt as worthwhile. For anyone living in poverty an effort to change his condition involves a recognition that the condition *can* be changed, and the acceptance of at least partial responsibility inasmuch as he has made no previous effort, or inasmuch as those efforts have failed or met with only limited success. Undoubtedly many low income consumers pass through several stages as their exploitation continues; their attitude degenerates from frustration to bewilderment to resignation to an abandonment of responsibility.

Thus the typical low income consumer is not a hardened penny pincher employing all his skill and ingenuity to stretch his meagre income as far as he can. He is an increasingly frustrated and embittered man, with $10,000 desires, $5,000 essential needs, and $2,000 income, alternately groping for a standard of living he cannot possibly afford and resignedly paying exorbitant prices for his daily essentials.

In sum, the new wave of informational legislation will be of little help to the poor because it presupposes values, motivation and knowledge which do not generally exist among them. The actual problem is not just a shortage of a narrowly defined sort of information—such as the price per pound of prepackaged food—but a total breakdown in the function the consumer is supposed to play in the market. "Bad buys" are the rule and price and quality competition the exception. As one merchant in New York put it: "People do not *shop* in this area. . . . It is just up to who catches him."

The resulting problems consumer purchases generally

Because of their dissimilarity to the ideal consumers of modern economics and legislation, the poor pay prices for food, rent, medicine and durables almost always exceeding those paid by the more affluent, and usually exceeding those needed to yield a fair return on the businessman's investment. This comes about in several ways:

Neighborhood price levels

Food stores in low income areas consistently charge higher prices than food stores in middle and upper income areas for comparable items. The low income consumer pays between 5% and 10% more for the same groceries purchased in his own neighborhood than does a middle income consumer. The average small grocery store charges a median 10% more than large middle income area chain stores, and the low income chain stores charge about 5% more than the middle income area chains. There are significant price differences among branches of the same chain, reflecting in part the commission basis upon which store managers are employed. Some other stores, such as co-operatives or private stores selling in particularly high volume have prices more than 15% below those predominating in the low income areas. Low income neighborhood stores usually price durables 50% to 100% above the going rate in more affluent areas, employing markups of 300 or 400% and giving commissions running as high as 100% of the value of the goods. Notwithstanding the resulting preclusion of comparative shopping, the poor buy a substantial portion of their furniture and appliances from door-to-door peddlers. Because of this preclusion, and because peddlers prey on the least competent of the poor shoppers, peddler prices are uniformly substantially above those of store owning merchants.

Quality

The low value which the poor receive for their money results not only from these above average prices, but also from the below average quality of the goods which are sold in low income areas. Grocery stores in the low income areas are less sanitary than their middle income counterparts; fruit and vegetables are more often damaged, meat commonly brown around the edges, and milk and eggs occasionally sold past the time recommended by the producer. As with prices, variations in the condition of food exist between stores of the same chain, the branch in the low income area generally having the lesser quality. Durables purchased by the poor are of a similarly low quality; both appliances and furniture have to be replaced or repaired frequently. Neighborhood stores and peddlers rarely deal in brand name goods, in part because a markup comparable to that on the low quality goods they normally sell would make brand name goods prohibitively expensive. Service on the purchased items is inadequate, warranties are rarely given, and the merchants often disclaim responsibility for goods, asserting that the salesman is no longer with them or that the line has been dropped. Often the firm is no longer even in business, at least under the same name.

Sales methods

A number of questionable merchant and peddler techniques are used to maintain high prices and poor quality. In low income areas of New York City food prices rise abruptly and temporarily on the 1st and 16th of each month, when welfare payments are made and the poorest (and least competent) of the poor do most of their shopping. Prices are not generally marked on furniture and appliances sold in poor neighborhoods, and the prices quoted verbally are tailored to the customer. One recent survey found differences as great as 60% for the same item; Negro and Puerto Rican shoppers were charged the higher amounts. Both merchants and peddlers commonly use high pressure techniques, while the law often penalizes those few customers who change their minds and revoke the contract before delivery. Customers are lured into a store by an advertised bargain which the merchant had little or no intent of actually giving, and are talked into a much more expensive purchase. Salesmen frequently misrepresent the nature of items being sold, their prices, the nature of documents being signed, and other relevant facts, and purposely deliver goods other than those purchased by the customer. Low income consumers are particularly susceptible to these and other forms of fraud, since they are less likely to detect it and to act to protect their rights. There is evidence to suggest that low income area businessmen and merchants occasionally resort to price fixing.

Resulting losses

The effect of area sales techniques and price and quality levels is compounded by the low income consumer's failure to shop around even within his neighborhood or to buy in large economic quantities. As a result of selling practices and poor shopping habits the typical low-income consumer is probably paying one-third to one-half more for his food than he would if he shopped with diligence in a middle income area. Durables probably cost the poor at least one and one-half to two times as much as they would if they bought in more affluent neighborhoods, especially at discount houses.

Credit and Loans

Two thirds of the purchases of major durables made by low income consumers involve the use of credit or loans, a portion comparable to that for middle income consumers. Seventy-five per cent of low income consumers have used credit for at least one purchase of a major durable, and a lesser number of them use it for food or clothing. Most low income families are presently in debt and will remain in debt; for them the only bill which never comes is the last one. The cost of credit is thus an important element in the budgets of most low income families.

Lending practices vary widely with the relevant state laws. New York has perhaps the best system of credit and loan regulation in the country; the problems in other states are generally worse. State law sets maximum rates for both credit and loans in New York, with penalties for overcharges. The Retail Installment Sales Act voids any clause in a credit purchase agreement which provides for an acceleration of payment in the absence of default, a power of attorney, a confession of judgment, an authorization to breach the peace in repossessing goods, or a waiver of defenses against the seller, and provide that the contract must clearly state the cost of the goods and of the credit. "Balloon payments"—progressively large payments often intended to force the purchaser into default—are discouraged. All these provisions have, however, fallen far short of adequately protecting the low income consumer.

The ceilings on credit charges are high. In theory the maxima are 10% for the first $500 and 8% for the rest of the debt, but since the interest can be computed in advance and added to the amount due ("add-on") the actual ceilings are close to 20% and 16% where the debt is to be paid within one year. Even these limits, however, do not appear to affect significantly the cost of low income consumer credit. Local stores frequently charge a higher price for goods being sold on credit in lieu of being able to openly charge a higher credit fee. Testimony before the Senate Committee studying the Truth-in-Lending Bill suggested that Negroes and Puerto Ricans are systematically and automatically charged a higher rate of interest than whites, and this regardless of their individual credit rating. This pattern is confirmed by the finding that non-whites buying on credit from local dealers and pedlers pay higher prices (*i.e.,* higher covert credit charges) than do low income whites making similar purchases, although the non-whites are not substantially more likely to default on their obligations. The high *de facto* rates reflect not only deliberate exploitation, but also the loss incurred when the consumer's promise to pay is sold to a bank or finance company for 70% or 80% of its face value.

In other instances exorbitant interest rates on credit or loans involve violations of the letter as well as the spirit of the law. Senator Douglas' committee, several years after the passage of the Retail Installment Sales Act, discovered credit charges in excess of 100% in New York City. Loan sharks, often charging as much as 1000% a year, continue to work and flourish in low income areas.

These exorbitant rates, yielding profits far above the normal level, continue to exist for several reasons:

(1) Many low income consumers do not and cannot engage in comparative shopping for either credit or loans.

(2) Those who do so are more concerned with the size of the weekly payments than with the total cost or interest that they will have to pay.

(3) Low income consumers are often totally unaware of the interest or the service charge which they are paying, either from a failure to request it or because of a purposeful concealment by the merchant.

(4) Where any information is given it is usually the total credit charge, as required by law, rather than the interest rate which is much more important for comparative shopping.

(5) Even those low income consumers who do feel that they are paying excessive credit charges are not aware that a violation of the law may be involved.

(6) Low income consumers are unwilling to endanger what may be their only source of credit by complaining to the lender, let alone to the law.

(7) The penalty provision of the Retail Installment Sales Act in New York is emasculated by a provision permitting the seller to avoid all penalties if he reforms the contract in conformity with the law within 10 days of written notice by the buyer of the violation.

Beside the credit charge itself, credit raises the costs of goods indirectly in other ways. The unavailability of credit outside of the low income area forces low income families to shop at the more expensive stores. Banks encourage consumers who do have savings to borrow for their purchases anyway in order to leave their savings "intact." The remoteness of the ultimate payment of goods and services induces low income consumers to spend more than they can afford.

Post-Sale Legal Conflicts

Existing legal institutions and practices fall far short of insuring reasonable protection for the low income consumer.

Where the low income consumer is the potential plaintiff, it is most unlikely that suit will even be brought. Most low income consumers are unaware of the existence of either legal aid or the small claims court and simply do not think in terms of invoking legal processes on *their* side. Where the low income consumer is sufficiently irate to take action, he is likely to stop payment as a form of pressure on or retaliation against the merchant—and usually just worsen his own position thereby. For those few who do attempt to invoke legal processes the obstacles that must be overcome are substantial: (1) The merchant may have gone out of business (and re-entered under a new name). (2) Legal aid societies may be reluctant to help because they do not in general take plaintiffs' cases. (3) Private attorneys' fees would often be so high as to eat up any possible gain. (4) Alleged warranties may not have been in writing. (5) Frequently written documents will have been lost.

When merchants or finance companies wish to sue, rather than invoke extra-legal pressures, the situation is very different; for them the legal process is a broad and easy road to garnishment. Merchant-initiated suits virtually never come to trial; the overwhelming majority —97% in the case of Harlem merchants—end in default judgments because the defendant never answers the summons or complaint. In most cases—legal aid attorneys estimate 75%—this is because the defendant never received the summons. The common procedure has come to be known as "sewer service."

In the few instances where process is actually served on the defendant it may still go unanswered, because he does not understand it, because he is unwilling to take time off from work to go to court, because he is afraid of all legal institutions, because he knows of no source of legal help, or because he feels that he will lose anyway. Clearly none of these reasons, except possibly the last, has anything to do with the usual theories behind refusal to re-open most default judgments.

Once the default judgment has been obtained the merchant proceeds as quickly as possible to garnishment of the defendant's salary. Often repossession and/or attachment of the defendant's property may have to precede garnishment, but the value of repossessed property usually falls far short of the price, and the impoverished debtor rarely has valuable property to attach. As a result of sewer service, default judgments, and failure to attach property, the defendant frequently first hears of the proceeding against him when he is served with a notice of wage garnishment. In some states the judgment debtor must be notified before the garnishment is served, but in practice this is not often done.

The general effect of this system is to make the court system an indiscriminate stamp for all creditor claims against the poor.

In addition to his original debt, the low income consumer who is subjected to a default or other judgment will also be liable for sizable costs and attorney's fees. In New York for example, where these additions are limited more than in most states, the total costs and fees on a debt of $100 will be $40 *excluding interest.*

The few low income consumers who do get a trial of their case may find that most of their defenses, such as fraud by the seller or delivery of the wrong goods, are unavailable because they are being sued, not by the original merchant, but by a bank or finance company. Merchants in both middle and low income areas commonly sell the customer's promise to pay to a financing institution in order to get working capital and to avoid the trouble of collecting the debt themselves. In most states virtually no defenses are available against such a "holder in due course." In a few states the buyer can raise against the bank or finance company any defenses he could against the seller. However, another provision of these states' laws provides that the debtor may be given ten or fifteen days after proper notice in which to notify the finance company or bank of any mistake in the contract, of nondelivery of the goods specified, or of any other nonperformance by the seller. The consumer waives any defenses of which the holder in due course has not been notified. In practice this second provision vitiates the protection given by the first; consumers are unlikely to report any such nonperformance or error, either because defects in the product may not have yet appeared, or because they do not understand or read the notice. Only Oregon and Massachusetts adequately protect consumers against such holders in due course.

Problems of the Affluent

The affluent as well as the poor buy without asking prices, shop for status or games rather than value, purchase food on credit, and do not know the cost of the credit they often use. The high motivation assumed by the new consumer legislation is often lacking among the middle classes. Advocates of the Truth-in-Lending Act argued for it on the ground that people do not know the cost of the credit that they are using—but if those consumers really *cared* about the cost they could often find out what it was by refusing, for example, to complete an agreement until the cost and interest rate were stated. Similarly Senator Hart stressed that Truth-in-Packaging legislation was needed because college-educated shoppers *told* to get best buys and given almost 2½ minutes per item, still could not do so with consistency. But elsewhere in the debates it became clear that housewives were spending far less shopping time per item than this, perhaps 30 seconds or less. Clearly such consumers allow themselves no time to compare prices among ten or 20 varieties; they simply grab their "usual brand" and run. The proverbial slide rule which food shoppers would need to compare food prices has remained just that; no one has suggested that shoppers do or should try to compute prices per pound from available information, or to ask their grocer to do it for them. Appliances, among which only an occasional engineer could decide without detailed research, annually sell in the tens of millions while *Consumer Reports* sells hardly 950,000 issues. It seems clear that the vast majority of the country does not exert itself to make informed and rational purchasing decisions.

Addendum

The remainder of Mr. Schnapper's article contains a proposed Unfair Sales Practices Act. See the *Yale Law Journal* 76 (1967), 769–792, for this material as well as the footnotes which extensively document the preceding discussion.

26. The Merchant and the Low-Income Consumer

David Caplovitz

The visitor to East Harlem cannot fail to notice the 60 or so furniture and appliance stores that mark the area, mostly around Third Avenue and 125th Street. At first this may seem surprising. After all, this is obviously a low-income area. Many of the residents are on relief. Many are employed in seasonal work and in marginal industries, such as the garment industry, which are the first to feel the effects of a recession in the economy. On the face of it, residents of the area would seem unable to afford the merchandise offered for sale in these stores.

That merchants nevertheless find it profitable to locate in these areas attests to a commonly overlooked fact: low-income families, like those of higher income, are consumers of many major durables. The popular image of the American as striving for the material possessions which bestow upon him both comfort and prestige in the eyes of his fellows does not hold only for the ever-increasing middle class. The cultural pressures to buy major durables reach low- as well as middle-income families. In some ways, consumption may take on even more significance for low-income families than for those in higher classes. Since many have small prospect of greatly improving their low social standing through occupational mobility, they are apt to turn on consumption as at least one sphere in which they can make some progress toward the American dream of success. If the upper strata that were observed by Veblen engaged in conspicuous consumption to symbolize their social superiority, it might be said that the lower classes today are apt to engage in *compensatory consumption*. Appliances, automobiles, and the dream of a home of their own can become compensations for blocked social mobility.[1]

The dilemma of the low-income consumer lies in these facts. He is trained by society (and his position in it) to want the symbols and appurtenances of the "good life" at the same time that he lacks the means needed to fulfill these socially induced wants. People with small incomes lack not only the ready cash for consuming major durables but are also poorly qualified for that growing substitute for available

---

[1] I am indebted to Robert K. Merton for suggesting the apt phrase, "compensatory consumption." The idea expressed by this term figures prominently in the writings of Robert S. Lynd. Observing the workers in Middletown, Lynd noted that their declining opportunities for occupational advancement and even the depression did not make them class-conscious. Instead, their aspirations shifted to the realm of consumption.

"Fascinated by a rising standard of living offered them on every hand on the installment plan, they (the working class) do not readily segregate themselves from the rest of the city. They want what Middletown wants, so long as it gives them their great symbol of advancement—an automobile. Car ownership stands to them for a large share of the 'American dream'; they cling to it as they cling to self-respect, and it was not unusual to see a family drive up to the relief commissary in 1935 to stand in line for its four or five dollar weekly food dole. (The Lynds go on to quote a union official:) It's easy to see why our workers don't think much about joining unions. So long as they have a car and can borrow or steal a gallon of gas, they'll ride around and pay no attention to labor organization. . . ." (Robert S. Lynd and Helen Merrill Lynd, *Middletown in Transition* (New York: Harcourt, Brace and Co., 1937), p. 26. (See also pp. 447–448.)

It should be noted that the Lynds identify the installment plan as the mechanism through which workers are able to realize their consumption aspirations. Similar observations are to be found in *Knowledge for What?* (Princeton University Press, 1939), pp. 91, 198. Lynd's student Eli Chinoy also makes use of the idea of compensatory consumption in his study of automobile workers. He found that when confronted with the impossibility of rising to the ranks of management, workers shifted their aspirations from the occupational to the consumption sphere. "With their wants constantly stimulated by high powered advertising, they measure their success by what they are able to buy." Eli Chinoy, "Aspirations of Automobile Workers," *American Journal of Sociology,* 57 (1952), 435. For further discussion of the political implications of this process, see Daniel Bell, "Work and Its Discontents," in *The End of Ideology* (New York: The Free Press, 1960), p. 246ff.

cash—credit. Their low income, their negligible savings, their job insecurity all contribute to their being poor credit risks. Moreover, many low-income families in New York City are fairly recent migrants from the South or from Puerto Rico and so do not have other requisites of good credit, such as long-term residence at the same address and friends who meet the credit requirements and are willing to vouch for them.[2]

Not having enough cash and credit would seem to create a sufficient problem for low-income consumers. But they have other limitations as well. They tend to lack the information and training needed to be effective consumers in a bureaucratic society. Partly because of their limited education and partly because as migrants from more traditional societies they are unfamiliar with urban culture, they are not apt to follow the announcements of sales in the newspapers, to engage in comparative shopping, to know their way around the major department stores and bargain centers, to know how to evaluate the advice of salesmen—practices necessary for some degree of sophistication in the realm of consumption. The institution of credit introduces special complex requirements for intelligent consumption. Because of the diverse and frequently misleading ways in which charges for credit are stated, even the highly educated consumer has difficulty knowing which set of terms is most economical.[3]

These characteristics of the low-income consumer—his socially supported want for major durables, his small funds, his poor credit position, his lack of shopping sophistication—constitute the conditions under which durables are marketed in low-income areas. To under-

[2] A frequent practice in extending credit to poor risks is to have cosigners who will make good the debt should the original borrower default. The new arrivals are apt to be disadvantaged by their greater difficulty in finding cosigners.

[3] Professor Samuel S. Myers of Morgan State College has studied the credit terms of major department stores and appliance outlets in Baltimore. Visiting the ten most popular stores, he priced the same model of TV set and gathered information on down payments and credit terms. He found that the cash price was practically the same in the various stores, but that there were wide variations in the credit terms leading to sizable differences in the final cost to the consumer. (Based on personal communication with Professor Myers.)

In his statement to the Douglas Committee considering the "Truth in Interest" bill, George Katona presented findings from the consumer surveys carried out by the Survey Research Center of the University of Michigan. These studies show that people with high income and substantial education are no better informed about costs of credit than people of low income and little education. See *Consumer Credit Labeling Bill, op. cit.,* p. 806.

stand the paradox set by the many stores selling high-cost durables in these areas it is necessary to know how the merchants adapt to these conditions. Clearly the normal marketing arrangements, based on a model of the "adequate" consumer (the consumer with funds, credit, and shopping sophistication), cannot prevail if these merchants are to stay in business.

On the basis of interviews with 14 of these merchants, the broad outlines of this marketing system can be described.

Low-Income Area Merchandising

The key to the marketing system in low-income areas lies in special adaptations of the institution of credit. The many merchants who locate in these areas and find it profitable to do so are prepared to offer credit in spite of the high risks involved. Moreover, their credit is tailored to the particular needs of the low-income consumer. All kinds of durable goods can be obtained in this market at terms not too different from the slogan, "a dollar down, a dollar a week." The consumer can buy furniture, a TV set, a stereophonic phonograph, or, if he is so minded, a combination phonograph-TV set, if not for a dollar a week then for only a few dollars a week. In practically every one of these stores, the availability of "easy credit" is announced to the customer in both English and Spanish by large signs in the windows and sometimes by neon signs over the doorways. Of the 14 merchants interviewed, 12 claimed that from 75 to 90% of their business consisted of credit and the other two said that credit made up half their businesses. That these merchants extend credit to their customers does not, of course, explain how they stay in business. They still face the problem of dealing with their risks.

The markup and quality of goods

It might at first seem that the merchant would solve this problem by charging high rates of interest on the credit he extends. But the law in New York State now regulates the amount that can be charged for credit, and most of these merchants claim they use installment contracts which conform to the law. The fact is that they do not always use these contracts. Some merchants will give customers only a card on which payments are noted. In these transactions the cost of credit and the cash price are not specified as the law requires. The customer peddlers, whom we shall soon meet, seldom use installment contracts.

In all these cases the consumer has no idea of how much he is paying for credit, for the cost of credit is not differentiated from the cost of the product.

Although credit charges are now regulated by law, no law regulates the merchant's markup on his goods. East Harlem is known to the merchants of furniture and appliances in New York City as the area in which pricing is done by "numbers." We first heard of the "number" system from a woman who had been employed as a bookkeeper in such a store. She illustrated a "one number" item by writing down a hypothetical wholesale price and then adding the same figure to it, a 100% markup. Her frequent references to "two number" and "three number" prices indicated that prices are never less than "one number," and are often more.

The system of pricing in the low-income market differs from that in the buraucratic market of the downtown stores in another respect: in East Harlem there are hardly any "one price" stores. In keeping with a multiprice policy, price tags are conspicuously absent from the merchandise. The customer has to ask, "how much?," and the answer he gets will depend on several things. If the merchant considers him a poor risk, if he thinks the customer is naïve, or if the customer was referred to him by another merchant or a peddler to whom he must pay a commission, the price will be higher. The fact that prices can be affected by "referrals" calls attention to another peculiarity of the low-income market, what the merchants call the "T.O." system.

Anyone closely familiar with sales practices in a large retailing establishment probably understands the meaning of "T.O." When a salesman is confronted with a customer who is not responding to the "sales pitch," he will call over another salesman, signal the nature of the situation by whispering, "This is a T.O.," and then introduce him to the customer as the "assistant manager" [4] In East Harlem, as the interviewers learned, T.O.s extend beyond the store. When a merchant finds himself with a customer who seems to be a greater risk than he is prepared to accept, he does not send the customer away. Instead,

---

[4] The initials stand for "turn over." The "assistant manager" is ready to make a small concession to the customer, who is usually so flattered by this gesture that he offers no further resistance to the sale. For further descriptions of the "T.O.," see Cecil L. French, "Correlates of Success in Retail Selling," *American Journal of Sociology*, 66 (September 1960), 128; and Erving Goffman, *Presentation of Self in Everyday Life* (New York: Doubleday, Anchor Books, 1959), p. 178.

he will tell the customer that he happens to be out of the item he wants, but that it can be obtained at the store of his "friend" or "cousin," just a few blocks away. The merchant will then take the customer to a storekeeper with a less conservative credit policy.[5] The second merchant fully understands that his colleague expects a commission and takes this into account in fixing the price.[6] As a result, the customer who happens to walk into the "wrong" store ends up paying more. In essence, he is being charged for the service of having his credit potential matched with the risk policy of a merchant.

As for the merchandise sold in these stores, the interviewers noticed that the furniture on display was of obviously poor quality. Most of all, they were struck by the absence of well-known brands of appliances in most of the stores. To find out about the sales of better-known brands, they initially asked about the volume of sales of "high-*price* lines." But this question had little meaning for the merchants, because high prices were being charged for the low-quality goods in evidence. The question had to be rephrased in terms of "high-*quality*" merchandise or, as the merchants themselves refer to such goods, "custom lines." To quote from the report of these interviews:

> It became apparent that the question raised a problem of communication. We were familiar with the prices generally charged for high-quality lines and began to notice that the same prices were charged for much lower quality merchandise. The markup was obviously quite different from that in other areas. The local merchants said that the sale of "custom" merchandise was limited by a slow turnover. In fact, a comparable markup on the high quality lines would make the final price so prohibitively high that they could not be moved at all. A lower markup would be inconsistent with the risk and would result in such small profits that the business could not be continued.

The high markup on low-quality goods is thus a major device used by the merchants to protect themselves against the risks of their

[5] The interviewers found that the stores closer to the main shopping area of 125th Street generally had more conservative credit policies than those somewhat farther away. This was indicated by the percentage of credit sales the merchants reported as defaults. The high-rental stores near 125th Street reported default rates of 5 and 6%, those six or seven blocks away, as high as 20%.

[6] The referring merchant does not receive his commission right away. Whether he gets it at all depends upon the customer's payment record. He will keep a record of his referrals and check on them after several months. When the merchant who has made the sale has received a certain percentage of the payments, he will give the referring merchant his commission.

credit business. This policy represents a marked departure from the "normal" marketing situation. In the "normal" market, competition between merchants results in a pricing policy roughly commensurate with the quality of the goods. It is apparent, then, that these merchants do not see themselves competing with stores outside the neighborhood. This results in the irony that the people who can least afford the goods they buy are required to pay high prices relative to quality, thus receiving a comparatively low return for their consumer dollar.

In large part, these merchants have a "captive" market because their customers do not meet the economic requirements of consumers in the larger, bureaucratic marketplace. But also, they can sell inferior goods at high prices because, in their own words, the customers are not "price and quality conscious." Interviews found that the merchants perceive their customers as unsophisticated shoppers. One merchant rather cynically explained that the amount of goods sold a customer depends not on the customer but on the merchant's willingness to extend him credit. If the merchant is willing to accept great risk, he can sell the customer almost as much as he cares to. Another merchant, commenting on the buying habits of the customer, said, "People do not shop in this area. Each person who comes into the store wants to buy something and is a potential customer. It is just up to who catches him."

The notion of "who catches him" is rather important in this economy. Merchants compete not so much in price or quality, but in getting customers to the store on other grounds. (Some of these gathering techniques will shortly be described.)

Another merchant commented rather grudgingly that the Negroes were beginning to show signs of greater sophistication by "shopping around." Presumably this practice is not followed by the newer migrants to the area.

But although the merchants are ready to exploit the naïveté of their traditionalistic customers, it is important to point out that they also cater to the customer's traditionalism. As a result of the heavy influx of Puerto Ricans into the area, many of these stores now employ Puerto Rican salesmen. The customers who enter these stores need not be concerned about possible embarrassment because of their broken English or their poor dress. On the contrary, these merchants are adept at making the customer feel at ease, as a personal experience will testify.

Visiting the area and stopping occasionally to read the ads in the windows, I happened to pause before an appliance store. A salesman promptly emerged and said, "I know, I bet you're looking for a nice TV set. Come inside. We've got lots of nice ones." Finding myself thrust into the role of customer, I followed him into the store and listened to his sales pitch. Partway through his talk, he asked my name. I hesitated a moment and then provided him with a fictitious last name, at which point he said, "No, no—no last names. What's your first name? . . . Ah, Dave; I'm Irv. We only care about first names here." When I was ready to leave after making some excuse about having to think things over, he handed me his card. Like most business cards of employees, this one had the name and address of the enterprise in large type and in small type the name of the salesman. But instead of his full name, there appeared only the amiable, "Irv."

As this episode indicates, the merchants in this low-income area are ready to personalize their services. To consumers from a more traditional society, unaccustomed to the impersonality of the bureaucratic market, this may be no small matter.

So far, we have reviewed the elements of the system of exchange that comprise the low-income market. For the consumer, these are the availability of merchandise, the "easy" installments, and the ressurance of dealing with merchants who make them feel at home. In return, the merchant reserves for himself the right to sell low-quality merchandise at exorbitant prices.

But the high markup on goods does not insure that the business will be profitable. No matter what he charges, the merchant can remain in business only if customers actually pay. In this market, the customer's intention and ability to pay—the assumptions underlying any credit system—cannot be taken for granted. Techniques for insuring continuity of payments are a fundamental part of this distinctive economy.

Formal controls

When the merchant uses an installment contract, he has recourse to legal controls over his customers. But as we shall see, legal controls are not sufficient to cope with the merchant's problem and they are seldom used.

REPOSSESSION.   The merchant who offers credit can always repossess his merchandise should the customer default on payments. But repossession, according to the merchants, is rare. They claim that the merchandise receives such heavy use as to become practically worthless in a short time. And no doubt the shoddy merchandise will not stand much use, heavy or light. One merchant said that he will occasionally repossess an item, not to regain his equity, but to punish a customer he feels is trying to cheat him.

LIENS AGAINST PROPERTY AND WAGES. The merchant can, of course, sue the defaulting customer. By winning a court judgment, he can have the customer's property attached. Should this fail to satisfy the debt, he can take the further step of having the customer's salary garnisheed.[7] But these devices are not fully adequate for several reasons. Not all customers have property of value or regular jobs. Furthermore, their employers will not hesitate to fire them rather than submit to the nuisance of a garnishment. But since the customer knows he may lose his job if he is garnisheed, the mere threat of garnishment is sometimes enough to insure regularity of payments.[8] The main limitation with legal controls, however, is that the merchant who uses them repeatedly runs the risk of forfeiting good will in the neighborhood.

DISCOUNTING PAPER. The concern with good will places a limitation on the use of another legal practice open to merchants for minimizing their risk: the sale of their contracts to a credit agency at a discount. By selling his contracts to one of the licensed finance companies, the merchant can realize an immediate return on his investment. The problem with this technique is that the merchant loses control over his customer. As an impersonal, bureaucratic organization, the credit agency has recourse only to legal controls. Should the customer miss a payment, the credit agency will take the matter to court. But in the customer's mind, his contract exists with the merchant, not with the credit agency. Consequently, the legal actions taken against him

[7] It is of some interest that the low-income families we interviewed were all familiar with the word "garnishee." This may well be one word in the language that the poorly educated are more likely to know than the better educated.

[8] Welfare families cannot, of course, be garnisheed, and more than half the merchants reported that they sell to them. But the merchants can threaten to disclose the credit purchase to the welfare authorities. Since recipients of welfare funds are not supposed to buy on credit, this threat exerts powerful pressure on the family.

reflect upon the merchant, and so good will is not preserved after all.

For this reason, the merchant is reluctant to "sell his paper," particularly if he has reason to believe that the customer will miss some payments. When he does sell some of his contracts at a discount, his motive is not to reduce risk, but rather to obtain working capital. Since so much of his capital is tied up in credit transactions, he frequently finds it necessary to make such sales. Oddly enough, he is apt to sell his better "paper," that is, the contracts of customers who pay regularly, for he wants to avoid incurring the ill will of customers. This practice also has its drawbacks for the merchant. Competitors can find out from the credit agencies which customers pay regularly and then try to lure them away from the original merchant. Some merchants reported that in order to retain control over their customers, they will buy back contracts from credit agencies they suspect are giving information to competitors.[9]

CREDIT ASSOCIATION RATINGS.   All credit merchants report their bad debtors to the credit association to which they belong. The merchants interviewed said that they always consult the "skip lists" of their association before extending credit to a new customer.[10] In this way they can avoid at least the customers known to be bad risks. This form of control tends to be effective in the long run because the customers find that they are unable to obtain credit until they have made good on their past debts. During the interviews with them, some consumers mentioned this need to restore their credit rating as the reason why they were paying off debts in spite of their belief that they had been cheated.

But these various formal techniques of control are not sufficient to cope with the merchant's problem of risk. He also depends heavily on informal and personal techniques of control.

---

[9] Not all merchants are particularly concerned with good will. A few specialize in extending credit to the worst risks, customers turned away by most other merchants. These men will try to collect as much as they can on their accounts during the year and then will sell all their outstanding accounts to a finance company. As a result, the most inadequate consumers are apt to meet with the bureaucratic controls employed by the finance company. For a description of how bill collectors operate, see Hillel Black, *Buy Now, Pay Later* (New York: William Morrow and Co., 1961), chap. 4.

[10] See *Ibid.*, chap. 3, for a description of the world's largest credit association, the one serving most of the stores in the New York City area.

Informal controls

The merchant starts from the premise that most of his customers are honest people who intend to pay but have difficulty managing their money. Missed payments are seen as more often due to poor management and to emergencies than to dishonesty. The merchants anticipate that their customers will miss some payments and they rely on informal controls to insure that payments are eventually made.

All the merchants described their credit business as operating on a "fifteen-month year." This means that they expect the customer to miss about one of every four payments and they compute the markup accordingly. Unlike the credit companies, which insist upon regular payments and add service charges for late payments, the neighborhood merchant is prepared to extend "flexible" credit. Should the customer miss an occasional payment or should he be short on another, the merchant considers this a normal part of his business.

To insure the close personal control necessary for this system of credit, the merchant frequently draws up a contract for weekly payments which the customer usually brings to the store. This serves several functions for the merchant. To begin with, the sum of money represented by a weekly payment is relatively small and so helps to create the illusion of "easy credit." Customers are apt to think more of the size of the payments than of the cost of the item or the length of the contract.

More importantly, the frequent contact of a weekly payment system enables the merchant to get to know his customer. He learns when the customer receives his paycheck, when his rent is due, who his friends are, when job layoffs, illnesses, and other emergencies occur— in short, all sorts of information which allow him to interpret the reason for a missed payment. Some merchants reported that when they know the customer has missed a payment for a legitimate reason such as illness or a job layoff, they will send a sympathetic note and offer the customer a gift (an inexpensive lamp or wall picture) when payments are resumed. This procedure, they say, frequently brings the customer back with his missed payments.

The short interval between payments also functions to give the merchant an early warning when something is amiss. His chances of locating the delinquent customer are that much greater. Furthermore, the merchant can keep tabs on a delinquent customer through his knowledge of the latter's friends, relatives, neighbors, and associates, who are also apt to be customers of his. In this way, still another informal device, the existing network of social relations, is utilized by the neighborhood merchant in conducting his business.[11]

The weekly payment system also provides the merchant with the opportunity to sell other items to the customer. When the first purchase is almost paid for, the merchant will try to persuade the customer to make another. Having the customer in the store, where he can look at the merchandise, makes the next sale that much easier. This system of successive sales is, of course, an ideal arrangement—for the merchant. As a result, the customer remains continuously in debt to him. The pattern is somewhat reminiscent of the Southern sharecropper's relation to the company store. And since a number of customers grew up in more traditional environments with just such economies, they may find the arrangement acceptable. The practice of buying from peddlers, found to be common in these low-income areas, also involves the principle of continuous indebtedness. The urban low-income economy, then, is in some respects like the sharecropper system; it might almost be called an "urban sharecropper system." [12]

The Customer Peddlers

Characteristic of the comparatively traditional and personal form of the low-income economy is the important role played in it by the door-to-door credit salesman, the customer peddler. The study of merchants found that these peddlers are not necessarily competitors of the store owners. Almost all merchants make use of peddlers in the great competition for customers. The merchants tend to regard peddlers as necessary evils who add greatly to the final cost of purchases. But they need them because in their view, customers are too ignorant, frightened, or lazy to come to the stores themselves. Thus, the merchants'

---

[11] The merchant's access to these networks of social relations is not entirely independent of economic considerations. Just as merchants who refer customers receive commissions, so customers who recommend others are often given commissions. Frequently, this is why a customer will urge his friends to deal with a particular merchant.

[12] The local merchants are not the only ones promoting continuous debt. The coupon books issued by banks and finance companies which underwrite installment contracts contain notices in the middle announcing that the consumer can, if he wishes, refinance the loan. The consumer is told, in effect, that he is a good risk because presumably he has regularly paid half the installments and that he need not wait until he has made the last payment before borrowing more money.

apparent contempt for peddlers does not bar them from employing outdoor salesmen (or "canvassers," as they describe the peddlers who work for one store or another). Even the merchants who are themselves reluctant to hire canvassers find they must do so in order to meet the competition. The peddler's main function for the merchant, then, is getting the customer to the store, and if he will not come, getting the store to the customer. But this is not his only function.

Much more than the storekeeper, the peddler operates on the basis of a personal relationship with the customer. By going to the customer's home, he gets to know the entire family; he sees the condition of the home and he comes to know the family's habits and wants. From this vantage point he is better able than the merchant to evaluate the customer as a credit risk. Since many of the merchant's potential customers lack the standard credentials of credit such as having a permanent job, the merchant needs some other basis for discriminating between good and bad risks. If the peddler, who has come to know the family, is ready to vouch for the customer, the merchant will be ready to make the transaction. In short, the peddler acts as a fiduciary agent, a Dun and Bradstreet for the poor, telling the merchant which family is likely to meet its obligations and which is not.

Not all peddlers are employed by stores. Many are independent enterprisers (who may have started as canvassers for stores).[13] A number of the independent peddlers have accumulated enough capital to supply their customers with major durables. These are the elite peddlers, known as "dealers," who buy appliances and furniture from local merchants at a "wholesale" price, and then sell them on credit to their customers. In these transactions, the peddler either takes the customer to the store or sends the customer to the store with his card on which he has written some such message as "Please give Mr. Jones a TV set." [14] The merchant then sells the customer the TV set at a

---

[13] A systematic study of local merchants and peddlers would probably find that a typical career pattern is to start as a canvasser, become a self-employed peddler, and finally a storekeeper.

[14] According to a former customer peddler, now in the furniture business, the peddlers' message will either read "Please *give* Mr. Jones . . ." or "Please let Mr. Jones *pick out*. . . ." In the former case, the customer is given the merchandise right away; in the latter, it is set aside for him until the peddler says that it is all right to let the customer have it. The peddler uses the second form when his customer is already heavily in debt to him and he wants to be certain that the customer will agree to the higher weekly payments that will be necessary.

price much higher than he would ordinarily charge. The "dealer" is generally given two months to pay the merchant the "wholesale" price, and meanwhile he takes over the responsibility of collecting from his customer. Some "dealers" are so successful that they employ canvassers in their own right.[15] And some merchants do so much business with "dealers" that they come to think of themselves as "wholesalers" even though they are fully prepared to do their own retail business.

Independent peddlers without much capital also have economic relations with local merchants. They act as brokers, directing their customers to neighborhood stores that will extend them credit. And for this service they of course receive a commission. In these transactions, it is the merchant who accepts the risks and assumes the responsibility for collecting payments. The peddler who acts as a broker performs the same function as the merchant in the T.O. system. He knows which merchants will accept great risk and which will not, and directs his customers accordingly.

There are, then, three kinds of customer peddlers operating in these low-income neighborhoods who cooperate with local merchants: the canvassers who are employed directly by the stores; the small entrepreneurs who act as brokers; and the more successful entrepreneurs who operate as "dealers." A fourth type of peddler consists of salesmen representing large companies not necessarily located in the neighborhood. These men are, for the most part, canvassers for firms specializing in a particular commodity, e.g., encyclopedias, vacuum cleaners, or pots and pans. They differ from the other peddlers by specializing in what they sell and by depending more on contracts and legal controls. They are also less interested in developing continuous relationships with their customers.

Peddlers thus aid the local merchants by finding customers, evaluating them as credit risks, and helping in the collection of payments. And as the merchants themselves point out, these services add greatly to the cost of the goods. One storekeeper said that peddlers are apt to charge five or six times the amount the store charges for relatively inexpensive purchases. Pointing to a religious picture which he sells

---

[15] One tiny store in the area, with little merchandise in evidence, is reported to employ over a hundred canvassers. The owner would not consent to an interview, but the student-observers did notice that this apparently small merchant kept some four of five bookkeepers at work in a back room. The owner is obviously a "dealer" whose store is his office. As a "dealer," he has no interest in maintaining stock and displays for street trade.

for $5, he maintained that peddlers sell it for as much as $30. And he estimated that the peddler adds 30 to 50% to the final sales price of appliances and furniture.

Unethical and Illegal Practices

The interviewers uncovered some evidence that some local merchants engage in the illegal practice of selling reconditioned furniture and appliances as new. Of course, no merchant would admit that he did this himself, but five of them hinted that their competitors engaged in this practice.[16] Several of the consumers we interviewed were quite certain that they had been victimized in this way.

One unethical, if not illegal, activity widely practiced by stores is "bait" advertising with its concomitant, the "switch sale." In the competition for customers, merchants depend heavily upon advertising displays in their windows which announce furniture or appliances at unusually low prices. The customer may enter the store assuming that the low offer in the window signifies a reasonably low price line. Under severe pressure, the storekeeper may even be prepared to sell the merchandise at the advertised price, for not to do so would be against the law. What most often happens, however, is that the unsuspecting customer is convinced by the salesman that he doesn't really want the goods advertised in the window and is then persuaded to buy a smaller amount of more expensive goods. Generally, not much persuasion is necessary. The most popular "bait ad" is the announcement of three rooms of furniture for "only $149" or "only $199." The customer who inquires about this bargain is shown a bedroom set consisting of two cheap and (sometimes deliberately) chipped bureaus and one bed frame. He learns that the spring and mattress are not included in the advertised price, but can be had for another $75 or $100. The living-room set in these "specials" consists of a fragile-looking sofa and one unmatching chair.[17]

The frequent success of this kind of exploitation, known in the trade as the "switch sale," is reflected in this comment by one mer-

---

[16] Events are sometimes more telling than words. During an interview with a merchant, the interviewer volunteered to help several men who were carrying bed frames into the store. The owner excitedly told him not to help because he might get paint on his hands.

[17] In one store in which I inspected this special offer, I was told by the salesman that he would find a chair that was a "fairly close match."

chant: "I don't know how they do it. They advertise three rooms of furniture for $149 and the customers swarm in. *They end up buying a $400 bedroom set for $600 and none of us can believe how easy it is to make these sales.*"

In sum, a fairly intricate system of sales-and-credit has evolved in response to the distinctive situation of the low-income consumer and the local merchant. It is a system heavily slanted in the direction of a traditional economy in which informal, personal ties play a major part in the transaction. At the same time it is connected to impersonal bureaucratic agencies through the instrument of the installment contract. Should the informal system break down, credit companies, courts of law, and agencies of law enforcement come to play a part.

The system is not only different from the larger, more formal economy; in some respects it is a *deviant* system in which practices that violate prevailing moral standards are commonplace. As Merton has pointed out in his analysis of the political machine, the persistence of deviant social structures can only be understood when their social functions (as well as disfunctions) are taken into account.[18] The basic function of the low-income marketing system is to provide consumer goods to people who fail to meet the requirements of the more legitimate, bureaucratic market, or who choose to exclude themselves from the larger market because they do not feel comfortable in it. As we have seen, the system is extraordinarily flexible. Almost no one—however great a risk—is turned away. Various mechanisms sift and sort customers according to their credit risk and match them with merchants ready to sell them the goods they want. Even the family on welfare is permitted to maintain its self-respect by consuming in much the same way as do its social peers who happen not to be on welfare.

[18] Robert K. Merton, *Social Theory and Social Structure,* rev. ed. (New York: The Free Press of Glencoe, 1957).

B. The Extent of the Problem

27. Exploitation of Disadvantaged Consumers by Retail Merchants

Report of the National Commission on Civil Disorders

Much of the violence in recent civil disorders has been directed at stores and other commercial establishments in disadvantaged Negro areas. In some cases, rioters focused on stores operated by white merchants who, they apparently believed, had been charging exorbitant prices or selling inferior goods. Not all the violence against these stores can be attributed to "revenge" for such practices. Yet it is clear that many residents of disadvantaged Negro neighborhoods believe they suffer constant abuses by local merchants.

Significant grievances concerning unfair commercial practices affecting Negro consumers were found in 11 of the 20 cities studied by the Commission. The fact that most of the merchants who operate stores in almost every Negro area are white undoubtedly contributes to the conclusion among Negroes that they are exploited by white society.

It is difficult to assess the precise degree and extent of exploitation. No systematic and reliable survey comparing consumer pricing and

Reprinted from *Report of the National Commission on Civil Disorders* (New York: Bantam Books, 1968), 274–277.

credit practices in all-Negro and other neighborhoods has ever been conducted on a nationwide basis. Differences in prices and credit practices between white middle-income areas and Negro low-income areas to some extent reflect differences in the real costs of serving these two markets (such as differential losses from pilferage in super-markets), but the exact extent of these differential real costs has never been estimated accurately. Finally, an examination of exploitative consumer practices must consider the particular structure and functions of the low-income consumer durables market.

Installment Buying

This complex situation can best be understood by first considering certain basic facts:

(1) Various cultural factors generate constant pressure on low-income families to buy many relatively expensive durable goods and display them in their homes. This pressure comes in part from continuous exposure to commercial advertising, especially on television. In January 1967, over 88% of all Negro households had TV sets. A 1961 study of 464 low-income families in New York City showed that 95% of these relatively poor families had TV sets.

(2) Many poor families have extremely low incomes, bad previous credit records, unstable sources of income, or other attributes which make it virtually impossible for them to buy merchandise from established large national or local retail firms. These families lack enough savings to pay cash, and they cannot meet the standard credit requirements of established general merchants because they are too likely to fall behind in their payments.

(3) Poor families in urban areas are far less mobile than others. A 1967 Chicago study of low-income Negro households indicated their low automobile ownership compelled them to patronize primarily local neighborhood merchants. These merchants typically provided smaller selection, poorer services, and higher prices than big national outlets. The 1961 New York study also indicated that families who shopped

outside their own neighborhoods were far less likely to pay exorbitant prices.

(4) Most low-income families are uneducated concerning the nature of credit purchase contracts, the legal rights and obligations of both buyers and sellers, sources of advice for consumers who are having difficulties with merchants, and the operation of the courts concerned with these matters. In contrast, merchants engaged in selling goods to them are very well informed.

(5) In most states, the laws governing relations between consumers and merchants in effect offer protection only to informed, sophisticated parties with understanding of each other's rights and obligations. Consequently, these laws are little suited to protect the rights of most low-income consumers.

In this situation, exploitative practices flourish. Ghetto residents who want to buy relatively expensive goods cannot do so from standard retail outlets and are thus restricted to local stores. Forced to use credit, they have little understanding of the pitfalls of credit buying. But because they have unstable incomes and frequently fail to make payments, the cost to the merchants of serving them is significantly above that of serving middle-income consumers. Consequently, a special kind of merchant appears to sell them goods on terms designed to cover the high cost of doing business in ghetto neighborhoods.

Whether they actually gain higher profits, these merchants charge higher prices than those in other parts of the city to cover the greater credit risks and other higher operating costs inherent in neighborhood outlets. A recent study conducted by the Federal Trade Commission in Washington, D. C., illustrates this conclusion dramatically. The FTC identified a number of stores specializing in selling furniture and appliances to low-income households. About 92% of the sales of these stores were credit sales involving installment purchases, as compared to 27% of the sales in general retail outlets handling the same merchandise.

The median income annually of a sample of 486 customers of these stores was about $4,200, but one-third had annual incomes below $3,600, about 6% were receiving welfare payments, and another 76% were employed in the lowest paying occupations (service workers, operatives, laborers, and domestics)—as compared to 36% of the total labor force in Washington in those occupations.

Definitely catering to a low-income group, these stores charged significantly higher prices than general merchandise outlets in the Washington area. According to testimony by Paul Rand Dixon, Chairman of the FTC, an item selling wholesale at $100 would retail on the average for $165 in a general merchandise store, and for $250 in a low-income specialty store. Thus, the customers of these outlets were paying an average price premium of about 52%.

While higher prices are not necessarily exploitative in themselves, many merchants in ghetto neighborhoods take advantage of their superior knowledge of credit buying by engaging in various exploitative tactics—high-pressure salesmanship, bait advertising, misrepresentation of prices, substitution of used goods for promised new ones, failure to notify consumers of legal actions against them, refusal to repair or replace substandard goods, exorbitant prices or credit charges, and use of shoddy merchandise. Such tactics affect a great many low-income consumers. In the New York study, 60% of all households had suffered from consumer problems (some of which were purely their own fault), about 43% had experienced serious exploitation, and 20% had experienced repossession, garnishment, or threat of garnishment.

Garnishment

Garnishment practices in many states allow creditors to deprive individuals of their wages through court action without hearing or trial. In about 20 states, the wages of an employee can be diverted to a creditor merely upon the latter's deposition, with no advance hearing where the employee can defend himself. He often receives no prior notice of such action and is usually unaware of the law's operation and too poor to hire legal defense. Moreover, consumers may find themselves still owing money on a sales contract even after the creditor has repossessed the goods. The New York study cited earlier in this chapter indicated that 20% of a sample of low-income families had been subject to legal action regarding consumer purchases. And the Federal Trade Commission study in Washington, D. C., showed that retailers specializing in credit sales of furniture and appliances to low-income consumers resorted to court action on the average for every $2,200 of sales. Since their average sale was for $207, this amounted to using the courts to collect from one of every 11 customers. In contrast, department stores in the same area used court action against approximately one of every 14,500 customers, assuming their sales also averaged $207 per customer.

Variations in Food Prices

Residents of low-income Negro neighborhoods frequently claim that they pay higher prices for food in local markets than wealthier white suburbanites and receive inferior quality meat and produce. Statistically reliable information comparing prices and quality in these two kinds of areas is generally unavailable. The U. S. Bureau of Labor Statistics, studying food prices in six cities in 1966, compared prices of a standard list of 18 items in low-income areas and higher-income areas in each city. In a total of 180 stores, including independent and chain stores, and for items of the same type sold in the same types of stores, there were no significant differences in prices between low-income and high-income areas. However, stores in low-income areas were more likely to be small independents (which had somewhat higher prices), to sell low-quality produce and meat at any given price, and to be patronized by people who typically bought smaller-sized packages which are more expensive per unit of measure. In other words, many low-income consumers in fact pay higher prices, although the situation varies greatly from place to place.

Although these findings must be considered inconclusive, there are significant reasons to believe that poor households generally pay higher prices for the food they buy and receive lower quality food. Low-income consumers buy more food at local groceries because they are less mobile. Prices in these small stores are significantly higher than in major supermarkets because they cannot achieve economies of scale, and because real operating costs are higher in low-income Negro areas than in outlying suburbs. For instance, inventory "shrinkage" from pilfering and other causes is normally under 2% of sales, but can run twice as much in high-crime areas. Managers seek to make up for these added costs by charging higher prices for good quality food, or by substituting lower grades.

These practices do not necessarily involve "exploitation," but they are often perceived as exploitative and unfair by those who are aware of the price and quality differences involved, but unaware of operating costs. In addition, it is probable that genuinely exploitative pricing practices exist in some areas. In either case, differential food prices constitute another factor convincing urban Negroes in low-income neighborhoods that whites discriminate against them.

28. Economic Report on Installment Credit and Retail Sales Practices of District of Columbia Retailers

Federal Trade Commission

This report presents the results of a survey of installment credit and sales practices involving household furnishings and appliances in the District of Columbia. The purpose of the survey was to obtain a factual picture of the finance charges, prices, gross margins and profits, legal actions taken in collecting delinquent accounts, and the assignment relationships between retailers and finance companies. The survey covered those D.C. retailers of furniture and appliances having estimated sales of at least $100,000 for the year. The 96 retailers providing data had combined sales of $226 million, which represented about 85% of the sales of furniture, appliance, and department store retailers in the District of Columbia.

Use of Installment Credit

Sixty-five retailers with combined sales of $151 million indicated regular use of consumer installment sales contracts. The remainder sold

Reprinted from *Economic Report on Installment Credit and Retail Sales Practices of District of Columbia Retailers* (Washington: Superintendent of Documents, 1968), ix–xvi and 1–24.

only for cash or on a regular or revolving charge account basis. This report focuses primarily on retailers using installment contracts. These retailers were classified into two groups: those appealing primarily to low-income customers and those appealing to a more general market.

District of Columbia stores varied widely in their use of install- ment credit. Some general market discount appliance stores made very few sales on credit. At the other extreme, a number of low-income market retailers sold entirely on installment credit.

Installment credit was used much more extensively by retailers selling to low-income consumers than by retailers selling to other con- sumers. Low-income market retailers used installment credit in 93% of their sales. The comparable figure for general market retailers was 27%.

Customer Characteristics

A sample of installment sales contracts and credit applications was analyzed to identify the customer characteristics of low-income market retailers. The analysis revealed substantial differences between cus- tomers of the low-income market retailers and all residents of the Dis- trict of Columbia. The average family size was larger—4.3 persons compared to an average of 3.5 persons for the District of Columbia. Almost half of the families of customers in the sample had five or more members. The median family income of the same customers was $348 per month. This is very low considering the larger than average size of the families. The Bureau of Labor Statistics recently estimated that the maintenance of a moderate standard of living for four in Washington, D.C., requires a monthly income of $730.

Most customers were engaged in low-paying jobs. The largest proportion, 28%, were Service Workers, such as waitresses and jani- tors. Second in importance were Operatives (including such occupa- tions as taxi drivers and laundry workers). Laborers and Domestic Workers also represented a significant share of the sample. Together, these four major occupational groups accounted for 75% of the customer sample. In comparison, only 36% of the general population in the District was classified in these low-paying occupational groups. There were 31 welfare recipients in the sample, accounting for 6% of all customers in the sample. There were also a number of customers in the sample dependent on social security, alimony, support pay- ments, and income received from relatives.

A review of credit references noted in the 486 contracts subjected to detailed analysis revealed that 70% indicated no credit references or references with low-income market retailers only. Only 30% of the customers of this retailer, therefore, had established credit with general market retailers.

Gross Margins and Prices

The survey disclosed that, without exception, low-income market retailers had high average markups and prices. On the average, goods purchased for $100 at wholesale sold for $255 in the low-income market stores, compared with $159 in general market stores.

Contrasts between the markup policies of low-income and general market retailers are most apparent when specific products are compared. Retailers surveyed were asked to give the wholesale and retail prices for their two best-selling models in each product line. These price data are typical of the large volume of products sold by each class of retailer.

For every product specified, low-income market retailers had the higher average gross margins reported. When similar makes and models are compared, the differences are striking. For example, the wholesale cost of a portable TV set was about $109 to both a low-income market and a general market retailer. The general market retailer sold the set for $129.95, whereas the low-income market retailer charged $219.95 for the same set. Another example is a dryer, wholesaling at about $115, which was sold for $150 by a general market retailer and for $300 by a low-income market retailer.

Operating Expenses and Net Profits

Despite their substantially higher prices, net profit on sales for low-income market retailers was only slightly higher and net profit return on net worth was considerably lower when compared to general market retailers. It appears that salaries and commissions, bad-debt losses, and other expenses are substantially higher for low-income market retailers. Profit and expense comparisons are, of course, affected by differences in type of operation and accounting procedures. However, a detailed analysis was made for retailers of comparable size and merchandise mix to minimize such differences.

Low-income market retailers reported the highest return after taxes on net sales, 4.7%. Among the general market retailers, department stores had the highest return on net sales, 4.6%. Furniture and home furnishings stores earned a net profit after taxes of 3.9%, and appliance, radio, and television retailers were the least profitable with a net profit of only 2.1% on sales.

Low-income market retailers reported an average rate of return on *net worth* after taxes of 10.1%. Rates of return on net worth varied considerably among various kinds of general market retailers. Appliance, radio, and television retailers reported the highest rate of return after taxes, 20.3% of net worth. Next in order were furniture and home furnishings retailers with 17.6% and department stores with 13% on net worth.

Assignment of Contracts

Low-income market retailers typically held their installment contracts and did not assign them to finance companies or banks. Only one fifth of the total contracts were assigned by low-income market retailers. Among general market retailers, appliance stores assigned almost all (98%) of their contracts to finance companies and banks. General market furniture stores assigned somewhat more than half of their contracts (57%). Among the retailers surveyed, only the department store category involved no contract assignment.

Finance Charges

There is considerable variation in the finance charges of D.C. retailers of furniture and appliances, particularly among the low-income market retailers. Most of the retailers surveyed determined finance charges in terms of an "add-on" rate based on the unpaid cash balance. When calculated on an effective annual rate basis, finance charges of general market retailers varied between 11% and 29%, averaging 21% when contracts were assigned and 19% when retailers financed their own contracts. Finance charges by low-income market retailers imposing such charges ranged between 11 and 33% per annum, averaging 25% on contracts assigned to finance companies and 23% on contracts the retailers held themselves.

One low-income market retailer made no separate charge for installment credit. All of his finance charges were, in effect, included in the purchase price. Other low-income market retailers kept finance charges below the actual cost of granting credit. This practice of absorbing credit costs can give the illusion of "easy" credit, but the customer may be paying a great deal for such installment credit in the form of much higher prices.

Judgments, Garnishments, and Repossessions

One of the most notable facts uncovered by the study relates to the frequency with which a small group of retailers utilized the courts to enforce their claims with respect to installment contracts. Eleven of the 18 low-income market retailers reported 2,690 judgments. Their legal actions resulted in 1,568 garnishments and 306 repossessions. For this group, one court judgment was obtained for every $2,200 of sales. In effect, low-income market retailers make extensive use of the courts in collecting debts. While general market retailers may take legal action as a last resort against delinquent customers, some low-income market retailers depend on legal action as a normal order of business.

Conclusions

Installment credit is widely used in marketing appliances and home furnishings to low-income families. Often these families purchase durable goods, such as furniture, television sets, and phonographs, through the mechanism of "easy" credit. Low-income market retailers specialize in granting credit to consumers who do not seek or are unable to obtain credit from regular department, furniture, or appliance stores. As a group, low-income market retailers made about 93% of their sales through installment credit.

The real cost of this "easy" credit is very dear, however. Primarily it takes the form of higher product prices. Credit charges, when separately stated, are not notably higher than those imposed by general market retailers. Though some low-income market retailers imposed effective annual finance charges as high as 33%, others charged much less or nothing at all. Markups on comparable products, however, are often two or three times higher than those charged by general market retailers.

The findings of this study suggest that the marketing system for distribution of durable goods to low-income consumers is costly. Although their markups are very much higher than those of general market retailers, low-income market retailers do not make particularly high net profits. They have markedly higher costs, partly because of high bad-debt expenses, but to a greater extent because of higher salaries and commissions as a per cent of sales. These expenses reflect in part greater use of door-to-door selling and expenses associated with the collection and processing of installment contracts.

The high prices charged by low-income market retailers suggest the absence of effective price competition. What competition there is among low-income market retailers apparently takes the form of easier credit availability, rather than of lower prices. Greater credit risks are taken to entice customers. Insofar as the problem for low-income consumers is availability of credit, merchants who sell to them focus on this element.

The success of retailers who price their merchandise on such a high markup in selling to low-income families leads inevitably to the conclusion that such families engage in little comparative shopping. It would appear that many low-income customers lack information or knowledge of their credit charges and credit source alternatives, or of the prices and quality of products available in general market retailing establishments. To the extent that door-to-door sales techniques are utilized, such families frequently make crucial purchases without leaving the home and without seeing the products they commit themselves to buy. The fact that low-income market retailers emphasize the use of door-to-door salesmen both reflects and encourages such behavior. The Commission is well aware that door-to-door selling, as well as home-demonstration selling, provides an opportunity for deceptive and high-pressure sales techniques. Moreover, such selling methods are also very high-cost methods of distribution. It would appear, therefore, that the low-income consumers who can least afford mistakes in their buying decisions face two serious problems when they are confronted with a door-to-door or home-demonstration sales approach— (1) the high cost of this sales technique will ultimately be borne by the purchaser, and (2) the opportunity for high pressure or deceptive selling is great, thus discouraging comparative shopping and enhancing the probability that the consumer will agree to purchases he would otherwise not want.

While public policy can help solve the problems of low-income consumers, legislation alone may not be sufficient. Legislation aimed at disclosure and regulation of finance charges will help low-income as well as other consumers make more rational buying decisions. Intensified programs on both state and Federal levels to eliminate all deceptions and frauds in the advertising and oral representations of the terms of sale and credit charges will also help to ensure that their money is spent advantageously. The poor, to a considerable extent, however, are not sophisticated shoppers. Many cannot afford the luxury of "shopping around" because their potential sources of credit are limited. Others, because of inadequate consumer education or lack of mobility, simply do not engage in comparison shopping.

Thus, in attempting to deal with the phenomenon of the poor paying more for consumer goods, every effort should be made to improve consumer counseling. Many customers continue to buy from low-income market retailers even though they have sufficient income to qualify for credit at stores selling for less. Greater community effort in consumer education is needed.

Beyond the matter of education is the question of credit availability. Many low-income families are quite capable of making regular payments. They should have the option of making payments on reasonably priced merchandise. Local community effort in the development of effective credit sources could contribute materially to freeing individuals from dependence on "easy" credit merchants. Moreover, perhaps general market retailers can take steps to make it easier for low-income families to apply for and receive credit. Some retailers have already found that they can do so economically. Various community business organizations might consider ways of more actively encouraging low-income families to seek credit from retailers selling for less.

Increased competition for the patronage of low-income consumers would go a long way toward resolving many of the problems confronting them in the low-income market. Public policy should consider the various ways by which new entrants could be encouraged into these markets to increase the competitive viability of these markets.

While the availability of credit is perhaps the major reason why low-income families purchase from the low-income market retailers, it is only logical to conclude that the sales techniques of these retailers are also an important factor. Low-income market retailers have every incentive to continue these techniques since their risk of loss is substantially reduced by their virtually unopposed access to judgment and garnishment proceedings to enforce payment or secure repossession. The 2,690 actions taken by eleven low-income market retailers suggest a marketing technique which includes actions against default as a normal matter of business rather than as a matter of last resort. At present, in the face of default, creditors can seek both repossession and payment of the deficiency, including various penalties. It may be appropriate to require creditors to choose one or the other of these legal remedies, and not to have the option of pursuing both courses simultaneously. Repossession would then fully discharge the merchant's claim. It is equally necessary to ensure that purchasers receive *actual* notice of any such proceedings and have legal counsel available to defend them in court. Perhaps, consideration should also be given to some form of negotiation before a court-appointed neighborhood referee as a compulsory prelude to a default judgment.

It is apparent that the solution to the problem of installment credit for the poor requires a variety of actions. A requirement that finance charges be clearly and conspicuously stated is a necessary but not a sufficient solution to the problem of installment credit for those consumers who are considered poor credit risks and are unsophisticated buyers. Among the complementary steps which might be considered are the following: (1) make reasonable credit more accessible; (2) provide counseling services which will encourage customers to practice comparison shopping; (3) equalize the legal rights of buyers and creditors in installment credit transactions; (4) encourage additional businesses to enter the low-income market; and (5) intensify consumer protection activities on both Federal and local levels to eliminate all fraud and deceptions in the advertising and offering of credit.

29. Similarity of Ghetto and Nonghetto Food Costs

Burton H. Marcus

Recent findings by researchers such as Caplovitz [1] and Sturdivant [2] have indicated that the poor pay more. Other studies, such as that by Goodman [3] and the Bureau of Labor Statistics, [4] have indicated that the poor may not pay more. Similarly, this article attacks one of the major issues with which Americans are currently concerned, i.e., Do the poor pay more?

The Caplovitz and Sturdivant studies focus on durable goods prices. The Goodman and BLS studies are primarily about food prices. This study resembles the last in that it investigates the cost of food. However, although each of the studies just cited represents an investigation of a rather limited selection of items (which in one case could

[1] David Caplovitz, *The Poor Pay More,* New York: The Free Press of Glencoe, 1963.

[2] Frederick D. Sturdivant, "Better Deal for Ghetto Shoppers," *Harvard Business Review,* 46 (March–April, 1968), 130.

[3] Charles S. Goodman, "Do the Poor Pay More?" *Journal of Marketing,* 32 (January, 1968), 18.

[4] U.S. Department of Labor, Bureau of Labor Statistics, National Commission on Food Marketing, "Retail Food Prices in Low and Higher Income Areas," *Special Studies in Food Marketing,* Technical Report No. 10, June 1966.

Reprinted from the *Journal of Marketing Research,* Vol. 6 (August, 1969), 365–368, published by The American Marketing Association.

have distorted the findings), the selection priced here is more comprehensive.

Objective and Hypothesis

The objective of this research was to determine if the poorer ghetto dwellers paid more than the more affluent nonghetto shoppers for comparable foodstuffs.

Geographic area

Specifically, it was hypothesized that the cost of foodstuffs listed in the *Consumer Price Index* (CPI) is no higher in Watts than in Culver City.[5]

Watts was chosen because of its recognition as a poverty area by Federal, state, and local government authorities as well as private interest groups (business, etc.). Also, findings of several other researchers are partly based on data drawn from this area.[6]

Culver City, an area ten miles from Watts, is a geographical island surrounded by Los Angeles. It was selected as a comparison city because of its similar retail business structure, only somewhat similar (but relatively more affluent) economic structure, and its dissimilar (nonminority, white) ethnic structure.[7]

Stores

Lists of food stores in the Watts and Culver City areas were obtained from the Pacific Telephone Company and the City Licensing Department. A total of 16 stores, of which seven were superchain stores [8]

---

[5] The items listed in the CPI were used as a guide for two major reasons. The CPI is a relative measure frequently used and well accepted as a fairly accurate approximation of the relative prices between areas and over time. Therefore, comparison of the cost of items that comprise a section of this index should constitute a relatively meaningful reference. The opportunity for comparison with statistics collected by the Bureau of Labor Statistics was also recognized.

[6] Chester R. Beverly, *A Study of Negro and Mexican-American Businessmen and Their Businesses,* Economic and Business Development Center, Research Department, Los Angeles, Calif., 1967, Sturdivant, *op. cit.*

[7] A branch of the Small Business Association, the Economic and Business Development Center of Los Angeles, used these two areas for comparison purposes in several of their studies.

[8] Chain stores are defined as stores with multiple outlets capable of centralized buying and distribution. Only one superstore in each area was not a member of a parent organization, i.e., they were independent superstores.

and nine were Ma and Pa stores,[9] were audited in Culver City. A total of 33 stores, of which six were superchain stores and 27 Ma and Pa stores, were audited in the Watts area.

Items sampled

The CPI, an accepted and useful economic indicator, served as a guide. This index is often referred to as the Cost of Living Index, and is ". . . a statistical measure of changes in prices of goods and services bought by urban wage earners and clerical workers, including families and single persons." [10]

By using the CPI market basket as a guide, prices and statistics could be compared with data collected by and available from the Department of Labor. The list of 86 items drawn from the CPI market basket excluded only those items that, because of the season, were not available and consequently could not be priced.

On the basis of findings from a sample survey conducted in Watts and Culver City area stores, the most prevalent brands and container sizes were determined. When only one brand, size, and kind was stocked in every store, that one was priced. For instances in which more than one brand, size, and kind was carried in every store, or for those in which no particular brand, size, and kind could be found in every store, the least expensive item of that kind was priced. This procedure was adopted because it was believed likely that the lowest priced foods would be within grasp of the greatest number of people.

The price recorded was the price stamped on an item, listed adjacent to it, or reported by the store manager when either of the former was unobtainable.

Findings

Generally, prices in both areas were quite similar. On the basis of the data collected for food items in general, the poor do *not* pay more; in fact, as Line 1 of Table 1 reveals, the cost of food in the ghetto area is actually slightly lower than in the nonghetto area.

If two categories—meat and produce—are excluded from the

---

[9] Ma and Pa stores are small, individually owned grocery stores. All but one Ma and Pa store in Culver City and three in Watts carried meat as well as other foodstuffs.

[10] U.S. Department of Labor, Bureau of Labor Statistics, *Consumer Price Index,* Washington, D.C., 1963.

Table 1. Percentage by which prices for foods are higher (lower) in Watts than in Culver City

Product group	Ma and Pa	Chain	All stores
All goods	(0.5%)	(0.9%)	(0.7%)
Meats and produce excluded	7.0	1.2	4.0

data, the conclusion stated earlier is reversed. That is, with meat and produce excluded, the cost of food in Watts is 4.0% higher than in Culver City. Moreover, a greater disparity between the prices charged in the two store types is also evident.

Product

Six categories were used to group the various food items surveyed: (1) cereal and bakery goods, (2) meat, poultry, and fish, (3) dairy, (4) produce, (5) canned fruits and vegetables, and (6) other foods.

In three of these categories, most or all of the items were fully comparable; brand, size, and grade could be held constant, leaving only price to vary. These three categories were cereal and bakery goods, canned fruits and vegetables, and other foods (including such items as margarine, coffee, salad dressing, and sugar).

Table 2 clearly indicates that the cost of comparable items in these three categories is consistently higher in the ghetto area than in

Table 2. Percentage by which prices are higher (lower) in ghetto versus nonghetto area

Product group	Ma and Pa	Chain	All Stores
Comparable product groups			
Cereal and bakery	6.0%	1.3%	3.7%
Canned fruits and vegetables	9.0%	0.3%	4.6%
Other foods	10.1%	1.5%	5.8%
Non-comparable product groups			
Meat, poultry, and fish	(11.5%)	(3.2%)	(7.4%)
Produce	(10.6%)	(6.5%)	(8.6%)
Dairy product			
Dairy	2.6%	0.9%	1.7%

the nonghetto area.[11] The greatest difference in cost to the consumer can be traced to higher prices charged by the Ma and Pa outlets in Watts.

In two other categories, meat and produce, the items were not comparable because of major differences in brand, grade, or size. Table 2 also indicates that, in contrast to the preceding findings, prices for meat and produce are lower in Watts than in Culver City. Again, the greatest cost differential is attributable to the Ma and Pa outlets.

Finally as seen from Table 2, dairy goods were priced slightly higher in Watts than in Culver City, with the major price differential traceable to the Ma and Pa outlets.

Discussion

This section will discuss: (1) several underlying causes for the evident price discrepancies, (2) the CPI as a vehicle for judging and comparing prices in ghetto versus nonghetto areas, and (3) the possible significance of consumer shopping behavior in terms of the conclusions.

Two hypotheses on price discrepancies

The following are two major and identifiable factors that might be directly related to price discrepancies evident in the data: (1) insurance rates and (2) pilferage.

Because of the 1965 Watts riots, insurance policies carried by proprietors were either cancelled or the rates raised. Hence, to protect against possible catastrophic losses, some proprietors attempt to compensate for the unusually high casualty risk by charging higher prices. Economically, such action is logical and rational, although at the same time it may appear unsympathetic or even inhuman.

Similarly, the ghetto proprietors' attempts to cover losses from pilferage can also be viewed as economically rational. Pilferage is an increasing problem for business in general, but to the ghetto merchant it represents a battle for survival. During this study, the interviewers personally observed blatant examples of pilferage. In some cases the proprietors themselves brought the act to the interviewer's attention and indicated that they knew many of the offenders but chose not to take action to avoid possible retaliation.

Other reasons that may contribute to the higher cost of food items

---

[11] Individual items vary widely but the exception can be found as always.

are unsatisfactory collection on credit accounts [12] and poor management. The first is probably not a major factor since it is estimated that less than 10% of sales volume is transacted on credit. The last factor, however, may well be significant. Research indicates that the majority of ghetto businesses are owned by men and women who were pushed into ownership by retirement, unemployment, fear of unemployment, disability, etc. It is also evident that many proprietors have given little thought to such vital factors as store location, retail operating principles, or even the kind of business for which they are personally best qualified to run.[13]

Item quality

Disparity in the quality of meat and fresh produce offered in the two areas was a major concern in the study. These items, representing approximately two-fifths of the total market basket cost, vary widely in comparability. Freshness, grade or cut are both difficult to determine and hard to hold constant.

In general, Culver City stores carried choice meats, but Watts stores typically featured commercial grades. Meat carried in the Culver City stores was fresh smelling and attractively displayed; that featured in the Watts stores was too often "green," i.e., meat appeared brown and aged, and was poorly displayed. Although the selection offered in nonghetto stores was varied, that in the ghetto stores was generally limited.

Similarly, produce in the Watts stores appeared to be of lower quality than that in the Culver City stores. Apples, oranges, grapefruit, and tomatoes, for example, were smaller. Vegetables and fruits were shriveled and bruised. Flies were also observed around unsprayed produce sections of the Watts stores. These conditions serve to confirm the BLS study, which reported that "stores located in the low income areas tend to be somewhat less orderly and clean than those located in higher income areas, and meats and produce do not appear as fresh." [14]

---

[12] The number of stores offering credit and the incidence of unsatisfactory collection on credit accounts were not investigated.

[13] See Burton H. Marcus and Don Spyrison, "The School of Business and Poverty Area Businessmen," Unpublished paper, Fall, 1968; C. Wilford White, "Can the Small Smalls Be Saved?", *Advanced Management Journal,* 31 (January, 1966), 34–41.

[14] Goodman, *op. cit.*

Thus, although prices were lower in the ghetto area, the quality appeared to be disproportionately lower. Hence, the relative price based on a price/quality comparison would indicate that the ghetto shoppers were actually paying a high price for the food obtained. This factor increases the magnitude of the discrepancies in price between areas and highlights the distortion in the derived overall statistic based on all foods.

Market basket

Finally, the items that constituted the contents of the market basket for the comparison study, which of course were the same as those used to calculate the CPI, deserve special attention. The market baskets of nonghetto and various cultural ghetto areas may vary significantly enough to justify inclusion of different items in any calculation for comparative costs. For instance, prices of expensive cuts of meat in poverty areas may be meaningless. Inclusion of pig's feet, pig's knuckles, chitterlings, beans, chilies, etc., however, not only may be appropriate, but may also lead to different conclusions. In this respect, both this and the BLS study contain weaknesses, since they only investigated items included in the CPI market basket. The BLS study included a sample of 18 foods; this study included 86 items—all except a few seasonal items not available for pricing.

The *real* difference in the cost of dissimilar but actual cultural market baskets of food items may be less (or more) than the *measured* difference in cost when identical but inappropriate baskets are used.

Consumer shopping behavior

It was noted in the findings that major price differences were attributable to the Ma and Pa outlets. The extent to which these outlets reflect actual higher costs depends on the shopping behavior of ghetto dwellers. If consumers only shop at the Ma and Pa stores for emergency items or if only a small percentage of the ghetto dwellers regularly shop at these stores, the importance of the price differential is less. If a large proportion of ghetto dwellers shop outside their immediate area, the significance of the differential also diminishes. This would be consistent with Goodman's findings [15] which indicate that ghetto dwellers do much of their shopping outside their immediate area.

[15] Goodman, *op. cit.*

Conclusions

This study once again points to the conclusion that the poor pay more. Although theoretically the hypothesis was not disproven (i.e., the statistic for all foods combined did not indicate that ghetto dwellers paid more than nonghetto dwellers), analysis by product group with a quality factor considered highlighted the inappropriateness of conclusions drawn from aggregate comparisons.

The degree to which ghetto dwellers pay more, the market basket used to determine relative costs, the reasons for price differentials, and consumer shopping behavior should be considered in evaluating the findings. This study indicates that the additional amount paid for food by Watts ghetto dwellers does not appear to be as great as that indicated for durable items by other researchers.

This author believes the time has come to shift emphasis. Questions that should concern future investigators include:

Are price differentials justified?

What are their underlying causes?

How can inequities be rectified?

C. Possibilities for Solution

30. Better Deal for Ghetto Shoppers

Frederick D. Sturdivant

However remote and unreal the newspaper photos of large numbers of looters carrying furniture, groceries, appliances, and other merchandise through the streets of many of this nation's major cities may seem, their message for U.S. business is profound. "Such poverty as we have today in all our great cities degrades the poor," warned George Bernard Shaw in 1928, "and infects with its degradation the whole neighborhood in which they live. And whatever can degrade a neighborhood can degrade a country and a continent and finally the whole civilized world . . ." [1]

Over the past few years an epidemic of this contagious disease has struck with great violence in Los Angeles, New York, Rochester, Chicago, San Francisco, Newark, Detroit, and other large U.S. cities. There is the threat of more riots to come. A major share of the responsibility for halting the epidemic and preventing further assaults on the structure of society rests with the business community.

No informed citizen questions the presence of large numbers of people living in poverty in the United States. Indeed, most Americans

[1] *The Intelligent Women's Guide to Socialism and Capitalism,* Garden City, New York: Garden City Publishing Co., Inc., 1928, page 42.

Author's note: The research for this study was partially supported by a National Defense Education Act grant and funds provided by the University of Southern California Research Institute for Business and Economics.

have tired of the debate which attempts to quantify and measure a state of existence that is too qualitative and miserable to be measured precisely. Many companies have participated in private and governmental programs by hiring and training individuals from disadvantaged areas.[2] In fact, efforts to deal with the dilemma of the underskilled and unemployed have represented the major thrust of the business community's commitment. In some areas of high unemployment such programs have led to significant improvements in local conditions.

While few would question the importance of training and employing the disadvantaged, a fundamental point is generally ignored. *The most direct contact between the poor and the business community is at retail level.* The greatest opportunity to assist and to revolutionize the daily lives of the poor rests in the retailing communities serving poverty areas.

While it is a great step forward to create jobs for the unemployed or to train men for better-paying jobs, such improvements can be nullified when the worker and members of his family enter the marketplace as consumers. Very little may be gained if they are confronted with a shopping situation that generally offers them higher prices, inferior merchandise, high-pressure selling, hidden and inflated interest charges, and a degrading shopping environment. Such conditions are closely related to the frustrations that have produced the spectacle of looted and burned stores throughout the nation.

A Tale of Two Ghettos

The first of the terribly destructive and bloody Negro riots took place in the south central section of Los Angeles in August 1965. In the aftermath of the nearly week-long Watts riots, which seemed to set the pattern for subsequent revolts around the country, it was apparent that retail establishments had been the primary target of the rioters. Of the more than 600 buildings damaged by looting and fire, over 95% were retail stores. According to the report of the Governor's Commission on the Los Angeles Riots, "The rioters concentrated primarily on food markets, liquor stores, furniture stores, department stores, and pawnshops." [3]

---

[2] See Alfonso J. Cervantes, "To Prevent a Chain of Super-Watts," *Harvard Business Review* (September–October 1967), 55.

[3] The Governor's Commission on the Los Angeles Riots, *Violence in the City—An End or a Beginning?* (Los Angeles, December 1965), 23–24.

Manufacturing firms and other kinds of business facilities in the area, which in many cases contained valuable merchandise and fixtures, were virtually untouched, as were public buildings such as schools, libraries, and churches. Not one of the 26 Operation Head Start facilities in the Watts area was touched.

Even a cursory survey of the damage would indicate that a "vengeance pattern" might have been followed. The various news media covering the riots reported many interviews which revealed a deep-seated resentment toward retailers because of alleged exploitation. The possibility that the rioters were striking back at unethical merchants was reinforced by the fact that one store would be looted and burned while a competing unit across the street survived without so much as a cracked window.

In the fall of 1965, facts and questions like these prompted a two-year study of consumer-business relations in two disadvantaged sections of Los Angeles:

1. As the center of the Los Angeles riots, Watts was an excellent place to begin the study. Consumers and merchants were very willing to discuss their experiences and to explore the causes of the riots. Civil rights groups and merchants' organizations were eager to cooperate with an "objective" research effort which would vindicate their respective points of view. In effect, there were a number of advantages in studying the conditions in Watts while the rubble still littered the streets and participants in the destruction were seeking to be heard.

2. But Watts by itself was not sufficient for an objective investigation. The basic retail structure of the area had been virtually destroyed, and it was impossible to contact many of the merchants who had been burned out by the rioters. In addition, feelings were so intense on both sides that the danger of distortion was greatly magnified. Since the population of the area was heavily Negro, the investigation might have become a study of exploitation of this minority rather than an analysis of the relations between business and the poor in general. Therefore, a second study area was selected—a disadvantaged section of the Mexican-American community in east Los Angeles.

In each area, more than 25% of the population fell below the government's $3,000 poverty line. In addition, each area had high unemployment (7.7% for Mexican-Americans and 10.1% for Negroes), a high incidence of broken homes (17.2% for Mexican-

Americans and 25.5% for Negroes), and the many other household and community characteristics which are associated with ghettos.[4]

Over a period of two years, more than 2,000 interviews were held with consumers and merchants in these two poverty areas, numerous shopping forays were conducted, and price-quality comparisons were made with stores serving the more prosperous sections of Los Angeles and surrounding communities. Although there were a number of interesting differences between the findings in the two areas (the differences were based for the most part on cultural factors), the evidence points to two basic flaws in local retailing which were present in each of the areas:

1. The prevalence of small, inefficient, uneconomical units.
2. A tendency on the part of many stores to prey on an undereducated and relatively immobile population with high-pressure, unethical methods.

These findings, I believe, apply rather generally to the retail segments serving disadvantaged areas in U.S. cities. Let us look at each of them in more detail.

Inefficient "Moms and Pops"

One of the cruelest ironies of our economic system is that the disadvantaged are generally served by the least efficient segments of the business community. The spacious, well-stocked, and efficiently managed stores characteristic of America's highly advanced distribution system are rarely present in the ghetto. The marvels of mass merchandising and its benefits for consumers normally are not shared with the low-income families. Instead, their shopping districts are dotted with small, inefficient "mom and pop" establishments more closely related to stores in underdeveloped countries than to the sophisticated network of retail institutions dominant in most of the U.S. economy.

With the exception of one outdated supermarket, no national or regional retailing firms were represented on the main street of Watts before the 1965 riots. Following the riots, when 103rd Street was

---

[4] California Department of Industrial Relations, *Negroes and Mexican-Americans in South and East Los Angeles* (San Francisco, July 1966); these data understate both the income and unemployment problems since they cover the entire area and not just the poorest sections analyzed in this study.

dubbed "Charcoal Alley," not even that lone supermarket remained. On Brooklyn Avenue, the heart of the poorest section in east Los Angeles, one found such establishments as Factory Outlet Shoes, Nat's Clothing, Cruz Used Furniture, Villa Real Drugs, and Chelos Market, ranging in size from 315 square feet to 600 square feet. Of the 175 stores in the shopping district (this figure excluded service stations), only five were members of chain organizations, and two of these firms traced their origins back to a time when the neighborhood was a middle-class district.

Lacking economies of scale and the advantages of trained management, the "moms and pops" muddle through from day to day and, in the process, contribute to the oppressive atmosphere of such neighborhoods. Their customers generally pay higher prices, receive lower-quality merchandise, and shop in shabby, deteriorating facilities.

Inflated prices and . . .

The most controversial of these conditions is pricing. The phrase, "the poor pay more," was popularized by Columbia University sociologist David Caplovitz's widely read book with that title.[5] Unfortunately, in addition to being an eye-catching title, it describes reality. While the small, owner-operated stores do not have a monopoly on high prices in the ghetto, they contribute significantly to the inflated price levels. Consumers in Watts, for example, can expect to pay from 7% to 21% more for a market basket of 30 items if they shop for groceries in one of the small local stores than would a family shopping in a supermarket in affluent Beverly Hills. Similar or even greater price differentials prevail in most merchandising categories.

Comparative pricing analyses of the disadvantaged area and the more prosperous sections in a city are very difficult to make because of quality differences. When national brands are carried by a ghetto appliance dealer, for example, he generally stocks only the lower end of the line. Retailers in higher income areas usually concentrate on the middle and upper price ranges of the product line. Furthermore, off-brand merchandise tends to make up a substantial part of the ghetto dealer's line. Since these lines are not carried in other areas, direct price comparisons are impossible. In food stores, the problem is particularly acute with respect to meat and produce items. Commercial

---

[5] David Caplovitz, *The Poor Pay More,* New York: The Free Press of Glencoe, 1963.

grades of meat are generally carried by ghetto stores, and visual comparisons reveal major qualitative differences in the produce carried, but precise measurements of these quality distinctions are impossible.

Depressed looks

The physical setting also does little to enhance ghetto shopping. Resentment over the appearance of stores is deeply felt in Watts. I have encountered many reactions like these:

"The manager of that grocery store must think we are a bunch of animals," charged one middle-aged Negro woman with whom I talked. She continued, "The floors are filthy, there are flies all over the place, they handle our food with dirty hands and never say thank you or nothing that's nice."

Commenting on the shabby appearance of the stores on 103rd Street, one young Negro activist said, "The merchants don't give a damn about Watts. They take our money back to Beverly Hills and never spend a cent fixing up their stores."

While such charges are influenced by emotion, the reasons for the bitterness become understandable when one takes a walk down "Charcoal Alley" with its many vacant lots, one dozen or so vacant stores, two thrift shops, six liquor stores, one dime store, one drugstore, one pawnshop, one record shop, one appliance-dry goods store, and a few bars. Although the number and variety of stores along Brooklyn Avenue in east Los Angeles is greater, 53% of the stores are more than 20 years old and have had no apparent improvements made since their construction. Of these stores, 6% are in obvious need of extensive repair and remodeling.

Parasitic Merchants

While the deteriorated condition of shopping facilities obviously does little to attract shoppers from outside the area, the ghettos do act as magnets for high-pressure and unethical merchandisers who become parasites on the neighborhoods. Take New York, for example. Because of the predominance of parasitic merchants in the ghettos of Manhattan, Caplovitz describes business communities there as "deviant" market systems "in which unethical and illegal practices abound." [6]

The parasitic merchant usually deals in hard goods and emphasizes

[6] Ibid., p. 180.

Table 1. Ghetto shoppers pay more for appliances

Product	Watts area	Prices East L.A. area	Control area
1. Zenith portable TV (X1910)	$170	—	$130
2. Olympic portable TV (9P46)	$270	$230	—
3. RCA portable TV (AH0668)	$148	—	$115
4. Zenith portable TV (X2014)	—	$208	$140
5. Emerson portable TV (19P32)	$210	$200	$170
6. Olympic color console TV (CC337A)	—	$700	$630
7. Zenith clock radio (X164)	—	$42	$19
8. Eureka vacuum (745a)	—	$35	$30
9. Fun Fare by Brown (36" free standing gas range)	—	$200	$110

Note: Prices for items 1–4 are averages computed from the shopping experiences of three couples (Mexican-American, Negro, and Anglo-White) in three stores in each of the three areas. The three couples had nearly identical "credit profiles" based on typical disadvantaged family characteristics. The stores located in the Mexican-American and Watts areas were selected on the basis of shopping patterns derived from extensive interviews in the areas.

Items 5–9 are the only prices obtainable on a 24-item shopping list. One low-income Anglo-White couple shopped 24 randomly selected stores in the disadvantaged areas.

All prices are rounded.

"easy credit." He stocks his store with off-brand merchandise, uses bait-switch advertising, offers low down payments and small installments, employs salesmen who are proficient at closing often and fast, and marks up his merchandise generously enough to assure himself of a very good return for his effort. Again, direct price comparisons are difficult because of brand differences, but Table 1 reflects the higher prices paid by ghetto shoppers compared with store prices in a middle to lower-middle class suburb of Los Angeles.

Data gathered on markups further confirm the presence of exploitation. The major furniture store serving the Watts area and its unaffiliated counterpart in east Los Angeles both carried Olympic television model 9P46. This model wholesales for $104. The retail price in the Watts area store was $270, a markup of 160%, and $229.95 in east Los Angeles, a markup of 121%. The latter store also carried a Zenith model number X1917 priced at $269.95, or 114% above the wholesale price of $126.

Are such substantial markups justified because of the higher risks associated with doing business in a ghetto? It would seem that such risks are more than offset by the interest charges on the installment contract. The rates are highly volatile, but never low. A Mexican-American couple and a Negro couple with virtually the same "credit profile" shopped a number of furniture and appliance stores in the two disadvantaged areas as well as stores in the middle-class control area. An "easy payment" establishment serving south central Los Angeles applied the same high-pressure tactics to both couples, who shopped for the same television set. The retailer charged the Negro couple 49% interest on an 18-month contract, while the Mexican-American couple really received "easy terms"—82% interest for 18 months!

Charges of this magnitude go well beyond any question of ethics; they are clearly illegal. In California, the Unruh Retail Installment Sales Act sets the maximum rate a dealer may charge on time contracts. For most installment contracts under $1,000, the maximum service charge rate is five-sixths of 1% of the original unpaid balance multiplied by the number of months in the contract. Accordingly, the legal rate for the television set selected by the two couples was 15%.

While it is true that most ghetto merchants do not exceed the legal limits, their customers still pay higher credit charges because of the inflated selling prices on which the interest is computed.

How they get away with it

Parasitic merchants are attracted to disadvantaged areas of the cities by the presence of ill-informed and generally immobile consumers. Operating from ghetto stores or as door-to-door credit salesmen, these merchants deal with consumers who have little understanding of contracts or even of the concept of interest. Given their low-income status, one dollar down and one dollar a week sounds to the buyer like a pretty good deal. The merchants are not at all reluctant to pile their good deals on their customers with the prospect of repossessions and garnishments.

Comparative shopping outside his own neighborhood would, of course, provide a ghetto resident with a vivid demonstration of the disadvantages of trading with the local merchants. Unfortunately, the idea of comparing prices and credit terms is little understood in the ghetto. And for those residents who can appreciate the advantages of comparative shopping, transportation is often a barrier. In Watts, less than half of the households studied had automobiles. The public transportation facilities, which are inadequate at best throughout the city of Los Angeles, are archaic. Infrequently scheduled, time-consuming, and expensive bus services are of little value to the area's shoppers.

In east Los Angeles, the Mexican-Americans have greater mobility; 73% of the households studied had an automobile, and bus services were better than in Watts. The Mexican-Americans also have relative proximity to modern shopping facilities. However, there are strong cultural ties that encourage residents to forgo shopping advantages offered in other areas. They choose, in effect, to be reinforced continually in the existing cultural setting by frequenting stores in the disadvantaged area where Spanish is spoken. Whether for reasons of transportation problems or self-imposed cultural isolation, the local merchant enjoys a largely captive market.

Shunning Depressed Areas

Not all merchants in disadvantaged areas are there for the purpose of exacting all they can from a neighborhood of undereducated and poor consumers. As noted before, many of the small shops offer their customers higher prices and lower quality because of inefficiency, not by design. The great villain, say the retailers, is the cost of doing business in disadvantaged areas. For example, it is said that small merchants normally cannot afford insurance protection. Of the merchants interviewed in Watts, fewer than 10% had insurance before the riots. Retailers in slum areas have always paid higher insurance rates. According to California's insurance commissioner, rate increases of 300% following the riots were not uncommon. In this respect, the riots throughout the country have only magnified the problem of good retail service, not relieved it.

Since so few small merchants attempt to insure their businesses, the major effect of the abnormally high rates is to deter larger organizations from investing in ghetto areas. An executive responsible for corporate planning for a retail chain would be hard pressed to justify

building a unit in Watts or east Los Angeles when so many opportunities and excellent sites are available in fast growing and "safe"
Orange County (in the Los Angeles area). A parallel could be drawn
with building in the South Side of Chicago as opposed to the prosperous and rapidly expanding suburbs on the North Shore, or in
virtually any central city slum area contrasted with the same city's
suburbs. Large retailers not only are frightened away by insurance
costs, but also point to personnel problems, vandalism, and alleged
higher incidences of shoplifting in disadvantaged districts.

This is not to suggest that there are not profits to be made in such
areas. Trade sources, especially in the supermarket industry, have
pointed to unique opportunities in low-income neighborhoods.[7] The
managements of supermarket chains such as Hillman's in Chicago and
ABC Markets in Los Angeles admit that, while there are unique merchandising problems associated with doing business in depressed areas,
their profit return has been quite satisfactory. It might also be noted
that companies that do a conscientious job of serving the needs of low-
income consumers are highly regarded. For instance, interviewees in
Watts were virtually unanimous in their praise for ABC Markets.
Perhaps the most dramatic affirmation of the chain's position in the
community came during the riots: not one of the company's three units
in the area was disturbed during the week-long riots.

My interviews with executives of Sears, Roebuck and Co. and
J. C. Penney indicate that these companies have been highly successful
in adapting to changing conditions in transitional areas. Those of their
stores located in declining neighborhoods have altered their merchandising programs and the composition of their work forces to adjust to
the changing nature of the market area. The result has been profits for
both firms.

Yet, in most cases, such opportunities have not been sought out by
large retailers, but stumbled on; they have been happily discovered by
older stores trying to readapt themselves in areas where the racial and
economic markup is changing. New stores are built only in trading
areas where the more traditional competitive challenges are to be
found. As one executive said, "Our target is the mass market, and we
generally ignore the upper 10 per cent and the lower 15 per cent to
20 percent of the market." The upper 10%, of course, can be assured

[7] See, for example, "Supermarkets in Urban Areas," *Food Topics* (February
1967), 10–22.

that Saks Fifth Avenue, Brooks Brothers, and a host of other such firms stand ready to meet their needs. The poor, however, are left with "moms and pops" and the easy-credit merchants.

A Workable Solution

Most critics of business-consumer relations in disadvantaged areas have called for legislation designed to protect consumers and for consumer education programs. Indeed, laws designed to protect consumers from hidden and inflated interest charges and other forms of unethical merchandising should be passed and vigorously enforced. Consumer economics should be a part of elementary and secondary school curricula, and adult education programs should be available in disadvantaged areas. However, these approaches are hardly revolutionary, and they hold little promise of producing dramatic changes in the economic condition of the disadvantaged.

A crucial point seems to have been largely ignored by the critics and in the various bills introduced in the state legislatures and in Congress. This is the difficulty of improvement so long as the retailing segments of depressed areas are dominated by uneconomically small stores—by what I call an "atomistic" structure. Indeed, many legislators seem eager to perpetuate the system by calling for expanded activities by the Small Business Administration in offering assistance to more small firms that do business in the ghettos. Another common suggestion is for the Federal Government to offer low-cost insurance protection to these firms. This proposal, too, may do more to aggravate than relieve. If the plight of the ghetto consumer is to be dramatically relieved, this will not come about through measures designed to multiply the number of inefficient retailers serving these people.

Real progress will come only if we can find some way to extend into the ghettos the highly advanced, competitive retailing system that has so successfully served other sectors of the economy. To make this advance possible, we must remove the economic barriers that restrict entry by progressive retailers, for stores are managed by businessmen, not social workers.

How can these barriers be removed?

Investment Guarantee Plan

Since shortly after the close of World War II, the Federal Government has had a program designed to eliminate certain barriers to investment by U.S. corporations in underdeveloped countries. In effect, the government has said that it is in the best interests of the United States if our business assists in the economic development of certain foreign countries. In a number of Latin American countries, for instance, the program has protected U.S. capital against loss through riots or expropriation. The investment guarantee program does not assure U.S. firms of a profit; that challenge rests with management. But companies are protected against the abnormal risks associated with building facilities in underdeveloped countries. If a guarantee program can stimulate investment in Colombia, why not in Watts or Harlem?

I propose a program, to be administered by the Department of Commerce, under which potential retail investors would be offered investment guarantees for building (or buying) a store in areas designated as "disadvantaged." A contract between the retail firm and the Commerce Department would guarantee the company full reimbursement for physical losses resulting from looting, burning, or other damages caused by civil disorders as well as from the usual hazards of natural disasters. In addition, the contract would call for compensation for operating losses sustained during periods of civil unrest in the area. To illustrate:

A Montgomery Ward store established in the heart of Watts would, under this program, be insured for the book value of the establishment against damages caused by natural or human events. If the firm emerged from a period of rioting without suffering any physical damages, but was forced to cease operations during the period of the riots, Montgomery Ward would be compensated for operating losses resulting from the forced closure.

The costs to a company for an investment guarantee would be minimal in terms of both financial outlay and loss of managerial autonomy. An annual fee of 0.5% of the amount of insured assets would be charged. There is no actuarial basis for this rate; rather, the fees are charged to cover the costs of administering the program and building a reserve against possible claims.

There would be no restriction on either the size of the investment or the term of the guarantee contract. The contract would be terminated by the Government only if the firm violated the terms of the agreement or if the economic character of the area improved to the point that it was no longer classified as disadvantaged.

In addition to paying annual premiums, the participating companies would be required to conform to state and local laws designed to protect consumers (or minimum Federal standards where local legislation is not in effect). A participating retailer found guilty of violating state law regarding, let us say, installment charges would have his contract terminated.

In effect, the ethical merchandiser would find no restrictions on his usual managerial freedom. So long as he abided by the law, his investment would be protected, and he would have complete freedom in selecting his merchandise, setting prices, advertising, and other areas of managerial strategy.

Enlarged investment credit

The guarantee program would offer the manager maximum discretion, but it would not assure him of a profit. The guarantee phase of the program merely attempts to place the ghetto on a par with nonghetto areas with respect to investment risk. The final barrier, the high costs associated with doing business in such areas, would have to be offset by offering businesses investment credits. Credits of perhaps 10% (as compared to the former 7% under other programs) could be offered as an inducement to outside retailers. Firms participating in the guarantee program would be eligible for such investment credits on all facilities constructed in disadvantaged areas.

The more generous investment credits would serve as a source of encouragement not only for building new facilities, but also for expanding and modernizing older stores that had been allowed to decline. For example, the Sears Roebuck and Penney stores located (as earlier mentioned) in transitional and declining areas would be likely targets for physical improvements.

Key to transformation

Perhaps the most important characteristic of the investment guarantee and credit program is the nature of the relationship that would exist between the Government and the business community. The Government is cast in the role of the stimulator or enabler without becoming involved in the management of the private company. The program is also flexible in that incentives could be increased or lowered as conditions warrant. If the investment credits should fail to provide a sufficient stimulus, additional incentives in the form of lower corporate income tax rates could be added. On the other hand, as an area becomes increasingly attractive as a retail location, the incentives could be reduced or eliminated.

If implemented with vigor and imagination, this program could lead to a dramatic transformation of the retail segment serving ghetto areas. While size restrictions would not be imposed, the provisions of the program would be most attractive to larger retail organizations. Thus, the "atomistic" structure of the retail community would undergo major changes as the marginal retailers face competition with efficient mass distributors. The parasitic merchants would also face a bleak future. The study in Los Angeles revealed no instance in which a major retail firm was guilty of discriminatory pricing or inflated credit charges. In addition, the agency administering the investment program could make periodic studies of the practices of participating firms, and use these investigations to prod companies, if necessary, to assure their customer of equitable treatment.

Conclusion

No one program will solve a problem as basic and complex as that of the big-city ghetto. A variety of projects and measures is needed. While the program I propose has great potential, its promise is more likely to be realized if it is supported by other kinds of action to strengthen local businesses. For instance:

Various "activist" groups have been bringing pressure on unethical retailers. In Watts, some limited efforts have been made to boycott retailers who do not conform to a code of conduct that has been promulgated. In Washington, D.C., a militant civil rights organization, ACT, has launched a national campaign to encourage bankruptcy filings by the poor in order to deal a severe blow to parasitic retailers.

In Roxbury, Massachusetts (a part of Boston), Negroes are organizing buying cooperatives. Such cooperatives have limited potential, but many people believe they can compensate for at least some of the problems of smallness and inefficiency which plague "mom and pop" stores in the area.

Some corporate executives are trying to help Negro businessmen develop managerial knowhow. Business school students have recently got into this act, too. A group of second-year students at the Harvard Business School, with the financial backing of The Ford Foundation, is providing free advice and instruction to Negroes running retail stores and other firms in Boston. The instruction covers such basic matters as purchasing, bookkeeping, credit policy, tax reporting, and pricing.

Some large stores are reportedly considering giving franchises to retailers in ghetto areas. Assuming the franchises are accompanied by management asistance, financial help, and other advantages of a tie-in with a large company, this step could help to strengthen a number of local retailers.

Some of the large-scale renewal projects undertaken by business have, as a secondary benefit, introduced residents of run-down areas to progressive retailing. In the 1950's, a 100-acre slum section of south Chicago was razed and turned into a 2,009-apartment community with a shopping center. In the shopping center were branches of various well-known organizations—Goldblatt's Department Store, Jewel Tea Supermarket, Walgreen Drug Stores, and others. Similarly, if a group of Tampa business leaders succeed in current plans to rebuild part of Tampa's downtown business district, such leading stores as Macy's, Jordan Marsh, Bon Marché, and Sears, Roebuck plan to open branches in the new buildings. In both cases, residents of the poor areas adjoining the shopping sections would be able to take advantage of progressive retailing. Projects like the foregoing would be welcome allies of the program proposed in this article. For this program, despite its many great advantages, will not be easy to carry out. The major retailers attracted to disadvantaged areas will face many challenges. Studies will have to be undertaken to help them adapt successfully to local conditions. Creative and imaginative managers will be needed at the store level.

The new program should be good for retailers from the standpoint of profits. In addition, retail leaders should derive a great deal of satisfaction from demonstrating that U.S. enterprise is capable of contributing significantly to the solution of the major domestic crisis of the twentieth century. An efficient and competitive retail community in a ghetto would certainly discourage ineffective and unethical store managers in the area. And while the new program would not solve all of the problems of the nation's cities, it could do a great deal to reduce the injustices suffered by the poor and to eliminate the bitterness that feeds the spreading civil disorders.

Reference Bibliography

After experiencing considerable difficulty in locating materials for this book, we concluded that there was a need to bring together and classify the disparate sources explored. Hopefully, this will permit the reader with a strong interest in one aspect of consumerism to become conversant with that area with a minimum of search effort.

Materials were included only if they showed promise of general and lasting value, and were not too shrill or chauvinistic in approach. There was also a bias toward interpretative materials that placed the topic of discussion in a larger context. These criteria excluded a number of good but narrowly technical articles from law and economics sources. To locate these articles we particularly suggest the *Law Periodical Index* or the bibliography in *The Law and the Low Income Consumer* by Carol Katz (New York: New York University Press, 1968). Also excluded were articles on "How to become a better consumer or financial planner." The best guide to this material is the *Consumer Education Bibliography* prepared for the President's Committee on Consumer Interest and issued in April 1969 by the Superintendent of Documents (Washington: U.S. Government Printing Office). Other bibliographies and sources which we found helpful were the U.S. Department of Commerce

(Business and Defense Services Administration), *Bibliography on Marketing to Low Income Consumers,* which is available from the U.S. Government Printing Office, and *The Consumer Interest* by John Martin and George Smith (London: Pall Mall Press, 1968). The latter is a useful guide to international sources.

Consumerism is a volatile area which sees action on one or more fronts almost daily. For those who wish to keep abreast of current events we particularly recommend the following periodicals: *Consumer Reports, Consumer Bulletin, U.S. Consumer, Advertising Age,* and *Business Week.* For information on Government actions the *Congressional Quarterly* and *Of Consuming Interest* are very useful. Because the material from these sources has a very short life it has not been included in this reference bibliography.

Finally, we have not included articles on consumer motives, decision processes, and information processing capabilities from the rapidly growing consumer behavior literature. Nonetheless we feel that this work has much long-term potential for expanding our understanding of the basic issues, even though it may seem rather remote at the present. For those interested in pursuing this connection we recommend the following references:

Steuart Henderson Britt, *Consumer Behavior and the Behavioral Sciences,* New York: Wiley, 1966.
James F. Engel, David T. Kollat and Roger D. Blackwell, *Consumer Behavior,* New York: Holt, Rinehart, 1968.
John A. Howard and Jagdish N. Sheth, *The Theory of Buyer Behavior,* New York: Wiley, 1969.
Harold Kassarjian and Thomas S. Robertson, *Perspectives in Consumer Behavior,* Glenview: Scott, Foresman, 1968.
Joseph W. Newman, *On Knowing the Consumer,* New York: Wiley, 1966.

The classification system used in this bibliography is consistent with the overall organization of the book.

Part One

The Scope of the Problem

American Trial Lawyers Association, *An In-Depth Study of Consumer Protection* (1966 Annual Seminar, Kansas City), Omaha, Nebraska: Woodbury-Woodbury, 1966.

Barber, Richard J., "Government and the Consumer," *Michigan Law Review*, 64 (May, 1966), 1203.

Baum, Daniel J., "The Consumer and the Federal Trade Commission," *Journal of Urban Law*, 44 (Fall, 1966), 71.

Bell, Carolyn S., *Consumer Choice in the American Economy*, New York: Random House, 1967.

Bell, Carolyn S., "Consumer Economic Power," *Journal of Consumer Affairs*, 2 (1968).

Borrie, Gordon J., and Aubrey L. Diamond, *The Consumer, Society and the Law*, London: MacGibbon and Kee, 1966.

Britt, Steuart H., *The Spenders*, New York: McGraw-Hill, 1960.

Campbell, Persia Crawford, *The Consumer Interest: A Study in Consumer Economics*, New York: Harper, 1949.

Chase, Stuart and Frederick Schlink, *Your Money's Worth: A Study in the Waste of the Consumer's Dollar*, New York: Macmillan, 1927.

Clasen, Earl A., "Market Ethics and the Consumer," *Harvard Business Review*, 45 (January, 1967), 79.

Collazzo, Charles J., *Consumer Attitudes and Frustrations in Shopping*, New York: Retail Research Institute, 1965.

Comment, "The Consumer in the Marketplace—A Survey of the Law of the Informed Buyer," *Notre Dame Lawyer*, 38 (1963), 555.

Comment, "Need for Protection of the Consumer of Services," *Buffalo Law Review*, 18 (1968–1969), 173.

Congress and Consumer Protection Proposals, Washington: Congressional Digest Corporation, March 1968.

Consumer Advisory Council, *Consumer Issues '66: A Report to the President from the Consumer Advisory Council*, Washington, D.C.: Government Printing Office, 1966.

"Consumer Protection Symposium," *Ohio State Law Journal*, 29 (Summer, 1968), 593.

Consumer Union, *Consumer Education in Lincoln High School*, Mount Vernon, New York: Consumers Union, 1965.

Consumer Rights: A World View, The Hague, Holland: International Organization of Consumers Unions, 1968.

408

Reference Bibliography

Coston, Dean W., "The Role of the Department of Health, Education, and Welfare," *Food, Drug, Cosmetic Law Journal*, 22 (June, 1967), 336.

Crown, Paul, *Legal Protection for the Consumer*, New York: Oceana, 1963.

Denenberg, "Insurance Regulation: The Search for Countervailing Power and Consumer Protection," *Insurance Law Journal*, 69 (May, 1969), 27.

Dervin, Brenda, *The Spender Syndrome* (Case Studies of 68 Families and Their Consumer Problems), Madison: University of Wisconsin Center for Consumer Affairs, 1965.

Dichter, Ernest, *The Strategy of Desire*, Garden City: Doubleday, 1960.

Directory of Government Agencies Safeguarding Consumer and Environment, Alexandria, Virginia: Serina Press, 1968.

East, Marjorie, *Consumer Education for Family Life*, Washington, D.C.: National Education Association, Department of Home Economics, 1962.

Fargis, Paul M. (editor), *The Consumers' Handbook*, New York: Hawthorn Books, 1967.

Federal Trade Commission, *Report on District of Columbia Consumer Protection Program*, Washington: U.S. Government Printing Office, 1967.

Fitzsimmons, Cleo, *Consumer Buying for Better Living*, New York: John Wiley & Sons, 1961.

Foote, W. E., "The Department of Consumers," *Vanderbilt Law Review*, 20 (October, 1967), 969.

Fulop, Christina, *Consumers in the Market*, London: Institute for Economic Affairs, 1967.

Fulop, Christina, *Competition for Consumers*, New York: Transatlantic Arts, 1965.

Furness, Betty, "Responsibility in Marketing," from a speech given at the AMA Conference, Washington, D.C., Reprinted in *Changing Marketing Systems*, Chicago: American Marketing Association, 1967, 25.

Galbraith, John Kenneth, *The Affluent Society*, Boston: Houghton Mifflin, 1958.

Galbraith, John Kenneth, *The New Industrial State*, Boston: Houghton Mifflin, 1968.

Gentry, Curt, *The Vulnerable Americans*, New York: Doubleday, 1966.

Golden, L. L., "Consumer Protection," *Saturday Review*, 51 (April 13, 1968), 93.

Gordon, Leland J., "Some Current Issues in Consumer Economics," *The Journal of Consumer Affairs*, I (Summer, 1967), 52.

Gotscall, Gale P., "Help! Help! or Why FTC Seeks Aid of the Attorneys General in Combatting Consumer Deception and Unfair Competition," Santa Fe, New Mexico: remarks before the Western Conference, National Association of Attorneys General, September 2, 1966.

A Guide to Federal Consumer Services, Washington: President's Committee on Consumer Interests, 1967.

Hamilton, David B., *The Consumer in Our Economy,* Boston: Houghton Mifflin, 1962.

Hobson, John A., *Economics and Ethics,* Boston: Heath, 1929.

Holton, Richard H., "Government-Consumer Interest: Conflicts and Prospects (The University Point of View)," *Changing Marketing Systems,* Chicago: American Marketing Association, December, 1967, 15.

Hopkinson, Thomas, "New Battleground—Consumer Interest," *Harvard Business Review* (September–October, 1964), 97–104.

Howard, Marshall, *Legal Aspects of Marketing,* New York: McGraw-Hill, 1964.

Johnson, Arno H., *The American Market of the Future,* New York: NYU Press, 1966.

Johnson, C. C., Jr., "Future of Consumer Protection," *Food, Drug, Cosmetic Law Journal,* 23 (December, 1968), 831.

Kallen, Horace M., *The Decline and Rise of the Consumer,* New York: Packard, 1946.

Koch, George W., "Government-Consumer Interest: From the Business Point of View," *Changing Marketing Systems,* Chicago: American Marketing Association, 1967, 18.

Lavidge, Robert J. and Robert J. Holloway (editors), *Marketing and Society: The Challenge,* AMA Reprint Series, Homewood, Illinois: Richard D. Irwin, 1969.

Levitt, Theodore, "Why Business Always Loses: A Marketing View of Government Relations," *Marketing for Tomorrow . . . Today,* Chicago: American Marketing Association, 1967, 14.

Margolius, Sidney, *How to Make the Most of Your Money,* New York: Appleton-Century, 1966.

Margolius, Sidney, *The Innocent Consumer vs. the Exploiters,* New York: Trident Press, 1967.

Margolius, Sidney, "Consumer Rights: the Battle Continues," *American Federationist* (April, 1967), 1.

Masters, Dexter, *The Intelligent Buyer and the Telltale Seller,* New York: Alfred A. Knopf, 1966.

Matthews, Joseph B., *Guinea Pigs No More,* New York: Conice, Friede, 1936.

McClellan, Grant S. (editor), *The Consumer Public,* New York: H. W. Wilson Company, 1968.

Nader, Ralph, "Consumer Protection and Corporate Disclosure," *Business Today* (Autumn, 1968), 20.

Nelson, J. Russell and Audrey Strickland (editors), *Ethics and Marketing* (lectures from the Cohen Symposium), Minneapolis: University of Minnesota, April, 1966.

O'Connell, John J., "Consumer Protection in the State of Washington," *State Government,* 39 (Autumn, 1966), 230.

Packard, Vance, *The Status Seekers,* New York, David McKay, 1959.

Packard, Vance, *The Waste Makers,* New York: David McKay, 1960.

Pei, Mario, *The Consumer's Manifesto*, New York: Crown Publishers, Inc., 1963.

Peterson, Esther, "Representing the Consumer Interest in the Federal Government," *Michigan Law Review*, 64 (May, 1966), 1323.

Piel, Gerard, *Consumers of Abundance*, Santa Barbara: Center for the Study of Democratic Institutions, 1961.

President's Committee on Consumer Interests, *Guide to Federal Consumer Services*, Washington, D.C.: U.S. Government Printing Office, 1967.

President's Committee on Consumer Interests, *The Most for Their Money*, Washington, D.C.: U.S. Government Printing Office, 1965.

President's Committee on Consumer Interests, *A Summary of Activities, 1964–1967*, Washington, D.C.: U.S. Government Printing Office, 1967.

Preston, Lee, *Social Issues in Marketing*, New York: Scott Foresman, 1968.

Sinclair, Upton B., *The Jungle*, New York: Heritage, 1966 (first published in 1906).

Smith, Ralph L., *The Bargain Hucksters*, New York: Thomas Crowell, 1963.

Sorenson, Helen Laura, *The Consumer Movement: What It Is and What It Means*, New York: Harper, 1941.

Starrs, J. E., "Consumer Class Action," *Boston University Law Review*, 49 (Spring, 1969), 211.

Symposium, "Consumer Protection," *Ohio State Law Journal*, 29 (Summer, 1968), 593.

Troelstrup, Arch W., *Consumer Problems and Personal Finance*, New York: McGraw-Hill, 1957.

Trump, Fred, *Buyer Beware*, New York: Abingdon Press, 1965.

Walton, Clarence C., "Ethical Theory, Societal Expectations, and Marketing Practices," *The Social Responsibilities of Marketing*, Chicago: American Marketing Association, December 1961, 7.

Weiss, E. B., "Consumerism and Marketing" (an 8-part series appearing in *Advertising Age* from May 8–July 3, 1967)—titles of the articles: "Consumerism and Comsat" (May 8), "From Caveat Emptor to Caveat Vendor" (May 15), "Pious Posturing—Marketing's Most Dangerous Posture" (May 29), "Association Programs for the Consumerism Trend" (June 5), "Giveaways Go Thataway" (June 12), "The Manufacturer's New Liabilities" (June 19), "Advertising's Crisis of Confidence" (June 26), and "Advertising's Triple Economic Threat" (July 3).

Weiss, E. B., *A Critique of Consumerism*, New York: Doyle, Dane, Bernbach, 1967.

Weiss, E. B., "Marketers Fiddle while Consumers Burn," *Harvard Business Review* 40 (July–August, 1968).

"We're Learning," *Economist* (January 29, 1966), 436.

"Why Consumerists Think Advertising Is a Waste," *Printer's Ink* (September 10, 1965), 51.

Part Two

The Pre-Purchase Phase: The Availability and Quality of Information

Alexander, George J., *Honesty and Competition: False Advertising Law and Policy under FTC Administration,* Syracuse: Syracuse University Press, 1967.

Anderson, John W., *Trade Trickery: Tool of Monopoly,* Washington: Quality Brands Associated, 1965.

Armbrister, Trevor, "Land Frauds: The Ads Promise Wonders but Look Before You Buy," *Saturday Evening Post* (April 27, 1963), 17.

Bauer, Raymond A. and Stephen A. Greyser, *Advertising in America: The Consumer View,* Boston: Division of Research, Graduate School of Business Administration, Harvard University, 1968.

Burditt, George M., "Fair Packaging and Labeling—The Cost to Consumers," *Food, Drug, Cosmetic Law Journal,* 22 (October, 1967), 543.

Butler, N. E., "Truth and Confusion in Lending," *Commercial Law Journal,* 74 (March, 1969), 64.

Byers, Theodore E., "Fair Packaging and Labeling Act," *Food, Drug, Cosmetic Law Journal,* 24 (January, 1969), 60.

Clark, B., "Revolution in Consumer Credit Legislation," *Denver Law Journal,* 45 (Fall, 1968), 679.

Coles, Jessie V., *Standardization of Consumer's Goods,* New York: Ronald Press, 1932.

Coles, Jessie V., *Standards and Labels for Consumers' Goods,* New York: Ronald Press, 1949.

"Consumer Credit Reform: A Symposium," *Law and Contemporary Problems,* 33 (Autumn, 1968).

Cook, James G., *Remedies and Rackets,* New York: W. W. Norton, 1958.

"Credit Bureaus Near a Day of Judgment," *Business Week* (August 17, 1968), 44.

Curran, Barbara A., "Legislative Controls as a Response to Consumer's Credit Problems," *Industrial and Commercial Law Review,* 8 (1967), 409.

Curran, Barbara A., *Trends in Consumer Credit Legislation,* Chicago: University of Chicago Press, 1965.

Dunham, A., "Consumerism, Competition and Consumer Credit: Action Now," *Illinois Bar Journal,* 57 (May, 1969), 718.

Dunkelberger, H. Edward, "Fair Packaging and Labeling Act—Some Unanswered Questions Two Years after Enactment," *Food, Drug, Cosmetic Law Journal,* 24 (January, 1969), 17.

"Fair Packaging Law? What's That?," *Modern Packaging,* 41 (November, 1968), 92.

Federal Trade Commission, *Report to Congress Pursuant to the Federal Cigarette Labeling and Advertising Act* (June 30, 1967).

Felsenfeld, "Some Ruminations about Remedies in Consumer-Credit Transactions," *Industrial and Commercial Law Review,* 8 (1967), 535.

Forte, W. E., "Fair Packaging and Labeling Act: Its Legislative History, Content and Future," *Vanderbilt Law Review,* 21 (October, 1968), 76.

Freedom of Choice—An Action in the Public Interest, New York: Magazine Publishers Association, 1968.

Freedom of Information in the Marketplace, Columbia, Missouri: Freedom of Information Center, 1967.

Friedman, Monroe Peter, "Predicting Short-Term Effects of Truth-in-Lending Legislation on Consumer Behavior: An Experimental Study in a Simulated Environment," *Proceedings of the American Psychological Association,* 76th Annual Convention, 1968.

Friedman, Monroe Peter, "Rational Choice in the American Supermarket: An Empirical Study of the Effects of Packaging and Pricing Practices," Selected Proceedings of the 13th Annual Conference of the Council of Consumer Information, 1966.

Giles, Robert E., "The Fair Packaging and Labeling Act of 1966," *Food, Drug, Cosmetic Law Journal,* 22 (March, 1967), 168.

Goodrich, William W., "The Fair Packaging and Labeling Act," *FDA Papers,* 1 (March, 1967), 21.

Goodrich, William W., "The Issues We Face in Carrying Out the Fair Packaging and Labeling Act," *Food, Drug, Cosmetic Law Journal,* 22 (March, 1967), 158.

"The Great Sandpaper Shave," *Fortune,* 70 (December, 1964), 30.

Grayser, Stephen A. and Raymond A. Bauer, "Americans and Advertising: Thirty Years of Public Opinion," *Public Opinion Quarterly,* 30 (Spring, 1966).

Harris, Ralph and Arthur Seldon, *Advertising in a Free Society,* London: Institute of Economic Affairs, 1959.

Harris, Richard, *The Real Voice,* New York: Macmillan, 1964.

Hollander, Stanley C. and James L. Fri, "A Debate: The Quality Stabilization Bill," *Business Horizons* (Spring, 1964), 5.

Holloman, Herbert, "The Role of the Department of Commerce," *Food, Drug, Cosmetic Law Journal,* 22 (June, 1967), 327.

"How to Tell the Truth without Getting Caught," *Marketing Communications* (October, 1967), 102.

Johnson, Robert W., "The Implications of the Proposed Uniform Consumer Credit Code," *Proceedings June 1967 Conference,* Chicago: American Marketing Association, 1967.

Johnson, Robert W., "Regulation of Finance Charges on Consumer Installment Credit," *Michigan Law Review,* 66 (November, 1967), 71.

Jordan, Robert L. and Warren, William D., "Disclosure of Finance Charges: A Rationale," *Michigan Law Review,* 64 (May, 1966), 1285.

Kintner, Earl, "Federal Trade Commission Regulation of Advertising," *Michigan Law Review,* 64 (May, 1966), 1269.

Koch, Walter R., "Time Sales Contracts and Other Pitfalls of Installment Lending," *Texas Bar Journal,* 28 (March, 1965), 181.

Koltman, E. J., "A Semantic Evaluation of Misleading Advertising," *Journal of Communication,* 14 (1964), 151.

Leonard, William N., "Is There Really an Antitrust Case against Advertising," *Challenge* (May–June, 1967).

Maleson, "Consumer Credit Legislation," *Albany Law Review,* 23 (1959), 297.

Millstein, Ira, "The Federal Trade Commission and False Advertising," *Columbia Law Review,* 64 (1964), 444.

Mors, Wallace P., *Consumer Credit Finance Charges: Rate Information and Quotation,* New York: Columbia University Press, 1965.

Morse, *Truth in Lending,* Council on Consumer Information, Pamphlet No. 17, 1966.

Morse, Richard L. D., "Consumer Looks at Labeling," *Selected Proceedings of the Third Annual Conference, Council on Consumer Information,* Greeley, Colorado: Council on Consumer Information, 1957.

Note, "The Consumer in the Marketplace—A Survey of the Law of Informed Buying," *Notre Dame Law Review,* 38 (1963), 555.

Note, "Fair Packaging, Fair Labeling, and the Federal Trade Commission: An Exercise in Consumer Protection," *Georgia Law Review,* 1 (Spring, 1967), 525.

Pease, Otis, *The Responsibility of American Advertising,* New Haven: Yale University Press, 1958.

"Private Branding by Retailers" (Chapter 6), *Organization and Competition in Food Retailing,* Technical Study Number Seven, National Commission on Food Marketing, Washington: U.S. Government Printing Office, 1966, 129.

Prosser, William L., "The Fall of the Citadel," *Minnesota Law Review,* 50 (April, 1966), 791.

Schur, Jerome, "A Study of Consumer Credit Legislation," Municipal Division of the Circuit Court of Cook County, Illinois (1966).

Shay, R. P., "Uniform Consumer Credit Code: An Economist's View," *Cornell Law Review,* 54 (April, 1969), 491.

Spanogle, "How Much Truth in What Kinds of Lending," *Journal of Public Law,* 16 (1967), 296.

Stern, Louis W., "The New World of Private Brands," *California Management Review* (Spring, 1966), 43–50.

"Symposium: Consumer Credit Reform," *Law and Contemporary Problems,* 33 (Autumn, 1968), 639.

"Symposium: Consumer Credit: Developments in the Law," *Industrial and Commercial Law Review,* 8 (1967), 387.

Sweeny, Charles A., "Packaging Responsibilities of the FTC," *Food, Drug, Cosmetic Law Journal,* 22 (March, 1967), 165.

Till, Anthony, *What You Should Know before You Buy a Car,* Los Angeles: Sherbourne Press, 1968.

"The Truth about Truth-in-Packaging," *Nation's Business,* 54 (October, 1966), 75.

Weston, Glen E., "Deceptive Advertising and the Federal Trade Commission: Decline of Caveat Emptor," *Federal Bar Journal,* 24 (Fall, 1964), 548.

Weir, Walter, *Truth in Advertising and Other Heresies,* New York: McGraw-Hill, 1963.

White, Irving S., "The Perception of Value in Products," in Joseph Newman (editor), *On Knowing the Consumer,* New York: John Wiley, 1966.

Willging, Thomas E., "Installment Credit: A Social Perspective," *Catholic University Law Review,* 15 (January, 1966), 45.

Willier, "Protection Instalment Buyers Didn't Get," *Industrial and Commercial Law Review,* 2 (1961), 287.

Young, Ralph A., *Personal Finance Companies and Their Credit Practices,* New York: National Bureau of Economic Research.

Part Three
The Purchase Transaction

Answers to Some Frequently Asked Questions about the Sperry-Hutchinson Company and S & H Green Stamps, Sperry Hutchinson Company (February, 1967).

Berger, Robert A., "The Bill Collector and the Law—A Special Tort, At Least for a While," *DePaul Law Review,* 17 (Winter, 1968), 327.

Bromley, James D. and William H. Wallace, *The Effect of Trading Stamps on Retail Food Prices,* Kingston: University of Rhode Island, 1964. (See also Milton Alexander, *Analysis of a RIU Study of Trading Stamps and Prices,* New York: Sperry and Hutchinson, 1965.)

Brown, F. E., "Pricing Movements Following Discontinuance of Trading Stamps," *Journal of Retailing* (Fall, 1967).

Brown, George, "Wage Garnishment in California: A Study and Recommendations," *California Law Review,* 53 (1965), 1214.

Charlton, Samuel E., "How a Game Is Run," *Advertising and Sales Promotion* (September, 1968), 25.

Comment, "Unconscionable Contract Provisions: A History of Unenforceability from Roman Law to the UCC," *Tulane Law Review,* 42 (1967), 193.

Comment, "Waiver of Defense Clauses and Consumer Protection in Installment Sales Contracts," *Fordham Law Review,* 36 (1967), 106.

Cross, Jennifer, "Groceries, Gas, and Games," *The Nation* (March 24, 1969), 370.

Crowther, Sam and Irwin Wirehouse, *Highway Robbery,* New York: Stein and Day, 1969.

Davidson, John R., "FTC, Robinson-Patman, and Cooperative Promotional Activities," *Journal of Marketing,* 32 (January, 1968), 14.

Dole, Richard F., Jr., "Merchant and Consumer Protection: The Uniform Deceptive Trade Practices Act," *Yale Law Journal,* 76 (January, 1967), 485.

Facts on Quacks—What You Should Know about Health Quackery, American Medical Association, Department of Investigation, 1967.

Federal Trade Commission, *Installment Credit and Retail Sales Practices of District of Columbia Retailers* (March, 1968).

"Flimflam: The 10 Most Deceptive Sales Practices of 1968—So Far," *Sales Management* (September 15, 1968), 33.

Fox, Harold W., *The Economics of Trading Stamps,* Washington, D.C.: Public Affairs Press, 1968.

415

"Games Mean Gallonage, But for How Long?," *National Petroleum News* (July, 1967).

"Games People Play at Gas Stations," *New Republic,* 159 (July 20, 1968), 15.

"Gas Games: Fraud on the Consumer?," *Business Today* (Autumn, 1968), 58.

Gentry, Curt, *The Vulnerable Americans,* Garden City: Doubleday, 1966.

Hammer, Richard, "Will Trading Stamps Stick?," *Fortune,* 62 (August, 1960), 116.

Hanlon, Thomas, "Who Wins Marketing Promotion Games?," *Fortune* (February, 1969), 104.

Haring, Albert and Wallace Yoder, *Trading Stamp Practice and Pricing Policy,* Bloomington: Foundation for Economic and Business Studies, Indiana University, 1958.

Jordan and Yagla, "Retail Installment Sales—History and Development of Regulation," *Marquette Law Review,* 45 (1962), 555.

Jung, Allen F., "Variations in Automobile Prices: Lessons for Consumers —A Reply," *Journal of Business* (April, 1962), 205.

Kaplan, Jack, "Doctor Abrams—Dean of Machine Quacks," *Today's Health,* 44 (April, 1966), 21.

Kessler, Fredrich, "The Protection of the Consumer under Modern Sales Law," *Yale Law Journal,* 74 (December, 1964), 261.

Leff, Arthur A., "Unconscionability and the Code—The Emperor's New Clause," *University of Pennsylvania Law Review,* 115 (February, 1967), 485.

Lefkowitz, Louis J., *Report of Bureau of Consumer Frauds and Protection,* New York: Department of Law, State of New York, 1966.

Mathews, H. Lee and John W. Slocum, "Social Class and Commercial Bank Credit Card Usage," *Journal of Marketing,* 33 (January, 1969), 71.

"Margins, Stamps, and Profits," *Progressive Grocer* (August, 1963), 64.

Mayne, E. Scott, "Variations in Automobile Prices: Lessons for Consumers," *Journal of Business,* 35 (April, 1962), 201.

McCracken, Paul W., *et al., Consumer Installment Credit and Public Policy,* Ann Arbor: University of Michigan Press, 1965.

Metcalf, Lee and Vic Reinemer, *Overcharge,* New York: David McKay Company, 1966.

Metz, Robert, *How to Shake the Money Tree,* New York: G. P. Putnam and Sons, 1966.

Mindell, Stephen, "The New York Bureau of Consumer Frauds and Protection—A Review of its Consumer Protection Activities," *New York Law Forum* (Winter, 1965), 603.

Moore, Dan Tyler, *Wolves, Widows and Orphans,* New York: World, 1967.

Mowbray, A. Q., *The Thumb on the Scale; or the Supermarket Shell Game,* Philadelphia: Lippincott, 1967.

National Congress on Medical Quackery, Sponsored by the American Medical Association and the Food and Drug Administration, First:

October 6–7, 1961; Second: October 25–26, 1963; Third: October 7–8, 1966.

Note, "Express Warrantees and Greater Consumer Protection from Sales Talk," *Marquette Law Review*, 50 (August, 1966), 88.

Note, "Unconscionable Contracts under the UCC," *University of Pennsylvania Law Review*, 109 (1961), 401.

"Playing the Games," *New Republic*, 156 (January 21, 1967), 10.

"Prices: Picketers and the Picketed," *Newsweek* (November 14, 1966), 78.

Roberts, E. F., "The Case of the Unwary Home Buyer—The Housing Merchant Did It," *Cornell Law Quarterly*, 52 (Summer, 1967), 835.

Sanford, D., "Looking into the Green Stamp Business," *New Republic* (October 16, 1965).

Schlink, F. J. and M. J. Phillips, *Don't You Believe It*, New York: Pyramid, 1966.

Shanker, Morris G. and Mark R. Abel, "Consumer Protection under Article 2 of the Uniform Commercial Code," *Ohio State Law Journal*, 29 (1968), 689.

Skilton, Robert H. and Orrin L. Helstad, "Protection of the Buyer of Goods under the Uniform Commercial Code," *Michigan Law Review* 65 (May, 1967), 1465.

Smith, Ralph Lee, *Bargain Hucksters*, New York: Thomas Y. Crowell, 1962.

Tatkon, Daniel, *The Great Vitamin Hoax*, New York: Macmillan, 1968.

"Trading Stamps; Organization and Competition in Food Retailing," Technical Study No. 7, National Commission on Food Marketing, June, 1966, chap. 21, 437.

Trading Stamps and Their Impact on Food Prices, Washington: Department of Agriculture, 1958.

Trump, Fred, *Buyer Beware!*, New York: Abingdon Press, 1965.

U.S. Post Office Department, "How the Postal Inspection Service Protects You against Mail Fraud," Washington, 1964.

Volid, Peter, "The Activist Consumer-Housewife," speech before American Marketing Association (Cincinnati Chapter), January 10, 1967.

Vredenburg, Harvey and Howard Frisinger, "The Value of Trading Stamps as Measured by Retail Prices," *Journal of Retailing* (Fall, 1965), 32.

Waddell, Frederick E., "The Case against Trading Stamps," *Journal of Consumer Affairs*, 2 (Summer, 1968), 21.

"Why Gas Stations Keep Up Games," *Business Week* (September 21, 1968), 62.

Young, James Harvey, *The Medical Messiahs, A Social History of Health Quackery in Twentieth-Century America*, Princeton: Princeton University Press, 1967.

Part Four

Post-Purchase Experience

Bailey, Henry J., III, "Sales Warranties, Products Liability and the UCC: A Lab Analysis of the Cases," *Willamette Law Journal*, 4 (Spring, 1967), 291.

Boehm, George A. W., "He Is Shaking 'Food and Drug" Well before Using," *The New York Times Magazine* (May 15, 1966), 23.

Boyd, Harper W., Jr. and Sidney Levy, "Cigarette Smoking and the Public Interest," *Business Horizons*, 6 (Fall, 1963), 37.

Bylinsky, Gene "The Search for a Safer Cigarette," *Fortune* (November, 1967), 146.

Carper, Jean, "At Last—Clothing That Won't Burn," *Family Safety*, 24 (Spring, 1965), 10.

Carper, Jean, *Stay Alive!*, Garden City, New York: Doubleday and Company, Inc., 1965.

Condon, William J., "Product Liability—1968," *Food, Drug, Cosmetic Law Journal*, 24 (April, 1969), 164.

Condon, William J., "Product Liability—1967," *Food, Drug, Cosmetic Law Journal*, 23 (March, 1968), 114.

"Confusion Persists about Product Warranties," *Appliance Manufacturer* (June, 1967), 67.

Cook, Fred J., *The Corrupted Land*, New York: Macmillan, 1966.

Cudahy, Richard O., "Limitations of Warranty under the Uniform Commercial Code," *Marquette Law Review*, 47 (Fall, 1963), 127.

Dale, William M. and Frank H. Hilton, Jr., "Use of the Product—When Is It Abnormal," *Willamette Law Journal*, 4 (1967), 350.

DeChaine, Dean A., "Products Liability and the Disclaimer," *Willamette Law Journal*, 4 (Spring, 1967), 364.

Dickerson, F. Reed, *Products Liability and the Food Consumer,* 1951.

Dickerson, F. Reed, "Products Liability: How Good Does a Product Have To Be?," *Indiana Law Journal*, 42 (Spring, 1967), 501.

Dickerson, F. Reed, *Product Safety in Household Goods*, Indianapolis: Bobbs-Merrill, 1968.

"Estimates of Injuries Associated with Products, Equipment, and Appliances in the Home Environment," Washington: Injury Control Program, Public Health Service, Department of Health, Education and Welfare (August 18, 1966).

"Extended Warranties Big Puzzle to Caloric," *Merchandising Week*, (August 21, 1967), 8.

Federal Trade Commission, *Staff Report on Automobile Warranties*, 1968.

Freedman, Warren, "Defect in the Product—The Necessary Basis for Product Liability in Tort and in Warranty," *Tennessee Law Review,* 33 (Spring, 1966), 322.

Gray, "Express Warranties and Greater Consumer Protection from Sales Talk," *Marquette Law Review,* 50 (August, 1966), 88.

Hirsh, Robert D., "The Products Liability Problem," *Journal of Marketing* (October, 1963), 9.

"Household Service Life of Appliances," *Journal of Home Economics* (December, 1957), 787.

James, Fleming, Jr., "The Untoward Effects of Cigarettes and Drugs: Some Reflections on Enterprise Liability," *California Law Review,* 54 (October, 1966), 1550.

Jaeger, Walter, H. E., "Product Liability: The Constructive Warranty," *Notre Dame Law,* 39 (August, 1964), 501.

Johnson, George, *The Pill Conspiracy,* Los Angeles: Sherbourne Press, Inc., 1967.

Kahn, Helen, "FTC Vows Action on Warranties," *Automotive News* (February 17, 1969), 2.

Kahn, Helen, "Nader Releases Warranty Report Hidden by FTC," *Automotive News* (November 11, 1968), 1.

Kallet, Arthur and Frederick Schlink, *100,000,000 Guinea Pigs,* New York: Vanguard, 1933.

Katz, Harold A., "Liability of Automobile Manufacturers for the Unsafe Design of Passenger Cars," *Harvard Law Review,* 69 (March, 1956), 863.

Katz, Harold A. "Negligence in Design: A Current Look," *The Insurance Law Journal,* 5 (January, 1965), 9.

Kearney, Paul, *Highway Homicide,* New York: Thomas Y. Crowell Co., 1966.

Keats, John, *The Insolent Chariots,* New York: Lippincott, 1958.

Keeton, Page, "Products Liability—Some Observations about Allocation of Risks," *Michigan Law Review,* 64 (May, 1966), 1329.

Kessler, Fredrich, "Products Liability," *Yale Law Journal,* 76 (April, 1967), 887.

Lamb, Ruth de Forest, *American Chamber of Horrors: The Truth About Food and Drugs,* New York: Farrar-Rinehart, 1936.

Lewiston, Robert R., *Hit from Both Sides,* New York: Simon and Schuster, 1967.

Magnuson, Warren G., "Establishment of a National Commission on Product Safety," *Congressional Record* (February 8, 1967), S. 1755.

"Marketing Credibility Gap," *Sales Management* (June 15, 1968).

The Medicine Show, Mount Vernon: Consumers Union.

Mintz, Morton, *By Prescription Only,* Boston: Houghton-Mifflin Company, 1967.

Mintz, Morton, *The Therapeutic Nightmare: A Report on the Roles of FDA,* New York: Houghton, 1965.

Mooney, Booth, *Hidden Assassins,* New York: Follett, 1966.

Morris, R. and B. Block, "The Instability of Quality: As Revealed in the
    Consumer Union Studies of Sunburn Preventatives, 1936–66," *The
    Journal of Consumer Affairs,* 1 (Summer, 1968), 39.
Nader, Ralph, *Unsafe at Any Speed,* New York: Pocket Books, 1968.
Nader, Ralph, "The Engineer's Professional Role: Universities, Corpora-
    tions, and Professional Societies," *Engineering Education* (February
    1967), 450.
Nader, Ralph, "Patent Laws: Prime Source to Secure Safer Auto Design
    to Reduce Highway Deaths," *Trial* (December/January, 1964), 28.
National Commission on Product Safety, Interim Report Recommending
    Enactment of *The Child Protecting Act of 1969,* Washington, D.C.:
    1969.
National Safety Council, *Accident Facts,* 1967.
Neal, Harry Edward, *The Protectors: The Story of the Food and Drug
    Administration,* New York: Julian Messner, 1968.
Neuberger, Maurine B., *Smoke Screen: Tobacco and the Public Welfare,*
    Englewood Cliffs: Prentice-Hall, 1963.
Noel, Dix, "Manufacturers Negligence of Design and Directions for Use
    of a Product," *Yale Law Journal,* 71 (April, 1962), 841.
Note, "The Contractual Aspect of Consumer Protection: Recent Develop-
    ments in the Law of Sales Warranties," *Michigan Law Review,* 64
    (May, 1966), 1430.
Note, "Effect of Advertising on Manufacturer's Liability to Ultimate Pur-
    chases," *Marquette Law Review,* 42 (1959), 521.
O'Connell, Jeffrey and Arthur Myers, *Safety Last—An Indictment of the
    Auto Industry,* New York: Random House, 1966.
Ogilvy, David, "What's Wrong with Your Image—and What You Can Do
    About It," speech to National Automobile Dealers Association, Las
    Vegas, February 3, 1965.
Press, Edward, "Wringer Washer Machines Injuries," *American Journal
    of Public Health,* 54 (May, 1964), 812.
"Products Liability," *Machine Design* (March 28, 1968), 20.
Products Liability and Reliability: Some Management Considerations,
    Washington, D.C.: Machinery and Allied Products Institute and Coun-
    cil for Technological Advancement, 1967.
"Quality Control, Warranties, and a Crisis in Confidence," *Consumer
    Reports* (April, 1965), 173.
"Rattles, Pings, Dents, Leaks, Creaks—and Costs," *Newsweek* (Novem-
    ber 25, 1968), 92.
Ridgeway, James, "Big Fish That Get Away," *The New Republic* (October
    23, 1965), p. 15.
Rinesch, G., "Warranties for the Protection of the Consumer," *Business
    Lawyer,* 24 (April, 1969), 857.
Rugaber, Walter, "Tire Safety: The Controversy and Outlook for Federal
    Code," *New York Times* (July 5, 1966), 1.
Shafer, Ronald G., "Who Should Write Industry Standards?," *Wall Street
    Journal* (February 11, 1969), 14.

"Smog Over Auto Accord," *Business Week* (January 18, 1969), 28.

"Standards and the Public Interest," *Magazine of Standards* (March, 1967), 67.

Senate Committee on Commerce, *Toy Safety Act 1969,* U.S. Congress, Washington, D.C., 1969.

Toy Manufacturers Association, Report to Senate Commerce Committee on Toy Safety Act 1969, Washington, D.C., 1969.

"Warranties: The Promise and the Reality," *Consumer Reports* (April, 1967), 194.

Part Five

Discrimination Between Segments:
The Case of the
Ghetto Consumer

"Aiding the Poor," *Wall Street Journal* (January 4, 1968).

Baum, Daniel Jay, "The Federal Trade Commission and the War on Poverty," *UCLA Law Review*, 14 (May, 1967), 1071.

Beackett, Jean C., "Intercity Differences in Family Food Budget Costs," *Monthly Labor Review* (October, 1963), 1189.

"Better Deal for Ghetto Growing Up," *Economist* (August 6, 1966), 578.

Bivens, Gordon E., "Food Price Competition in a Local Market: Milwaukee, A Case Study," presented at 12th Annual Conference of Council on Consumer Information, Minneapolis, April 21, 1967.

Brunn, George, "Wage Garnishment in California: A Study and Recommendations," *California Law Review*, 53 (December, 1965), 1214.

Caplovitz, David, "The Other Side of the Poverty Problem," *Challenge* (September–October, 1965), 12.

Caplovitz, David, "On the Value of Consumer Action Programs in the War on Poverty," Office of Economic Opportunity, March 8, 1966.

Colazza, Charles J., Jr., "Effects of Income upon Shopping Attitudes and Frustrations," *Journal of Retailing* (Spring, 1966), 1.

Consumer Action and the War on Poverty, Office of Economic Opportunity Community Action Program, President's Committee on Consumer Interest, Washington: U.S. Government Printing Office, 1965.

Consumer Problems of the Poor: Supermarket Operations in Low-Income Areas and the Federal Response, 90th Congress, Second Session Hearings, October 12–November 25, 1967, 352 pp.

The Crisis in America's Cities: A Report on Civil Disorders in 1967, The American Retail Federation (September 6, 1967).

CUNA International, "The Poor Don't Have to Pay More," *Everybody's Money* (Spring, 1967).

". . . Do the Poor Pay More?," *The Food Industry Report* (August, 1968).

Dixon, Donald F. and Daniel J. McLaughlin, Jr., "Do the Inner City Poor Pay More for Food?," *The Economic and Business Bulletin*, SBA Temple University (Spring, 1968), 6.

Federal Trade Commission, *District of Columbia Consumer Protection Program*, Report by the FTC, Washington (June, 1968).

"Fleecing the Consumer," *New Republic* (August 21, 1965), 7.

"Food Prices in High and Low Income Areas," Technical Study No. 10, National Commission on Food Marketing (June, 1966).

Goodman, Charles S., "Do the Poor Pay More?," *Journal of Marketing* (January, 1968), 18.

Goodman, Charles S., "Marketing in the Low-Income Neighborhoods," *AMA Proceedings,* Changing Marketing Systems: Consumer, Corporate, and Government Interfaces, Chicago: American Marketing Association, 1968.

Hamilton, Walter A., "Ghetto Marketing: Voluntary Versus Mandatory Improvements," from a speech given at the American Marketing Association Conference, Denver (August, 1968).

Howell, Kenneth, "Most Chains Not Tailoring Techniques to Negro Needs," *Supermarket News* (November 16, 1964), 5.

"The Inner City," *Food Topics* (October, 1967), 19.

"Inside Negro Buying Habits," *Grocery Manufacturer* (November, 1967), 9.

Irelan, L. M. (editor), *Low Income Life Styles,* Washington: U.S. Government Printing Office, 1966.

Katz, Carol H., *The Law and the Low Income Consumer* (Project on Social Welfare Law), New York: NYU School of Law, 1968.

"Law and the Ghetto Consumer," *Catholic Lawyer,* 14 (Summer, 1968), 214.

Levitan, Sar A., *Programs in Aid of the Poor,* Washington: The Upjohn Institute, 1965.

"Merchants Count Up the Losses," *Business Week* (August 5, 1967), 28.

Miller, Herman P., *Rich Man, Poor Man,* New York: Thomas Y. Crowell Company, 1960.

Miller, Herman P. (editor), *Poverty American Style,* Belmont: Wadsworth, 1966.

Miller, Merlin G., "Increasing Low-Income Consumer Buying and Borrowing Power by Cooperative Action," *Ohio State Law Review,* 29 (Summer, 1968), 709.

Morse, Richard L. D., "The Lengthening Distance between the Haves and and the Have-Nots," *Journal of Home Economics* (October, 1967).

"New Chain for Ghetto Shopper," *Chain Store Age* (March, 1968), 78.

1965 Law and Poverty, Washington, D.C.: Report of the National Conference on Law and Poverty, June 23–25, 1965.

Note, "Installment Sales: Low Income Plight," *Columbia Journal of Law and Social Problems,* 2 (June, 1966), 1.

Note, "Installment Sales: Plight of the Low-Income Buyer," *Columbia Journal of Law and Social Problems,* 2 (1966).

Oppenheim, Irene, *Conference on Buying and Consumption Practices of Low Income Families,* New York: NYU Press, 1964.

Peterson, Esther, "Equality in the Marketplace," Los Angeles: Remarks before the National Conference of the NAACP, July 7, 1966.

Petrof, John V. "Customer Strategy for Negro Retailers," *Journal of Retailing* (Fall, 1967), 30.

Poverty and Deprivation in the United States: The Plight of Two Fifths of the Nation, Conference on Economic Progress (1962).

Ratner, Cynthia, "Educating the Low-Income Consumer: Some Viewpoints from an Action Program," *The Journal of Consumer Affairs,* 2 (Summer, 1968), 107.

Real Estate Research Corporation, *Retailing in Low-Income Areas,* prepared for the Chicago Small Business Opportunities Corporation, Vol. 2 of 2 (August, 1967).

"The Riot Peril," *The Journal of Insurance* (November–December, 1967), 13.

Rosenthal, Richard, "After the Riots—A Position Paper for Retailing," *Stores,* the NRMA Magazine (December, 1967), 11.

Sawyer, B. E., "An Examination of Race as a Factor in Negro-White Consumption Patterns," *Review of Economics and Statistics* (May, 1962), 217.

Schrag, Philip G., "Ghetto Merchants: A Study in Deception," *New Republic,* 159 (September 7, 1968), 17.

"Should Supermarkets Take a New Look at Urban Areas?," *Food Topics* (February, 1967), 10.

Shriver, Sargent, *What the War on Poverty Means to Americans and to Advertisers,* A.A.A.A. Eastern Annual Conference, New York City, October 10–11, 1967.

"State Consumer Protection: A Proposal," *Iowa Law Review,* 53 (1967), 712.

Sternlieb, George, "Household Research in the Urban Core," *Journal of Marketing* (January, 1968), 25.

Sturdivant, Frederick D. and Walter T. Wilhelm, "Poverty, Minorities, and Consumer Exploitation," *Southwestern Social Science Quarterly* (December, 1968), 643.

A Survey of Attitudes of Detroit Negroes after the Riot of 1967 sponsored by the Detroit Urban League, coordinated by the Detroit Free Press.

"There is No Evidence That Poor Pay Higher Prices for Drugs," *American Druggist* (August 1, 1966), 18.

Toyer, Aurelia, "Consumer Education and Low-Income Families," *The Journal of Consumer Affairs,* 2 (Summer, 1968), 114.

The Urgent Need for Consumer Protection in Our Inner Cities, address by Commissioner Mary Gardner Jones, FTC, Minneapolis, May 24, 1968.

U.S. Department of Commerce, Bureau of the Census, *Characteristics of Families Residing in Poverty Areas,* Series p-23, No. 19, Washington: U.S. Government Printing Office, August 24, 1966.

U.S. Department of Health, Education & Welfare, Division of Research, *Low Income Life Styles,* Washington: U.S. Government Printing Office, 1966.

U.S. Department of Justice and Office of Economic Opportunity, *National Conference on Law and Poverty,* Washington: U.S. Government Printing Office, 1965.

U.S. Department of Labor, *Levels of Living among the Poor,* BLS Report #238-12 (August, 1965).

U.S. Department of Labor, Bureau of Labor Statistics, *A Study of Prices Charged in Food Stores Located in Low and Higher Income Areas of Six Large Cities* (February, 1966).

Wald, *Law and Poverty: 1965*, report to the National Conference on Law and Poverty, 1965.

Wright, John S. and Carl M. Larson, *A Survey of Brand Preferences among Chicago Negro and White Families*, Urbana: University of Illinois, 1967.

Index